Dancing to the Drum Machine

Dancing to the Drum Machine

How Electronic Percussion Conquered the World

Dan LeRoy

BLOOMSBURY ACADEMIC
NEW YORK • LONDON • OXFORD • NEW DELHI • SYDNEY

BLOOMSBURY ACADEMIC
Bloomsbury Publishing Inc
1385 Broadway, New York, NY 10018, USA
50 Bedford Square, London, WC1B 3DP, UK
29 Earlsfort Terrace, Dublin 2, Ireland

BLOOMSBURY, BLOOMSBURY ACADEMIC and the Diana logo are trademarks of Bloomsbury Publishing Plc

First published in the United States of America 2023
Reprinted 2023

Copyright © Dan LeRoy, 2023

For legal purposes the Acknowledgments on pp. xiii–xvi constitute an extension of this copyright page.

Cover illustration © Jason Anscomb

All rights reserved. No part of this publication may be reproduced or transmitted in any form or by any means, electronic or mechanical, including photocopying, recording, or any information storage or retrieval system, without prior permission in writing from the publishers.

Bloomsbury Publishing Inc does not have any control over, or responsibility for, any third-party websites referred to or in this book. All internet addresses given in this book were correct at the time of going to press. The author and publisher regret any inconvenience caused if addresses have changed or sites have ceased to exist, but can accept no responsibility for any such changes.

A catalog record for this book is available from the Library of Congress.

ISBN: HB: 978-1-5013-6727-4
PB: 978-1-5013-6726-7
ePDF: 978-1-5013-6729-8
eBook: 978-1-5013-6728-1

Typeset by Newgen KnowledgeWorks Pvt. Ltd., Chennai, India
Printed and bound in Great Britain

To find out more about our authors and books visit www.bloomsbury.com and sign up for our newsletters.

Allan Schwartzberg, who's a great session drummer, comes in one day late for a gig. He's sweating bullets and he's out of breath. He looks terrible.

He says, "Guys, I'm sorry I'm late. I had the worst night last night. I couldn't sleep a wink." And we're just waiting.

Finally, he says, "I had this terrible dream that I came home, and found my wife in bed with a drum machine."

Late Night with David Letterman bassist Will Lee

Contents

Foreword by Nick Rhodes: Timing Is Everything		x
Acknowledgments		xiii
Prologue		xvii
1	From Boats to Babies: How Drum Machines Began	1
2	The Rhythm Aces	13
3	Beat Brothers: Sly Stone and J. J. Cale	27
4	The Machines Are Fighting Back	35
5	Teutonic Sonics: Germany and Programmed Rhythm	47
6	Turn the Beat Around: Eno, Disco, and the Drum Machine	55
7	Our Drum Machine Could Be Your Band	65
8	The Drum Machines That Weren't	79
9	Punch the Clock: The Joy and Pain of Drum Machine Programming	89
10	Without Me, You Would Not Have Even Thought About Writing This Book	109
11	Give the (Electronic) Drummer Some	117
12	Inside and Outside the Box: The Linn Revolution	129
13	Have You Seen This New Drum Machine? *Shit!*	143
14	808 State	159
15	Hip Hop's Electric Guitar	171
16	Worker Bees of the DMX	185
17	Destination Emulation	207
18	Mr. K's Last Laugh	225
19	The Mammals Arrive: The Linn 9000 and the End of the Drum Machine	241
20	Computer Love	261
21	Time Out of Time	275
Appendix: I Am Echo		287
Index		289

Dan LeRoy is the author of several books, including a volume for Bloomsbury's 33 1/3 Series about the Beastie Boys album *Paul's Boutique*. His work has appeared in *The New York Times, Rolling Stone, Newsweek, The Village Voice*, and *Esquire* online. His speculative fiction has been published in several anthologies and has been featured on the *No Sleep* podcast. Since 2006, he has been the director of the Writing and Publishing Department at Lincoln Park Performing Arts Charter School in Midland, PA.

Foreword: Timing Is Everything

The skies once provided our only source of guidance for a sense of time; the sun, moon, and stars closely informing daily routines.

A sundial became the pinnacle of technology around 1500 BCE. Our pursuit for more precision continued for centuries: water clocks, hour glasses, early oscillating devices … and then the pendulum, first drawn by Leonardo da Vinci in the 1490s, developed further by Galileo and finally realized in 1656 by Christiaan Huygens, whose clocks were controlled by harmonic oscillators. Progress toward the watch was slow, but by the mid-1950s we had atomic clocks, which still remain our most accurate time-keeping devices. We are now connected to a global network where phones, tablets, and computers are all synchronized, giving us a precise readout any second we care to look.

The first signs of human life are a rhythm, a heartbeat. Our lives are inextricably linked to time, which elapses at a finite rate. Time, beats, pulses, and rhythms are important to us, they are in our blood. When we are excited, our heart rate increases.

We respond to rhythm by moving our bodies, tapping our feet, clapping our hands, or dancing. It's an instinct. We rarely think about it; we just react. In a club, if the DJ plays a popular song, there is an instant response on the dance floor and those who are not there often rush to join in. It's a joyful sensation. Music has always been a powerful form of communication.

As far as we know, the earliest drums and percussion date back even further than 5500 BCE. It took a while longer for the first snare drum to arrive, around 1650, then a few hundred years passed before a basic drum kit was invented in 1909. A little more than a decade later this was supplemented by a hi-hat.

Live drums and percussion will forever remain an exciting spectacle in musical performance, but as technology developed we were gifted an alternate new species of rhythm: the drum machine.

Music is mathematical; it's measured by tempo, the number of beats in a bar and a time signature. Aside from the occasional Jazz artist, most musicians aspire to play in time. As early as 1815, metronomes were used for practice to improve accuracy and technique.

In 1957 the electronic rhythm revolution began seriously with the Chamberlin Rhythmate, which was able to produce a selection of sophisticated beats using tape loops of real drums and percussion. Tempo was controlled by speeding up and slowing down the tapes. Only two years later the Wurlitzer Side Man became the first drum machine to create rhythms mechanically. Throughout the 1960s and 1970s a growing number of products were developed and the market expanded rapidly from the home organ enthusiasts toward musicians using these machines as creative tools, in myriad ways, across many genres.

I can personally isolate significant moments when I first heard drum machines on records, and I have no doubt that each of those instances had an impact upon decisions I made musically in the years that followed. Many of these records you will read about in this book: George McCrae's "Rock Your Baby," Kraftwerk's "Autobahn" (and everything they produced after this), Iggy Pop's "Nightclubbing," Grace Jones's "La Vie en Rose," Suicide's "Frankie Teardrop," Ultravox's "Hiroshima Mon Amour," Blondie's "Heart of Glass," Marvin Gaye's "Sexual Healing," Herbie Hancock's "Rockit," Prince's "When Doves Cry," New Order's "Blue Monday." And I could continue with the list.

I experienced all of these artists' songs firsthand when they were released, with just one important exception, which had a profound effect on me when I discovered the band more than a decade later. That was Sly and the Family Stone. Most notably, they used a drum machine on the pioneering song "Family Affair" in 1971, but I found their music around 1984, through the album *Fresh*, initially released in 1973. This was the continuation of their artistic journey combining drum machines with live drums, achieving the funkiest sound imaginable. The track "In Time" remains an astonishing masterpiece.

Between 1977 and 1978, the advent of electronic drums also had an extraordinary effect on music. In my opinion, the song "I Feel Love," by Donna Summer, is possibly the single most influential track that dictated the future direction of dance music. Whilst they remained cult records, "Warm Leatherette" by The Normal and "Being Boiled" by The Human League are also landmark songs.

During this period, in the summer of 1978, I witnessed the band Suicide perform at Birmingham's Top Rank venue, supporting The Clash. They were thrilling, unique, and uncompromising—a duo with just a drum machine, an organ, and a lead vocal. Much to my dismay, the angry punk audience had little patience for their sound and subsequently they were subjected to a relentless barrage of bottles, cans, and other projectiles being hurled at them. They withstood the rain of missiles and held their ground for several songs, but were eventually forced to retreat off stage. I was enormously disappointed, as I loved their album, and although punk was of the moment, the future was beckoning.

Several months later that same year, I stepped on stage for the first time, aged sixteen, at an art college. I pressed play on my Kay R-8 Rhythmer drum machine. Those were the first sounds anyone ever heard from Duran Duran. Our singer at this time was Stephen Duffy.

Some lineup changes and a couple of years later, when Simon Le Bon had been recruited as our singer, for our premier performance at the Rum Runner club, we opened the show with a cover version of the song "I Feel Love," which also featured a drum machine.

There are a few tracks in the first Duran Duran album on which I used drum machines, including "Night Boat," "To the Shore," and the song "Girls on Film," which became our most successful single from that record. By the time we made the follow-up album, *Rio*, in 1982, I had bought one of the earliest Roland TR-808s, which features on several songs, but most notably on "The Chauffeur," where the entire track was built around the drum pattern I programmed and synced to a sequencer. At this point, drum machines were deeply embedded in the musical DNA of Duran Duran, and undoubtedly many other artists from that period too ... though I don't think any of us could have possibly predicted how some years later, that one device, the TR-808, would have spawned an entirely new musical genre: hip hop.

The evolution continued with the introduction of widely used Linn drums and then the Roland TR-909, which was largely responsible for inspiring techno, acid, and house music. Rhythm became a dominant force in music.

Drum machines all have their own personalities and they have become as essential to modern music as any other instrument. Some musicians talk about vintage guitars and amps, others speak about analogue synth and drum machines.

If I have to wake up early (for me), I set my alarm for 8.08.

After all, timing is everything ...

Nick Rhodes
London
January 2022

Acknowledgments

What I'm about to say must be true for most authors: my favorite part of writing a book is the people I meet while I do it. Over and over again, I'm humbled and heartened by the window that a project like this provides into the best parts of human nature. Writing is a lonely job, but most books are the work of a cast of hundreds, if not thousands. Getting to know the following people in that cast—or getting to know them better—has been a blessing.

Let me begin, then, by offering my appreciation to the more than 130 people who agreed to be interviewed for this book. The fact that many are musical heroes of mine makes their participation even more gratifying. Sincere thanks to: Steve Albini, Dave Allen, David M. Allen, Carlos Alomar, Billy Amendola, Jon Astrop, Juan Atkins, Arthur Baker, Wally Badarou, Gordon Bahary, Afrika Bambaataa, Michael Beinhorn, Bryan Bell, Pete Bellotte, Benge, Mark S. Berry, Boris Blank, Jimmy Bralower, Martin "Red" Broad, Justin Broadrick, Evan Brooks, Greg Broussard, Arthur Brown, Paul Buchanan, Ed Buller, Hugo Burnham, Cally Callomon, Julie Campbell, Chris Carter, Ben Cenac, Suzanne Ciani, Kenny Clayton, Bernadette Cooper, Ian Curnow, Andy Dalby, Iva Davies, Wally De Backer, Eric Debris, Jimmy Destri, Thomas Dolby, Bill Drummond, Sly Dunbar, Rusty Egan, Greg Errico, Larry Fast, Bruce Forat, Keith Forsey, John Foxx, Joe Galdo, David Gamson, David Garibaldi, Mike Garson, Andy Gill (RIP), Joe Goretti, Reggie Griffin, Robin Guthrie, Phil Harding, Richie Hawtin, Nancy Heyman, Mike Howlett, Linden Hudson, Jack Hues, Roy Mayorga, Chris Merrick Hughes, J. J. Jeczalik, Marshall Jefferson, Jellybean Johnson, Gareth Jones, Michael Jonzun, cEvin Key, Jon King, Erdal Kizilcay, Craig Krampf, Gary Langan, Daniel Lanois, Bill Laswell, Keith LeBlanc, Will Lee, Don Lewis, Stephen Lipson, Fred Maher, Stephen Mallinder, Robert Margouleff, Derrick May, George McRae, Sammy Merendino, Jason Miles, Daniel Miller, Moby, Stephen Morris, Mark Mothersbaugh, James Mtume, Martin Newell, Hugh Padgham, Man Parrish, Chrissi Poland, Steve Porcaro, Thommy Price, David "Davy DMX" Reeves, Blaine L. Reininger, Martin Rev, Hans-Joachim Roedelius, Susan Rogers, Michael Rother, Gordon Rudd, Marcus Ryle, Schoolly D, Eric "Vietnam" Sadler, Kevin Saunderson, Will Sergeant, Steven Singleton, Dave Smith, Steve Stevens,

Chuck Surack, Richard Tilles, Paul Waaktaar-Savoy, Asmus Tietchens, Martyn Ware, Rob Warr, Steven Wolf, and David Z (Rivkin).

I especially want to thank the following people, who kindly consented to multiple interviews: Richard James Burgess, David Frangioni, David Frank, Tadao Kikumoto, Roger Linn, Andy Newmark, Dave Rossum, Sam Sever, and Art Wood. Extra special thanks to Nick Rhodes for the lovely foreword, and to the personable and insightful Warren Cann, who has thought more about drum machines than some people who've actually made one!

I also want to acknowledge Wolfgang Flür, who answered some technical questions; Bobby Z (Rivkin), who read a chapter of this manuscript; and Mario Caldato, Jr., whose contributions to my *Paul's Boutique* book came in handy again.

While there's a long list of publicists, managers, and agents who ought to be thanked individually, I'm especially grateful to Zoe Miller of ZOPF PR, who arranged many of the interviews for this book.

Thanks to everyone at Bloomsbury, including Amy Martin, Rachel Moore, and Leah Babb-Rosenfeld, who commissioned this book. The volume I wrote for Bloomsbury's 33 1/3 series continues to open new and surprising doors, and I'm proud to have the chance to work once again with such a great publisher.

The readers who supplied feedback for my proposal happen to be an all-star team of fellow writers: Samantha Bennett, Jim Daniels, Neil McCormick, and Greg Renoff. I'm incredibly appreciative of their helpful suggestions. A shout out as well to Simon Reynolds, who helped get this whole project going by connecting me with Wally De Backer, a.k.a. Gotye.

Mankind has made undreamed-of advances over the centuries. We still haven't figured out a way to make transcription suck less—except for having someone else do it. These people did, and I can't tell them how much it means: Greer LeRoy, Cindy West, and Erin Brody. Thanks as well to Rhodri Marsden for recommending Transcribe, which saved me (and the aforementioned folks) some miserable hours.

It's my continued good fortune to work with the administration, faculty, staff, and students at Lincoln Park Performing Arts Charter School and Lincoln Park Performing Arts Center. The other two current and former members of the Writing and Publishing Department, Deanna Baringer and Cindy West, will never know how much they contributed to this book through their patience, talent, and friendship.

My students in the Writing and Publishing Department have had to put up with me working on two books over the past three years. That involves considerable sacrifice on their part, even when they might not have realized it. They are what makes my current day job the best I've ever had.

The priests and parishioners of St. Monica and St. Blaise remain some of my true blessings. Thank you sincerely to Fr. Kim Schreck, Fr. John Naugle, Fr. Ladis Cizik, Fr. Bill Schwartz, and Deacon Harry DeNome for your leadership and witness.

To have talented fellow writers as close friends is a necessary condition of writing. They challenge you; they commiserate with you; they inspire you. To Michael Lipton, D. X. Ferris, Peter Relic, and Brian Coleman, my everlasting gratitude. And my thanks to the irrepressible Jon Sidel, an endless source of good humor and great stories. If you enjoy this book, you will probably get a kick out of our own collaboration, coming soon!

I share many of the musical memories in this book with my best friend, Stephen Catanzarite. He has my gratitude for many things, not least the countless patient hours he endured while I programmed the Alesis HR-16 that was the bedrock for many of the songs from our longtime songwriting partnership. My band in the prologue never really had a name, but Undiscovered Sons was a group that was both of, and ahead of, its time. (Aren't the best ones, always?) Stephen, his wife, Rachel, his sons, Thomas and Henry, and the rest of their family, helped make this book possible in ways impossible to count.

So did the members of my incredibly supportive family: my brother, Drew LeRoy, and my nephews Alex, Matt, and Connor; my brother-in-law Devin Nutter, his wife Melissa, and my niece Charlotte; Carolyn Tallman, Jamie Tallman, Heather, Chad, and Lily Sigmon; and Nancy, Steve, and Rachel Kovac.

Parents put up with so much, and mine put up with even more than most—including all the times I played Visage's "Beat Boy" at house-shaking volume just to revel in the snare sound! I can never repay my mom and dad, Polly G. and Louie D. LeRoy, what I owe them, but every book I write is some small offering, born of love and appreciation, against that debt.

To my children, Carys, Greer, and Grant: I love you three, sincerely and unreservedly. My wish is that you've each had the sort of childhood that might someday inspire a project like this one.

No one makes a book more possible than a spouse. No one suffers more when one is written. And the payoff might be a book they don't even want to read! My own beloved wife, Kiena Nutter, probably feels that way about this one. That she not only consented to its creation, but supported it every step of the way, is more (unnecessary) proof that I married up—and married right.

Notes

All quotations in this book are from interviews conducted by the author, unless otherwise noted.

As a reader who often looks first at the endnotes of a book, it kills me a little to have to exclude most of them here. The decision was made to save space—and to get as much information as possible into the text of the book. However, there are tons of fascinating stories, sidelights, and supplemental details to be found in the original endnotes I wrote. Those complete endnotes can be found on Bloomsbury's website, https://www.bloomsbury.com/us/dancing-to-the-drum-machine-9781501367267/. I hope if you've enjoyed this book that you'll check out the notes!

Working on this project has convinced me that it's important to document drum machine history—especially as many of its pioneers age. To that end, I hope you'll consider subscribing to my Substack newsletter, *Dan LeRoy's Bonus Beats*, at danleroy.substack.com. I'll be offering exclusive content: brand-new interviews with drum machine creators and users; stories that didn't make it into this book; full interview transcripts from *Dancing to the Drum Machine*; and the proverbial "much, much more." The goal is for as much of this material to reach the public as possible, to preserve this singular era and document the way it continues to shape our music and culture.

Prologue

Autumn, 1984

1.

We all locked eyes and held a collective breath.

Then Monte released his finger from the pause button of my cassette deck. Scott poised his hands atop a tiny Casio keyboard. And Jay began to tap out a rhythm, with drumsticks, on the gray plastic pads of the box he held in his lap.

It was the beginning of the first and only song that our unnamed group would record, there in my crowded bedroom one October afternoon.

It was also the beginning of this book, though I wouldn't realize this for decades.

What I understood almost immediately was that I had made a terrible mistake. An even worse mistake than the series of horrible errors I was about to commit to tape, using my newly purchased bass guitar.

As we started recording, I suddenly grasped that it should have been *me* holding that black box, tapping out the beats on the Mattel Synsonics Drums. (If I'd known that Kraftwerk had actually used these toy drums on a recording, I might have been even more envious. Luckily, I barely knew who Kraftwerk were.)

Regardless, I stared at the Synsonics drums so intensely that I almost missed my entrance. I didn't, though. Another mistake.

My Harmony bass, featured in the pages of J. C. Penney's Fall 1984 Catalog, was a homage to my heroes, John Taylor of Duran Duran and the jazz fusion great Marcus Miller. With the best, misguided intentions of all young musicians—especially the ones who've read just enough about punk to be truly dangerous—I was sure I could teach myself how to simulate the popping bass sounds on the records I loved. With no lessons. Or practice. On the spot. As soon as the red "Record" light glowed.

Immensely proud of our gritty, hard-hitting hip hop debut—a song titled, with elegant simplicity, "Life Ain't Right"—we took our tape to the local McDonald's. There, we played it for a group of our friends.

When people heard the programmed drums, their eyes lit up. True, the flecks of white noise making the sounds of Synsonics Drums were just weak pops on our cassette. Even I, at the height of my delusional stage, knew this was no LinnDrum. It was no DMX. It wasn't even a Dr. Rhythm.

But in 1984, drum machines were still novel for musicians. And they were almost unheard of for teenagers. So they connected you, in some mystical way, to the people using LinnDrums and DMXs. In a way that, say, using a bass did *not* connect you to John Taylor and Marcus Miller.

My bass playing, especially, made no such connection. It was what clearly wasn't right with "Life Ain't Right." The second the bass entered, like some clueless, uninvited party guest, the mood among the listeners changed.

"WHAT. IS. THAT!!!" a girl demanded. She looked as if she'd been hearing a confession of pedophilia, instead of my recorded debut. Everyone pointed at me.

I refrained from pointing at myself. Instead, I was calculating how many weeks of delivering newspapers it would take to buy myself some Synsonics Drums.

2.

The simplest way to view drum machines is that they are an exercise in control. They promise mastery of that most elusive entity: time. But many musicians have also been snared by the otherworldly siren song of electronic rhythm. When those two qualities collided, the effect could be irresistible.

Listen to Ultravox's Warren Cann, as he describes the first time he and his bandmates heard a drum machine—a Roland TR-77—plugged in through an amp. The band gathered around the machine in their London rehearsal room, sometime in 1976, and pushed the silver "Start" bar.

"It was pure fuckin' magic," Cann says, his face aglow at the memory. "We were all kind of entranced. We'd never really heard perfect rhythm before. It was a drug invented by God."

Blaine L. Reininger, the former frontman of the San Francisco avant-garde band Tuxedomoon, was also mesmerized. It's the thing, he says, that kept the early users of drum machines inspired to overcome the devices' multiple—sometimes heartbreaking—limitations.

"You had to be *dedicated* to it. You had to really love the sound of electronic music, you know? That's the thing that few people talk about," Reininger says. "How seductive these sounds are."

Hip hop artist Man Parrish speaks, perhaps, for all of the pioneers in this book.

"Nobody *understands* what I had to go through," he says in a mock-whine. The tone is joking; the sentiment isn't. "I deserve a *plaque*."

3.

If you think of drum machines as a dated artifact of a dated moment in pop music history, you're absolutely correct and incredibly misguided.

The reign of the drum machine was short: at most, it lasted two decades. Their peak was shorter still: five or six years at most. Drum machines didn't truly fulfill their destiny until programmability became possible toward the end of the 1970s. And by the mid-1980s, sampling expanded the possibilities of drum machines so far and so fast that the standalone drum machine was already on the way out.

So if your idea of drum machines is the inexorable thump of a LinnDrum, or the twitching rhythms of a Roland 808 from somewhere between 1983 and 1984, you're not wrong—not completely. That truly was the high-water mark for these devices, though no one realized it at the time.

By 1985, the game had already changed. And while standalone drum machines were still very much around in the second half of the 1980s, they had become a retro curiosity less than a decade later. Just as computers began to open up the limitless possibilities of the internet, they promised musicians an unending banquet of choices, through the magic of digital recording and plug-ins that simulated any sound. Including drum machines.

But the drum machine is something like a dead star, which went supernova ages ago, but continues to shine in the night skies. The glow of drum machines illumines nearly every genre of music today, even if the standalone machines that started it are mostly vanished.

And paradoxically, the earliest rhythm units—which once promised perfection—are now prized precisely because they didn't quite deliver.

"The joy of primitive machines lies almost completely in their imperfections and limitations," says John Foxx, the former singer of Ultravox, who's been a dedicated drum machine user for more than forty years. "They invite you to use them ingeniously, in ways they were not designed to operate.

"Imperfection is character," Foxx adds, "becomes identity, and adds fascination."

4.

Four locations are the primary setting for the story of drum machines. Two of these sites are where most of the drum machines mentioned in this book were conceived and built: Japan and the United States. And two other places contributed immeasurably to the development of electronic percussion: Germany and the UK. Within, and between, these spots on the map, drum machines forged secret—and sometimes unexpected—connections.

In the twentieth century, rhythm units were first developed by a fussy, avant-garde classical composer. They were next marketed to Everyman and his family, from Grandma and Grandpa down to the kids, for singalongs around the organ. When the novelty wore off, this technology was appropriated by maverick musicians of every persuasion. It was then refined by some of the brightest minds in the budding technological hubs of Japan and America, and became the cornerstone of some of the most extreme new musical genres imaginable.

And ultimately, the desire that had driven Henry Cowell, that fussy, avant-garde classical composer, to want a drum machine in the first place—the desire for perfect, unchanging, hypnotic rhythm—led electronic percussion to ultimate victory.

5.

What you've just read may, if you're feeling generous, convince you that I am a credible candidate to write a book about drum machines. What it may not convince you of is the need for such a book in the first place.

If so, you're not alone.

For almost every musician who greeted my interview request like Daniel Lanois—"I got kind of excited," he told me. "Nobody ever asks about beat boxes much!"—there was a good-natured skeptic.

"I'm not aware at all whether, or how important it'll be, for the public to get informed about drum machines and the way musicians used them in the past," contends Hans-Joachim Roedelius.

Roedelius made use of some of the earliest rhythm boxes in the hugely influential Krautrock bands Kluster and Harmonia. So his disavowal might seem surprising.

But many of the drum machine users interviewed for this book are well into their seventies now. Roedelius himself will soon be eighty-seven. Some memories of machines and how they worked are simply unrecoverable.

And in some cases, the machines were, and always will be, secondary to the creative impulse. A means to an end, in other words—and therefore not to be studied. Or even, in some cases, remembered at all.

As Roedelius puts it, gut instinct trumps note-taking. "I'm working out of the belly, deciding in the very moment what to do," he says, "what to use, and how."

6.

Without being too reductive, it seems important to say at the beginning what this book is not.

First, there's inevitable overlap between drum machines and other forms of electronically manipulated percussion. There are electronic drums, of course. But there are many other devices to consider. Musical workstations like the Fairlight CMI and the Synclavier. Samplers, drum triggers, and loop generators. Analog synthesizers that can generate rhythmic pulses, and keyboards with built-in drum machines. And computer recording programs that can instantly provide anyone a library of vintage rhythm units.

Almost all of these devices operated simultaneously with standalone drum machines during the 1980s, the period that dominates this book. But to cover fully each of these subjects would require a separate volume for each. My goal here is to talk about those developments within the context of drum machines. That is, how did these devices *anticipate* drum machines? How did these devices *complement* drum machines? And how and why, in some cases, did these devices *replace* them?

Second point: when musicians have spoken about drum machines over the years, they've often simply referred to them as "the drum machine," with no reference to make or model.

I've made every effort to nail down those details in these pages. However, I did not always succeed. I went several rounds with many patient musicians who looked over pictures of old drum machines and tried to pick their devices out of the proverbial lineup. But the effort didn't always pay off.

We tend to think that musicians and producers have photographic memories of every instrument and every session. As the quote from Hans-Joachim

Roedelius above reminds us, they don't. And that leads to another unfortunate truth about drum machines.

There are far more variations of, and variants among, drum machines than even a professional musician probably knows. To catalogue them all would have meant writing a completely different sort of book, or doubling the length of this one.

I've tried to include as many significant machines as possible here. But for me, the most interesting part of drum machine history is not only how they were made, but how they were employed. The story of the most high-tech endeavor is still the story of people. When in doubt, I have erred on the human side in this book. After all, drum machines inevitably reflect the humanity of their creators.

Fortunately, there already exist books that catalog a huge variety of drum machines and electronic percussion instruments, including their technical specifications. New Zealand musician and producer Alex Graham has written four illustrated volumes that track drum machines from their earliest preset days to the modern era. This quartet of books was invaluable in my research, and I can't recommend them highly enough. (For those able to track it down, Joe Mansfield's coffee table book *Beat Box: A Drum Machine Obsession* is also a worthy addition to any music library.)

This volume tries to do something different. I knew drum machines affected music. I also knew they affected me—deeply and personally. So I wanted to find out more about others who were so affected. I wanted to tell the untold story of drum machines, from the perspective of the people who made them. Who used them. Who cursed them, frequently. But who also loved them. As I did, and still do.

7.

"Everybody's talking to computers/They're all dancing to a drum machine," Rick Springfield sang back in 1983, in the hit "Human Touch." He even made a *Star Wars*-style video to illustrate his point.

George Orwell's magical year of 1984 was then just months away. So it was popular at the time to predict that Orwell's dystopia was just around the corner, too. No one could have guessed that it would be MTV heartthrob Rick Springfield who'd make the most prescient observation of the era.

Obviously, everybody's talking to computers. But we're also all dancing to a drum machine, of some sort. We have been, for a long time—even when we didn't know it.

Chances are that you're fascinated by drum machines like me, and like the far more interesting people who are the subjects of this book. Even if you're not—perhaps *especially* if you're not—thanks for being willing to follow the beat of this very different drummer.

1

From Boats to Babies:
How Drum Machines Began

There is music wherever there is rhythm, as there is life wherever there beats a pulse.

Igor Stravinsky

I think drum machines are huge. I was watching this program the other night and when the waves hit the floor of the ocean, the skin of the Earth moves. And it's all rhythmic, and the Earth's skin makes a sound like a drum.

Musician and drum machine user Arthur Brown

1.

In the beginning, there was rhythm.

And immediately *after* the beginning, there was someone complaining that the rhythm was a little too fast, or a little too slow.

Probably not long after that came the first drummer joke. And probably not long after *that*, the laughter subsided, and someone started thinking about how nice it would be if there were a way to make rhythm steady, and regular. And perfect.

2.

If rhythm is joined inexorably to water, as Arthur Brown suggests, then it makes sense that the first drum machine depended on water, as well.

Some might call Ismail al-Jazari the Muslim Leonardo da Vinci. This would be a mistake. That's because al-Jazari lived and worked more than three centuries before da Vinci. As *National Geographic* points out, da Vinci was more like the Italian al-Jazari.

Like da Vinci, Ismail al-Jazari was a polymath: an artisan, an engineer, a mathematician, and an inventor. It's that last category that brings him to our attention.

In *The Book of Knowledge of Ingenious Mechanical Devices*, which appeared at the start of the thirteenth century, al-Jazari gives us all the biographical information we possess about him. His full name was Badi al-Zaman Abu al Izz Ismai'l al-Razzaz al-Jazari. "Badi al-Zaman" means "Prodigy of the Age" and it was a term used for lots of well-known men. Few deserved it as much as al-Jazari.

The name "al-Jazari," meanwhile, is a reference to his homeland: al-Jazira, otherwise known as upper Mesopotamia. But when *The Book of Knowledge of Ingenious Mechanical Devices* appeared, in 1206 CE, al-Jazari tells us he had been working for nearly thirty years in what is now Turkey. Like his father, he served al-Din, the king of Diyar Bakr.

Fifty of Al-Jazari's experiments—for devices called *shaki*—are collected in *The Book of Knowledge of Ingenious Mechanical Devices*. The book, al-Jazari tells us, came by royal command of King al-Din. It would apparently be one of his final acts; he died the same year it was presented to the king. In the book, he acknowledges his debt to earlier creators, and is careful to note that he has only included experiments that he actually built and tested. "I found that some of the earlier scholars and sages had made devices and had described what they had made. They had not considered them completely nor had they followed the correct path for all of them," he wrote, "and so wavered between the true and the false." These new experiments include early camshafts and crankshafts, the rotating devices that power engines. They feature escapements, the pendulum-and-gear mechanisms used in clocks and watches, which produce that familiar ticking sound. And they boast complex systems of pumps, used to regulate the many water-based machines that al-Jazari created. His most famous invention was probably a water clock featuring an elephant and its driver.

Al-Jazari was fascinated with automata—mechanical creatures. He's sometimes called the father of modern robotics because he used his devices to power artificial beings. These figures were constructed of wood, of beaten copper, and of papier mache. Some were animals: cows, elephants, serpents.

Some were humans, from slave girls to swordsmen. Many were musicians. And some of those musicians were drummers.

The most significant device for us is a boat that contained several automata. Four are musicians: two tambourine players, a harpist, and a flautist. The boat would have floated on a lake, providing automated entertainment at royal drinking parties. (This was a big deal in the court of King al-Din. A whole subsection of al-Jazari's book is titled "Vessels and Figures Suitable for Drinking Sessions.")

The musicians were made of jointed copper. The two tambourine players had been fitted with axles. One end was fastened to the sleeve of their robes. The other end contained two wooden pegs. When the boat's reservoir was filled with water, the axles turned, and the pegs struck levers that created rhythms. This would provide musical accompaniment for about a half hour, until the reservoir drained and had to be refilled.

Most notable, though, is the fact that the pegs could be removed and reconfigured. Doing this would change the rhythms of the tambourine players. "The movement of the hand," al-Jazari wrote, "gives two beats and one [beat]." But these beats could be altered by moving the pegs.

"In other words," as a publication from the University of Sheffield pointed out, "it is a programmable drum machine."

Faculty member Noel Sharkey, an emeritus professor of artificial intelligence and robotics in the school's computer science department, built a model of al-Jazari's boat in 2007. He limited his automata to a single drummer. But he was particularly interested in the potential programmability of al-Jazari's creation.

"Whether or not al-Jazari dynamically programmed his machines is an intriguing question," Sharkey said. "It is quite likely that he used this method, at the very least, for fine-tuning the rhythm of the musicians."

This method of using pegs as a way to program rhythms definitely traveled down the centuries. Since 1206, al-Jazari's rhythmical fine-tuning has been on the minds of musicians everywhere.

3.

It apparently stayed in the *back* of their minds for some time, however.

It wasn't until 1930—nearly eight hundred years after the birth of al-Jazari— that someone got fed up enough to try developing a new drum machine.

That someone was American composer Henry Cowell. Along with contemporaries like Charles Ives and Edgard Varese, Cowell was looking beyond the limitations of Western music.

He opened up the piano lid to generate sounds from the instrument's insides. He invented the concept of the "tone cluster"—a sound made by playing notes right next to each other on a keyboard, sometimes with a fist or other object.

But Cowell had a surprisingly traditional—which is to say, precise—view of rhythm. His friend Nicholas Slonimsky, a Russian conductor and composer, noted that Cowell was "annoyed by the wistful realization that … human players will still be human—that is, inaccurate, psychologically limited, rhythmically crippled, and unwilling to reform." The answer, Cowell thought, was "an instrument which would faithfully reproduce all kinds of rhythms and cross-rhythms."

The idea for this instrument was first proposed by Cowell in his 1930 book *New Musical Resources*:

> It is highly probable that an instrument could be devised which would mechanically produce a rhythmic ratio, but which would be controlled by hand and would therefore not be over-mechanical. For example, suppose we could have a keyboard on which when C was struck; a rhythm of eight would be sounded; when D was struck, a rhythm of nine; when E was struck, a rhythm of ten. By playing the keys with the fingers, the human element of personal expression might be retained if desired. It is heartily proposed that such an instrument to play the scale of time-values given at the end of this chapter be constructed.

Cowell, however, was not the right person to construct it. So he turned to his friend Leon Theremin.

Born Lev Sergeyevich Termen in St. Petersburg, Russia, Theremin became best known for the device that bears his name. Patented in 1928, the theremin was the first mass-produced electronic instrument. Without it, as his biographer Albert Glinsky notes, "there could have been no synthesizer." Users control two oscillators for volume and frequency by waving their hands. This instrument would later become the signature element of such songs as The Beach Boys' "Good Vibrations."

The basic idea of what would become the Rhythmicon was Cowell's. He imagined a photoelectric cell powering a beam of light. When users pressed a key, rotating wheels inside the machine would break up the light beam into patterns. These patterns would trigger the sounds and rhythms of the instrument. In March 1931, Cowell gave Theremin $200 to put this idea into practice.

Theremin created a machine that looked like a small home organ. Each of its sixteen keys played a rhythm, with the number of notes increasing as you went up the keyboard. The lowest key sounded one note per beat, all the way up to the sixteenth key, which played sixteen notes per beat. "Essentially," Glinsky writes, "it was a prototype of an early drum machine."

The Rhythmicon had another feature that made it similar to early drum machines. It was polyphonic, which meant that multiple rhythms could be played by pressing multiple keys.

Cowell and Russian composer Joseph Schillinger debuted the Rhythmicon in January 1932 at New York's New School for Social Research. It was less than a year after its commission—an impressive achievement. But critics focused on complaints that would dog many future drum machines.

Musical America conceded that the "theoretical interest is high." But its reviewer had his doubts about a machine focused exclusively on rhythm. "The ear, being more accustomed to listen for melody than rhythm," he wrote, "is apt to ignore the latter."

The sound of the Rhythmicon didn't wow the press, either. The *Musical Courier* described it as something like "a strong flute in the high register; or a strong bassoon in the low register." When Cowell took the instrument to a demonstration at Stanford University, *The San Francisco Chronicle* gave an even less flattering report. The sounds of the low keys were like "a cross between a grunt and a snort." In the higher keys, the Rhythmicon approximated "an Indian war whoop."

Marc Blitzstein of *Modern Music* sounded like many a later drum machine critic. "Insofar as one is constrained to represent a single rhythm always upon the same repeated note, and without deviation from the regular beat," Blitzstein wrote, "the limitations far outweigh the advantages, from a practical point of view."

Composer Charles Ives tried to address some of these complaints by commissioning Theremin to build a second Rhythmicon. This one had two sliding controls: one to regulate pitch, the other to control tempo.

Cowell came up with a notation system for his instrument, and even wrote a four-movement score for Rhythmicon and orchestra called *Rhythymicana*. Yet this early drum machine never caught the public's imagination.

Theremin's first prototype fell into disrepair at Stanford, and was junked in 1938. The second, improved unit survived, and can be seen today at the Smithsonian Institution. A third unit was built by Theremin in Moscow, where it is now housed in the Theremin Museum. He remained proud of his invention, and made special mention of this third and final model when the *New York Times* interviewed him in 1967.

"It can produce any combination of complex rhythms," he told the paper's Harold Schonberg, during a tour of his lab. "Let me play you seven against nine. Or would you like to hear five against 13? Very important. A conductor can stand here and learn to beat four with one hand, and five with the other." But the need for a machine that would play simpler rhythms, with improved sounds, left the market open for another inventor.

4.

The instrument for which Harry C. Chamberlin is remembered today is not a drum machine. It's the Mellotron, a keyboard that revolutionized music when it appeared in the 1960s. Chamberlin came up with the concept, which involved using magnetic tape loops to simulate the sounds of instruments like strings and woodwinds.

When you pressed the keys, you could have, as *Crawdaddy* magazine put it in 1976, a "Phantom Orchestra at your Fingertips." The Beatles' Paul McCartney made unforgettable use of the Mellotron during the intro of "Strawberry Fields Forever," when he used it to simulate the sounds of flutes. And many people have called Chamberlin the father of sampling, thanks to his use of tape loops.

But not everyone knew that Chamberlin was actually responsible for the Mellotron. One of his salesmen, Bill Fransen, had grown frustrated at the design flaws that plagued Chamberlin's invention. In the early 1960s, he took a model of Chamberlin's Model 600 keyboard to England, trying to find someone who could improve it.

The trio of brothers who fixed the problem mistakenly believed that Fransen also owned the patent to Chamberlin's keyboard. They formed a company called Mellotronics, which began manufacturing the Mellotron soon afterward. But Chamberlin held a US patent for his invention, and worked out a royalty deal with Mellotronics. He went on to develop his own line of Chamberlin keyboards—which he always said sounded better than Mellotrons.

However, the Mellotron had actually begun life as a drum machine. In fact, it was the first one available for sale, although Chamberlin rarely talked about this.

Undoubtedly feeling burned by his experience with Mellotron, Chamberlin gave only few interviews during his lifetime. One of the most substantial occurred in *Crawdaddy*, when he was seventy-four years old.

Chamberlin was an Iowa native who bounced around the Midwest during the 1920s and the Depression. He told *Crawdaddy*'s Len Epand that he'd worked at a Milwaukee electronics factory, installed heating and refrigeration equipment in Illinois, and had insulated buildings in Lacrosse, Wisconsin.

He was also interested in music, and formed an eight-piece dance band, in which he played saxophone and clarinet. But he also revealed to Epand that he'd had a nervous breakdown at age twenty-five, when he was "burning the candle at both ends." Some of the burning might have been invention related: Chamberlin claimed to have built his own speedboat and a car windshield washer that he failed to patent.

In 1949, he was back in Lacrosse. He'd bought a home organ, which had become increasingly popular following the Second World War. In the interim period between the decline of radio and the widespread adoption of television, companies like Hammond and Lowrey marketed their organs to families as entertainment devices. These instruments were also increasingly easy to use. Hammond debuted the chord organ in 1950, allowing users to play full chords with the touch of a button.

Chamberlin was making a tape recording of the organ to send to his parents in California when he had his great revelation. "For heaven's sake," he told *Crawdaddy*, "if I can put my finger down and get a Hammond organ note, why can't I pick a guitar note or trombone note and get that under the keys somehow, and be able to play any instrument? As long as I know how to play the keyboard, I could play *any* instrument!"

But the first instrument he tried to play with his tape-loop system was a drum kit. At some point around 1949, Chamberlin moved to California, to join his parents. In his garage in the Los Angeles suburb of Upland, he began constructing a machine he called the Model 100. It used fourteen quarter-inch tape loops, each of which played a prerecorded drum pattern.

Housed in a wooden cabinet with an amplifier and 12-inch speaker, the Model 100 made ingenious use of its tape loop system. The short tape loops could be sped up or slowed down to control tempo. And the drum loops sound very similar to the sorts of beats that hip hop and dance music producers would later plunder en masse.

But Chamberlin only built between four and ten Model 100s, by most estimates. With his next invention, the Model 200, Chamberlin expanded his sound palette to other instruments, paving the way for the Mellotron. He would not return to dedicated rhythm units again until he developed a line of Rhythmate units during the 1960s. Manufactured at Chamberlin's Ontario, California workshop, these machines were also tape-loop based.

However, technology was moving toward more streamlined designs and by then, Chamberlin had other concerns. He was not only fighting for his Mellotron patent: his products were also the target of bans from musicians' unions.

Since they first appeared in the 1950s, Chamberlin's inventions had prompted the unions' ire. Their complaints centered more around Chamberlin's tape loops replacing string and horn players. But the accusations were exactly the same as those that would someday be used against drum machines. "Actually, I was told by authorities that if I would sue 'em, they wouldn't have a chance," Chamberlin told *Crawdaddy*. "But I didn't have the money to fight those guys, you know. Cause they would keep you goin' and goin' until you're broke ... I'm retired now. I don't want to go back."

The way forward in drum machines was taken up instead by the Wurlitzer Company. Founded in Cincinnati, Ohio by German immigrant Rudolph Wurlitzer in 1853, the company became famous in the early years of the twentieth century for its pipe organs, which were often used in theaters. During the big band era, Wurlitzer jukeboxes were so popular that the company name became synonymous with the invention. And in the 1950s, Wurlitzer joined the home organ market to compete with companies like Hammond, Lowrey, and Baldwin.

The Side Man, which debuted in 1959, was a standalone, "electro-mechanical" rhythm machine that could be used alongside an electronic organ. "Now you can be a combo all by yourself!" an ad for the Side Man promised. "Flip a switch ... and there's a full rhythm section at your side!"

The Side Man was similar in construction to the Chamberlin. Its guts were enclosed by a mahogany cabinet, which contained an amp and speaker. But the Wurlitzer ads were quick to point out that "the Side Man uses no tapes or recordings."

This was an advantage in some ways, though not in others. Because it wasn't using drum loops, the Wurlitzer was the first drum machine to include individual drum hits. Vacuum tubes and a valve amplifier powered the sound-generating circuits to create ten individual instruments: a bass drum, three tom-toms, two temple blocks, a wood block, claves, maracas, a brushed snare, and a cymbal.

The sounds were triggered in patterns by an internal mechanism that looked like a clock. The clock "face" was a disc with electrical contact points mounted in various configurations. When one of the ten preset patterns was selected, a motorized dial swept across the face of the disc, like the hand of a clock. The contacts on the dial triggered the appropriate contacts for the ten preset patterns, including a metronome.

Adjusting the tempo was simple: when the internal dial sped up, so did the pattern. You could go from 34 beats per minute to 150. The internal motor was noisy, however, and there was sometimes lag in the rotation of the dial.

Yet the Side Man might have been the first rhythm machine to truly strike fear into the hearts of drummers. Motown producer Hal Davis recalled buying a Side Man in the early 1960s, and using it for a restaurant gig when his drummer called off:

> After plugging it in, I was trying out some of the rhythms before getting ready to resume playing our next set. The others of the group were busy watching while I tried to set it up. Suddenly, I looked up and saw three couples on the dance floor dancing to the rhythm of the Side Man all by itself.
>
> Have you ever had the feeling that you might be expendable?

Davis, who would later produce drum machine users like Stevie Wonder and Michael Jackson, did outlast the Side Man. But it was the first drum machine to be widely available to consumers. It retailed for just under $400 when it debuted—roughly $3,500 today—and Wurlitzer continued to manufacture the unit well into the 1960s. That's when transistors changed the world of drum machines, as well as the world at large.

5.

The first commercial recordings that featured a drum machine weren't directed at fans of pop, or disco, or hip hop, or EDM. They were targeted instead at the parents of babies—and at the babies themselves.

The three volumes of *Soothing Sounds for Baby* don't seem like the place where you'd encounter groundbreaking rhythm units. They also don't seem like the place where you'd meet the great unknown genius of electronic music.

These three LPs, released in 1964, were the creation of Raymond Scott. Today, many people view them as ancestors of ambient music and techno.

Scott was a Julliard School of Music graduate, a composer, and a bandleader. But he spent most of his life, and his fortune, inventing electronic devices that should have made him a household name.

They didn't. Even today, lots of books about electronic music barely mention Scott—or ignore him altogether. That's partly because Scott had a mania for privacy. He kept much of his work hidden from even his subordinates. And partly it's because Scott made the name he has—at least to those who are familiar with him—because of his gift for simple, catchy riffs.

Even if you've never heard of Scott, you know his songs. His compositions were adapted by the arranger Carl Stalling and used in more than a hundred Looney Tunes and Merrie Melodies cartoons. Later animated series like *The Simpsons* and *The Ren and Stimpy Show* would also use of Scott's work.

To some, this feels like an outrage. "Raymond Scott should have been as famous as Dolby or Moog or even Stockhausen," writes jazz critic Ted Gioia. "Instead he's unfairly pigeonholed as accompanist to Bugs Bunny and Porky Pig."

But as Gioia also points out, Scott was a relentless undercutter of his own legend. "In 1963, he developed a drum machine, but decided to name it 'Bandito the Bongo Artist,'" Gioia writes. "How could you take this technology seriously?"

Scott, at least, certainly did. Born Harry Warnow in Brooklyn, New York, Scott changed his name to avoid charges of nepotism. That's because his older brother Mark was a conductor and musical director for the radio show *Your Hit Parade*. Raymond wanted to follow in his brother's footsteps, and joined the CBS house orchestra. Later he would write for Broadway, compose pop songs, and try his hand at classical music. But when his brother died in 1949, Scott took over the *Your Hit Parade* orchestra. His second wife, Dorothy, became the show's featured vocalist.

It was a well-paying gig, and Scott used the money to finance his inventions. In 1946, he'd established Manhattan Research, a company he called "a dream center where the excitement of tomorrow is made available today." He always thought big. In 1949, he promised, "Someday, perhaps within the next hundred years, science will perfect a process of thought transference from composer to listener."

Within a decade, Scott had created a literal "Wall of Sound" at his Manhasset, New York, home. The wall was dominated by what an astonished young Columbia University student named Bob Moog realized was a huge electromechanical sequencer. Moog, who designed circuits for Scott and later went on to develop the first commercial synthesizer, was an admiring witness to many of Scott's other inventions.

One of them, the Clavivox, adapted the theremin into a keyboard instrument. Another, the Electronium, became Scott's lifetime project. This invention tried to bridge the gap between man and machine. It allowed for a "duet" between a composer and the Electronium: the composer would make choices from a set of variables, and the machine would use this data to craft a real-time composition.

Scott's two rhythm-based machines, meanwhile, anticipated much later technologies. The first such device, which appeared in 1960, was simply called the Rhythm Synthesizer. The second, Bandito the Bongo Artist, was invented in 1963, although it wasn't patented until 1968.

Scott described Bandito in the application as a "device that automatically and performs bongo-like drum improvisations, an infinite variety of pitches, rhythms, and colors—comparable to—and frequently more exciting than the most brilliant bongos anywhere." It contained eight oscillators, "all long-pitched, bongo-like." As they played in sequence, the pitch, accent, rhythm, and tempo of these sounds could be "occasionally, but randomly and attractively" changed by random trigger generators.

You can hear this process on "Bandito the Bongo Artist," a 90-second song included on the posthumous Scott compilation *Manhattan Research, Inc.* And Bandito was probably the rhythm unit showcased on the three volumes of *Soothing Sounds for Baby*, each of which is geared toward a specific age range.

The three volumes of *Soothing Sounds*, however, all flopped. For author David Stubbs, Scott was simply a man out of time. "Here was Scott's problem: he was stranded in futurist space in the 1960s, having arrived too early," Stubbs writes, "too ahead of a society that in the tumult of the decade had mentally deferred the dreams of the Tomorrow People."

Scott died of pneumonia in 1994, far less known than a man of his accomplishments deserved. A letter apparently written near the end of his life is a poignant reminder. It was unaddressed, but it seemed to be pitching a story to a publication about Scott's invention of the sequencer. It shows that even Scott realized his fears of having his work stolen might have been overblown.

"I was so secretive about my development activities—perhaps neurotically so," lamented Scott. "Now, with the passing of years, I guess I regret my secrecy and would like for people to know of what I accomplished."

The next wave of drum machine inventors would certainly build upon Scott's many innovations—even if his furtive nature meant he wouldn't get the credit he deserved.

✳✳✳

2

The Rhythm Aces

1.

The young man is listening to the radio he built, wearing headphones so he won't disturb the other patients. He loves music, and he's always wanted desperately to play an instrument.

That, however, is the least of his worries today. The young man has tuberculosis. He's been confined at this sanitarium in Osaka, Japan for the past three years. And his condition isn't improving. He's lost nearly 50 pounds from his original weight of 132.

The young man is an electronics genius. During his hospitalization, he's managed to build a prototype TV receiver. Television is new and incredibly novel in 1953 and parts are expensive. But he was able to make most of them himself, and he convinced his aunt to loan him the money for the picture tube. Other patients in the sanitarium crowded around his bed to watch the strange new device.

Now, however, his hands shake, and he finds the work he loves to do almost impossible. Even the good news—an antibiotic cure called streptomycin, developed by Dr. Selman Waksman at Rutgers University—quickly turns bad. The black-market price for injections is 10,000 yen per shot. That's twice the average monthly salary of a Japanese office worker. And the young man needs forty shots for a full recovery.

Then a miracle occurs. Because he's so near death's door, the young man is chosen as a test subject for the streptomycin injections. And not only does the treatment work, the results are almost instantaneous. He regains his appetite, and begins putting on the lost pounds. He's strong enough to start studying English again.

Less than a year after being discharged from the sanitarium, the young man has married his fiancé. He's become a father. And he's opened a small appliance shop in Osaka. Best of all, he's been spared an occasional, but dreadful, side effect of the streptomycin treatments: deafness.

"So I could continue my relationship with musical instruments," the young man would write, many years later.

That relationship would ultimately change every aspect of music-making. And had Ikutaro Kakehashi died of tuberculosis, instead of living to the ripe old age of eighty-seven, much of the music we know and love might never have existed. Neither would this book.

2.

In 2001, Ikutaro Kakehashi was interviewed at the NAMM conference. NAMM stands for National Association of Music Merchants, and the conference is the world's biggest musical trade show.

Kakehashi had been a regular guest since the mid-1960s. Some of his most revolutionary inventions had been unveiled over the years at NAMM. And at age seventy-one, he'd become such a momentous figure in music that most people now simply knew him as "Taro" or "Mr. K."

During this interview, however, he turned reflective. Growing up in Japan during the Second World War, Kakehashi explained, music education was nonexistent. "So I miss many, many chance," he said. An earnest expression spread across his broad face at the memory.

Even after the war, "I want to play, you know?" he asked his interviewer, stretching his hands across an imaginary keyboard, then dropping them. "But violin? Too late. Piano? No place to [play]."

His first response to this dilemma was to learn how to build radios. Then he could at least *hear* the music that fascinated him. But an even better idea presented itself. "I start to build musical instruments," he said. "Electronics only." No one else was doing it. And he saw his opportunity.

Ikutaro Kakehashi learned early on that he had to seize his chances. Both his parents died when he was two, and he was raised by his grandparents. In 1945, when he was fifteen, their home in Osaka was firebombed. The family lost everything, including Kakehashi's extensive model railroad collection. "Strangely, I didn't feel angry or sad when I came across fragments of the collection in the ashes of the house," he wrote in his 2002 autobiography, *I Believe in Music*. "Instead, I decided to start fresh with a new hobby." That hobby would first be the repair of watches. In postwar Japan, with new products in short supply, "people had no alternative but to fix what they had," Kakehashi wrote, "so the demand for repair work was quite large."

Kakehashi had moved with his family to rural Kyushu, Japan's southernmost island. He became an apprentice at a local clock repair shop. But his master refused to teach him how to repair watches. So Kakehashi left after just a few months to start his own business, Kakehashi Watch Shop. There's a photo showing the bold young entrepreneur, just sixteen, standing proudly in sandals and baggy trousers outside his tiny storefront.

Learning how to repair watches from a mail-order manual, Kakehashi found immediate success. He used the profits, however, to pursue a more significant interest: building radios.

When postwar shortages eased in 1950, Japan relaxed its policy about allowing people to return to big cities. Kakehashi quickly liquidated his watch repair shop and went back to Osaka, so he could study electronics at university. Then tuberculosis intervened.

At the end of Kakehashi's four-year sanitarium stay, he'd changed his mind about higher education. And since no one would hire an undernourished-looking former TB patient, he started his own electronics shop in Osaka, assembling and repairing radios and TVs. It was, once again, a successful business. But it still wasn't close enough to Kakehashi's true love: music.

In 1960, he established Ace Electrical Co. Ltd., and made a fateful decision. He wouldn't just repair musical instruments: he would *make* them.

He would start with organs. And he would build them for people with a love of music, but limited musical training, like himself. Inspired by the sounds of an electronic organ he heard in church, Kakehashi began experimenting with prototypes of monophonic organs. These organs had simple keyboards that could only play one note at a time—perfect for amateurs.

Years later, he would admit that the sounds those early instruments produced "probably were not particularly good." Just as he'd done with watches, radios, and televisions, Kakehashi taught himself by taking apart existing products and then duplicating them. He had no choice: getting technical information from the West was a process that could take years. But he was finally following his passion—and learning more with every experiment.

He realized these primitive organs would be even better if they generated their own rhythms. That observation would transform Kakehashi from follower to innovator.

3.

In *Tales of Suspense* #39, which appeared on newsstands in early 1963, the millionaire industrialist Tony Stark amazes a US army general with his new invention: a magnet that can rip open a locked bank vault. The secret? The magnet is powered by transistors.

"My tiny transistors are so powerful that they can increase the force of any device a *thousandfold!*" Stark tells his awestruck audience. Little does he know that these devices will soon help transform him into the superhero Iron Man—and save his own life. But that's another story.

Comic books are well known for taking liberties with science. But in this case, Marvel Comics impresario Stan Lee was pretty accurate. Transistors had emerged from Bell Laboratories in New Jersey at the end of the 1940s. They were the project of three physicists who would win the Nobel Prize for their efforts. By 1963, transistors *were* changing the world—and their possibilities *did* seem limitless.

Transistors are made from silicon, a chemical element that acts as a semiconductor. Transistors can essentially do two jobs. They can act as amplifiers, boosting electrical currents. This makes them useful in devices like hearing aids.

But they can also act as on-off switches. In this way, they're a little like the neurons in your brain. Transistors store information in zeroes and ones. And when electrical currents flow through them, they can be turned on and off individually to access this information. This is why transistors became crucial to the development of computer memory.

Size really did matter when it came to transistors. These switches were small—and kept shrinking. Computer memory chips the size of a dime can now contain millions—perhaps even billions—of transistors. When it came to memory storage, this was revolutionary. No longer did data have to be stored and accessed from bulky physical components, like punch cards or magnetic drums. So the gadgetry that housed these transistors could be shrunk as well.

Ikutaro Kakehashi recognized this when he studied the Wurlitzer Sideman. Its bulk was necessary to house the many components, including the vacuum tubes that produced its ten drum sounds. Meanwhile, the internal mechanics were noisy. And because the machine's patterns were triggered by the rotation of an internal dial, it was also slow.

Another Japanese company called Keio-Giken had already tried to top the Sideman. Accordionist Tadashi Osanai had become frustrated with the

Wurlitzer unit during his Tokyo nightclub sets. He convinced his boss, club owner Tsutsomu Katoh, that they could make their own rhythm unit.

In 1963, the pair debuted the Donca Matic DA-20. It improved on the Sideman by including a whopping twenty-six preset rhythm patterns. And it incorporated a small piano-style keyboard that could be used to play individual drum sounds.

But the Donca Matic used the same internal mechanics as the Sideman. So it was still a large, bulky device, which included an amplifier and speaker designed for onstage accompaniment. And its price approached the average household income in Japan at the time. With smaller, lighter transistors, Kakehashi knew he could do better.

He developed a machine he called the Ace Tone R-1 Rhythm Ace, one of the first transistorized drum machines. The R-1 had a simple push-button front panel, and brackets allowing it to be side-mounted to an organ.

In the summer of 1964, Kakehashi packed up the R-1 and the prototype of an electronic organ called the Canary, and flew to Chicago. There, he would exhibit Ace's transistor powered innovations at the NAMM exhibition. His room at the Conrad Hilton would be his booth.

Nervous, jet-lagged, and overwhelmed by the amount and variety of goods on display, Kakehashi waited anxiously for a knock on his door. But there were almost no visitors. So before the convention opened on the third day, he slipped handwritten messages touting his products—"Transistor Rhythm Machine & Melody Keyboard"—under the doors of hotel rooms where organ companies were exhibiting.

His luck changed a little: the next day, representatives of ten companies, including Hammond, Lowrey, and Baldwin, visited his room. Yet he left Chicago having only sold eight sets of samples. That was enough to keep him going. But he'd recognized a significant flaw in the design of the R-1.

The machine had no preset patterns. Instead, each of the six drum sounds—maracas, claves, wood block, cymbal, and two tom-toms—had to be played manually by pushing the buttons on the front of the unit. This made it highly impractical for an organist who wanted accompaniment while playing. Yet solving this problem "presented a serious technical challenge," Kakehashi soon realized.

To form patterns using transistors, electrical pulses had to trigger each sound. To trigger the sounds at a rate that would allow the playing of complex rhythmic patterns without any lag, Kakehashi calculated, each bar of music had to be subdivided into forty-eight separate parts. How could this much memory be loaded into a small, compact, and affordable rhythm unit?

Kakehashi and his team at Ace developed a diode matrix circuit. Think of the diode matrix as a wire grid that contains chains of diodes. When a current runs through the wires, it triggers a particular string of diodes that store preprogrammed information. Diode matrixes provided RAM—random-access memory—in many early computers. In Kakehashi's new drum machine, the diode chains contained rhythmic patterns that were triggered with the push of a button.

The result of this innovation was the Ace Tone FR-1 Rhythm Ace. The "F" stood for "full automatic," since this machine could now play sixteen preset patterns. But it could do even more than that.

The diode matrix circuit allowed for more than one chain of diodes to be triggered simultaneously. This was an innovation that countless FR-1 users would seize upon. It allowed them, in effect, to radically expand their selection of preset rhythms. Now they could press the buttons for "Rock'n'Roll" and "Tango," or perhaps "Bossa Nova" and "Foxtrot," to create an entirely new, combined pattern.

The FR-1 also included a "cancel" feature that allowed the muting of four different sounds—Cymbal, Claves, Cowbell, and Bass Drum. Once again, this allowed users more rhythmic variety.

Weighing about 15 pounds, the FR-1 even had a handle for portability. The price was around $300—not cheap in 1969, but not unreasonable for a game-changing piece of gear.

"The FR-1 was clearly a turning point for me and for the business," Kakehashi wrote in his autobiography. It impressed a young German sales manager named Erik Gramkow, who became instrumental in spreading Ace products throughout Europe. It also led to a partnership with Hammond Organs, which adopted the Rhythm Ace for its new line of keyboards.

Kakehashi took over a rundown factory in Hamamatsu to keep up with the increased demand for Ace products. And he traveled to Chicago every year for NAMM, becoming better and better known.

During the 1969 convention, Kakehashi attended a Hammond showcase. A flashy young organist entertained the crowd with his playing. But Kakehashi was more interested in the sounds coming from the organist's Ace Tone rhythm unit.

He heard patterns that he hadn't programmed into the Rhythm Ace. And the organist was somehow able to accentuate certain drum sounds by raising their volume.

Fascinated, Kakehashi approached the young man after his set. "This *looks* like my rhythm unit," he said, examining the Rhythm Ace. "But it doesn't *sound* like my rhythm unit!"

The organist pulled out a set of tools, took the cover off the Rhythm Ace, and proceeded to show the flabbergasted Kakehashi all the modifications he'd done. "His eyes were all lit up," the organist recalled, years later. "It was like this soulmate that we found in each other."

These two musical soulmates—Ikutaro Kakehashi and an American keyboardist and inventor named Don Lewis—became more than lifelong friends. Together, they started drum machines on a path to world domination.

4.

The first word that strikes you when talking to Don Lewis is *ebullient*.

Even if you've never seen him perform, you can tell immediately that he's a born entertainer. With a ready smile and an infectious laugh, he embodies that old cliché: "He lights up the room."

You'd never guess that Don Lewis is eighty years old. You'd also never suspect that he spent years fighting a long, bitter battle against the American Federation of Musicians (AFM) during the 1980s.

The local union protested Lewis's performances with LEO, which stood for Live Electronic Orchestra. The LEO was a groundbreaking, integrated collection of synthesizers, drum machines, and sound modules that allowed Lewis to become a one-man band like no other before him.

When threatened with new technology like drum machines and synthesizers, unions usually—and reflexively—fought back. In the short term, the AFM won its battle with Don Lewis. It was an ugly affair, not without racial overtones. Lewis stopped playing and put LEO in mothballs.

Over the long run, however, Lewis came out on top. His story is told in a 2020 documentary called *The Ballad of Don Lewis*. Director Ned Augustenborg concludes the film with vindication. The union finally apologizes. Lewis rebuilds LEO and gives a special performance at the Museum of Making Music in Carlsbad, California, where his invention is now displayed. It's a real-life happy ending. And if the experience left scars, Lewis isn't one to display them.

"If you understand the life, the culture of African-Americans, seemingly nothing has changed for the most part," Lewis explains from his Bay Area studio, his thousand-watt grin momentarily dulled. "We learned to live with this stuff, and it just becomes a part of our armor to do it. And if you sit around and indulge in self-pity, that really doesn't help anybody.

"So you take the disappointments," he concludes, "and you turn them around."

It's necessary to know all that about Don Lewis first. Multiple challenges faced him in the development of drum machines. But he had the right outlook to turn them around instead.

A native of Dayton, Ohio, Lewis grew up listening to Saturday radio broadcasts of the Metropolitan Opera with his mother. He became truly captivated by music, though, after watching the organist at his church.

Piano lessons followed, but Lewis's path to music would be a roundabout one. He studied electrical engineering at the former Tuskegee Institute. Then he served as a nuclear weapons specialist in the US Air Force during the early 1960s. When he was discharged, Lewis relocated to Denver, where he worked as an engineer at Honeywell and directed his church choir on weekends.

His first encounter with a drum machine occurred by accident, when he accompanied a singer on a local TV show. The singer rented an organ for Lewis. And the organ came with its own rhythm unit: a Kinsman Rhythm King.

This early drum machine was the last official act of Kinsman, a musical instrument company based in Laconia, New Hampshire. Beset by financial troubles—in part because of the pains it took to develop the Rhythm King—Kinsman was taken over by the jukebox manufacturer Seeburg, which was starting to manufacture home organs.

The Rhythm King, which debuted in 1962, turned out to have been worth the effort, though few people realized it. It was most likely the first transistor-based drum machine in the world. So it was a surprisingly compact unit, boasting sixteen preset rhythms.

Lewis was entranced. He bought a Seeburg organ that included the Rhythm King, and began using it for gigs at a local Mediterranean restaurant.

Not long afterward, Lewis quit his engineering job and became a salesman for Hammond. In 1968, Hammond debuted a new organ: the X77. "I wanted that organ because it looked *good*," says Lewis, grinning at the memory. "So I traded in my Seeburg and got this Hammond. But it didn't have a rhythm unit."

He approached a fellow salesman for advice, and was directed to the Ace Tone FR-2L. This was a version of the FR-1 designed to sit atop an organ. It even had a wire music stand.

Lewis was happy with his purchase—but not satisfied. Getting the schematics of the X77 and FR-2L had been a condition of buying them. Now he got out his toolbox, delved into the guts of the machines, and went to work.

He was frustrated by the lack of volume control on the rhythm unit. Lewis discovered that the X77 had four separate outputs. Two of these outputs were run through a rotating Leslie speaker, which gave the Hammond organ its trademark vibrating sound. But two other outputs—for bass and percussion—were routed to stationary speakers.

Lewis split the signal from the Rhythm Ace and sent it through these two outputs. Both outputs were affected by the organ's "Expression" foot pedal, which allowed an organist to increase the volume of a passage. Now Lewis could control the volume of the drum machine by pumping the organ's foot pedal. He could accent certain drum sounds to give the preset patterns more variety and life.

"I could just sit there, and I could play the rhythm unit solo, just by pumping the pedal back and forth. That was a part of my act!" he says. "Even though you have a canned sequence, you can make it sound like it's *not* canned, if you add accents to it. And that's what bowled over Mr. Kakehashi."

Lewis also found that each of the percussion instruments in the Rhythm Ace was equipped with a tiny trim pot. By turning the knobs, a user could raise or lower the pitch of an instrument. "It's just like a drummer tightening up their drum heads to get a certain pitch," Lewis explains.

An even more significant modification was Lewis's creation of his own custom rhythm patterns. He was able to do this by using the machine's schematic to figure out the pulse sequence of the diode matrix. Lewis was then able to change the way the drum sounds were triggered internally. Instead of triggering a snare drum on beats two and four of a bar, for example, he might change the pattern so that the snare was triggered on beats two, three, and four.

Lewis and Ikutaro Kakehashi corresponded frequently over the next two years. Then in 1971, Kakehashi invited Lewis to Japan to play a series of concerts. He thought it would be a perfect way to publicize Ace Tone's partnership with Hammond.

"I came to Japan with my Rhythm Ace," Lewis recalls. "When I left, Mr. Kakehashi wrote me and said, 'They had a run on the factory. They couldn't build those rhythm units fast enough.' But he also said, 'Some people will be disappointed because your rhythm unit doesn't sound like theirs.'"

During the 1970s, Kakehashi and Lewis made regular trips across the Pacific to trade ideas about rhythm units. Meanwhile, Lewis was sent new products, and gave feedback to the engineers. Their ultimate collaboration between these two men would be the product of a brand-new company—a company that would establish a peerless drum machine pedigree.

5.

Like many young and ambitious companies, Ace Electronics had entered into investment deals designed to hasten its expansion. In the early 1970s, one of those deals turned sour. A major investor was taken over by Sumitomo Chemical Company—which suddenly became the majority owner of Ace.

"It was terrible to have to work with employees dispatched by Sumitomo Chemical," Kakehashi lamented. "They did not understand music or the music business, and they were not interested in learning." Kakehashi stoically tried to endure the "utter insensitivity" of his Sumitomo bosses. But by 1972, his patience had run out. "I had no option but to walk away from Ace Electronics, the company I had personally started in a storefront 20 years before," he wrote.

"If I had not committed myself to a life's work in electronic music," Kakehashi added, "I probably would have gone into an entirely different business." Now in his early forties, he resolved instead to start over with a new company.

Kakehashi thought the first letter of a company's name set the tone for its success. Opening a dictionary for ideas, he was struck by the name "Roland." It had two syllables, which he thought was the ideal number for customers to remember. And the name was connected to a legendary figure: Roland was a Frankish military leader, whose fictionalized life became the subject of poems and songs throughout medieval Europe. "We would not be a company that followed trends," Kakehashi insisted of Roland. "Rather, we would seek to discover and define new market sectors with creative products that gave musicians wonderful new avenues of expression."

The first such product from Roland, naturally, was a new rhythm unit. It was called the TR-77: "TR" for "transistor rhythm," and "77" in honor of the Hammond X77 organ that Don Lewis played. One difference in the TR-77 and past drum machines was the use of tuned resonant circuits. When these circuits are triggered, they "ring" like a drum. The snare drum of the TR-77 combined one of these circuits with white noise to create a punchier sound.

Two years later, the TR-66 Rhythm Arranger appeared. It was a square box in a woodtone cabinet, with a row of distinctive colored buttons. The TR-66 also boasted a few more analog percussion sounds—a total of ten.

The major improvement was that the TR-66 offered a wider variety of rhythm patterns. The eighteen main presets could be combined with one or more patterns from an additional menu of nine choices, from Slow Rock to Jazz. Each of those twenty-seven patterns included further variations, via the "arrange" selector for which it was named.

What the TR-66 didn't have was the one thing Don Lewis—and many other musicians—wanted most: programmability. "Always, it was about the money. You gotta remember that computer chips were just so expensive in those days," Lewis says. "But I was on Mr. K about that from the very beginning, in 1969," he adds, chuckling. "And his quote was always, 'Yes—but not yet.'"

In the meantime, drum machine users would make do with what they had—beginning the same year Ikutaro Kakehashi and Don Lewis struck up their very rhythmic friendship.

6.

In December 1967, Jimi Hendrix had just released *Axis: Bold as Love*, the second album from his Experience. But the guitarist "was still full of creative juices," remembered engineer Eddie Kramer. "And he wanted to get in the studio and try some things on his own."

So Hendrix entered Olympic Studies in London to test his ideas. "This is the first time there's a record of him coming in the studio, by himself, and creating a drum track, playing guitar, playing bass," said Kramer. "Playing all the parts. Doing everything."

Kramer pulled up the faders on the demo of a song called "Angel." Then he briefly isolated the drum track. The sound of a preset drum machine—it might have been an Ace Tone FR-1—could clearly be heard. This demo version, titled "Sweet Angel," appeared in 1997 on the compilation *South Saturn Delta*. It's a reminder that forward-looking musicians had already grasped the possibilities of rhythm units.

The first American chart single that featured a drum machine, meanwhile, was one of the most unlikely hits imaginable. In July 1969, pianist Dick Hyman grazed the Top 40 with "The Minotaur." The song came from Hyman's album

Moog: The Electric Eclectics of Dick Hyman, a showcase for the new and novel Moog synthesizer.

"The Minotaur" wasn't the first recording to feature a Moog. But the synthesizer overshadowed the truly groundbreaking part of the recording: the drum machine. "Originally it was just an improvisation done with three overdubs on top of a drum machine track," Hyman told *Tape Op* magazine. "We added the melody line, the bass, and finally the drone. The drum machine beat was an odd result of combining a waltz with a bossa nova. It was a lucky inspiration, all around."

The first truly big hit to feature a drum machine, however, probably wouldn't have happened without a bitter sibling disagreement. It occurred in January 1969, when The Bee Gees released the single "First of May," from their forthcoming album *Odessa*.

Robin Gibb, the younger brother of Barry and fraternal twin of Maurice, was deeply hurt by this decision. Just nineteen years old and "unduly sensitive" by his own admission, Robin felt that "Lamplight"—one of his vocal features—should have been *Odessa*'s lead single. Instead, the group chose "First of May," which featured Barry backed by an orchestra.

So Robin left the group and headed into De Lane Lea Studios in Soho to record his solo debut. Originally he planned to call it *All My Own Work*, an obvious declaration of independence. Ultimately the collection was titled *Robin's Reign*.

If that sounds grandiose, the first single lived up to Gibb's ambition. Drenched in strings, the romantic "Saved By the Bell" became a Number 2 hit in the UK that June.

Most noteworthy, however, was that "Saved By the Bell"'s stately rhythm was provided by the "Slow Rock" setting of the Ace Tone FR-1 Rhythm Ace. The song thus became the first major hit to be powered by a drum machine, beating later contenders by at least a year.

In fact, four more of the eleven baroque pop songs on *Robin's Reign* feature the Rhythm Ace—or what we assume is the same machine that appears on "Saved By the Bell." "If indeed Gibb was using a Rhythm Ace machine," authors Mark Brend and Tom Conway write in the book *Strange Sounds*, "he made careful use of the preset-combining and sound-canceling features."

But as Brend and Conway also point out, *Robin's Reign* is a mysterious album. Gibb did several interviews at the time of its release, but talked surprisingly little about the album itself.

And in later years, Gibb rarely returned to the subject of his first solo release. Perhaps he ultimately viewed it as an embarrassment. The second single, "One Million Years," which also included a drum machine, failed to chart in Britain. When asked by a journalist about the album's prospects, older brother Barry didn't hold back. "As for it being a very commercial hit record," he said, "frankly, I just can't agree."

Robin's Reign is now regarded as a minor masterpiece of late-1960s chamber pop. But in the short term, Barry was proven right. Meanwhile, Robin's follow-up solo album, *Sing Slowly Sisters*, was shelved and didn't appear until 2015. By the next summer, presumably chastened, Robin had rejoined Barry and Maurice in a reformed Bee Gees.

Sadly, many of the people involved with *Robin's Reign* are no longer with us—including Gibb himself, who passed away in 2012, and his manager Vic Lewis, who conducted the orchestra. Arranger Kenny Clayton, now in his eighties, is hardly more eager to discuss the subject than Gibb once seemed to be. Contacted at his East Sussex home, Clayton offers few recollections of the sessions—and almost no memories of the drum machine that played an important role in them. "All I remember is trying to get it done as quickly as possible, because I wasn't particularly in love with the song," Clayton says of "Saved By the Bell." "So I went home and wrote out the arrangement." As for the drum machine and who was responsible for it, Clayton casts some doubt as to Gibb's role. "He probably stood by the operator and said, 'That one,' when he heard something he liked," Clayton suggests.

Asked who the drum machine operator might have been, if not Gibb himself, Clayton's patience runs out. "I must tell you right now I do not remember a thing about it," he says. "I think the proper thing to do is to terminate this conversation, because I don't have a single piece of information. It is a complete waste of time."

So *Robin's Reign*, and the drum machine it featured so prominently, remain an enigma. But the increasing influence of Ikutaro Kakehashi, Don Lewis, and their rhythm units during the next decade is no mystery at all.

***

3

Beat Brothers: Sly Stone and J. J. Cale

1.

One was a Californian as colorful as the stage outfits he and his "family" wore, and as larger-than-life as the psychedelic soul anthems they created. The other was a reclusive Oklahoman with a singing voice as gentle as a sigh, whose understated music matched his laid-back personality.

Both men wound up retreating from the limelight, though their songs resonated in their absence. And the beat of their drum machines provides a rhythm that forever links these two unlikely pioneers.

2.

The first Number 1 single to feature a drum machine occurred in 1971. The way its creator used drum machines would forever alter the course of recorded music of every genre.

The cost of these innovations for Sylvester Stewart, AKA Sly Stone, was high. The retreat he made into the studio at the same time he discovered drum machines is a retreat from which he has never completely emerged. His sporadic public appearances over the past fifty years have usually generated more questions than answers.

Some even speculate that the isolation assisted by the drum machine helped splinter one man, already being squeezed in the vice of fame, into two distinctly personalities. "You know, it's Jekyll and Hyde," recalls Richard Tilles, the engineer who helped midwife *There's A Riot Goin' On*, the album that introduced millions of listeners to the drum machine. "I mean, he was Sylvester doing Sly Stone." Even Sly himself admitted to a case of split personality, confessing to TV host Dick Cavett in June 1970 that "I look in the mirror when I write. The reason I do that is ... I can react spontaneously before I realize that I'm going along with what I'm doing."

If Sly Stone became the increasingly drug-addled Mr. Hyde, then Sylvester Stewart was the introverted Dr. Jekyll, the genius who took studio technology to new heights during marathon sessions. "Sly, you know, he's always searching for new sounds. I mean, he is really a *sound* guy," Tilles observes. "He was a brilliant mixer. When he's mixing, it's like he's playing piano. When he was on, there was no one better." But right from the start, the freedom and solitude that drum machines allowed revealed a darker side of Sly to emerge. The music turned inward; as author Jeff Kaliss notes in his book about Sly, "The popular judgment on *Riot* is that it's evidence of Sly's fall from a state of sunlit grace into a miasma of dark introspection, fueled by chemical self-indulgence."

Yet the studio was also an escape from the increasing pressures of fame and hangers on. "At this point, for Sly, the studio was his home," says Tilles, who spent untold hours recording with Sly between 1970 and 1972. "I mean, he didn't do much *except* go to the studio."

"He and I talked a lot. He was having a tough time," adds Tilles. "I'd just lost my dad, and I got a divorce right at time I met Sly. So I escaped to the studio also, because as long as I was high on music and whatever, I didn't have to think about the sadness going on around me."

"And I remember talking to Sly, and I said, 'God, I'm going through all this stuff,' and he said, '*Tell* me about it. You should see what *I'm* going through!' We had some great talks when no one was around. But, you know, he was in torment."

3.

The mansion at 783 Bel Air Road, where Sly Stone took up residence in 1970, was a perfect representation of how he must have been feeling at the time.

Family Stone saxophonist Jerry Martini thought the structure strongly resembled the home of TV's Munster family. The gloomy, Gothic-style residence had been hastily vacated by John and Michelle Phillips of the Mamas and Papas. Martini and other band members discovered LSD, Ouija boards, and occult paraphernalia strewn throughout the house. Not surprisingly, some of the new occupants concluded that the place was haunted.

Not that these occupants—especially not Sly Stone—were pursuing a sunny, carefree lifestyle. There was now a cache of firearms stashed in the pool house, a terrifying pit bull named Gun roaming freely, and bodyguards and wild animals prowling the grounds.

"There were sometimes great moments there, but there were some really ugly moments too," Tilles says. "A lot of people were hanging around, and not all of them, you know, were great people. But I had a ball making that music."

Today, Richard Tilles works at the opposite pole of his former rock 'n roll lifestyle. He provides financial guidance to clients of Wells Fargo Advisors in San Diego. Sporting a distinguished white beard and a calm, reassuring demeanor, he seems like a guy you could trust with your money.

In 1970, he was the guy that Sly Stone trusted with his music. Tilles was then a 28-year-old second engineer honing his craft at Village Recorder, a now-legendary Los Angeles recording studio housed in an old Masonic temple.

Sly first visited Village Recorder to work on a series of singles for his Stone Flower imprint. This was a boutique label through which Sly could introduce a series of Family Stone-related acts to the public. Among them were Little Sister, a female R&B trio fronted by Sly's little sister Vet; Bay Area singer–songwriter Joe Hicks; and the multiracial rock group 6ix.

These singles also allowed Sly the freedom to experiment with a radical new toy: the Maestro Rhythm King MRK-2. Manufactured in Kalamazoo, Michigan by Gibson, Inc's Electronics Division, this drum machine was a push-button unit with eighteen preset rhythms and a pitch control.

Where did Sly get this machine, which he would later christen his "Funk Box"? Even he can't remember. As he told researcher Alec Palao, "I saw it in the corner [of the studio], and I didn't even know what it was, but I got it and started making beats, something like that, because it was new."

Whichever studio Sly found the Maestro in, it wasn't Village Recorder. "It was really limited at the Village," recalls Tilles, who normally worked with Sly upstairs in Studio C. "There was a piece of shit console. It wasn't even close to being state-of-the-art."

This, Tilles would soon learn, was exactly what attracted Sly. "He wasn't into fidelity," Titles says. "He liked it because it created different sounds. So we recorded there, and then to mix down, we had to go somewhere else. We mixed a couple of songs at CBS, and all the rest of them were mixed at the Record Plant."

Sly took the young engineer with him, beginning a partnership that would last for an intensely productive three years. Sly took advantage of Tilles's inexhaustible patience, and he also took advantage of the Maestro, which offered him the control he craved. Finally, he could do everything himself.

To this point, multitrack recordings had almost always followed the drummer, the timekeeper of the song. And no matter how steady the drummer was, there were always variations in time. The drum machine introduced a completely new element into recording. Its timing—in theory, at least—never wavered.

"Basically, Sly used the drum machine as a metronome," Tilles says. This made overdubs easier, since Sly could add and discard parts without having to worry about matching tempos. It was an early preview of the click track, a steadying pulse which was often used to prevent drummers from speeding up or slowing down.

Sly was smitten. As he confessed to Alec Palao. "The people that intimidated me the most were fourteen-, fifteen-year-old white kids that I saw playing music on the computer. I said, I gotta find out how to do this."

But Sly's drum machine was alienating fellow musicians. One of them was his longtime drummer, Greg Errico.

Errico had been the engine of all the Family Stone's biggest hits. Nicknamed "Hands and Feet" because of his amazing dexterity on the kit, he understandably took a skeptical view of the Maestro. "At first when I heard it, I said, 'Oh, a drum machine. This is kind of lame,'" remembers Errico. For Errico, as for many drummers, the machine conjured up a single image: "Some keyboardist in a Holiday Inn lounge." Like many of his bandmates, Errico was in the process of departing the Family Stone during a tumultuous 1971. He remembers taking calls from Sly, realizing that they were offers to record alongside the drum machine, and deciding to stay away.

"It started out that he would use it so he could have a rhythm so he could write," Errico says. "But he heard opportunities to make it more creative than it would have been in its natural state."

Two of those creative opportunities were copied—knowingly or accidentally—by countless other users of preset drum machines. First, the Maestro allowed multiple preset buttons to be pushed, and triggered, at once. Doing so would instantly create a more complex polyrhythm, as both beats played simultaneously.

Sly mostly chose patterns from the seven red buttons that produced Latin rhythms. "The only ones he didn't use were the bolero and the tango because they went *duh-duh-duh-DUH*," Tilles says. "He just wanted something steady."

The more radical innovation was even simpler. Many of Sly's basic tracks from this time, Tilles recalls, began with the Rhythm King and Sly playing organ.

By simply beginning the song on an offbeat—on the second, third, or fourth beat of a rhythm, instead of starting naturally on the first—Sly would automatically invert the machine's pattern, creating, in effect, a whole new rhythm.

One of those offbeat rhythm tracks from the Stone Flower sessions also marked the real beginning of the drum machine era. "Somebody's Watching You," a Little Sister single, became a Top 10 R&B hit in November 1970 and grazed the Billboard Top 40 by year's end.

It was proof for Sly that his critics—the musicians, especially, who said, "'You gonna use that fake stuff?'"—had underestimated the drum machine, and the man who was controlling it.

"If you look at it and you let it run you, it will be fake," he observed decades later. "But if you beat the shit out of it and you make it do how your heart feels, if it can represent how you feel, then it's cool."

4.

Increasingly nervous CBS executives waited throughout 1971 for Sly to deliver his new album. It was provisionally—and presciently—titled *The Incredible and Unpredictable Sly and the Family Stone*. "At some point, I started getting concerned about stories I heard about Sly's personal habits," admitted Clive Davis, the head of Sly's label, Epic. "But every time I met with him, he was on top of his game."

The place where Sly reached his peak during this revolutionary year was the attic of 783 Bel Air Road. Sly reveled in the freedom of recording there in the studio that John Phillips had constructed, and that Tilles had upgraded. Hidden behind a sliding bookcase, the studio boasted a sixteen-track console and the luxury of unlimited time to tinker. And while cocaine and PCP became common in and outside the sessions, Sly also became addicted to overdubs—so many that, as Jeff Kaliss wrote, they "actually threatened to wear out the magnetic oxide coating on the recording tape."

That was of little concern to Sly, who loved the sound of grit—much to Tilles's chagrin. In fact, the real audio concern was not deteriorating tape, but audio leakage. That is, sounds that "leaked" onto other tracks, blurring the separation that multitrack recording was designed to ensure.

"Sly would record everything in the control room. When he was doing vocals, the drum machine would be playing through the speakers. The leakage from the drum machine would go into his microphone. The leakage from the drum machine would go into his pickups on his guitar.

"And I was like, 'Sly, *no!*,'" recalls Tilles with a rueful grin. "But he liked it." Author David Hepworth poetically describes this leakage as a patina that "lay on the surface of the finished record like the glaze of ages on a Rembrandt."

The track that perfectly encapsulates this era, including its use of the drum machine, is the bittersweet "Family Affair." The song used a similar rhythm pattern to Little Sister's "Somebody's Watching You." However, Tilles made several crucial contributions that made the sound of "Family Affair" singular.

With only a single mono output that went straight into the studio's mixing board, the Maestro offered few options for altering its signal. But Tilles found one: he cut the treble equalization, so the sixteenth notes of the machine's hi-hat pattern were muted.

This decision met Sly's immediate disapproval. "I brought it to Sly at Bel Air and played to him. The first thing he did, he went to his stereo and he boosted the treble. He said, 'I want those sixteenth notes,'" remembers Tilles with a smile.

But Tilles prevailed, as he did in two other instances that gave the song its unique character. First, he convinced Sly to abandon the James Brown shout in which he'd originally sung the track. Instead, Tilles had Sly lie on a couch at the Record Plant and murmur a far more sedate vocal.

Then Tilles flaunted protocol by applying echo to every track—including the Rhythm King. This decision panicked him when he heard the first mixes. "I said, 'This is worst thing I've ever heard!'" he says. "Because it was so different."

But when the single was released in October 1971, it quickly climbed to the Billboard summit, hitting Number 1 on December 3. Greg Errico, listening to "Family Affair" on the radio as the year drew to a close, shook his head in admiration.

"The drum machine was the intro," remembers Errico. "And it stopped you. 'Oh, wow. What's that?' He took this corny sound and made it a thing that caught the ear."

5.

Around same time that Sly Stone and Richard Tilles were conducting their initial drum machine recordings in 1970, a similar experiment was taking place across the country in Tennessee.

The experimenter was a singer and guitarist named John Weldon Cale. He was better known as J. J.—although "better known" was a misnomer. For more than a decade, the 31-year-old Cale had been trying to break into the music business. Now that elusive success was about to occur.

Eric Clapton had just released a cover of Cale's 1966 composition "After Midnight" on his long-awaited solo debut. Adding gospel backing vocals to Cale's blues shuffle, Clapton turned the tune into a Top 20 hit.

For Cale, who was "deathly poor" and had returned home from Los Angeles, Clapton's cover version was "like discovering oil in your backyard." Now Cale and producer Audie Ashworth were in the studio, trying to capitalize on this stroke of good fortune.

The resulting album, *Naturally*, was deceptively unnatural. On the opening "Call Me the Breeze," Cale counted in the band over a simple rhythm pattern generated by an Ace Tone Rhythm Ace drum machine. "I have an old Japanese drum box called an Acetone. It just goes bomp-chink, bomp-chink, bomp-chink," Cale told *Vintage Guitar* in 2004. "When we did the first album, most people didn't realize that was an electric drum machine – or that there even was such a thing." Yet despite a similar metronomic rhythm, "Crazy Mama" became Cale's first authentic hit, as well as his biggest, reaching Number 22 on the Billboard pop charts in April 1972.

Using the drum machine was a simple matter of expediency, as Cale later recalled. "I didn't use a real drummer because I had no money." Recording the single-output Rhythm Ace was similarly low-frills. "I ran it into a '65 blackface Fender Twin amplifier," Cale said, "and put a microphone on it."

The unassuming Cale didn't mind leaving the Rhythm Ace in place on the finished tracks because, he explained, he and Ashworth "didn't care if the records sold or not; that's why I always called them demos."

Cale would continue to use drum machines to write songs, and they occasionally turned up on record—like "Ridin' Home" on the 1973 follow-up album *Really*. Yet *Naturally* was really the beginning of a whole new chapter in drum machine history.

By the early 1970s, Cale's fellow Oklahoman, pianist and songwriter Leon Russell, had established himself as an L.A. session musician, becoming a member of the famed Wrecking Crew. He'd also produced hits for Gary Lewis and Joe Cocker, begun a solo career, and helped establish the "Tulsa Sound" through the label Shelter Records.

Russell was also fascinated by Cale's drum machine. Studying Cale's "cheesy Ace Tone machine," Russell suggested that it could be improved by adding several features—like the ability to pan individual sounds to different parts of the stereo field.

In short, Russell "wanted to make a fancy drum machine," Cale said. And Russell had the perfect person in his band to conduct this experiment: a young guitarist and songwriter from California named Roger Linn. As Cale noted, "Roger was an electronics nerd," a visionary who'd already seen the musical potential of computers.

Improving the Rhythm Ace would become a personal project for Linn—one that ultimately affected nearly all musicians.

6.

For some listeners, *There's a Riot Goin' On* was Sly Stone's swan song. As early as the month of its release, *Rolling Stone*'s Vince Aletti judged the slippery, slurred and disorienting album "a testament to two years of deterioration rather than two years of growth."

More recently, author David Hepworth made a similar observation about post-*Riot* Sly. Hepworth contends Sly was "wrung dry" by the experience of making this landmark album. "Although Sly made and continues to make records," Hepworth notes, "he never wrote anything significant again."

That assessment is too harsh, and not just because it dismisses some authentically great music. The follow-up to *Riot* is an even more important album in the story of recording technology and drum machines. It's one of three hugely innovative projects from 1973, all of which proved those little black boxes were here to stay.

***

4

The Machines Are Fighting Back

1.

In the Bel Air bedroom, the drummer waited, unsure of what might happen next.

Several other people were standing around, unsmiling, arms folded. The mood in the room, the drummer later recalled, was "very heavy, and sinister, and weird, and dark."

All eyes were on the man sprawled across a huge waterbed. Finally, Sly Stone drawled out an introduction.

"You're a drummer?" he asked the drummer, who nodded.

"Are you *funky*?" Sly inquired.

"Yes," the drummer replied.

Next to the waterbed was a tiny set of Remo practice pads. Sly eyed the makeshift kit, then the drummer.

"Play," he commanded.

The drummer was then employed by up-and-coming soft rocker Carly Simon. In fact, he'd been brought to this Bel Air mansion between Simon's sets at the Troubador. "I knew I'd have about 20 seconds to make an impression," the drummer remembered, "so I just played the funkiest beat I could."

The change was immediate and electric. Sly bounced off the waterbed and began dancing around wildly.

"This is the new drummer," he declared to the onlookers. "Tell the other guy he's fired."

And just like that, Andy Newmark became the brand-new drummer in Sly and the Family Stone. What he didn't realize was that this was the beginning of the pivotal role he'd play in the story of drum machines.

This role would also foreshadow major changes in how music came to be created and recorded. Newmark's partnership with Sly Stone lasted for only one album. But it produced a recording that might have had just as powerful an impact as the previous *There's a Riot Going On*.

Today, Newmark has little interest in retelling stories about his famous employers, like David Bowie, John Lennon, and Bryan Ferry, in addition to the mercurial Sly. He confesses he's "interviewed out."

The subject of drum machines is different, and Newmark warms to it quickly. "They're really fun to play along with, because there's a great little groove in these machines. They're just dead easy to accompany. I mean, that's what you're doing," Newmark points out. "The drummer is not the captain. The machine is the captain; the drummer is an accompanist."

This is a significant admission. Though he's lived in England for years, Newmark is still a pull-no-punches New Yorker. Playing second fiddle to a machine doesn't seem like it would be his first instinct.

Newmark admits as much. Sweatshirt clad and unshaven, he runs a hand through his spiky grey hair and grins. His initial response to drum machines, it turns out, was exactly the same as that of his predecessor, Greg Errico.

"Listen, initially, I associated the Rhythm Ace with something very corny and tacky and square," he says. "But I quickly realized that it wasn't."

2.

Despite Sly Stone's fascination with mechanical rhythm, Newmark was certain he would be playing with "one of the most amazing live acts ever. They could pretty much blow anybody off the stage. That was the thrill for me."

He soon discovered the Family Stone had become mostly fiction. "Half of the band was gone by that time," Newmark recalls. Among the defectors were Errico, and Larry Graham, who developed the thumb-popping sound of slap bass.

So the follow-up to *There's a Riot Goin' On* would be a surprisingly minimalistic affair. There would be occasional overdubs from various band members. Most of the record, though, would be a three-man show: Sly, Newmark, and the drum machine Sly called his "Funk Box." "There was never a conversation. He didn't have much to say conversationally, ever," Newark says. "We went in the studio one day. It was just me and him and an engineer, and he played a track with the Rhythm Ace on it. And just said, 'Play.'"

Richard Tilles served as the engineer for some of these sessions, working on most of the basic tracks. But the stresses of *Riot* had taken a considerable toll. He was also unhappy that Sly had begun to experiment with other drum machines like the Ace Tone Rhythm Ace, which Tilles felt were inferior to the Maestro Rhythm King. Faced with another recording process that threatened to stretch into infinity, Tilles decided he'd had enough.

Newmark can't recall which track kicked off the sessions for *Fresh*. Perhaps it was "In Time," the song that would begin the album. After a two-count from the drum machine, with a synthesized snare fill and claves, Newmark adds his kick drum to the mix. He plays off the beat with a series of snare and hi-hat accents before joining his entire kit to the track.

The hybrid is a revelation: the bubbling drum machine holds down the time, while Newmark improvises an irresistibly loose, stop–start pattern. The funky syncopation was so striking that Miles Davis forced his band to listen to the song repeatedly.

The first song recorded might also have been "If You Want Me To Stay," a hit single that begins with a drum machine pattern playing on the offbeats before Newmark's kick drum establishes the one. Or perhaps it was "Let Me Have It All," which reworks the complex syncopation of "In Time" at a slower tempo.

The fact that Newmark doesn't remember which song came first points to the thoroughly modern way that *Fresh* was made. The unshakeable pulse at the heart of the songs not only allowed overdubbing, it *invited* it.

"I put a drum track down on something, and two weeks later I'd come back in and he would have changed the bass and the voice," Newmark remembers. "And he'd be like, 'Okay, Andy, do the drums again, because I've rewritten a song around this.'

"The only thing that remained consistent on all these songs was the Rhythm Ace. Everything else kept evolving," throughout 1972 and well into 1973. "Until Epic Records cut him off and said, 'No more money for recording. You have to mix the record and hand it in.'"

Newmark realized early on the potentially destructive seeds of this freedom. But when *Fresh* finally appeared in June 1973, it had an effect that went well beyond its sales—even though it was Sly's final Number 1 album.

"It became a musician's record," Newark says. "Like a Miles Davis album, you know? Musicians were digging on this record, so it became a great calling card for me."

One of those musicians was guitarist Ronnie Wood, who was in between jobs with The Faces and The Rolling Stones when he recorded his first solo album in 1974. Two songs on *I've Got My Own Album to Do* could have been outtakes from

Fresh. "Shirley" and the Willie Weeks-penned instrumental "Crotch Music" use a funky combination of drum machine patterns and Newmark's drumming that was clearly inspired by Sly.

"Ronnie had a little rhythm box, a Rhythm Ace probably," Newmark recalls. "He'd bought it just to mess around with at home. It became, very quickly, a songwriters' tool.

"Because it did the two things most drummers couldn't do," says Newmark with a wry grin. "It didn't talk back. And it kept perfect time."

The overdubbed story of *Fresh* soon became the story of nearly all popular music. And it happened because of the way Sly Stone saw the hidden value of a humble piece of technology.

Even Sly couldn't always admit to fellow musicians what he was up to in those days. "I'd have to lie at first and say, 'Rhythm box, no, I'll never do that!'" he acknowledged in 2014. "I'd get all kinds of musicians saying, you're crazy, you're tripping, what kinda weed you got?'

"But then the songs started getting popular," he added, "and I just told them the truth, yeah."

With that truth revealed, others would soon follow Sly's lead.

3.

James Mtume is insistent. He wants his interviewer to listen immediately to "Phase 1," a track from his first solo album. The song is forty seconds of congas played through a Mu-Tron phaser effect. The result is a waterfall of tumbling drum hits, like a brief rain shower in some tropical forest.

"I think it'll blow your mind," the 75-year-old Mtume says, in a gravely voice, before commanding, "Call me right back when you've heard it."

The pride Mtume takes in this percussive innovation is evident. So you can imagine how he feels about being the musician who introduced the drum machine to jazz.

He did it while serving as the percussionist in Miles Davis's band during the early 1970s. Davis's exquisite, muted trumpet solos and equally stylish suits had made him a household name over the past two decades. But even at his most popular, he'd always been an envelope-pushing musician.

On the 1970 double album *Bitches Brew*, Davis began incorporating rock and funk elements into a dense, uncompromising brand of jazz fusion. Mtume joined the Davis band for 1972's *On the Corner*, which showed Miles had been listening closely to Sly Stone.

Though just twenty-three, Mtume boasted his own jazz legacy. Born James Forman in South Philadelphia, he was the son of saxophonist Jimmy Heath, and the stepson of pianist James "Hen Gates" Forman. But Mtume quickly learned it would take far more than connections to impress his new boss.

"So I'm the young buck. And I'm like, 'Man, we only had three practices, and we're about to go to Europe. We need to practice more,'" remembers Mtume. "So Miles told everybody to leave, and he told me to stay. And he said, "Mother*fucker*, I pay you to practice *onstage*.""

"He said, 'I don't want you to overlearn stuff, because I don't want you to *overcook the meal*.' I'll never forget those words. He wanted every night to be an adventure. Some nights, shit happens and you don't always get there. But you learn somethin' along the way."

That thought traveled with Mtume to Japan, where the *On the Corner* band toured during June of 1973. During their visit, they were invited to visit a Yamaha factory.

"Yamaha had just started making instruments," remembers Mtume. "So each cat in the band got an instrument. And then they said, 'We got this thing called a drum machine'—a Yamaha. So I said, 'Give me *that*!'"

The device in question was probably the EM-90 Ensemble Mixer. More than just a drum machine, it also contained a six-channel mixer with a built-in spring reverb.

But it was the drum machine, which contained eight preset patterns, that fascinated Mtume. "I said, lemme see what I can do with this. And in the context of that *On the Corner* band, the only thing you can do is somethin' that hasn't been done."

That meant Mtume would use the machine to generate atmosphere, not tempo. "I would play maybe four rhythms at the same time," he says. "So it became more of a texture, a *whoosh-whoosh-whoosh-whoosh*. I'd use four beats, and I'd run 'em through these phase shifters and wah-wahs. If I didn't tell you it was a drum machine, you'd never know.

"Texture and ambience. That's what I was after. Especially because we were so far out there by 1973," he says. "We weren't tryin' to find new sounds. We were tryin' to find new *planets*!"

You can pick out that texture and ambience on the series of live recordings Davis released from this period. The machine is particularly prominent in the

"Hip Skip" section of a live performance Miles gave on January 22 1975, at Shinjuku Kohseinenkin Hall in Tokyo.

But the best place to hear Mtume's contributions is on the studio outtake "Turn of the Century." Recorded in February 1975, with the touring band but minus Miles, it's a hard-hitting, but straightforward, funk-rock workout.

What vaults it into the stratosphere are the frequent interjections from Mtume's drum machine. With its tempo cranked to hyperspeed, and with a heavy dose of Mu-Tron processing, the EM-90 creates skittering electronic rhythms that ricochet crazily around the mix. These sounds wouldn't be heard again for another two decades, until the advent of double-time dance music like jungle.

But none of these recordings capture the reaction of Miles, when Mtume debuted the drum machine live in Japan. "The first time, when I got with the engineers and sound guys, and hooked up all the pedals and boxes—when he first heard it, he just *looked* at me," Mtume recalls, chuckling at the memory.

"And he just had this broad smile. Like, 'Shit, motherfucker, *where you goin'?*', you know?"

4.

This was a question Arthur Brown was also asking of his drummer. But Martin "Slim" Steer's decision to run off with his band's van had a surprisingly large effect on drum machine history.

Steer called Brown, the singer in his band Kingdom Come, that summer of 1972, with two pieces of news. Steer had not only absconded with the group's transport—he'd taken bassist Phil Shutt's wife with him. And after suffering through "three troublesome drummers" in Kingdom Come, Brown decided he'd had enough.

So Brown and his bandmates didn't find some*body* in to replace their drummer. Instead, they found some*thing*—a Bentley Rhythm Ace. On the 1973 album *Journey* and its related tours, they established a whole list of drum machine firsts.

They were the first band to completely replace a drummer with a machine on record, and in concert. And they were even the first band to give their drum machine a human pseudonym: Ace Bentley. The machine's punning nickname, Brown jokes, might have been the beginning of artificial intelligence. But Ace Bentley was at least smart enough not to run off with a van.

"We just felt like," Brown says, "it will be nice to get something that is going to be *stable*."

5.

More than fifty years after the Crazy World of Arthur Brown blazed across the musical firmament with "Fire," Brown's brief superstardom remains imprinted on the retinas of pop. The song hit Number 1 in the UK and a spot lower in America, and its catchphrase—"*I am the god of hellfire!*"—became Brown's calling card.

At age seventy-nine, he radiates a Gandalfian quality, with his floppy hat and scarf, pointed white goatee, and enigmatic smile. But Brown admits that his partnership with Ace Bentley was more practical than mystical.

Kingdom Come, the band he'd formed after the Crazy World of Arthur Brown disbanded in 1969, had released two albums of progressive psychedelia. The lineup had shifted around Brown and guitarist Andy Dalby. Now those two musicians—along with bassist Phil Shutt (nee Curtis) and American synthesist Victor Peraino—needed percussion for Kingdom Come's third release.

It was probably Dalby's idea to try a drum machine. "I've always liked tech toys," he says. The band's first machine, he recalls, was a somewhat obscure unit called the "Status." Dalby preferred it to the Bentley Rhythm Ace. However, "I think Arthur liked the controls on Bentley better," Dalby says. "He had to play it, after all!"

The Rhythm Ace in question was the FR-8L, now owned by a friend of Dalby's. Designed to sit atop an organ, the FR-8L had fifteen preset rhythms, tempo and volume controls, and individual volume sliders for the bass drum, snare, guiro, and cymbal/hi-hat/maracas.

The Bentley was, in fact, an almost identical British twin of the Ace Tone Rhythm Ace machines. Bentley Organs in the UK distributed the machines—intended for use with the company's keyboards—and rebranded them.

Brown had been thinking a lot about new technology. An interview Jim Morrison had done with *Rolling Stone*'s Jerry Hopkins in 1969 stuck in his mind—so much that he references it even today.

The Doors frontman had predicted music's brave new world with what now seems like startling prescience. "I can see a lone artist with a lot of tapes and electrical … like an extension of the Moog synthesizer—a keyboard with the complexity and richness of a whole orchestra, y'know?" Morrison said. "There's somebody out there, working in a basement, just inventing a whole new musical form."

Minus the basement, that described the new Kingdom Come. And Brown enthusiastically promoted Ace Bentley, bringing the machine to a June 1972 interview with Steve Peacock of *Sounds*.

"Ace sat immobile between Arthur's knees. Slick and black, he says nothing, but he's a neat little fellow," a bemused Peacock wrote. "He'll slip from a tango to a slow rock beat in a split second, keeps perfect time throughout, and never has volume problems.

"A rhythm ace drumming machine may not be the most soulful of instruments," Peacock continued, "but in the context of Kingdom Come's latest mutation it seems to fit perfectly well."

Brown explains, "We wanted to have a sound that was the equivalent in rock of a string quartet, where all the sounds were clearly audible. And where everything had the same equivalence. And of course, with a drummer, that's not usually how it goes."

The Bentley, which had a stable volume as well as tempo, was the answer. But Brown quickly realized this stability had immediate effects on the music the group played.

"Because there is no give in a drum machine. It's not like you can catch up a little with the drums," he says. "And in fact, the bass player, Phil Curtis, used to get a headache every night because you had to be so much *on*, and there was no way out of it."

"And so it was a discipline for us," Brown admits, "but actually, it encouraged a lot of experimentation."

Not everyone was convinced. Showing that complaints against drum machines have remained consistent through the ages, *Melody Maker* warned, "Beware—the machines are fighting back!" Speaking for Luddites everywhere, *Melody Maker* added, "In an age of mechanization, as the handloom gradually gives way to the water-powered wheelbarrow—so the drummer is being replaced by an electronic robot."

Undaunted, Kingdom Come embarked on a UK tour later in 1972, making the surprising decision to play primary schools and mental institutions. It was a particularly bold choice, as Andy Dalby recalls. "I remember a mental hospital gig where someone came up after and told us he'd been in there since a bad trip at one of our previous gigs," he says. "Very sad."

Clad in black velvet jumpsuits, gold face paint, and transparent helmets, the group presented a space-age image perfectly aligned to the technology onstage. Yet from the very first gig, at the London School of Economics, there were significant obstacles. One occurred when keyboardist Goodge Harris quit the band shortly before this performance. The remaining trio soldiered on and received, Brown recalls, a standing ovation afterward.

The drum machine presented a longer-standing set of challenges. For one thing, Brown—one of rock's most dynamic and unpredictable frontmen—was now tethered to the most important piece of gear onstage. He had to start and stop the machine on cue, sometimes at various places within the song. He was also responsible for manually controlling the tempo shifts—and there were several—in the complex new compositions.

Dalby notes dryly, "Arthur was working the machine, so we were at his mercy on gigs. We just had to adapt to whatever went on, right or wrong."

A perfect example was a jam-packed show at London's Marquee Club. At this hot and sweaty gig, condensation from the low ceiling dripped onto the Bentley. The moisture scrambled the machine's circuitry, and Ace Bentley truly took on a persona of his own. Brown quickly realized, "We're going to have to follow the machine."

It could have been disastrous, but the group stayed cool in the overheated Marquee. "By that time, everybody in the band was so accustomed to listening ferociously, that it was not that difficult to move along with it. So we basically improvised the whole set," Brown concludes with a shrug, "and the audience loved it. And we started to get a cult following."

Certain followers couldn't quite believe their ears, however. "It was a time when nobody had seen a band based around a drum machine," Brown says. "So some people would rush to the dressing room after a show, claiming, 'You've got a drummer in *here* playing!'"

"Or people would say, 'It's tapes! You've got it all recorded!'" Brown continues, shaking his head. "It took a while for people to go, 'It really *is* a drum machine.'"

One of the journalists who knew the difference was Charles Shaar Murray, who took in a December 1972 show at Hounslow Heath Junior School and wrote about it in *New Musical Express*. After introducing the group, he came to the fifth and most unusual member: Ace Bentley.

"No one has ever seen him. He sounds like drums, and is concealed in a small box on which Arthur presses buttons," wrote Murray. He admitted, "I don't really understand Ace, as he is never available for interviews, but then neither is David Bowie."

6.

That autumn, Kingdom Come decamped for Rockfield Studios in the wilds of Wales. There, the acid-fueled recording of *Journey* was overseen by a young musician named Dave Edmunds. Edmunds had recently recorded his own Number 1 single at Rockfield—a 1970 Christmas hit called "I Hear You Rockin'."

"We all loved his stuff," Dalby says, "and Rockfield was his home studio, so we figured he'd get the best out of it." One of Edmunds's main challenges was recording the Bentley. "It only had one output, so it was very difficult to get a good sound on all the parts at once. Not easy on an analogue 16-track," recalls Dalby. "We did used to spin things in, but timing was very delicate."

Nevertheless, "Time Captives" begins the album by putting Ace Bentley front and center: the machine's electronic heartbeat, unadorned, opens the first minute of the record. Thirty seconds later, the kick drum is joined by the Bentley's synthetic snare, and the track begins speeding up, the first of multiple mechanical time changes.

Even in an era of experimentation, this was far from the usual fare. But Kingdom Come had road-tested "Time Captives," beginning their sets with it, and Ace Bentley had passed with flying colors.

Overall, *Journey* was greeted with the response usually given to such far-reaching works: it was largely ignored. But at least one young listener came away believing that drum machines really were the future.

"I went to an Arthur Brown gig at a small youth club in North London. At one point Arthur set light to his elaborate headdress and started running around the room, totally freaking the kids out," recalls Chris Carter, who was then designing lights and visual effects for progressive rock outfits like Yes and Hawkwind.

> But what was more interesting to me was that the setup the band had on stage was quite unusual for the kind of music they were playing. They had a drummer, but they were also using a Mellotron, a VCS3 synth and Rhythm Ace drum machine. I remember thinking how cool it all sounded, even without the flaming head piece.

Within a few years, Carter would play his own role in early drum machine history, as a member of industrial provocateurs Throbbing Gristle. "That was my transition," he says, "from head-banging prog-rocker to tech head."

Following a final show at London's Rainbow Theater in June 1973, Kingdom Come's journey was over. "Unless they had a great imagination," Brown concludes, "I don't think drum machines were the thing that most people thought would be catching on."

But thanks in some significant part to Arthur Brown—and, of course, Ace Bentley—they did.

***

5

Teutonic Sonics: Germany and Programmed Rhythm

1.

When you say "drum machines" and "Germany," another word usually follows.

It's a word many of the people interviewed for this book used at some point during our conversations. In German, it means "power plant." But to some, "Kraftwerk" is synonymous with "drum machine," instead.

The connection is understandable. Of all the avatars of electronic music, Kraftwerk have always seemed to have the closest connection to the mechanical.

The two founding members of Kraftwerk, Ralf Hütter and Florian Schneider, did much to perpetuate this link. There was the fascination with robots—including the creation of doppelgängers that sometimes stood in for the band. There was the impenetrable secrecy of the group's headquarters, Kling Klang Studio, in the industrial section of Düsseldorf. There was the aversion to interviews, a policy that continues to this day.

But the person who brought programmed rhythms to Germany was a flesh-and-blood human named Michael Sauer. Sauer was an employee of Farfisa, an Italian company best known for its line of compact electric organs.

Like many organ manufacturers, Farfisa had begun including rhythm units with some of its organs. One of them was called the Rhythm 10. It was a transistorized machine with ten preset rhythms, five drum sounds, and the ability to cancel sounds within a preset pattern. It could also run on battery power.

In the early 1970s, Farfisa had a German branch. And Sauer, who worked there, sold Farfisa Rhythm 10s to an all-star lineup of Krautrock artists. One of the musicians who bought one was a guitarist named Michael Rother.

In 1971, Rother had just left an early incarnation of Kraftwerk. Teaming with drummer Klaus Dinger, who had also just departed the group, he formed Neu! The group's debut was produced by Conny Plank. Plank is often credited as

Neu!'s unofficial third member, and he also played a pivotal role in the sound of Kraftwerk.

Rother and Plank join most of the strands of the West German music that became known as Krautrock. They're also the common elements in German drum machine history.

Rother, now seventy-one, is a lively and solicitous conversationalist. He still remembers the special offer he received from Sauer, the "junior boss" of Farfisa Germany. "He was very interested in musicians. He gave away Farfisa instruments for a 50 percent discount—not making money, but just for promotional purposes—to bands like Can, Kraftwerk, and Neu!"

So it wasn't long before the machines began turning up on their records—which in turn inspired countless new drum machine users.

"I bought several machines at Farfisa," Rother adds. "Because the price—what do you say?—I couldn't refuse that offer!"

Rother was less satisfied with the sound of the Rhythm 10. "It sounded—well, it sounded terrible," he says with a laugh. "It was so stupid, to put it bluntly."

Two factors changed Rother's opinion. He notes, "It was nicer to play along to something that you could imagine was a drummer, rather than a metronome." And the machines "really came to life once you started to manipulate the sounds through the output. The sound was sent through filters, through wah-wah, even sometimes through delay, and a small pedal for tremolo.

"And when you sync them in a certain way," says Rother, "there was a whole new world of sound and rhythms. Which was fascinating!"

2.

In early 1972, a song titled "Spoon" sold more than 300,000 copies in Germany. It was the theme to a popular TV detective series called *Das Messer*. The band responsible was named Can. And this unexpected success was sparked by the Farfisa Rhythm 10.

Can had already used the Farfisa on a song from their second LP, a double album called *Tago Mago*. Nearly twelve minutes long, "Peking O" combined passages of live drumming from Jaki Liebezeit with Latin presets from the Rhythm 10.

Liebezeit was one of Krautrock's most legendary drummers. He was one of the architects of the repetitive, *motorik* beat that came to characterize the music. "He is more than the drum machine," bassist Holger Czukay once said admiringly. "He can absolutely repeat something forever."

Not surprisingly, Liebezeit was initially reluctant to use the Rhythm 10 on "Spoon." But like Sly Stone, Can guitarist Michael Karoli had discovered a trick to make drum machines more versatile.

Keyboardist Irmin Schmidt recalled that Karoli used the Farfisa machine "against its rhythm. So not starting on the 'one' that's indicated, but on the two or whatever," Schmidt said. "And that became so interesting … that Jaki really joined in."

For his part, Liebezeit insisted, "I don't mind drum machines. To make a synthetic attempt to have a real drum there, that idea I don't like so much." Of the Farfisa, he recalled, "It was fun—we didn't take it too seriously."

Others who'd bought the Rhythm 10, however, certainly did.

3.

The story of Kraftwerk and its electronic percussion proves that the showroom dummies of myth are not, and never were, robots. It shows that the members of Kraftwerk had hearts all along—and within them resided the very human emotions of jealousy, hurt feelings, and betrayal.

The group's classic lineup of Ralf Hütter, Florian Schneider, and percussionists Wolfgang Flür and Karl Bartos, began to splinter when Flür left in 1986, followed by Bartos in 1990. The main reason, Flür said, was simply boredom.

"I remember that [Bartos] and I were waiting thousands of times in the studio after dark—waiting for Ralf and Florian," Flür told me in 2006. "I claim that Ralf and Florian had lost interest in their own musical project then."

Even Schneider finally departed the group he had helped cofound, before dying of cancer in 2020. That left Hütter and a collection of replacements. As biographer David Buckley puts it, "Ralf was always the acknowledged leader." Now there was no doubt.

But there remains plenty of controversy about who developed the electronic drums that generated Kraftwerk's cyborg rhythms. Enough controversy, in fact, that Hütter and Schneider's lawyers successfully halted publication of Flür's 1999 autobiography. *I Was a Robot* had, to that point, been selling well in Germany. Flür's former bandmates had several objections to the book. But a major sticking point was that Flür claimed to have created the band's electronic drum kit.

The controversy occurred, according to the book's editor, Manfred Gillig-Degrave, because Hütter and Schneider "seem to have a patent" on the drum kit. "That was something they [Ralf and Florian] wanted to have absolutely not in this book, because at least in America, Wolfgang Flür, if he had ... [a] good lawyer ... he could have claimed royalties from the patent."

I Was a Robot was eventually republished, and Flür stood by his claims. What seems beyond dispute is that after Michael Rother and Klaus Dinger left Kraftwerk in 1971, Hütter and Schneider turned to their newly acquired Farfisa Rhythm 10 to provide most of the percussion for their next two albums. "In 1971 Kraftwerk was still without a drummer, so I bought a cheap drum machine giving some pre-set dance rhythms," Hütter told an interviewer in 1981. "By changing the basic sounds with tape echo and filtering, we made the rhythm tracks for our second album."

Kraftwerk 2, released in 1972, used the Farfisa most notably on the seventeen-minute opening track, "Klingklang." As biographer Pascal Bussy notes, "The track's constantly shifting tempo is due to the changing beat of the drum machine, giving the impression that for the first time it is a machine that is actually driving the music forward. ... To most people, the very idea that a machine could dictate the form and shape of a piece of music was an alien concept."

The next year, *Ralf und Florian* also employed the unit's preset rhythms. They were especially notable on the gentle "Tanzmuzik." It's an October 1973 performance of this song, from the German TV show *Aspekte*, where the quantum leap forward occurs.

Schneider plays the song's melody on his flute, while a long-haired, bespectacled Hütter sits shyly behind his keyboard. The star is clearly Flür, the newest member of the band. Using what seem to be a huge set of knitting needles, he raps at a foil-covered board studded with metal discs.

The sounds had been transplanted, like the brain of Frankenstein's monster, from a drum machine. There has been debate over the source of the sounds, but Flür says this machine was the Farfisa Rhythm 10.

"Important to me were the separated sound keys," he says today. These individual sounds, Flür says, "I had separated and cable-connected with the metal plates on my drum pads board."

The debate remains: who actually assembled the drum kit? Rother recalls that even before he left Kraftwerk in 1971, "I remember Florian having some kind of contact, metal things, which he used just to get a pulse to some electronic sound. Which was the very embryonic start of the Kraftwerk drum machines."

"I really don't want to talk about who invented what," Rother adds. "But of course Florian was an inventive guy, always looking for new sounds. He was an edgy, strange guy. So that led him to look for unusual and edgy stuff."

In his autobiography, Flür notes that one night in 1973, during rehearsals, he discovered

> a small beat box that Florian had bought in a shop. Because he and [Ralf] had so often had problems with drummers before, he had been unable to pass by a device like this, which was probably an accessory for organists. I asked Florian to connect the box to a loudspeaker so that I could hear how it sounded. The fixed settings of the styles sounded artificial and quite electronic, but there were some keys on the upper side of the casing that each triggered a single impulse of a sound, and these were what interested me. Like a proper drum kit, there was a bass drum, a snare, tom toms, crash and ride cymbals, claves and a hi-hat. These sounds, triggered individually by the keys, had a really naturalistic sound, and the bass drum sounded particularly good—above Ralf's plump bass horn, it was indescribably rich and dry, ringing out in a wonderfully leathery way. If I pressed the key repeatedly, I thought that, with a little practice, I'd be able to play my own rhythms with my fingertips. Although it wasn't a very comfortable device to play, it had an electrifying sound, and it was quite advanced for the time.

It was this machine, Flür claims, that he used to provide the sounds of that first electronic kit.

> Florian and I were deeply enthusiastic, and that evening we played the drums totally live, without the pre-programmed rhythms. How could we arrange things so I could play it more comfortably, perhaps like a proper drum kit? After a lot of toing and froing, it occurred to us that we could detach the contact cables leading to the small keys and link them to other contacts. Ultimately, they were only interrupted contacts that triggered a new contact if reconnected, so all we needed to do was to solder a metallic object to both sides. If these objects were then brought together, the same function would be created as that of the keys. I had to find out how these two metal parts could be fashioned so that they could be played by a drummer in a controlled, regular way to produce a beat.

The key, Flür writes, was the metal drumsticks. They needed to be made of a conducting metal like copper, and connected to cables carrying a low-voltage current. This would allow the sounds to be triggered by striking the metal drum plates, which were salvaged from a junkyard.

This was not the first electronic drum kit. But it was the first one many listeners ever heard—on "Autobahn," the 1974 single that turned Kraftwerk from hippie experimenters to actual pop stars.

Named after the famous German motorway, "Autobahn" became an unexpected hit in both the UK and the United States. In its full-length version, the song is "a serene 22-minute journey of swerves and curves, gentle gradients and blaring horns, tarmac-rumbling rhythms and doppler-shift effects that simulate the sensory whoosh of passing vehicles," writes *Uncut*'s Stephen Dalton.

Who created those "tarmac-rumbling rhythms" became another sticking point for Schneider and Hütter. They disputed Flür's claim, in his autobiography, that he played the electronic drum kit on "Autobahn."

But in the song's immediate aftermath, harmony reigned in Kraftwerk. The group added Karl Bartos, a trained percussionist, to the group in 1975. Flür claims to have built Bartos an electronic drum kit similar to his own: "The principle was just the same, although the sounds from his box were different." And Hütter touted the kit during his infrequent interviews, giving credit to Flür for playing it—if not inventing it.

In late 1975, Kraftwerk released the album *Radio-Activity*. When David Bowie heard it, he offered Kraftwerk the opening slot on his *Station to Station* tour. Hütter and Schneider turned him down. Instead, the quartet namechecked Bowie and his sidekick, Iggy Pop, on their next release, *Trans-Europe Express*, which rocketed Kraftwerk even further into the future.

The electronic drums were now more than just a TV novelty. If "Kraftwerk" meant "power plant," then Kraftwerk's special drum kit had become a big part of the *kraft*.

4.

While the cream of the Krautrock crop purchased Farfisa drum machines, at least one collective didn't follow the trend.

Keyboardists Dieter Moebius and Hans-Joachim Roedelius formed Kluster with multi-instrumentalist Conrad Schnitzler in 1969. The three met at Berlin's Zodial Free Arts Lab, and released a trio of experimental albums pressed in limited quantities and heard by few listeners. When Schnitzler left, the band became Cluster, and started to get notice.

Rhythm units didn't turn up in Cluster's work until "Im Süden," on the 1972 LP *Cluster II*. This thirteen-minute epic contained, as Moebius would say with some understatement, "a very fast drum machine." The machine in question, heavily treated with reverb, was an Elka Drummer One.

This device, like the Farfisa, was a product of Italy. It debuted in 1969, and boasted a fairly standard set of sixteen patterns and nine drum sounds. However, each drum sound was equipped with an individual volume control, which offered users a surprising amount of rhythmic variations.

"It was the first [drum machine] I owned," Roedelius says today. "But I don't know anymore where I got it and how." What he does recall is the ability to combine presets, which Cluster frequently used to create layered polyrhythms.

Roedelius also remembers that Cluster had the full support of Conny Plank, listed on *Cluster II* as an official third member of the group. The bearded, long-haired Plank was a free-spirited bear of a man, always willing to experiment in the studio. "Conny was as flexible as we were," Roedelius says. "Using a machine was no problem for him."

"Open-minded doesn't say enough about Conny," adds Michael Rother. "He was humble. His famous quote was that saw himself a 'midwife,' helping the musician give birth to his ideas. And it's lucky, I suppose, because we wouldn't have accepted a producer who would have said, 'You can't use that drum machine.'"

Cluster and their families next settled into a trio of historic houses in Forst, a small town on the Weser River not far from the East German border. During the 1970s, while Cold War tensions were high, tanks rumbled daily down a nearby road, while NATO fighter planes often buzzed over the valley.

Yet Forst was a largely peaceful backwater where creativity blossomed. Cluster were joined on the riverside by Michael Rother, who had come to Forst in 1973 with an invitation. He'd gotten bored with the minimalistic sound of Neu!, the group he and Klaus Dinger formed after they both left Kraftwerk. And he was intrigued by the drum machine-enhanced sound of Cluster's "Im Süden." So he hoped Roedelius and Moebius would join him in an expanded version of Neu!

The music they made caused Rother to rethink his plans. He ended up not only producing Cluster's 1974 album *Zuckerzeit*: the three musicians also formed the group Harmonia. Many of the songs that ended up on Harmonia's two studio albums, 1974's *Musik von Harmonia* and 1975's *De Luxe*, began with jam sessions in a nearby barn. They were often inspired by beats from the Elka One and the Rhythm 10.

Harmonia's two releases are today considered milestones. They're lauded for their use of technology—including, of course, drum machines. But in the mid-1970s, that appreciation was a long way off.

"Harmonia was rejected to such an extent," Rother says frankly. "And it was difficult to understand for me. Because I always thought if I loved music, then everybody would love it. The reaction of the crowd, I couldn't make sense of."

Part of the problem, Rother thought, was that audiences had trouble accepting the drum machine, which was brought onstage at shows. "I think there was this idea that everything that was not made by hand was not right," he says. "The idea that music was meant to be played by living people, in that moment. Not from some canned sound source."

Rother became unnerved by the sounds of conversation in the audience, and the clear signs of disinterest. "As a musician, I sometimes have problems trying to imagine what non-musicians are hearing," he confesses. "As a musician, I heard the machine."

Those crowds may have been deaf to the possibilities. But other musicians, like Rother, heard the machine loud and clear.

***

6

Turn the Beat Around: Eno, Disco, and the Drum Machine

1.

In 1974, many listeners probably still weren't aware that drum machines existed. But as Andy Newmark pointed out earlier, musicians were a different story.

So it wasn't surprising that drum machines found their way onto the albums of several well-known artists that year.

On his sixth solo release, the double album *Todd*, the dependably eclectic Todd Rundgren used a drum machine on several tracks. Blue-eyed soul duo Hall & Oates, whom Rundgren would produce in 1974, featured "a primitive Roland machine" on a cover of the big Jamaican hit "Soldering." Even Elton John's double LP *Goodbye Yellow Brick Road*, the year's bestselling album in America, included a preset drum machine on the throwaway track "Jamaica Jerk Off."

The connection between drum machines and Jamaica was not accidental. Some of the most significant early experiments with drum machines occurred there. The man who conducted them was Aston "Family Man" Barrett, the bassist and musical director of Bob Marley's Wailers.

"The first time I heard a drum machine was Sly and the Family Stone, 'Family Affair,'" recalls drummer Sly Dunbar. "But the first time in *reggae*, it's 'Chim Cherie.' And that's Family Man."

The drum machine Barrett used on "Chim Cherie," a 1973 single for the Upsetters produced by Lee "Scratch" Perry, was equally revolutionary—and rare. The EKO ComputeRhythm is credited as the first programmable rhythm unit. It was made in Italy from 1972 to 1977, in extremely limited quantities. As author Alex Graham notes, probably "no more than 25 are in existence."

The ComputeRhythm contained twelve sounds, including a drum fill that features prominently on "Chim Cherie." It allowed users to program rhythms by use of a computer punch card. These punch cards were a primitive but useful way of storing patterns, since the rhythms were erased when the unit was turned off.

The following year, Barrett once again used a drum machine while working with a fellow reggae titan. This time it was Bob Marley himself. The songs "No Woman No Cry" and "So Nah S'eh" on *Natty Dread* both feature drum machine patterns. In this case, the unit in question appears to have been a Maestro Rhythm King, similar to the one Sly Stone used on *There's a Riot Goin' On*.

While drum machines would soon play a major role in Jamaican music, they never made any significant appearance again in Marley's catalog. This continued a pattern followed by many of the artists we've met thus far. Drum machines were still more novelty than necessity.

The same could not be said for Brian Eno. As the keyboardist in Roxy Music, Eno had been an early and conspicuous user of technology. His experiments with the EMS VCS 3—a semi-modular synthesizer contained in a wooden suitcase—helped define Roxy's sound. And as a solo artist, he became intrigued by programmed rhythms.

Eno's second solo album, 1974's *Taking Tiger Mountain (By Strategy)*, began with the sound of a drum machine. Most likely a Bentley Rhythm Ace, the unit opened "Burning Airlines Give You So Much More" before drummer Freddie Smith joined the track. Drum machine was audible on several other tracks—most ominously on "The Great Pretender," an unsettling little number about a housewife who's raped by a robot.

This use of preset rhythms was "a sound still rare in 1974," as Eno biographer David Sheppard points out. But as he prepared to record his third album, Eno was ready to give them a bigger role. "An import copy of Cluster's *Zuckerseit* LP had been on Eno's turntable consistently all summer," Sheppard writes. "Its most palpable influence on his new music was in its use of drum machines."

On 1975's *Another Green World*, "Eno would mimic and then expand upon the electronic rhythm processes pioneered by Cluster producer Michael Rother and studio engineer Conny Plank," writes Sheppard, "feeding drum machines through echo, delay and reverb units to create eccentric polyrhythms whose sound seemed forever poised on the cusp between industrial futurism and impossibly exotic ethnic percussion."

Some reviewers heard a link between the machines and Eno's growing interest in ambient sound. In *The Village Voice*, Lester Bangs perceptively noted that "those little pools of sound on the outskirts of silence seemed to me the logical consequence of letting the processes and technology share your conceptual burden."

Eno would continue these increasingly gentle experiments. But it would be another type of music entirely—one designed for filling dance floors—that truly allowed drum machines to share the conceptual burden.

2.

As he drove toward Hialeah, Florida in the wee hours that February morning in 1974, George McCrae Jr. thought his musical career was in the rearview mirror.

McCrae was nearly thirty, a Navy veteran and native of West Palm Beach. He'd started his career in the early 1960s with the R&B group the Jivin' Jets, and he and his wife, Gwen, had recorded as a duo for local entrepreneur Henry Stone's Alston label. Lately, both of them had contributed to Stone's new TK Records, a sort of "Miami Motown" operation where, as McCrae puts it, "everybody sang on everybody else's songs."

The new label got an instant boost when it distributed the debut of Miami singer Timmy Thomas in late 1972. Thomas cut the entire album with his Lowrey organ—and its built-in Rhythm Ace drum machine—for accompaniment. With his left hand, Thomas played organ chords; with his right, he handled the programmed percussion; and with his feet, he played bass by using pedals.

Thomas had honed this act at a Miami Beach club called Timmy's Lounge in the Lucerne Hotel. "People had seen trios," Thomas told author John Capouya, "but they had never heard one guy sound like three people."

One evening, Thomas debuted an original. It was a song he'd been inspired to write after watching anchorman Walter Cronkite deliver the nightly bad news from Vietnam. The tune was a simple, heartfelt plea for global unity: "No matter what color/You are still my brother." The crowd demanded an encore, and Thomas recorded "Why Can't We Live Together" soon afterward. The puzzled studio owner, Bobby Dukoff, asked, "Where's everybody else?" But Thomas convinced Dukoff that he could handle all the instruments. That included the programmed drums, courtesy of the Lowrey organ's onboard Rhythm Ace.

The single became a regional smash. And when Thomas recorded his debut album for Henry Stone at TK not long afterwards, the label's co-owner Steve Alaimo decided the drum machine should stay.

Why Can't We Live Together was the first full-length LP to use a drum machine. The spare, minimalistic sound deeply divided critics, but the title track topped the R&B charts and reached the Top 3 in the Billboard 100.

Yet TK's success seemed like it had little to do with George McCrae. He was driving to TK this February morning to listen to an album his wife had just cut for the label. McRae was managing her career, but was considering going back to school to study law enforcement. "Since I had a baby daughter, I had another mouth to feed," he recalls. "I thought it was time to give up singing, period."

That was, until he got to the studio. McCrae was greeted by two young men who wanted him to hear a track they'd just recorded.

Harry Wayne Casey and Rick Finch were an ambitious songwriting team. Casey was beginning to have some minor R&B hits with his group, KC and the Sunshine Band. Finch, meanwhile, had regularly skipped school to record more than a hundred singles for Stone before his seventeenth birthday. Finch was now twenty, and he and Casey had been pulling a studio all-nighter.

To write their new song, they'd commandeered Timmy Thomas's Lowrey organ and its built-in Rhythm Ace. There was just one problem: the tune was in the key of E flat—too high for Casey to reach the top notes.

"They said, 'We know you can sing it—you got that high voice,'" McRae remembers. "'We wanna produce you.'"

Finch gave McCrae a recording of the song, called "Rock Your Baby." Over the next week, McCrae listened carefully, asking advice from his mother and sister about how best to sing the romantic ditty. The next weekend, he drove back to TK and cut the song in a single take. Rick Finch played live drums atop the burbling Rhythm Ace. Casey handled keyboards, and guitarist Jerome Smith—paid just $15 for his contribution—rounded out the track.

Stone rushed the single out that spring, and it got an immediate reaction. "All the rich kids come down to Miami, Fort Lauderdale, for spring break. And at the time, everyone was doin' The Bump," McCrae says. "The DJs would say, 'Whenever we wanna pack the floor, we just put on 'Rock Your Baby.'"

"Rock Your Baby" went on to top the pop charts on both sides of the Atlantic, selling more than seven million copies worldwide. "Miracles," the 76-year-old McCrae marvels today from his home in Aruba, "really do happen."

One of the song's fans was a Connecticut boy named Richard Melville Hall. Years later, as the techno artist Moby, he would use drum machines to become a global star. Today, he traces that interest back to hearing "Rock Your Baby" at age nine. "That's probably where it started, you know," Moby reflects, "being in the car with my mom, listening to AM radio and hearing that song."

Disco songs didn't always begin with a programmed pulse. But thanks to "Rock Your Baby," the sounds of disco and the drum machine would be forever intertwined.

3.

Drum machines could keep perfect time. They'd proven to be a valuable songwriting tool. You could even have hit records with them. But 1975 was the year they found another purpose: extending orgies.

"It's quite a true story," affirms Pete Bellotte, sporting a black baseball cap and sitting in front of a bank of keyboards in his West Sussex studio.

The 77-year-old Bellotte knows a little about a good yarn. For the past few years, he's been preoccupied with literary endeavors, which include a collection of short stories. But he's been a musician since getting his first guitar as a teenager; among the artists he worked with early on was a young pianist named Reginald Dwight, a.k.a. Elton John.

Bellotte's real break, though, came when he joined an Italian-born, German-based singer named Giorgio—first as his assistant, then as his songwriting partner. Giorgio's last name was Moroder. And the breakthrough for him and Bellotte was a song they wrote called "Love to Love You Baby."

The singer was Donna Summer, an expatriate American who'd appeared in the German and Austrian productions of the hit musical *Hair*. But the real action was taking place beneath her gospel-tinged vocals. Moroder, Bellotte, and their team of studio musicians were sculpting a rhythm track that would define a new genre: disco.

"Moroder deliberately simplified funk's clustered beats," Simon Reynolds writes in *Bring the Noise: 20 Years of Writing About Hip Rock and Hip Hop*, "into an even flow of metronomically regular pulsations." In other words, the swinging drum patterns that dominated R&B in the early 1970s—the complex polyrhythms of artists like Sly Stone—were flattened out. The bass drum now played on every beat, so no one could ever lose their place. The result was a more user-friendly dance music.

When it came time to record "Love to Love You Baby," regular session drummer Keith Forsey was absent. His place was taken by Martin Harrison. "He was a very nice guy," Bellotte remembers, "and he wasn't a bad drummer. But when we recorded 'Love to Love You Baby,' I said to Giorgio, 'In the breakdown, you can hear the drummer slow down.'"

"I said, 'We've got to record the whole thing again. We can't let it out like that—we'll be ridiculed!' So then I thought, 'How can we keep a steady beat?' And I thought immediately of this little drum machine I'd seen."

Bellotte had heard it played in a local Italian restaurant. "So I found my friend Lupo, who ran a shop called The Music Shop in Munich. And I described what I wanted, and he said, 'Oh, I know what it is. It's a Korg. It's called a Minipops.' And I said, 'Could you send one up to the studio?'"

The Minipops came in many different models. All of them available in the late 1960s and early 1970s featured a cha-cha rhythm setting, which is the preset Bellotte recalls.

Whichever machine it was that Lupo sent to the studio, it clicked. "Because firstly, it got us in time," Bellotte says. "Absolutely, mechanically in time."

The timing of the drumming was now perfect. The timing of the single's release was not. "When we released it in England, it didn't do anything," recalls Bellotte. "It was kind of a flop."

But things changed when Neil Bogart, the president of Casablanca Records, heard the song. Bogart agreed to release "Love to Love You Baby" in the United States. And a cocaine-fueled bacchanal at his house had major ramifications for both disco, and drum machines.

"He phoned us on a Friday night at the studio to say that he was having this orgy," Bellotte remembers with a grin. "They were all using coke, and they were all getting it on to this song. But being a 45, they had to get up and keep putting it on and on again.

"So he suddenly had this thought. He'd like to have an extended version of the song—16 to 20 minutes, like 'In A Gadda Da Vida,' from Iron Butterfly. And he wanted it *now*."

This carnal, party-hardy inspiration was a long way from the experiences of Bellotte and Moroder. "I've never tasted a cigarette. I've never tasted alcohol," Bellotte confesses. "Giorgio rarely drinks." But within a week, Bellotte, Moroder, and Summer had done as Bogart requested—thanks to the Korg Minipops.

"All we had to do was elongate this four-minute drum machine track to five times [its length], and we could drop in wherever we wanted, and we would be perfectly in time," Bellotte says. "So it was the first time, I think you could say, that syncing was done with a drum machine."

The final mix clocked in at almost seventeen minutes. During that span, it was Summer's erotic vocals—recorded in a darkened, empty studio—that attracted the most attention. *TIME* magazine called the single "a marathon of 22 orgasms," and the BBC banned it. In spite, or perhaps because of, this attention, the edited single reached Number 2 on the Billboard Hot 100, and Top 5 in the UK.

The long version of "Love to Love You Baby," meanwhile, invented the extended dance mix. However, there were no tape loops involved in the recording. Once the drum machine rhythm was laid down on tape, Keith Forsey was responsible for overdubbing the entire seventeen-minute drum track.

The Korg Minipops wasn't audible on "Love to Love You Baby." And the next major single from Bellotte, Moroder, and Summer didn't exactly include a drum machine, either. But they didn't need one to create what might be the most influential recording in electronic music.

4.

After "Love to Love You Baby," Bellotte and Moroder continued to use the drum machine to lay down a click track for Keith Forsey. But the quantum leap forward arrived the following year, on the final track of the concept album *I Remember Yesterday*. Bellotte's thematic idea was to trace the history of popular music from the 1950s to the present—and beyond.

Duplicating past musical styles was easy enough. But how were Bellotte and Moroder to create the sound of the future? The answer came via a song titled "I Feel Love"—and via engineer Robbie Wedel. "He was the man," Bellotte says, "the true innovator. No one else had figured out how to do what he did."

Wedel had come along when Bellotte and Moroder rented the Moog Modular 3P from classical composer Eberhard Schoener. Wedel was Schoener's assistant, and he knew the workings of this massive modular synthesizer inside and out. Moroder himself admitted, "I needed him because even if I'd owned one, I wouldn't have been able to get any sound out of it."

Wedel knew how to do far more than that. He was able to sync the Moog Modular to the studio's Studer sixteen-track tape recorder. "He said, 'It's something I've figured out that even Bob Moog didn't know his machine was capable of, and now I've told him how it's done,'" said Bellotte. By recording a reference pulse on track sixteen, Wedel was able to lock together all the Moog's sounds in perfect tempo.

Those precisely linked sequencers, Bellotte remembers now, unnerved them all during the first playback of "I Feel Love." "It was the first song where we'd ever experienced inhumanity in a piece of music," he says. "It was so exact … it was kind of spooky, really."

Wedel was also able to craft drum sounds from the waveforms of the Moog. But while the snare and hi-hat were suitably futuristic, Moroder and Bellotte weren't satisfied with the Moog's bass drum. That meant Keith Forsey was drafted to play the kick drum—and the kick drum only—for more than eight minutes.

Today, Forsey admits he found the experience boring. The most difficult part was figuring out what to do with his hands. The answer was to play the hi-hat part on a phone book—"something that wouldn't bleed into the bass drum mic," he recalls. "Because you've got to get your whole body involved."

The entire recording had been a memorable experience. Yet Bellotte says that when the song was completed, "it was just one of the tracks on the album. We weren't jumping around or saying, 'What have we done here?' People have told me, 'You must have realized you were shaping the future.' And that's nonsense."

As proof of how Moroder and Bellotte viewed it, "I Feel Love" was originally just a B-side. But club DJs recognized the song's revolutionary qualities. In July 1977, it became Summer's biggest UK hit, when promoted as the single's A-side. In America, the song lodged inside the Top 10. Along with Kraftwerk's "Trans-Europe Express," it provided an alternative path to punk, one that scores of electronic musicians would follow.

But within two years, Bellotte, Moroder, and Summer would take a deliberate detour. Disco's massive success had triggered a backlash: now the music was mocked as brainless and repetitive. So Summer's 1979 album *Bad Girls* was deliberately more rock-oriented. "The main disco people were intransigent, doing the same things over and over again," Bellotte acknowledges. "I understood why things had to move on." Yet at the time, the widespread criticisms of disco wounded him deeply.

In 1980, Bellotte was staying in the Plaza Hotel in Los Angeles. When he entered the restaurant each day, he couldn't help but notice a familiar face. John Lennon was also a guest at the Plaza. "I would have gone up to him and said hello," Bellotte says. "But I thought he would have looked down on me, or spat on me, or whatever."

Yet just a day before this interview, Bellotte acquired a book that contained Lennon's 1980 playlist. He was amazed to find that Lennon loved Donna Summer's "Hot Stuff." "He sent someone out to buy it," Bellotte says. "And at another point, he's just bought [Summer's] *The Wanderer* album, and he's all thrilled."

Bellotte looks temporarily anguished. "I thought to myself yesterday, 'I could have *spoken* to him!' But that's what disco had done to me."

What Bellotte and Moroder had done to disco—and to music generally—was appreciated by more listeners than just John Lennon. The experiments of "I Feel Love" would directly inspire a new generation of electronic musicians and rhythm programmers.

***

Our Drum Machine Could Be Your Band

1.

First, he takes the subway, rumbling underneath the grey towers of Manhattan until it bursts free into the suburban greenery beyond. Then he rides a bus to reach this well-kept split-level home, where he now stands in the tidy basement.

He's traveled all this way to Queens—more than an hour from his tiny apartment in the city—because the price is right. Thirty dollars: all the money he has.

He inspects the box in front of him. The manufacturer is Seeburg, and the model is called a "Rhythm Prince." And when he pushes the start button, the thumping heartbeat of a bass drum leaps out into the basement.

"It was *so* strong," he remembers today. "Right away, I knew this was the one."

Curious, he asks the kindly older couple how they have come to own this drum machine.

"This was our daughter's," they tell him. "She wrote poems to this."

After a pause, they continue, quietly.

"And she has recently committed suicide."

Stunned, the man assesses the situation.

"The first thing I thought was, 'How advanced was she?' We're talking about a girl who was fifteen, sixteen years old, writing poetry to a drum machine," he says. "If girls were even in bands at that point, playing a regular instrument, that was something."

But the second, more important thing that Martin Reverby decides there in the basement is that he probably shouldn't share the name of his band. The group is five years old at that point, and still struggling to get a foothold.

It's called Suicide.

Riding back home that evening, the drum machine a comfortable weight across his lap, Reverby watches the lights blur outside his window and reflects.

"I was thinking, it's almost like she passed it on to us," he says. "That was the next place for it to go. What are the odds of that?"

What were the odds, indeed, that this drum machine would transform Martin Reverby—better known as Martin Rev—and his friend, vocalist Alan Vega, into one of the most iconic duos in music history?

These are questions that still haunt Rev to this day, at age seventy-four.

"I thought about them just the other night," he says of the couple, his Bronx accent softening at the memory. "I realized they probably didn't understand their daughter. I mean, how many parents would? But I realized if they had, they probably never would have sold the drum machine. Because it was so close to her."

But Rev still believes there's some link between Suicide and that unnamed teenage girl, who bequeathed them the instrument that changed their fortunes.

And just as Rev knew the machine was right when he heard it in that suburban basement, it made an instant and seamless transition into the band. Maybe it was fate; maybe it was destiny. But the drum machine was, without question, the missing piece for Suicide.

It was the missing piece for the three other bands in this chapter, as well: a thing that set them apart and helped give them their identity. In 1975, for the first time, bands emerged that were impossible to imagine without their drum machines.

"The next day, we rehearsed—we were rehearsing in a gallery then. I set it right up. No words were spoken about what we were doing. Alan got right into it," Rev recalls.

"And there it was. And there we went."

2.

Until that magical moment in 1975, it seemed like Suicide was going nowhere in particular.

Formed in 1970, the group had advertised its earliest shows as "Punk Music by Suicide"—becoming perhaps the first band to use the term. Suicide began as a quartet, but by 1972, they'd become a duo.

Rev, whose parents and brother were all musicians, had been playing piano and organ in free jazz combos around the city. He met Alan Vega, a Brooklyn born painter and sculptor, at a twenty-four-hour Manhattan gallery Vega helped found called MUSEUM: A Project of Living Artists.

But gigs were hard to come by. Suicide only played a handful of shows between 1972 and 1975. The music was demanding, and Vega's pugnacious attitude didn't help attract many fans. Having witnessed a revelatory Stooges show in 1969, Vega adopted Iggy Pop's no-holds-barred onstage persona. His demeanor was thrown into further relief by the implacable Rev, who stood behind his "instrument"—the collective name given to all his electronic odds and sods—peering out from behind huge, bug-eyed shades.

"I was totally confrontational," Vega told author Simon Reynolds. "Almost every time we played there was a riot." But the idea to bring a drum machine into the band was, at first, something Martin Rev devised to avoid a riot at home.

"More and more, Alan was feeling we should get a drummer. He would bring it up often," Rev says. "And I knew it was a good idea to clarify what we were doing, what was becoming more and more like songs. Drums seemed like an important ingredient of that."

Searching for a drummer, Rev invited his wife to sit in with the group. The former Mari Montgomery had been a waitress at The Village Vanguard, a fabled jazz venue. She had a broad musical knowledge and was up for the challenge. "She played in a session with us, and she sounded great," Rev recalls. However, she was not invited to join the group.

Chivalry then took over. "I realized that I wasn't going to bring in another drummer, and then come home and tell her that we got somebody else," Rev admits. "I just couldn't do that.

"And then it dawned on me," Rev recalls. "I remembered going to weddings, or bar mitzvahs, or confirmations. And the entertainment would be very minimal. Usually one guy with a keyboard or an organ … and a drum machine."

"I'd never thought about it. It was too square," he adds with a laugh. "But it hit me like a beautiful vision. *This was it!* I saw it right away as a whole new musical space."

3.

The Seeburg Rhythm Prince opened up this new musical space for Suicide almost immediately. With the drum machine plugged into one output of a Fender Bassman amp, and Vega's vocal mic feeding into the other, Suicide began writing new songs. They were rhythm-driven, and inspired by the primitive mythology of rock 'n' roll. Rev had acquired a Farfisa organ, which he augmented with noise from a transistor radio, feedback, and the occasional bash on a ride cymbal.

He jacked up the tempo on the Seeburg to provide the rhythm for one of these new tracks, a jittery travelogue about "riding around in a killer's car" called "Rocket USA." But that was nothing compared to the soundscape the Seeburg provided for a song first titled "Frankie Teardrop, The Detective Meets the Space Alien," a yarn about a detective at the racetrack. With the tempo button cranked to the limit, the drum machine's hi-hats and clave melted into an ominous hiss just beneath Vega's shaggy dog story.

Seeburg was better known for its jukeboxes when it entered the analog drum machine market, in partnership with the Gulbransen company, an Illinois manufacturer of player pianos and home organs. The Rhythm Prince was the first of several drum machines that emerged from this collaboration. The companies also produced the Select-A-Rhythm unit and a 1969 box called the Teeny Bopper, which was designed specifically for home organs.

The Rhythm Prince had a handle on top and was the approximate size of a guitar amp head—partly because it employed a bulky, rotating internal cylinder that electromagnetically triggered the various drum patterns, sound by sound.

With only eight preset rhythms—two fox trots, two marches, and rhumba, samba, cha-cha, and waltz—getting the most out of the Rhythm Prince was a constant challenge for Rev. "I didn't have that many beats that were worth using. Two, maybe three at the most," he remembers. "But at different tempos. And when you combined different tempos with each different riff, you had different songs.

"It was really back to basics, but in a different way. It was totally based on necessity."

4.

Speaking of simplicity, it's hard to imagine a more straightforward recording than the creation of Suicide's first album.

"The record was a live record, basically," says Rev. "That was our set, in order. So however long it was—forty minutes?—that was how long our sets were then." The album was recorded for less than $4,000 at Ultima Studios, a repurposed bowling alley in the tiny town of Blauvelt, New York.

As Rev recalls it, producer Craig Leon suggested recording all the instruments directly into the mixing board. So Rev plugged in his mishmash of gear: the Seeburg, the Farfisa organ, a chain of beat-up Electro Harmonix effects pedals, and his transistor radio.

There were few overdubs during the sessions, and only "Frankie Teardrop" underwent serious revisions. After reading a newspaper account of a laid-off factory worker who killed his entire family and then himself, Vega rethought his detective story. He turned the song into a chilling ten-minute psychodrama about "twenty-year-old Frankie," who can't make ends meet and is being evicted. Art imitates life: Frankie shoots his wife and son before taking his own life. "We're all Frankies/We're all lying in hell," Vega sobs, before unleashing one of rock's most memorable banshee screams.

It was the capper to an unforgettable debut. But when Leon was called away from the sessions after doing a preliminary mixdown of the songs, label owner Marty Thau and the band smoked up a bagful of weed and had another crack at the mixes. Thau, who had never produced before, said later, "I broke all the rules, but somehow my tinkering succeeded." Leon didn't agree, and was aghast when he heard the new versions of the songs, now swimming in echo and delay.

The one musical element Rev tried to keep clean of any effects was the Seeburg. "The drum machine sounded so good to me, it was so rich," he says. "I didn't wanna mess with that at all."

When *Suicide* was released at the end of 1977, the initial reviews were savage. *Rolling Stone*'s Michael Bloom complained, "I've heard stolen riffs before, but this is far worse: raping and pillage of entire concepts." The band's hometown *Village Voice* called the record "abstract-expressionistic pornography," and Robert Christgau dismissed Vega and Rev as the "Two Stooges."

The vitriol peaked during Sucide's 1978 tour of England, opening for Elvis Costello and The Clash. Even before the band started playing, the absence of a drum kit seemed to antagonize the gobbing punks. "People just didn't know what to make of Suicide," remembered British-born A&R man Howard Thompson, "and they weren't prepared to give it a shot because they didn't have guitars and drums."

Some listeners were indeed ready, however. One of the New York City punks who cheered Suicide was a young guitarist named Steven Schneider. Within a few years, rechristened Steve Stevens, he would become the right-hand man of singer Billy Idol. "The first time I saw someone use a drum machine live was Suicide," recalls Stevens. "And we all loved Suicide."

Meanwhile, during Suicide's disastrous British tour, a Liverpool guitarist saw his own future onstage. Within the year, Will Sergeant had purchased the drum machine that would become a founding member of Echo and the Bunnymen.

As the saying goes, all the criticisms of Suicide all wound up on the wrong side of history. In a little more than a decade, *Rolling Stone* concluded that Suicide might have been "the most influential and least accessible group to emerge from the New York punk scene," giving them credit for inventing "everything from synth-pop to industrialized disco."

After the first album was released, Marty Thau gave the duo a thousand dollars to buy new equipment. "Which was a *fortune* in those days," Rev recalls. He went shopping for a new rhythm unit, and returned with a used Univox drum machine, the SR-95. For Rev, the main attractions were, once again, simplicity and rock 'n' roll thriftiness.

"I've almost done no programming," he admits. "Because when I get a new machine, from the store, or used, even now, the first thing I do is turn it on, and see what beats are already in there. Maybe from the last person who had it. Because sometimes they were really good. And it's stuff you never would have thought of—because it wasn't you!"

It's hard to argue with that philosophy. A used drum machine, after all, was what gave Suicide a new lease on life.

5.

Now we cross the Atlantic. It's an afternoon in 1975, and three young men in Sheffield, a northern industrial town, are at a local music shop, trying to be industrious.

For the past couple of years, they've been recording a series of collages, manipulating tapes, random bits of junk, and found sounds. The result is a disorienting music that pays homage to the Dada movement of the early twentieth century. In fact, the three young men have named their group after the nightclub in Zurich that was the early headquarters of the movement: Cabaret Voltaire.

But their music lacks a consistent rhythm, and they're here today to address that shortcoming. So Stephen Mallinder and his friends, Richard H. Kirk and Chris Watson, are pricing the drum machines on offer. They have a hundred pounds between them to make the purchase. "Fuck knows which machine we were looking at," Mallinder says. "But we really didn't get anywhere with the salesperson."

That's because they've been joined at the counter by a seedy looking character straight out of a Charles Dickens novel. He even has a wooden leg. The man gives the three boys advice about the drum machines they're thinking about purchasing. The advice is the same about each machine: "*You don't want that one. It's rubbish. It don't work. It's shit.*"

Discouraged, the trio pocket their hundred quid and exit the music shop. The dodgy Dickensian character is waiting for them outside.

"The guy collars us, and takes us round the back of the shop, where he'd got his van," Mallinder recalls, a smile creasing his face at the memory. "And he opens up the back and says, 'There you go. You can have that one for fifty quid.'"

"That one" turns out to be the Farfisa Rhythm 10. Mallinder and his friends don't realize it yet, but this is the Italian-made machine that has helped Kraftwerk become international stars.

What the three men *do* know is that this machine is exactly what they've been searching for. It's battery operated by six 9-volt cells, so they can take it anywhere—including to gigs. It has ten preset rhythms, but there are also five red buttons on the top that trigger individual percussion sounds: a bass drum, snare, cymbal, claves, and bongo.

"That was the reason it was so important for us was, as well as having the presets, and a foot switch—an on–off switch, that allowed us to structure our sets a bit by turning the machine on and off," Mallinder explains. "All the individual drum sounds were in a row on the top. You could hit the drums individually. So it became this thing that was played. That was the importance of it.

"We'd use the percussion. We used the clave and a cabasa on some of the early records. And obviously we'd put them through delays, ring modulators. So it became a sort of sound source for us, really."

Today, Professor Stephen Mallinder has his PhD in music and popular culture, and lectures at the University of Brighton. Inside his cozy flat, a bass guitar propped against a wall, Mallinder grins at the recollection of that persistent drum machine salesman, whoever he was. As was the case with Suicide, acquiring a rhythm unit under unlikely circumstances was the turning point for Cabaret Voltaire.

Like so many electronic music pioneers, the Cabs got their start using tape recorders. Watson, a telephone engineer whose goal was "making music without musical instruments," began these experiments in his parents' attic in Totley, a

Sheffield suburb. Then he met Kirk, who played guitar and clarinet, and later Mallinder, who added bass and vocals.

Drum machines, Mallinder says, "really changed everything massively for us. All of a sudden, the impracticalities of constructing rhythms from tape loops disappeared. It meant we had something we could anchor live stuff to."

The band had already developed a library of rhythm tracks onto precisely edited cassette tapes. The Farfisa Rhythm 10 gave the group even more rhythmic options. "The early sets that we did—things like 'Talkover' 'Do the Mussolini'—were actually rhythms from these edited cassettes," Mallinder says. "Then when we got the drum machine, we'd augment the cassettes with it, and built the sets up that way."

However, the lack of a live drummer baffled more than a few soundmen. "The big eye-opener was in 1978, when we played the Lyceum with The Buzzcocks, John Cooper Clarke, The Slits. It was our first big gig, so there's a proper PA, and proper sound people," Mallinder says.

"So the first question is, 'Where's your gear?' And the second is, 'What d'you mean, you haven't got a drummer?' And we said, no, we've got a drum machine. And the sound people were like, 'Yeah, we've never seen *anything* like this before.'"

The Farfisa drove the four songs on *Extended Play*, a 1978 EP released on Rough Trade that was the label's third release. But adding a second preset drum machine—the Selmer MR-101 Auto Rhythm—proved to be just as momentous for the Cabs.

The Selmer included a button that triggered a programmed drum fill. This tom-tom roll became a signature element of 1979's "Nag Nag Nag," an aggressive single that sold more than ten thousand copies, and put the Cabs on the map.

Having seen the results drum machines could provide, Mallinder and Kirk went shopping for reinforcements. They came back with the Electro-Harmonix DRM-16, a 1978 machine made in the United States.

This lunchbox-sized analog device boasts sixteen patterns. DRM stands for "Digital Rhythm Matrix," which simply means that the sixteen rhythms are selected from a matrix table printed on the top of the machine. But the patterns are largely groove-oriented and reflect the new ubiquity of pop music—especially disco.

The Cabs chose the DRM-16 to provide the pulse for the 1980 single "Seconds Too Late," as well as its flipside, "Control Addict." The machine sits high in the mix, while vocoders and heavily treated vocals weave around its chilly electro-clop.

These three preset machines paved the way for Cabaret Voltaire's later experiments with more sophisticated, programmable drum boxes. But Mallinder also thinks they gave the Cabs something else even more important: a doorway that skeptical listeners could enter.

"Even though the music we were making at the time was very weird, and massively unconventional, rhythm gave people a way to comprehend it," he reflects. "People were sometimes hostile, but more often, people were bemused. And they did try to find a way in. In some way, the drum machine did that."

6.

Three hours south of Sheffield's steel mills, throughout 1975, punk was coalescing. So was a London group that helped create an entirely new musical genre—in which the drum machine played a central, punishing role.

Throbbing Gristle began its long, strange trip in the late 1960s, as COUM Transmissions. The term was invented by Neil Megson, a young man from Manchester. More accurately, the words were spoken to Megson in the backseat of the family car, on an outing to Wales. Maybe it was a daydream; maybe it was a hallucination; maybe it came from beyond. Whatever COUM was, it would change Megson's life.

Megson, a late bloomer who was then nearing thirty, was a dropout from Hull University. Adopting the name Genesis P-Orridge, he created an arts collective that was both performance spectacle and deliberately amateurish musical group. P-Orridge's motto was "the future of music lies in nonmusicians."

Cannily realizing that performance art was eligible for government grants, while the average rock band was not, P-Orridge and the rest of COUM— including his girlfriend, Christine Carol Newby—set out to shock the provinces. Audiences were fascinated and repelled by the antics of P-Orridge and Newby, who'd been punningly rechristened Cosey Fanni Tutti. The pair engaged in various types of sex onstage, while stage props—from severed chicken heads to used tampons—enhanced the atmosphere.

Frequently hassled by the authorities in Hull, P-Orridge and Tutti moved to London. They were joined in 1974 by Peter Christopherson, an artist, photographer, and designer. Christopherson worked for the design firm

Hipgnosis, and had helped create album artwork for such acts as Pink Floyd. But in COUM, he was given the name "Sleazy"—thanks to his interest in the group's flouting of sexual taboos.

Since COUM had received a grant from the Arts Council of Great Britain, its taboo-flouting attracted the notice of government officials. Nicholas Fairbairn, a conservative member of Parliament, complained, "These people are the wreckers of civilisation." But COUM wouldn't truly reach civilization-wrecking status until they became a full-fledged band.

The addition of Chris Carter, a North Londoner in his early twenties, marked the true beginning of that band: Throbbing Gristle. Carter was an example of something author Simon Reynolds observes: the link between 1960s and 1970s psychedelia, and what would come to be known in the 1980s as "industrial music." As Reynolds notes, one of the important similarities between the two styles was an obsession with sonic treatments—including drum machines.

Carter had been a fan of psychedelia during its 1960s heyday, having his mind blown on an LSD trip while watching Pink Floyd. A technology enthusiast since he was a boy, Carter became a sound engineer for such TV networks as Granada and Thames, and had started his own light show business.

But it wasn't until he witnessed Arthur Brown's Kingdom Come in 1973—as described in Chapter 4—that Carter considered the possibilities of the drum machine. Browsing at a music store in London's West End just a couple of weeks later, he came across a secondhand Bentley Rhythm Ace—the exact machine Brown had used as Kingdom Come's substitute drummer.

"It was about £20, which was like two weeks' wages back then," Carter recalls, "so for me it wasn't cheap. The funny thing, apart from it being so bloody massive when I actually saw it up close, was that when I got it home and plugged it in, it sounded so tame and, frankly, shitty."

To overcome his disappointment, Carter hooked up the Bentley to a battery of effects and began experimenting. "That machine was only ever half-decent sounding with extra processing, like echo and a fuzz box, a wah-wah or a phaser," he remembers. "I didn't keep it long, but I did make quite a lot of processed tape loops with it, which I still have."

Those tapes found their way into the sets of Throbbing Gristle—over the objections of P'Orridge. "Genesis, ever the technophobe, didn't like drum machines and wanted us to get a regular professional drum kit, because he wanted TG to sound more punk," says Carter. "But he was outvoted by the rest of us; we really didn't want to go down that road."

Spectators, however, didn't necessarily want to follow Throbbing Gristle down this new path. "We constantly had battles with audiences, sometimes physically. In those days, turning up at a venue with a stage full of gear but no drum kit seemed to broadcast an alert that really riled some crowds," Carter says. "It was like, 'What's wrong with this picture? We see a band, but there's no drums ... we want drums!'

"Punks in particular found it an issue, and it seemed they just couldn't identify with a band with no drummer. Without even hearing us, some audiences would assume, I guess, that we were going to be a shitty pop band or something, and they'd start causing trouble, heckling, shouting, booing," adds Carter. "Of course, our answer to that was to counteract their response with brute force, industrial-strength electronic rhythms, at maximum volume."

Those rhythms were generated from a variety of sources in Throbbing Gristle, and Carter was the primary generator. "I used to spend days on end putting rhythms together, in my little one-room bedsit in Crouch End, surrounded by bits of gear and tape decks," he remembers.

That gear included "a tape echo machine, more cassette decks, a couple of reel-to-reel tape machines, three custom DIY synths, a sequencer, a scratch-built drum box, and a Roland TR-66 drum machine." Another machine that was part of the TG arsenal for a time was a Korg Minipops machine that might have been acquired from Cabaret Voltaire. The two groups crossed paths frequently in those days, as kindred, programmed-percussion spirits.

Throbbing Gristle took its name from Yorkshire slang for an erect penis. But the members could hardly have chosen a better descriptor for their sound. On Throbbing Gristle's first two albums, released on their own Industrial Records, the throbbing percussion appears only sporadically, like words in a recognizable language emerging from a crowd in a foreign country. Many songs are grounded instead in gristly squalls of synth and found sounds. But a handful of tunes do employ treated drum machine. These include "Dead on Arrival" and the nearly synth-poppy "AB/7A" from 1978's *D. O. A.: The Third and Final Report of Throbbing Gristle*.

Just as Arthur Brown's early drum machine experiments helped launch Throbbing Gristle, a new wave of musicians was observing Carter and his bandmates, and taking notes. These artists would figure out ways to make the drum machine terrorize listeners even more effectively.

7.

In most histories of popular music, 1975 is The Year Before Punk Changes Everything—the last twelve months of prog pomp and dinosaur rock and glam nonsense. That is, of course, a reductive history, and the three bands mentioned so far in this chapter—all of which were well underway long before the Sex Pistols showed up—are proof enough of that.

Yet from the beginning, punk itself was driven by the rhythms of a drum machine. Paris's Métal Urbain had the same slashing riffs, the same raw-throated vocals, and the same calls for revolution, resistance, and anarchy as their British cousins The Sex Pistols, The Clash, and The Damned. Métal Urbain's inexorable pulse, however, was provided not by a drummer, but by a Korg Minipops 120P.

The influence of Métal Urbain extends further than many realize. There would be no industrial music as we know it without songs like "Panik," "Ghetto," and the gloriously noisy "Lady Coca-Cola." Lots of musicians have been quick to acknowledge that debt—something that occasionally frustrates vocalist and programmer Eric Débris.

When he first met American musician and producer Steve Albini of the 1980s industrial band Big Black, Débris was astonished when Albini fell to his knees in tribute.

"I was going to shake his hand, and he bowed down and said, 'I'm not worthy.'" Débris recalls, shaking his head at the memory. "The same thing happened with Jim and William [Reid] from the Jesus and Mary Chain. And Bobby Gillespie of Primal Scream, too."

"The thing is, it makes it really hard to talk to these guys. Because I'd like to tell them that I dig what they're doing." Débris shrugs helplessly—as if to say "What can you do?"—and grins.

When he laughs, the best way to describe Débris might be "cherubic." The French punk whose band once spat out anti-fascist lyrics like "Assassinate the state ... /I judge you the state against me" is now bald-headed and rosy-cheeked, with heavy eyebrows he wiggles expressively for comic effect.

Taking a break from his photography studio in Austin, Texas, Débris thinks back to the origins of the drum machine in Métal Urbain. It all started, he says, with the band's former drummer, Jean-Pierre Zing—nicknamed Zip Zinc. "Our drummer ... he doesn't want to play drums any more," Débris explains. "He says, 'The machine is the future.'"

To back up this belief, Zinc purchased a Korg Minipops 120P, a push-button machine housed in a black Tolex case with a carrying handle. (The "P" stood for "portable," to distinguish it from a similar version called the 120W, housed in a woodgrain cabinet.) Besides 16 rhythms, including four rock presets, the Minipops boasted two outputs and three jacks that could accommodate foot pedals.

Débris volunteered to beef up some of the sounds in the Minipops. Many machines of this time had tiny interior trim pots that could be adjusted to control drum sounds to a limited extent. Débris says he went further than this, although his explanation is, nearly fifty years after the fact, light on specifics.

"I take the cover off. I get a soldering iron. I change the sound of the snare drum. So it's not just this cha-cha beat," he says, making a dismissive gesture. "I add a few switches."

Did he have any background in electronics at the time? "No, not really. I'm an artist," Débris says with a shrug. "It's really just trial and error."

In the studio, Métal Urbain managed to avoid a common problem that drum machine users of the day encountered: skeptical engineers who had no idea how to record the device.

"We were lucky. We recorded at one of the biggest studios in Paris. The people there, they're interested in new things. Their goal is to get the best sound possible," Débris says. "So they thought, 'A drum machine? Hey, this is pretty cool.'"

That was not, Débris hastens to add, always true in the live setting. Like Suicide, Métal Urbain ran the drum machine through a Fender amp when playing live. "People in the recording studios, that's one thing," Débris says. "But the live sound engineer … well, you know the old joke: what's the difference between God and the live sound engineer?" Débris breaks into a throaty laugh as he delivers the punchline: "God doesn't think he's a live sound engineer."

The band's unusual sound, however, attracted influential fans in England. Métal Urbain's debut release on Cobra Records, "Panik," was named the *NME*'s Single of the Week in 1977. Also smitten with the group's electropunk was a frizzy-haired visionary named Geoff Travis, who had just started a record shop called Rough Trade on Ladbroke Grove in West London.

When the members of Métal Urbain showed up at Rough Trade on a trip to London, hoping to drum up interest in their new single, Travis decided to expand his business to include a record label.

Métal Urbain seemed like the right band for the label's first release: "We thought they were the French Sex Pistols," added Travis. Thus, "Paris Maquis," b/w "Clé De Contact," became serial number RT 001 on Rough Trade Records, which would become one of the most famous independent labels in history.

Notoriety came more slowly for Métal Urbain. It wasn't until 1981 that its collected works were released as the compilation *Les Hommes Morts Sont Dangereux (Dead Men Are Dangerous)*. By that point, the group no longer existed. Original singer Claude Perrone—a.k.a. Clode Panik—had departed in 1978. And Débris had taken the Minipops and formed a new group called The Metal Boys with programmer Charles Hurbier.

The next project from Débris, Doctor Mix and the Remix, retained the Minipops but slowed it down. With stripped-down covers of songs like David Bowie's "The Supermen," The Stooges' "No Fun," and The Velvet Underground's "Sister Ray," Dr. Mix became the missing link between Suicide and The Jesus and Mary Chain, and inspired a host of drum machine-driven revivalists of the 1980s.

The day the music died, however, came after a 1980 Doctor Mix and the Remix gig in London. The faithful Korg Minipops was accidentally abandoned on the curb outside the club. "It was a black box, sitting out there on the sidewalk," Débris recalls, still rueful at the memory, "and it got left behind. I never found out what happened to it."

Perhaps it was stolen by an unknowing thief. Perhaps it was simply trashed. Or perhaps like Suicide's Rhythm Prince, the historic Minipops that once belonged to Métal Urbain simply found itself another user who needed it more.

8.

The myth of 1976 as a decks-clearing Year One in pop music is an enduring one, but it does contain a kernel of truth. Massive musical changes were indeed on the way, and that was true in the field of drum machines as well.

But several people who'd grown tired of waiting for the future decided to take matters into their own hands first.

***

8

The Drum Machines That Weren't

1.

In his Berlin studio, Daniel Miller lights another cigarette and considers. "Maybe," he says with a smile, "I'm not the best person for your book."

What Miller means is this: "I was never a particularly big fan of using drum machines."

If you know anything about Miller's career, that might come as a shock. In 1977, recording as The Normal, he created a single that put synthesizer pop on the map. Miller went on to found Mute Records, a label that such electronic music titans as Depeche Mode, Erasure, and Moby have called home. So surely there's a cupboard full of drum machines somewhere there in Miller's sanctum sanctorum?

Nope. "There's lots of ways to make drum sounds here," says Miller, sweeping his gaze around the pristine white walls and the neatly organized gear. "But no actual drum machines."

Since his musical debut, Miller has preferred creating his own rhythms from scratch. In the early days of drum machines, this was a path that several brave and patient musicians chose. By using the sound-sculpting capability of analog synthesizers, Miller and others found a way around the limitations of 1960s and 1970s rhythm units.

One major limitation was, simply, the sound of those devices. In the days before sampling, analog drum machines used short, percussive bursts of white noise and modified waveforms to simulate the sounds of drums. And they offered few options for improving those generally unrealistic percussion sounds.

But you could also use an analog synthesizer, for example, to generate a square wave—an oscillating waveform with a square shape that gives it a naturally hollow, percussive tone. And you could then tweak that waveform to your heart's content.

Using envelope generators to change the attack, sustain, and decay of basic waveforms like sine, sawtooth, or triangle waves, an ambitious musician could create an entire synthetic drum kit. In other words, a "drum machine that wasn't."

Daniel Miller was the only child of two Jewish refugees, actors from Vienna who'd met in London. Miller caught the theatre bug from his open-minded parents, and at age sixteen, some of his sketches impressed an up-and-coming comedian named John Cleese. Cleese invited him and his friends to the taping of a brand-new sketch comedy program called *Monty Python's Flying Circus*.

By 1977, Miller was twenty-six years old, and life had turned more serious and mundane. He was working as an assistant film editor when he read a *Melody Maker* feature on the punk band Desperate Bicycles. The Bicycles aimed to democratize music: their slogan was "Now It's Your Turn!" Inspired by the message, if not the music, Miller decided it was time to make his move.

He was a fan of experimental German outfits like Kraftwerk, Neu!, and Can, as well as emerging electronic artists like Throbbing Gristle and Cabaret Voltaire. So Miller worked overtime at his editing job until he'd saved up enough to buy a secondhand Korg 700s.

The 700s was a monophonic analog synthesizer. It had thirty-seven keys and could only produce one note at a time. But it contained several onboard methods to shape sounds. There were two oscillators, which could generate sawtooth, triangle, and square waves. There were also low- and high-pass filters to modify those waveforms. In addition, the 700s contained an envelope generator and a ring modulator, which produced metallic overtones perfect for futuristic music.

What the 700s *didn't* have was a sequencer. So in his North London bedroom, Miller first laid down a click track on his four-track tape recorder. Then, using his fingers, he played the bass and snare drum sounds he'd created from the 700s, using the click track as a guide.

"You hear little mistakes. It's not perfect," Miller admits. "It's got a human element, shall we say? But in spite of my ineptitude, it didn't take me too long, surprisingly."

Miller could have chosen to buy one of the rhythm units then on the market. But this was at least a year before programmable drum machines started to become widely available. He didn't seek out a standalone drum machine "partly because I couldn't afford it. And partly because I wanted to try to generate all the sounds from the keyboard, in a purist sort of sense."

The result was two spare electronic songs that really got under listeners' skins. On "TVOD," Miller recites the tale of a television addict who "shoots up" using the antenna from his set. The even creepier "Warm Leatherette" is based on J. G. Ballard's novel about car wreck fetishists, *Crash*.

When Miller took a box of the singles to Rough Trade Records, owner Geoff Travis decided to audition the song in the crowded shop. Miller cringed. But Travis convinced him to press 2,000 copies of the single—and fronted him £ 300 to do it.

Jane Suck at *Sounds* got hold of a copy and dubbed it the "Single of the Century." And Miller, who'd put his address on the record sleeve, was bombarded with demo tapes from musicians who assumed he was running a record label. He wasn't, and had no interest in doing so—until he got a tape from a 21-year-old Londoner named Frank Tovey, who recorded as Fad Gadget.

Tovey had studied visual arts and mime at Leeds Polytechnic, and his tape recorder experiments intrigued Miller. He agreed to work with Tovey, whose 1979 single "Back to Nature" became the true beginning of Miller's label, Mute Records.

It was also Miller's first real experience working with a drum machine. Tovey had a Korg Minipops unit, and Miller struggled to manipulate the sound. Finally, he hit on a low-tech solution. "We split the output, and ran it into a stereo graphic equalizer," Miller recalls. "We took all the top off one side, and all the bottom off the other side, to have some control over the levels of the kick drum, the snare drum."

By this point, Miller had also acquired an ARP 2600. This was a semi-modular synthesizer, which meant that the basic components of the unit were prewired. Fully modular synths required users to connect patch cords to create individual sounds. However, users could operate the ARP with or without patch cords, using the synth's preset sounds.

For Miller, the ARP—when used with the sequencer he'd purchased with it—was a great source of drum sounds. Yet in 1979, he also purchased a KR-55, a drum machine made by Korg. The Rhythm 55, as it was called, was not programmable, offering forty-eight preset patterns, plus a selection of drum fills. But it did have one feature that appealed mightily to Miller: six mixer controls that controlled the volume for the unit's twelve individual drum sounds.

"That was quite revolutionary for the time," he recalls. "And so I used to use that in combination with the ARP. I would use the snare, or more conventional sounds like the hi-hat, from the KR-55, and the kick drum from the ARP. That was my big thing—kick drums from the ARP."

The KR-55 turned up occasionally on the first album of a young quartet called Depeche Mode from Basildon, Essex. Miller first saw them open for Fad Gadget in 1980. He introduced himself after the gig, and a long-standing partnership began.

The "Disco 2" pattern from the KR-55 became the basis of "Photographic," recorded for a compilation album on Some Bizarre. But when it came time to create Depeche Mode's 1981 debut album for Mute, *Speak & Spell*, the band chafed at the time it took Miller to craft drum sounds with the ARP 2600.

"I remember being really frustrated because it seemed to me that he'd spend all day doing a bass drum sound," primary songwriter Vince Clarke would say years later, in Jonathan Miller's band's biography, *Stripped*, "and I couldn't work out why that would be." His bandmate Andy Fletcher joked, "Danny would read a synthesizer manual; he reads them at home—probably on the toilet or something! That's his hobby."

Yet as Jonathan Miller noted,

> The band would come to thank Daniel Miller for his meticulousness. While admittedly time-consuming, Miller's mastery of the subtractive (analogue) synthesis system employed on a vintage ARP 2600 synthesiser—still the mainstay of the early Depeche Mode sound—gave the band an edge over their rivals. The bass drum sound and other percussive tones Miller achieved were unique; more importantly, they are able to stand the test of time—unlike commercially available drum machines such as Linn Electronics' LM-1, the first to feature digitally sampled sounds to simulate real drums.

By the time of the band's second album, 1982's *A Broken Frame*, the group and Miller expanded their percussion palette to include a Roland TR-808 drum machine, as well as Simmons electronic drum pads that were triggered from the ARP.

But Miller would always remain skeptical of mass-produced machines. "Every single record sounded the same," he says. "People weren't very imaginative in how they used them. And we wanted our own sound."

Miller's inspiration was Kraftwerk, whom he admired for "creating drum sounds that were very individual and specific to each track." In the north of England, during that pivotal year of 1977, that German foursome would inspire another impressionable young man with an interest in DIY rhythm.

2.

Sometime during the summer of punk, 21-year-old Martyn Ware attended a party in his hometown of Sheffield. The host was Richard Kirk, a member of the fledgling band Cabaret Voltaire.

Ware was a fan of Roxy Music. He loved the extravagance of Roxy's keyboardist, Brian Eno. And in his own dress and listening habits, he'd been rebelling against his city's gray, industrial drabness for years. His future bandmate Phil Oakey—no slouch in the sartorial stakes—later recalled, "Martyn was more daring than me: he'd be going through the toughest areas of town in green fur jackets and high-heel shoes."

Yet even while the Sex Pistols and Clash were raging around the UK, Ware was searching for a different sound. Then someone put on a record at the party. It was like nothing Ware had ever encountered: sleek, futuristic, and fully automated. Ware quickly discovered it was the Kraftwerk album *Trans-Europe Express*. And just like that, any thoughts about conventional instruments vanished.

Ware and his friend Ian Craig Marsh were regular visitors to a Sheffield arts lab called Meatwhistle, housed in an old elementary school. It was there, soon after the party, that the two decided to form a band. The heart of this group would be a semi-modular synthesizer that Marsh and Ware pooled their resources to buy.

The Roland System 100 set the duo back nearly $2,000. However, it became the engine that drove The Future, the short-lived trio they formed with tape operator Adi Newton. It then became the primary sound generator—including the source of drum tracks—for the much better-known band that followed, the Human League.

Today, Martyn Ware has ditched his old gear and his old wardrobe. With his black polo-neck, shaved head, and thick-rimmed spectacles, he resembles the academic he has, in fact, become. Ware serves as a visiting professor at London's Queen Mary University. He's also a Fellow of the Royal Society of Arts, and has an honorary doctorate degree.

As he readily admits, "I'm really not nostalgic." But Ware does confess to having kept a System 100. And his affection for this old, semi-modular synthesizer is apparent.

"The exciting thing is—we used to perform live with it. With different patch settings for different rhythm sounds. Between the songs, we had to re-patch *everything*," says Ware, miming the process of plugging in patch cords. "So quite regularly you'd miss something, or one of the slider settings would be five percent off. And because of that, you'd end up with something incredible, that you'd never have thought of!"

The System 100 combined two monophonic synthesizers—one with a keyboard; the other simply a "brain" with exposed patch cords. These two synthesizers housed oscillators, filters, envelope generators, and attenuators that could be used to create a wide variety of sounds. The System 100 also contained speakers, a four-channel mixer, and a twelve-step sequencer that allowed looped sequences of notes to be played.

It can't have hurt that when they bought the System 100, both Ware and Marsh had worked as computer operators. Yet Ware makes an important observation about Japanese instruments like the System 100—and the influence of Roland's founder, Ikutaro Kakehashi, a frustrated musician.

"The System 100 wasn't designed for professional musicians," Ware says. "The original manual was written in very plain English. There is no geek element to it at all. So that's what appealed to us, because it was pointed squarely at people had no experience at all. That was us."

Ware and Marsh had also acquired one of the earliest programmable drum machines. The Dr. Rhythm—made by Roland, and distributed under the brand BOSS—debuted in 1979. But Ware and Marsh made little use of the machine in the early Human League. Instead, they painstakingly crafted drum sounds using the controls available on the System 100.

The icy slap of the synthesized backbeat on the League's debut single, "Being Boiled," and the fat kick-snare thump of the group's third release, "Empire State Human," were miles ahead of the drum machines then available. These were sounds and patterns not yet available on any rhythm unit.

The System 100 provided almost all the percussion sounds on the League's 1979 debut album, *Reproduction*, and the 1980 follow-up, *Travelogue*. But neither record produced a breakthrough hit. Tensions within the band then reached an intolerable peak.

Lead singer Phil Oakey and Ware were at loggerheads over the direction of the band's third release, with Oakey arguing for a more commercial sound. Oakey sacked Ware early in 1981, then was shocked when Marsh followed him out the door. Manager Bob Last negotiated the breakup, which allowed Oakey and the rest of the group to keep the Human League name.

Ware and Marsh, meanwhile, formed a new group called Heaven 17. They would also receive 1 percent of the revenues from the next Human League album.

As Simon Reynolds notes, "It was likely to be 1 per cent of next to nothing." So Ware and Marsh turned their attention to their own career.

"When we left the Human League, we'd already been writing some new backing track material for the next album," Ware recalls. "Obviously, not realizing we were going to split up." That material would surface later in the year, when both Heaven 17 and the new Human League reappeared. The songs marked a deliberate move away from the System 100 and its made-from-scratch percussion sounds.

"We were looking for a radical change of direction. A *correction* from the Human League," Ware explains. "We just didn't want to be continuing the same stuff. So we decided to look at other ways of creating music."

Both groups, ironically, would hit upon the exact same new path—which would depend heavily on a brand-new drum machine we'll encounter soon.

3.

Synthesizers were one of the primary alternatives to drum machines, then, during the transitional period of the 1970s. But they weren't the *only* option for musicians dissatisfied with conventional drum sounds.

Long before punk, some bands had been experimenting with ways to bring drums into the future. Kraftwerk had devised a way to combine the electronic sounds of drum machines with a live percussionist. Yet while they were innovators, they weren't the first.

Akron, Ohio, became known as "The Rubber Capital of the World" early in the twentieth century. Each of the nation's four major tire manufacturers had their headquarters in the city. It was also the birthplace of Devo, one of the most subversive bands of the 1970s.

Frontman Mark Mothersbaugh and keyboardist Gerald V. Casale had been radicalized by the events of May 4, 1970, when National Guardsmen shot and killed four anti-war protestors at nearby Kent State University. Mothersbaugh and Casale had been among the demonstrators. When the university shut down for three months, Devo was born.

Wearing red flowerpot hats that became a trademark, Devo infiltrated the mainstream. In 1980, "Whip It" became a surprise Top 20 hit. But Devo was always a commercial square peg. Its philosophy of "de-evolution"—the idea that the human race was actually *de*volving—wasn't merely tongue-in-cheek.

Today, Mark Mothersbaugh may be as recognizable for his movie and TV scores as for his work with Devo. However, his enthusiasm for drum machines—and for unconventional ways of generating rhythm—goes back to the start of his career.

Well before Devo, Mothersbaugh and Casale were known around the Kent State campus for their performance art hijinks and outre musical experiments. For Mothersbaugh, those two worlds collided during an art show. The owner of the gallery where he was exhibiting gave him a copy of the 1966 Perrey-Kingsley album *The In Sound From Way Out*. The album's binaural sound and percussive tape loops fascinated Mothersburgh.

By this point, he'd also acquired a MiniMoog synthesizer, which he called his "M16 rifle"—a tool he could use to sculpt abrasive new sounds. But the key experimenter in the early incarnation of Devo was actually Mothersbaugh's younger brother, Jim. He quickly went "from being our drummer, to deep into being an inventor and circuit bender," Mark recalls.

Jim Motherbaugh's crowning creation, unveiled in 1973, was a full electronic drum kit. "These weren't things you could buy back then," his brother points out. "So he was taking practice drum heads and guitar pickups and gluing them together. And then he'd run them into a wah-wah, or an Echoplex, or maybe a fuzz tone pedal. And he did the same thing with his cymbals. His cymbals sounded so *crazy*!"

At his day job, working at a muffler shop, Jim Mothersabugh made a custom stand for his electronic drum kit. He used exhaust pipes that he bent and welded together.

"The other guys weren't really sure about the kit," Mark Mothersbaugh remembers. "But I thought that drum kit really defined the direction that Devo was gonna go."

Jim Mothersbaugh would leave the band in 1976, replaced by an "incredible, metronomic drummer" named Alan Myers. Jim continued to develop new audio products for the band, however. And you can still see and hear evidence of his groundbreaking drum set.

Watch the cover version of Johnny Rivers's "Secret Agent Man" in Devo's first film, *In the Beginning Was the End: The Truth About De-Evolution*. That's Jim Mothersbaugh bashing away at his standup electronic kit, with what look like xylophone mallets. The squelchy, distorted beats are unlike any sounds that a rhythm machine of the time produced.

Devo would later make use of programmable drum machines. But Mothersbaugh finds himself drawn to the period when his brother's homemade electronic drums provided the band's pulse. He recalls in particular one of Devo's earliest concerts—a hometown gig at Kent State in 1974, where they played before a screening of the John Waters shockfest *Pink Flamingos*.

"To me," he says, "that's the purest Devo art we ever made, was that show."

4.

If would be nearly a decade before sampling revolutionized drum machines, and rhythm generally. But in the late 1970s, some musicians were already using looped rhythms in songs.

One of the best-known examples came during the 1977 recording of the Bee Gees' disco classic "Stayin' Alive." As the group struggled to record without a drummer, keyboardist Albhy Galuten proposed making a one-bar loop of the drums from another song, "Night Fever," and using them on "Stayin' Alive." This loop had such irresistible feel that it was recycled for the song "More Than A Woman," as well as "Woman in Love," a Barry and Robin Gibb composition covered by Barbara Streisand in 1980.

There's another noteworthy example of pre-sample-era sampling, far more obscure than the Bee Gees' experiments. Yet it has much more in common with the way sampling would come to change music during the 1980s—when drum loops were sourced not from a live drummer in the studio, but from existing records instead.

Martin "Cally" Callomon is one of pop music's great raconteurs, and has worked with a "who's who" of rock iconoclasts. Start with his 1970s student days at Watford Art College, where he attended classes with the members of Wire and heard guest lectures by Brian Eno. As a sleeve designer, he worked on campaigns for U2, Tricky, and P. J. Harvey; as an executor, he oversaw the estate of the haunted genius Nike Drake. And don't forget the time Callmon spent managing mercurial British pop star Julian Cope.

It was Cope who recognized Callomon's secret identity, when the two men met at Phonogram Records in late 1983. "For fuck's sake," Cope would later write, in his memoir *Repossessed*, "this man was Nigel Simpkins."

Nigel Simpkins was the artist who, in 1978, had released one of the earliest sampling records: a three-song EP titled *X. ENC*. The A-side, "Time's Encounter," featured snippets from dozens of records, including several Krautrock classics.

Beneath the samples is percussion sourced from a "drum drop" record called *Pop Time*.

Drum drop records were designed primarily as tools for songwriters, in the days before programmable drum machines. They featured recordings of studio drummers playing unaccompanied drum tracks. But what Callomon did atop the two minutes of "Time's Encounter" is perhaps best—if not one hundred percent accurately—described by Cope himself.

Cope declared that "Time's Encounter" had "taken a drum demonstration record and added snippets of every hip record in the world to its Krautrock stew." He went on to contend that "'Time's Encounter' had sold truckloads and never been off the John Peel show." About these assertions, Callomon takes issue.

"I think Julian was being kind or had smoked one of those reefers," he laconically observes. "It did get a 'few' John Peel plays, perhaps two or three, and I reckon it must have sold 2,000 copies, no more. In those days that was the basic sales amount of any record you took into Geoff [Travis] at Rough Trade. 'I'll take them all,' he'd say, and wrote a cheque for them in his tiny lettering, there and then. That was no way to run a business—as he later found out."

But Nigel Simpkins will always hold an important place in sampling history. Nearly a decade later, another brilliant provocateur—a Liverpuldian named Bill Drummond—would offer a higher-tech version of Callomon's experiment. As The KLF, Drummond and partner Jimmy Cauty also borrowed freely from eclectic sources, setting these samples atop walloping drum machine beats.

Drummond and Cauty were sued for their unauthorized borrowing. But they also had a Number 1 hit in 1988 with "Doctorin' the Tardis," which mashed up the Doctor Who theme and Gary Glitter's "Rock and Roll (Part Two)."

It seems entirely appropriate that Callomon now looks after The KLF's affairs. And while "Time's Encounter" never reached the heights of those pop pranksters, it still provided its creator with some memorable moments.

"My favorite reaction was to be confronted by a bloke called Nigel Simpkins. He had been a student on Watford Art School's Design Induction course a few years before," Callmon remembers. "He was none too happy to read that I chose the name because it was so wimpy.

"He was nice about it, mad fool—he should have landed me one," says Callomon, before adding wryly, "Being a Nigel, of course, he couldn't."

***

Punch the Clock: The Joy and Pain of Drum Machine Programming

1.

In the sixties and seventies, if you couldn't spend thousands of dollars on electronic gear, you could build it yourself.

Companies like Heathkit, Allied Radio, and EMC offered do-it-yourself (DIY) kits that allowed you to construct everything from radios to robots to early computers. From the ranks of these DIY enthusiasts came the creators—Gates, Jobs, Wozniak—who built Silicon Valley and reshaped the world.

Musicians also took advantage of these mail-order kits, building homemade modular synths, amps, and effects units. A Moog or ARP synthesizer could run between $5,000 to $10,000. But a DIY synthesizer kit might only cost a couple hundred bucks.

One of these musical hobbyists was a New Jersey native named Larry Fast. And one of the kits he built had a dramatic effect on the popularity of drum machines.

Now sixty-nine years old, Fast is one of the giants of electronic music. Grey-haired and wearing a blue sweatshirt, he's sitting in his cluttered home office, where bulging files and stacks of manuals prop each other up on the bookshelves. But he rattles off complex recording processes as if he'd been in the studio yesterday.

As a high school junior during the late 1960s, Fast began working for an electronics company that imported Japanese musical instruments. This included some early drum machines, and Fast reviewed prototypes for the company's sales department. He was usually disappointed. "The preset rhythms were for an earlier generation. And I was a Beatles product," Fast remembers with a grin.

Fast continued working at the company through college, where he studied computer science and got a degree in history from Lafayette University. He kept the job after a fortuitous meeting with Yes keyboardist Rick Wakeman at a local radio station. Wakeman was so impressed by Fast's synthesizer expertise that he brought the young keyboardist to England, to assist with the synths on Yes's 1973 album *Tales from Topographic Oceans*.

And Fast was still working for the importer when he got a contract from Passport Records to record his own music, under the name Synergy. Fast was inspired—like many of the musicians interviewed for this book—by a seminal electronic album. *Switched-On Bach*, a 1968 collection of the great composer's melodies performed by Wendy (then Walter) Carlos on the Moog synthesizer, became a surprise bestseller.

Synergy's first album, 1975's *Electronic Realizations for Rock Orchestra*, might not have had quite the impact of *Switched-On Bach*. But it did reach the Billboard charts, as did the 1976 follow-up, *Sequencer*. No less an authority than Bob Moog declared that Fast's debut was the most important recording ever to use his synthesizer.

At first, Fast was only interested in generating occasional electronic percussion from his Moog. However, his bosses at the electronics importer had allowed him to keep one of the prototype drum machines. Fast was intrigued by a particular feature: a snare drum roll. He'd written a Synergy song where the roll might come in handy, and realized "this could save me a whole lot of programming on the Moog."

So Fast hacked into the drum machine and jury-rigged his own single-sound rhythm unit. The box played the snare drum roll, and also had a tempo control. "That got used on my third album in a bunch of places," he says.

By that point, Fast had joined Peter Gabriel as a keyboardist and programmer. He worked on the ex-Genesis singer's first two solo recordings. These albums were critically well-received and produced a minor hit—1977's "Solsbury Hill." But the sense was that Gabriel's adventurous spirit hadn't quite paid off yet. In *New Musical Express*, critic Nick Kent called him "a man whose creative zenith is close at hand."

So, it turned out, was Fast's. His drum machine experiments would be part of that renaissance.

2.

One of the companies that offered mail-order kits for musicians was an Oklahoma City outfit called PAiA. It's a Hawaiian term that means "noisy." The founder, John Stayton Simonton Jr., had been born in Honolulu in 1943, and liked the sound of the word.

Simonton grew up in New Orleans and graduated from Louisiana Tech with degrees in electrical engineering and psychology. He moved to Oklahoma in 1967 to work at Tinker Air Force Base, at the first computerized jet engine test facility. But Simonton was also a guitarist and dedicated music fan, and the next year, he founded PAiA Electronics.

The company started life in the back of a local bowling alley. Simonton slowly built PAiA into a close-knit outfit that became a dependable source of low-cost, high-tech gear.

While he was still in high school, Larry Fast had gotten to know Simonton. "He had worked for a company who made kits that I had built—amplifiers, strobe lights, all kinds of cool stuff. But he had a love for electronic music. He was just enthralled by it."

One of Simonton's first DIY kits was an early drum machine, which made the cover of *Popular Electronics* in 1971. The Drummer Boy, which had eleven preset rhythms and five instrument sounds, was a bargain at $59. But other than the bright orange casing of some models, the machine was similar to other transistorized push-button units.

The game changer came in 1975, when PAiA introduced the Programmable Drum Set. It took the drum machine to a new level with the microchip, which shrank transistors to microscopic size and embedded them onto silicon chips. Finally, computer memory was both small and affordable, and PAiA pounced.

The Italian-made EKO Computerhythm had been the first programmable drum machine. But that unit, which stored patterns on punch cards, was manufactured in extremely limited quantities.

The Programmable Drum Set was different. Retailing for just $84.95, the kit allowed users to program its seven drum sounds "in any conceivable combination." Its circuit board contained 256 bytes of memory. For comparison's sake, a byte is about enough memory to hold a single character. A single page of text would take about 2 kilobytes to store. The PAiA's internal memory was about a quarter of that amount.

That was enough, though, to store two eight-note sequences. The sequences could be repeated, and each had its own "bridge pattern"—an additional pattern that could be manually triggered.

With AC or battery power (four AA batteries, plus a nine-volt battery for the snare drum), the sounds of the PAiA Drum Set were generated by "ringing oscillators." Simonton explained the technique: "You have a filter that's very close to oscillating all by itself, and when you hit it with a little pulse to excite it, it rings the way a drum does."

Fast built one of the kits. "I didn't actually see a place for it in my own music," he says, "but I thought it was a really neat little thing." Then he remembered a recent conversation he'd had with Peter Gabriel, "talking about how on his wish list was something like this."

As sessions for Gabriel's second solo album came to a close in New York City, Fast showed Gabriel the PAiA Drum Set he'd built. "And he was thrilled. So I promised him, 'I'll get you one and I'll build it.'" Ultimately, Simonton and Jones offered to build the kit themselves, "and test it, to make sure it's all bulletproof."

Soon afterward, Fast presented Gabriel his own PAiA Drum Set, then forgot about it. Until he received the demos for what would be Gabriel's third album. "I was surprised, because when I started hearing these songs that would become 'Games Without Frontiers,' and 'Biko,' and 'No Self Control,' and a bunch of them, they were all based on these looping rhythms on the PAiA box."

When these songs were taken into the studio, they turned into an album that became more than just Gabriel's breakthrough. It also helped define percussion in pop music for the next decade.

3.

Hugh Padgham has a droll sense of humor that's surely served him well over his six decades as a producer and engineer. The Buckinghamshire native has won multiple Grammy Awards, and his client list is a virtual Who's Who of 1980s rock royalty: McCartney. Bowie. Genesis. Gabriel. Collins. The Police. Sting.

Padgham's work with two of those acts intersected during the summer of 1979 at London's Townhouse Studios. There, he engineered Peter Gabriel's third solo release. And Gabriel's former Genesis bandmate, Phil Collins, played drums on several tracks.

One of these songs, "Intruder," became famous for the gated drum sound Padgham created. It started as a happy accident. The SSL recording console at Townhouse was equipped with a "listening mic" to allow conversations between the studio and control room. The mic had a powerful compressor, which leveled out the differences between loud and soft noises.

Collins was playing one day while the mic was turned on, and Padgham was amazed by the gigantic drum sound the compressor created. But the ambience of the room also created lots of reverb, which made the drum sounds blur into one another.

So Padgham applied a noise gate to the sound of the drums. The gate abruptly cut off the reverb of the room. Now Collins's snare drum and toms still sounded massive. But because the decay of the reverb had been clipped off by the noise gate, the drum hits were also short, punchy, and distinct.

At this moment, the drum sound of the 1980s was born. Padgham's innovation would have appropriately massive ramifications—not just for the sound of acoustic drums, but for drum machines and electronic percussion as well.

Padgham has told and retold this story many times. So it's hardly surprising that he downplays it today. "When you're working on the coal face, so to speak, it doesn't seem like it's such a groundbreaking thing, does it?" he says good-naturedly.

But the coal face of *Peter Gabriel* included more ore than just "Intruder." The programmed rhythms of the PAiA Drum Set—and the way the live drummers integrated with them—also previewed the future of percussion.

Sometimes those rhythms could be incredibly simple. On "Biko," the hymn to martyred South African activist Stephen Biko, a conga pattern on the PAiA is combined with the sound of a Brazilian *surdo*—a bass drum—played by Collins. And sometimes, as on the Top 5 UK hit "Games Without Frontiers," the PAiA came to the forefront. The machine's hypnotic pattern was crucial to the uneasy atmosphere of the song, which interpreted warfare as a child's game.

"The sounds were so distinctive. And these are not big, fat, heavy sounds. This is the birth of a new aesthetic, with these thin, weedy sounds," contends Fast. "But interesting rhythms can be something of their own. And that was something that had not really been in the musical vocabulary before."

Gabriel's American label, Atlantic, believed this new vocabulary properly translated as "commercial suicide," and dropped him upon hearing the tapes. But Gabriel would have the last laugh: when it came out on Mercury, his third solo album finally catapulted him to solo stardom. He gave drum machines much of the credit.

"Over the course of the last two albums," he said in 1982, following the release of his fourth LP, *Security*, "I've got back into a rhythm consciousness. And the writing—particularly with the invention of these drum machines—is fantastic. You can store in their memories rhythms that interest you and excite you."

"And then the groove will carry on without you, and the groove will be exactly what you want it to be, rather than what a drummer thinks is appropriate for what you're doing."

Hugh Padgham saw firsthand how this enthusiasm overrode the challenges of working with an inherently limited device like the PAiA.

"I don't remember there being a lot of skepticism," he says. "Because the people I worked with—Peter Gabriel, Phil Collins—they embraced this technology. With open arms, joyfully."

4.

Few musicians have embraced technology as joyfully as Warren Cann and John Foxx. For nearly half a century, these former members of new wave pioneers Ultravox have been passionate advocates of drum machines.

Thinking back on his mid-1970s introduction to drum machines, Foxx reflects, "They were entirely new at the time and felt uniquely stark and alien. I really loved investigating all this.

"I always felt that real drums were such a cliché, when there were many other sounds that could be generated by synths and machines that could be much more powerful and interesting," he adds. "A drum machine seemed to offer the solution—switch it on, and off you go. A liberation from exhausting days of energy-absorbing tosh, and vast potential for further sonic mutation."

Cann, meanwhile, must be one of the only drummers ever to depart a group because he wanted to use *more* drum machines. And his devotion to rhythm units might be even more intense than Foxx's. Listening to Cann discourse from the study of his Los Angeles home, as strings of fairy lights twinkle in the background, is like getting a series of master classes about rhythm units.

Unlike the other members of Ultravox, Cann grew up in Vancouver. So his husky voice contains a mixture of Britishisms ("bloody," "rek-kord") and his native Canada ("sore-y" for "sorry"). He's been interested in electronics since he was a teenager, and at age seventy, the subject of drum machines is clearly still close to his heart.

"You can tell the depth of feeling because I'm starting to cuss a lot," Cann apologizes at one point. Where Foxx tends to enthuse, Cann is more critical. He speaks about these machines and their manufacturers with the disappointment of a teacher who just *knows* his star pupil is capable of so much more.

There were no drum machines on Ultravox's first, self-titled album, recorded in the fall of 1976. But there was Brian Eno, who helped produce with Steve Lillywhite. And Eno's philosophy helped make the group more receptive to these rhythm units, as Foxx explains.

"Brian was an extraordinarily prescient character. He'd been using a drum machine on *Another Green World*, and for me, that was a real breakthrough," says Foxx. "It acknowledged the joy of artificiality as a valid element of recording, rather than this dominant pretense of 'authenticity,' which was thought to be justified by recording 'real' instruments."

In addition, as Foxx points out, in the mid-1970s, "a studio would cost around £1,000 for each day, then you had to pay equipment transport, crew, and hire costs on top. Worst of all, though, getting a good recorded drum sound was a long and tedious process. Often the rest of the band might have to kick their heels for a day or more, and this leached the energy right out of the session. You can't make exciting music when you're bored to death. Also, even after enduring all that, you ended up sounding just like everyone else."

For Ultravox, one way to sound different came via the Roland TR-77. Foxx remembers using one to make demos for the band's second album, 1977's *Ha! Ha! Ha!*

One of these songs, a number called "Hiroshima Mon Amour," dropped aggressive guitars to reveal a wistful lyric—"Riding inter-city trains/Dressed in European grey"—and eerie synthesizer backing. Today, we can hear it as perhaps the true beginning of synth-pop. But at the time, "as usual, we recorded the song," Foxx says, "leaving the drum machine off the track."

Later, Foxx listened and wasn't happy. This tune, he thought, demanded a more futuristic drum sound. When it was rerecorded with the TR-77, "Hiroshima Mon Amour" became properly otherworldly. "The TR-77 certainly set the entire mood and atmosphere for the piece," Foxx says.

Cann threw himself wholeheartedly into the investigation of the TR-77's possibilities. "Warren was a precise drummer, and turned out to be good at synchronizing himself with machines," Foxx says. Cann began plugging the drum machine into a series of effects—flangers, distortion boxes, and phasers. He experimented with combining rhythms, punching in multiple buttons until he ran out of fingers. And he quickly grew exasperated with the machine's controls—especially the finicky tempo slider and the start/stop bar on top of the TR-77.

"All you had to do was *look* at that thing and the bloody machine would stop. Right in the middle of a song onstage!" Cann makes a comedic grimace. "Who in the world thought *that* was a good idea?" But Cann wouldn't admit defeat. If the machines couldn't be built to his specifications, he would bring them up to code himself.

The possibilities were too great not to try. Though it was only released as a B-side, "Hiroshima Mon Amour" was clearly, as Foxx puts it, "the distinct signpost for the future."

For Ultravox, and for drum machines, that future was about to arrive.

5.

Ikutaro Kakehashi and his team at Roland had been patient. But transistors had gotten smaller and smaller, and the microprocessor had finally arrived. In late 1971, Intel debuted the 4004, the first microprocessor to condense its data processing functions onto a single integrated circuit.

The next year, Intel introduced the 8008, an 8-bit microprocessor. A similar chip would become the brain of the CR-78, the programmable drum machine that Kakehashi's friend Don Lewis had been requesting for nearly a decade. It would also be the first drum machine powered by a microprocessor. (The PAiA had used TTL—Transistor-Transistor Logic—logic chips, which contained bipolar transistors.)

Like its predecessor, the CR-66, this new machine was housed in a square wooden box. There were colored buttons that allowed users to access the presets. And the breaks, fills, and variations offered more variety for users than ever before. There was even an "Accent" dial that allowed users to emphasize certain parts of a pattern. Don Lewis's signature innovation had finally found its way into a Roland machine.

It was called the CR-78. The "CR" stood for "CompuRhythm." That was a reference to the CR-78's claim that it was a "drum computer." Its 8-bit microprocessor allowed internal storage of user programs.

"You could only program four patterns," Lewis remembers. "That's how expensive memory was!" But Lewis wasted no time adding the CR-78 to his racks of gear in the Live Electronic Orchestra.

The CompuRhythm had fourteen sounds and twenty preset patterns. Even though it was programmable, the presets were catching up with musical trends. Six of the twenty stock rhythms were rock and disco patterns. A few of them—sped up, slowed down, and processed—would turn up on multiple hit records.

Both John Foxx and Warren Cann acquired the CR-78, although by this point, they were no longer bandmates. Foxx had left Ultravox following the group's first US tour in 1979, in support of their third album, *Systems of Romance*.

For Foxx, the path forward would definitely involve the CR-78, which he'd purchased at a music store on California's Sunset Strip. "By the end of 1977, I'd already realized I didn't want to be in a touring rock band at all—wasn't cut out for it—so I headed into a much more risky territory, but one I was far more comfortable with," he says. "A more completely electronic sound with no real drums or guitar."

Working at a small eight-track studio in Islington, and primarily using the CR-78 to create rhythms, Foxx's experiments turned into his solo debut, *Metamatic*, which reached the Top 20 in the UK in 1980.

While drum machines and synths allowed for a streamlined studio setup, making a record like *Metamatic* still wasn't easy. Recording engineers were suspicious of these automated studio interlopers. "I was often told that synths were not 'real instruments', that drum machines were simply cheap toys, not meant for recording at all, that the sounds they made were not of sufficient 'quality,'" Foxx recalls.

> I remember these engineers would often employ a sort of grim, silent mode when I persisted. Everything would go very slowly, and there'd be a lot of sighing—especially if I wanted to put the drums through a cheap guitar pedal. "What? A *flanger*! On drums? You know what they say—Phased, Flanged and Fucked," as I remember one engineer reacting.

But when Foxx was joined at Pathway by a new engineer, Gareth Jones, things changed. "He was a light in the dark. Intelligent, perceptive, enthusiastic, and energetic. He loved to experiment and delighted in new sounds and techniques," Foxx says. "Total eclipse of the past. Future here we come."

Read these quotes at his London studio, Strongroom, Jones laughs. He's probably known best for his work with Depeche Mode, and his clothing is sober black. But the paisley bandana on Jones's head, and the colorful tapestries on the walls and ceiling, are reminders of his days as a self-described "psychedelic hippie."

How did he remain so open-minded about drum machines in those early days? "I wasn't a punk," Jones explains. "But I took a lot from the punk ethos: *Let's just do it, man*. I'd worked a small studio and had been thrown into the deep end. Meanwhile, John had made several records already. He'd worked with *Conny*

Plank, for goodness sake! He'd met Brian Eno. As far as I was concerned, the dude was on a voyage, and there was a lot I could learn from him."

"And learning," Jones concludes, "is about doing new shit."

With Foxx gone solo, Ultravox had no choice but to try "new shit" as well. Dropped by their label, Island, they recruited Scottish guitarist and vocalist Midge Ure to replace Foxx. However, the band continued recording with German producer Conny Plank. Staying the course with Plank made sense: he was also open to using drum machines, having worked with such early adopters as Kraftwerk and Cluster.

The CR-78 played a significant role on *Vienna*, the new lineup's first outing for Chrysalis Records. The "Metal Beat" preset is the first sound on the opening instrumental, "Astradyne." Meanwhile, the mysterious "Mr. X" became a popular album cut, showcasing the CompuRhythm and a rare lead vocal by Cann. And the title track is built on a pattern Cann programmed.

That, by the way, was no simple feat. You could tap in rhythms from a plastic add-on pad called the WS-1. But the pad was incredibly finicky, and you couldn't correct what you tapped into the Compurhythm. "The best thing to do," Cann remembers, "was simply not to attempt to do too much."

Vienna did more than enough to vindicate the revamped Ultravox. The album and single went Top 3 in early 1981, and began a string of hits that continued over the next three years. Now the band would have to play these songs live. Here, Cann excelled himself.

He began with the biggest problem: how to control the tempo of the CR-78, regulated by a sensitive and unreliable knob. The answer was ingenious. Cann connected an electrician's voltage meter to the machine's tempo circuit. Then he made note of the voltage settings of individual songs, and worked out how these settings corresponded to tempos.

"I didn't have a digital readout on the machine to give me tempos," Cann explains. "But if I knew that a song was, let's say, 12.4 volts, I could set the voltage meter for 12.4, and that would correspond, roughly, to the correct tempo for the song."

Then Cann opened up the machine and began experimenting with the tiny ceramic trim pots that regulated the machine's tuning. He was able to correct one of his pet peeves: a floppy bass drum sound that boinged like "a giant beach ball" when amplified. The trim pot allowed him to tighten up the bass drum into a harder, cleaner thump.

These improvements made it possible for Ultravox to take *Vienna* on the road. However, Cann was dumbfounded by a conversation he had with some fans after a show. Because he was sometimes bent over running the machines instead of playing drums, they believed he was reading a book onstage. "I couldn't believe it!" he says, shaking his head. "So I recognized that I'd have to do something to combat that idea."

The answer was to double down on artifice. Removing the TR-77 and CD-78 from their wooden housing, Cann built a clear plastic case to contain them. Then he added strings of LED lights to the box, and synched the lights to the tempo of songs. "And *volia!*" he says, grinning. "No one thought I was reading onstage any more. And as a bonus, now people wanted to know more about the drum machines inside."

More gear would be added to the box, which became jokingly known as "The Iron Lung." As its caretaker, Cann had his share of hair-raising moments onstage. He recalls vividly one of them, when the CR-78 had to negotiate the most difficult passage in "Vienna," as the rhythm goes to double time.

"My drum machine just shat itself," he says. "It started playing ten different things at once. I looked at it. Everything's where it supposed to be. The only thing I could possibly do—can't possibly do any harm at this point!—is just slug it." He mimes a punch and shrugs.

This is why a criticism of Ultravox—that the band was too serious, or 'po-faced,' onstage—still rankles Cann. "In private life, we had a pretty good sense of humor. But we were 'po-faced' because we were *shitting* ourselves!" he exclaims. "We had gear connected all over the stage. And if something went wrong, there was a domino effect. It wasn't like an amp not working."

The space-age look of the Iron Lung, though, suited Ultravox. Especially because they'd jumped to the forefront of a fashionable new movement. Some called this group "Futurists." But the term that finally stuck was "New Romantics," and the CR-78 provided the heartbeat of their two national anthems.

One was "Vienna." The other was a song by a studio project that contained two members of Ultravox, and a drummer-turned-DJ with an ear for the next big thing.

6.

Londoner Rusty Egan had bought a CR-78 when he was in the post-punk band The Rich Kids, though it was only used as a click track. Egan thought, however, that the future of pop was synthesizers.

Before The Rich Kids broke up, he and guitarist Midge Ure had decided to take the group in a more electronic direction. Ure soon joined Ultravox as singer John Foxx's replacement. But Ure and Egan remained partners. They invited Ultravox violinist Billy Currie and three members of the group Magazine to join them in a studio band called Visage.

The face of this group would be vocalist Steve Strange, a Welshman best known for his outrageous fashion sense. Strange worked the door at various London clubs where Egan DJed. During these evenings, Egan spun tunes by Bowie, Roxy Music, Kraftwerk, and newer electronic groups like The Human League. Meanwhile, Strange might appear as a pirate, a gypsy, or a 1930s gangster, and he kept out people who couldn't meet his exacting standards of dress. On one memorable night, that included Mick Jagger.

Many clubgoers, however, were inspired by Strange's look. At a time of massive unemployment in Great Britain, the New Romantics offered the chance to dress up, and what Spandau Ballet guitarist Gary Kemp cannily noted was a "conceit that it all somehow meant something grander."

Now Visage would add their own music to the movement they'd helped begin. They began recording at producer Martin Rushent's Genetic Studios, located in a barn near his home along the River Thames in Berkshire.

One day, Currie brought in a synthesizer-heavy track that had emerged from soundchecks while he was touring with Gary Numan. He'd written the song with Numan's keyboardist, Chris Payne, and drummer Ced Sharpley. Despite its unpromising title—it was then known as "Toot City"—the tune was both haunting and danceable. And the percussion was provided by the "Disco 2" rhythm of Sharpley's CR-78.

Egan and Rushent considered replacing the machine. They finally realized, though, that "it's perfect—leave it from the demo," Egan recalls. So Egan played live hi-hats over the CR-78. Ure wrote the lyrics and melody, Strange supplied the vocal, and Egan's girlfriend Brigitte Arens added some evocative French phrases. The result was "Fade to Grey," a Top 10 hit in the UK in 1980.

As historian Dominic Sandbrook later reflected, "You were supposed to enjoy the disco-influenced rhythms, to savour the portentous French lyrics, to yield to the atmosphere, at once fey, funeral, and futuristic, as if Aubrey Beardsley had popped up in *Doctor Who*. It was ridiculous, of course. But it was fun."

7.

More than five thousand miles away, a San Francisco collective was working its way up to the CR-78—and to eventual comparisons to Ultravox.

The members of Tuxedomoon were fascinated by electronics, but they weren't New Romantics. Instead, they were part of what frontman Blaine L. Reininger once called San Francisco's late 1970s "Belle Epoque"—an arts scene where the avant-garde flourished. The group emerged from a commune called The Angels of Light, which had roots in underground theatre and film.

If all that makes Reininger sound "po-faced," think again. Speaking from his apartment in Athens, Greece, while his cat climbs on and off his shoulder, Reininger is charmingly down-to-earth. Now sixty-eight, he still sounds a lot like the Colorado teenager who had his mind blown by the Moog synthesizer solo on Emerson, Lake and Palmer's "Lucky Man." The effect, he admits with a grin, was enhanced by being "stoned on massive amounts of Sicilian pot sold by the Mafia."

Reininger, who played electric violin and guitar, met fellow multi-instrumentalist Steven Brown in an electronic music class at San Francisco's City College. Students had access to a variety of gear. That included, Reininger recalls, an old Korg drum machine that he and Brown processed by running it through the filters of a modular synth.

The group's first real rhythm machine was a PAiA Drum Set. Their manager and technical guru, a transplanted New York sculptor named Tommy Tadlock, built the kit. Afterward, Reininger became responsible for it onstage. Because the machine could only hold two short sequences, this involved punching in a new rhythm track before almost every song.

"So I invented a kind of programming shorthand—'B' for bass drum, and 'S' for snare, and 'R' for rest. That was about all you had," Reininger remembers. "There would be two-to-three-minute pauses between songs. And some people thought that was part of the music.

"One time we were doing a show at a theater, and I thought it'd be interesting and cryptic to include my programming notes as part of the program. So I wrote out, 'BBSSR, BBBRRR,' and so on. And some guy wrote on the program, and handed it back to us." Reininger smiles as he mimics an aggrieved hick voice. "It said, 'This is BS, BS, BS. *I want mah money back!*'"

The PAiA "got demoted," Reininger says, when Tuxedomoon acquired a CR-78. That machine appeared on several tracks from the group's 1980 debut,

Half Mute. At the time, the LP's synthesizers, syncopated basslines, eerie violin melodies, and CR-78 rhythms led to understandable comparisons to John Foxx and Ultravox. But there were differences in the two groups that went beyond geography.

An important one involved the use of the CompuRhythm. Whereas Foxx and Ultravox embraced the mechanical qualities of the unit, "we were trying mightily to make a drum machine sound like drums," says Reininger.

One of the most memorable efforts came on the song "Loneliness." The CR-78 was run through a notch filter on a Serge synthesizer. This eliminated all frequencies except the snare drum. "Then we ran the snare through an Auratone, a little speaker. Then we put a brick on the sustain pedal of a piano, and we miced that up," Reininger says. "And it gave us this huge sustain on the snare, this *KKSSSHH* sound."

Tuxedomoon, like Ultravox's Warren Cann and John Foxx, would soon move on to more sophisticated drum machines. But for Foxx, at least, the CR-78 became a "sonic signature"—and a machine that continues to reward his efforts.

"Every time I turn it on, it turns me on," Foxx says. "That's what you really want from a piece of equipment."

8.

Clearly, the CR-78 was what a lot of other musicians really wanted as well.

Even though drum machines had been the basis of several significant hits—including multiple Number 1 singles—they simply hadn't caught on. That changed with the introduction of the CR-78.

Roxy Music used the CompuRhythm to drive the hit "Dance Away" in 1979. Gary Numan featured the CR-78 on his albums *Telekon* and *Dance*. The first major synth-pop duo—Wirral's Orchestral Manoeuvres in the Dark—programmed their own beat into the machine. They took the song that resulted, "Enola Gay," to the UK Top 10 in 1980.

Back in the United States, Hall and Oates rode the CompuRhythm to a pair of Number 1 singles in 1981. The first was "Kiss on My List." The duo used the "Rock 1" preset on the machine, which John Oates later recalled was a "crude brown box that we used mostly to find tempos." It was such an off-the-cuff recording that the song was recorded at a slower speed to save tape. Yet the magic of the demo—and the CR-78—was undeniable.

"That little drum machine would make its sonic presence felt again to great effect on the next few albums," Oates conceded. The next time it appeared, the same preset was run through a bass amp and a delay effect to create the unforgettable opening of "I Can't Go For That (No Can Do)," which reached Number 1 in November.

But the earliest success story of the CR-78 began the year of its release. In the summer of 1978, the group Blondie was recording its third album at the Record Plant in New York. Singer Debbie Harry was a former Playboy Bunny and budding pop pinup, but the quintet had yet to experience mainstream success. They'd enlisted glam-rock producer Mike Chapman, who later recalled Blondie as "musically the worst band I ever worked with."

Keyboardist Jimmy Destri had a habit of visiting the many music stores in the city. Stopping at Manny's Music on West 48th Street one afternoon, he noticed a wooden box with rows of colored buttons. Destri thought the CR-78 might help with a song called "Once I Had Love" that Blondie had been trying to whip into shape for years.

The track began life as "The Disco Song," since it was inspired by the Hues Corporation hit "Rock the Boat." The band then tried it as a ballad, as a reggae tune, and a straightforward pop song. Nothing worked.

Destrti bought the CompuRhythm and brought it to the studio, where he'd been playing around with a riff on his Roland SH-1000 synthesizer. He struggled to "manually tie the repeating notes" to the rhythm of the drum machine. Guitarist Chris Stein heard the experiment and started playing along.

"I got pretty close to making it sound like a sequencer, without having one," recalls Destri. "And Chris would set the tremolo on his amp to the tempo of the CR-78." But trying to sync the synthesizer and the drum machine turned out to be futile.

"We tried to sync it with control voltage, pulse—whatever," adds Destri. "The only thing that would work was to 'fly in' the repeated notes over the rhythm sequence on the CR-78 manually."

Chapman, Destri remembers, "heard me and Chris fooling around with these toys, and that's how we started the song." Returned to its disco roots, the rewritten "Heart of Glass" became a worldwide chart-topper. It made Blondie stars, and once again showed the hit potential of drum machines.

Even today, you can't escape the song—or its CR-78. "Now it's a Nissan commercial," marvels Destri. "You never know."

9.

It might be the most famous drum fill in history.

It's also the moment where the two dominant percussion sounds of the 1980s—the drum machine and massive, gated drums—first collide. And it happens at precisely 3:41 of the 1981 Phil Collins song "In the Air Tonight."

"It's safe to say that no other drum fill has ever wormed its way as deeply into the popular consciousness as Phil Collins' descending 10-note tom-tom break," wrote *Rolling Stone*'s Hank Shteamer in 2021. As proof, Shteamer's story was written to celebrate forty years of "The Fill."

Collins himself has usually dismissed his iconic drum riff as luck. He's equated the fill to the sound of "barking seals," and noted that it was just one of several different fills he played when recording the song. But the tom-toms leap so spectacularly from the mix because of the other percussive element: the Roland CR-78.

The ominously ticking machine perfectly sets up the explosive entrance of the gated drums. As is so often the case, chance played a huge role in the juxtaposition.

In 1979, Collins returned home to Surrey from a tour to find his marriage over, and his wife and children gone. While he was in Japan, he and the other members of Genesis had been given Roland CR-78s. "I said I didn't want one," he recalled. "But when I got back to find that I had a lot of time on my hands because the family wasn't there, I rang up and said, 'Can I have my drum machine?' Because I had to start writing some of this music that was inside me."

Genesis unveiled the CR-78 a year before "In the Air Tonight." The unit provided the rhythmic bed of "Duchess," from the band's 1980 album, *Duke*. The machine is also the first thing visible in the song's music video, perched atop Tony Banks's piano. You can hear the seeds of "In the Air Tonight" when Collins's kit crashes in atop the drum machine. But the effect is far less dramatic.

At loose ends in Surrey, Collins developed a routine. He went to the local pub in the afternoons, then returned home each evening ready to write. "The way I write is, I need an atmosphere," he said. "Atmospheres will tell you where to go next." The CompuRhythm turned out to be an efficient atmosphere generator. "'In the Air Tonight' was just a drum machine pattern that I took off that CR-78 drum machine," Collins said. "You could eliminate certain sounds and program bass drums and snare drums, so I programmed a bass drum part into it, but basically the rest of it was already on there."

Collins took the demo to Hugh Padgham. Padgham had agreed to coproduce Collins's solo debut, *Face Value*, after working with Collins on Peter Gabriel's third release. "What happened was that Phil used the CR-78 on the demo. And we tried to duplicate that sound in the studio, but we were unable to capture it," Padgham remembers. "So we copied the drum track from Phil's eight-track recorder."

Yet "The Fill" was almost scrapped during the final mix. Ahmet Ertugen, the head of Atlantic Records, was unhappy with the understated sound of the drum machine. "Ahmet thought that the song needed more of a backbeat to be a single," recalls Padgham. "So we overdubbed some live toms to give it that sound."

This version of "In the Air Tonight," where the drums muscled out the CR-78, actually became the single. "But the DJs ended up playing the album track—the non-drums version," Padgham says. "And obviously, that became the version everyone knows."

While "In the Air Tonight" is certainly the most famous use of the CR-78 on *Face Value*, the machine informed much of the album. You can hear it at the start of "Hand to Hand" and the cover of The Beatles' "Tomorrow Never Knows." Even when it's not audible, Padgham says, the CompuRhythm is significant. He points out "This Must Be Love," a slow number with sparse hand percussion, as a song that Collins demoed with the CR-78.

Both Collins and Genesis would continue to use drum machines and electronic percussion of various types. Padgham would be there for most of those recordings. But *Face Value* was really the conclusion of their two-part drumming experiment, which began with Peter Gabriel's third album, and concluded with "In the Air Tonight."

The rest of the 1980s would be a continuing refinement of the hybrid these recordings pioneered: increasingly sophisticated drum machines, and increasingly large live drum sounds. Yet some imitators missed an important point: it was the audible gap between man and machine that really made the combination work.

"Obviously, it was to some extent trying to replace the drummer," Collins said of drum machines years later. "But the Roland machines kind of didn't really do that. They kind of just gave you percussion—and that, for a drummer, was great."

10.

As the 1970s drew to a close, Roland had set a new standard in drum machines. Aspiring musicians in every genre were adding the CR-78 to their arsenals.

In London, Chris Carter of Throbbing Gristle bought a CompuRhythm that became the band's main drum machine for the next three years. The group's 1979 album *20 Jazz Funk Greats* might have been misleadingly titled. But the rhythms of the CR-78 did bring Throbbing Gristle's confrontational sound a little closer to accessibility.

In Paris, a keyboardist named Wally Badarou also purchased the CR-78. Badarou would soon be heard around the world after playing on M's hit "Pop Musik." But Badarou got valuable electronics experience by using the CompuRhythm on his first solo album *Back to Scales Tonight*, a beguiling combination of reggae rhythms and synthesizer pop.

The CR-78's programmability was crucial to Badarou. Having control of rhythms "made me a full music composer," he thought. "Some stiffness could still remain despite the hard work put into it," he says, "but at the end of the day, I could look at myself in the mirror and say: this composition is fully mine, from the main melody down to the slightest hi-hat struck."

In Hamburg, an experimental composer named Asmus Tietchens had been intrigued by drum machines since a sunny afternoon in the mid-1950s. Listening to musicians at a garden party, the boy heard drums, yet didn't see a drummer. Puzzled, he asked his mother where the drums were. She replied, "Maybe in the organ." That began his fascination with what he calls the "Invisible Drummer."

As an adult, Tietchens was inspired by the electronic compositions of Karlheinz Stockhausen to create an uncompromising "absolute music." But this music didn't include drum machines.

"All drum machines I'd heard bored me to death," Tietchens explains. "Poor sounds, inflexible patterns, and mostly too expensive. Even the machine Cluster and Harmonia used—the Elka Drummer One—disappointed me."

That was until one night in 1979, when Titchens "goofed around a little bit" in the studio with his friend Okko Bekker's CR-78. "By chance, one of the mixing desk's channels was connected with the Eventide Harmonizer. And suddenly I heard the drum machine transposed an octave lower. Wow, that was a kind of epiphany!" he recalls.

Tietchens was so inspired by the CompuRhythm that he used it to record four albums for Sky Records. "Basically, all pieces began with the rhythm track," he explains. "That means heavily processed patterns of the CR-78. The rhythm tracks more or less inspired me for the melodies. In a way, the melodies were mostly 'slaves to the rhythm.'"

Tietchens calls the results "strange pseudo-pop." But those Sky albums are now widely considered classics. They became signposts for later electronic musicians and "invisible drummers."

Of course, with a list price of more than $1,000, the CR-78 was well out of reach for most amateur musicians. But the new programmable machine hadn't made preset rhythm boxes obsolete just yet. If not for these older machines, some of the most important acts of the 1980s might never have made it out of their hometowns.

***

10

Without Me, You Would Not Have Even Thought About Writing This Book

1.

One afternoon in early 1978, the keyboardist and guitarist of an ambitious new quartet are shopping for gear in their hometown of Birmingham, England. Suddenly, they stumble across a rhythm box in a local music store.

Made in Japan, the Kay R-8 Rhythmer covers all the basics for preset drum machines. It has eight preset rhythms. It has volume and tempo knobs. It even has the obligatory wood grain cabinet.

And the price is certainly right. "We didn't have a lot of money at that time," says the keyboardist, then just sixteen years old, "and 15 pounds for a rhythm unit seemed like a bargain even then."

What Nick Rhodes remembers most, though, is the sense of possibility when he and John Taylor powered up the R-8. "When I first pushed the buttons, I thought, 'Oh, okay. Interesting,'" he says with a laugh. "'This means we don't need a drummer at the moment!'"

That was a big deal for the fledgling Duran Duran, made up at the time of Rhodes, guitarist John Taylor, singer Stephen Duffy, and bassist/clarinetist Simon Colley. Onstage, Rhodes played a monophonic synthesizer called the Wasp, as well as a Crumar string synth. But he was also in charge of the mixing desk, as well as a reel-to-reel tape recorder on which "I'd just record very random things, church bells, or people walking upstairs, or conversations of people at parties. And I'd just fade them in and out during songs, whenever I thought they might sound good."

Now Rhodes was in charge of the drum machine as well. "I had to guess or mark with a pen where the tempos were for all the different songs," Rhodes recalls. "It was never quite the same every night, but I think that made it more interesting.

"It was used on all our early live shows with Stephen Duffy. It had a fantastic sound," he adds. "And it gave us our backing track for every song we had."

This incarnation of Duran Duran was a long way from global pop stardom. That would arrive after the band reshuffled its lineup, adding singer Simon Le Bon and guitarist Andy Taylor—and drafting Roger Taylor to replace its drum machine. Yet in those crucial early days, Rhodes thought the machine gave his group what it needed most: an anchor.

By the end of the 1970s, preset machines like the R-8 weren't just more affordable. They also put up uncomplainingly with the amateur incompetence that has sunk countless bands, whose names will never be recorded in pop music history.

"The drum machine," recalls guitarist Will Sergeant, thinking back on Echo and the Bunnymen's early days, "was the only professional among us."

2.

At almost exactly the same time that Nick Rhodes and John Taylor were buying their Kay R-8, Sergeant was also entering a music store. This one was 80 miles to the northwest of Birmingham, in Liverpool.

The shop was called Rushworth's. Paul McCartney's dad once traded in a trumpet there to get his son his first guitar. Sergeant's first guitar also came from this shop.

Sergeant was then working as an assistant at Bing's, a big department store around the corner. He usually stopped at Rushworth's during his dinner break to browse the new music gear. One day, in the glass cabinet where guitar strings and effects pedals were kept, he noticed a wooden box with colored buttons.

"I said to the geezer, 'What's that?' And he says, 'That's a drum machine.' A little light goes on in me head. A *drum machine—that's what Eno uses*."

Sergeant had heard Brian Eno's album *Another Green World*. He'd also heard drum machines before, in his village, as part of home organs. "We didn't think much about it," he confesses. "It was just something that old people had." But this standalone unit, a Korg Minipops Junior, seemed closer to Eno than easy listening.

The price was £80, and the Minipops was basic: five sounds and ten rhythms. And only two of those rhythms—Rock 1 and Rock 2—were really of any use. Regardless, the machine turned out to be a godsend for Sergeant and singer Ian McCulloch. The three of them formed a band called Echo and Bunnymen.

Within a year, joined by bassist Les Pattinson, they released their first single, "The Pictures on My Wall." Within two years, the *NME* was calling their debut album, *Crocodiles*, "one of the contemporary rock records of the year."

Even though the drum machine was only part of the band for ten shows, it was the glue that held them together when they needed it most. "Because we were messing up all the time," Sergeant says, "even with our primitive two-chord songs."

This drum machine also became a longstanding part of the group's mythology. Some people believed McCulloch was actually "Echo," which pissed him off. So he and Sergeant concocted a story about the drum machine being "Echo," instead.

The tale, Sergeant admits, was "rubbish. We were just kids, talking nonsense." But the story stuck, and the myth grew. Sometimes the band members themselves gave in and referred to the machine as Echo.

Whatever the Minipops was called, "it became a really valuable part of the band," Sergeant adds. "And I think it really did make us stand out when we did our very first gigs. There were still no real drum machines in a guitar band."

By the autumn of 1979, the Minipops had just about served its purpose. The Bunnymen's manager, Bill Drummond, insisted that a real drummer was necessary. So did Seymour Stein of Sire Records, who made getting a drummer a condition of signing the band to his new imprint, Korova. And despite McCulloch's reservations—"we were saying, 'Can't we just get a more expensive drum machine that does a few more things?'" he claimed in 1998—Sergeant found himself agreeing with Drummond and Stein.

"I loved the drum machine. But it became a bit limited," Sergeant says. "You couldn't build it up to a crescendo and then dip it back down. And you couldn't program stuff. We'd really exhausted all possibilities."

Drummer Pete DeFreitas became the replacement for Echo the Minipops. Sergeant sprayed the machine green, then gave it a coat of red paint. "And then it just vanished from our rehearsal rooms," he says.

There was no mourning period. The Minipops was replaced by a Roland TR-66. The Rhythm Arranger appeared on a couple of songs from the band's sophomore album, *Heaven Up Here*. On "Over the Wall" and "Turquoise Days," you can hear the machine ticking away underneath DeFreitas's drumming.

Sergeant still owns that Rhythm Arranger, although it's been some time since it worked properly. The band's drum machines, he reflects sadly, "all get stolen or left behind or broken or forgotten about."

This seems like an insufficiently sentimental farewell to Echo. But luckily, the band's former manager, Bill Drummond, has come to the rescue.

In response to questions about the machine, Drummond wrote a one-act play called *I Am Echo*. In it, the author costars with Echo the Minipops, who rather impertinently states, "Without me you would not have even thought about writing this book."

That may or may not be true, but the entire play is reproduced in its entirety in the Appendix. It's probably the most fitting epitaph a drum machine is ever likely to receive.

3.

Now we move even farther north, to Scotland. In Glasgow, three members of a recently disbanded group named McIntyre are rehearsing for some gigs. McIntyre had been a Steely Dan-influenced act. This new band, provisionally called The White Hats, has retained that sophistication. But their new sound is spacious—sparse, even.

That's partly because the White Hats have no drummer. So the singer, a thoughtful Edinburgh native named Paul Buchanan, has borrowed a drum machine from another local musician. This Roland CR-5000 is the only machine on loan in town, and Buchanan only has it for an afternoon.

Besides Buchanan, the White Hats also include keyboardist P. J. Moore and bassist Robert Bell. This afternoon, these three recent graduates of the University of Glasgow are putting together a set of cover songs: The Beatles; Tom Petty; Earth, Wind, & Fire; Talking Heads; Stevie Wonder. For each song, the musicians pick a drum pattern, time it out, and then commit it to a cassette.

Today, Buchanan can't recall who lent him the CR-5000, though he does remember that the machine's preset "merengue" pattern proved particularly useful. Over the years, he's admitted that the White Hats "mangled" their repertoire of covers. But he's also acknowledged that the taped drum machine rhythms helped the group survive. "The drum machine was so insistent and the songs so well known," he told band biographer Alan Brown, "that you could kinda hit a chord every few minutes and people were pretty happy."

The White Hats soon became The Blue Nile, a band legendary for the spaces in its sound. The Zen minimalism of albums like *A Walk Across the Rooftops* and *Hats* made them outliers during the busy 1980s. And Buchanan sees the sense in giving that first drum machine a bit of the credit. "I suppose it did help incline us towards space, or leanness," he says.

Halfway between Glasgow and Edinburgh, on the Firth of Forth, lies the refinery city of Grangemouth. There, Robin Guthrie, a shy seventeen-year-old guitarist, first heard a drum machine on the debut album by Suicide.

Then, in a local music shop, Guthrie happened onto a device that seemed too good to be true. It was a drum machine not only affordable—just under $200—but programmable as well.

"Of course, I owned this drum machine for two weeks before I realized you could program it," recalls Guthrie with a laugh. But buying the BOSS DR-55, more commonly known as a Dr. Rhythm, was a turning point for Guthrie and his band, the Cocteau Twins.

The group, which began as partnership between Guthrie and bassist Will Heggie, became a trio with the addition of vocalist Elizabeth Fraser. The Cocteau Twins then tried out a drummer for a week or two, but his requests for travel expenses ended the partnership. So Guthrie turned to the Dr. Rhythm. "I was a kind of nerdy guy anyway, building these fuzzboxes and things," he remembers. "So the drum machine was just an extension of that."

The BOSS company was a division of the Roland Corporation. Formed in 1973, it primarily manufactured effects pedals for guitarists. Yet when it was introduced in 1979, the Dr. Rhythm became a surprise success. The machine was limited to just four analog sounds: bass drum, snare drum, rimshot, and hi-hat. And the hi-hat could only play eighth or sixteenth notes, unless you decided to simply mute it.

But the Dr. Rhythm was tiny—just eight inches across and less than five inches deep—and light, weighing less than two pounds. It was also battery powered, and offered users the ability to overwrite its eight preset patterns with programmed rhythms of their own. It was an attractive choice for musicians who were looking for accompaniment—like Guthrie.

Quickly, however, the band's set list grew beyond the capability of the Dr. Rhythm. "There came a point where the eight memories were not enough for us to play a set of more than 20 minutes," Guthrie says. "So I bought a second drum machine."

This one was even smaller, and even cheaper. But the Japanese-made Sound Master SR-88 was also programmable, allowing users to arrange its four drum sounds into eight patterns. Guthrie was enamored of this little blue box—"That was the shit, that one!" he enthuses—and soon bought a second copy of this machine.

The Cocteau Twins soon recorded their first album, *Garlands*, at London's Blackwing Studios in 1982. But they replaced the Dr. Rhythm and the Sound Master with a new, much more high-tech machine—the Roland 808. "We wanted to have our beatbox going through a guitar amp," Guthrie says. "And they told us, 'No, no, it sounds terrible. Use this proper machine instead.'"

Later, Guthrie thought he should have stuck to his guns. "I was really into technology, so I was happy to use the 808. But the early, more aggressive sound was something that I really preferred at the time."

"I was young and I just wanted to do something different," Guthrie adds. "I didn't really know the rules." By the end of the 1970s, drum machines were allowing the young—and young at heart—to make their own rules, and remake music in the process.

4.

We end our tour back in England, in the kingdom of East Anglia. There, Martin Newell—the man many would call the patron saint of DIY recording and cassette culture—is wearing a natty red vest and paisley bandana, and considering the mysteries of drum machines.

"It struck me as a subject that's been very important to my life. And I hadn't really thought about it until I thought about it," reflects Newell. "They did kind of change my life and the way I made music."

Recording with various collaborators as The Cleaners From Venus, The Brotherhood of Lizards, and under his own banner, Newell has developed a reputation as one of England's finest songwriters. He's also a popular poet and author, and possesses a wicked sense of humor.

When Newell was the lead singer of 1970s bands like the hard-rocking Plod and the proggy Gypp, drum machines weren't really a laughing matter. "A lot of musicians I knew were very reactionary about them," he remembers. "Musicians in the first band I played in were sort of *outraged*. And I said, 'Well, we could have both drummers and machines, couldn't we?'"

But Newell didn't have to make that choice until drummer Lawrence "Lol" Elliot left the Cleaners From Venus in the early 1980s. When his musician friends asked, "'You going to get a proper drummer?' I thought, well, no," he says. "I'm a lo-fi studio rat. I'm doing drummers a favor by not involving them."

So Newell improvised, in his lo-fi way. "I hadn't really used a drum machine before, except a cheap one that was in a double cassette machine, that only had about 10 drum beats." Newell employed this device on "I Can't Stop (Holding On)," a song from the third Cleaners LP, 1982's *On Any Normal Monday*. "It occurred to me that there was no way not to make it sound like a cheap drum machine," he explains. "So we were going to have to make that a feature."

At the time, Newell was making a living through various means, including working as a dishwasher at a local restaurant. But he scraped together enough cash to buy a Sound Master SR-88—the same model Robin Guthrie was using in the Cocteau Twins.

The Sound Master proved its worth on "This Rainy Decade," from 1982's cassette release *Midnight Cleaners*. Newell supplemented the rhythms with various bits of hand percussion. "I overdubbed a tom-tom on it, and a very nasty little splash cymbal. I mean, all of this came out of genuine poverty. I couldn't have afforded to buy more gear," he says. "Until gradually, I began to realize that what I'd got, out of this junkyard kit, was a thing of its own."

On what were essentially solo cassette releases like 1985's *Songs for a Fallow Land*, Newell ran his Sound Master through "loads of cheap reverb," making no attempt to hide its mechanical origins. The following year, when keyboardist Giles Smith became a Cleaner for a time, he brought with him his own Sound Master, which he was also able to program.

The Cleaners had a brush with the big time on the albums *Going to England* and *Town and Country*—a story both poignant and hilarious, and expertly told by both Smith and Newell in their respective memoirs. Real drums were the order of the day on both releases, but Newell soon returned to the world of programmed rhythm.

His everyday rhythmic lineup is still determinedly modest. "I've got an [Alesis] SR-16 now. And I can't be bothered reading the manual. I just want a basic beat," Newell confesses. "Then I've got a 40 quid Zoom guitar pedal that has some beats in it the SR-16 hasn't got.

"And in my toy cupboard, I've some sleigh bells. Two types of tambourines. Sticks. Still have that horrible old cymbal. I have a jar of yellow split peas I use as a kind of shaker. And by adding these things, you can sort of make it sound like a human being is playing." He smiles. "Badly, sometimes."

Newell has a cupboard full of drummer jokes as well, but he's quick to dispel the usual stereotypes. "I don't work with drummers, not because they're not intelligent. On the contrary, they're *too* intelligent. All the drummers I've ever worked with have university degrees!" The problem, he adds, "is that they bung things in that you don't want."

Drum machines don't. That, for Newell, is their enduring appeal. "I didn't hate drummers," he says, giving a crooked grin. "But they're always going to be a problem for the home recordist."

***

11

Give the (Electronic) Drummer Some

1.

"I've still got it!"

Stephen Morris is talking excitedly about the pearl syncussion SY-1, one of the early electronic drum pads.

Morris has still got a *lot* of electronic percussion, in fact. He looks around his music room, where some of those devices sit, and shakes his head.

"I've got too much, really," he acknowledges. "But I get as far as, 'I should really sell some of this stuff.' And then you plug it in and go, 'Oh, that's a good sound. Whoa! Can't get rid of *this*!'"

What Morris cheerfully admits, however, is that it wasn't just the *sound* of the SY-1 that convinced him to buy it. It was also the *look*.

"It had a stand. It had a bag. It had sliders. It looked *really sophisticated*," says Morris with a knowing smirk. "It was cool. And I wasn't! I was the least cool person in the world. So I was hoping some of it would rub off."

It worked. As the drummer in the iconic post-punk bands Joy Division and New Order, Morris became a world-renowned percussionist. But he also grasped an important point early on. To have a drum kit is cool. To have an electronic drum kit is cooler.

Dr. Richard James Burgess had this same realization. That's how Burgess came up with idea for the hexagonal pads of the Simmons drum kits. Those honeycomb-shaped drum heads made the SDS 5 one of the most eye-catching elements in the early days of MTV. Even today, they remain the strongest link between the sound and vision of electronic percussion.

"For that brief period in the early 1980s, a nonstandard looking drum set was what everybody wanted, and the SDS 5 was it," says Burgess. "It was uncompromising and it was beautiful. It looked like a piece of art."

2.

When synthesizers allowed musicians to sculpt their own sounds in the late 1960s, it was only a matter of time before drummers and electronics collided with an amplified bang.

In 1971, The Moody Blues became the first band to get electronic drums onto vinyl. Drummer Graham Edge designed a transistorized kit with Brian Groves, an electronics professor from Sussex University. The kit survived long enough to be immortalized on "Procession," the leadoff track from the band's album *Every Good Boy Deserves Favour*.

The Moog 1130 Percussion Controller was marketed in 1973 as part of the company's "Sound Ensemble." It was a single Ludwig drum head that could trigger sounds from a Moog modular synthesizer, and the user could control volume and pitch. That same year, on the song "Toccata" from the Emerson, Lake and Palmer album *Brain Salad Surgery*, drummer Carl Palmer debuted an electronic kit he'd helped create. During his solo, Palmer used an octave divider to "play" a synthesizer's bleeps and whooshes, up and down the octaves.

But the turning point for electronic percussion came in 1975. Drummer Joe Pollard, who'd played with The Beach Boys and The Grass Roots, was tired of trying to compete with increasingly powerful guitar amps onstage. His efforts to have someone develop an electronic drum kit, however, had failed. Then he met a young engineer named Mark Barton, who worked for the Tychobrahe Sound Company in Hermosa Beach, California.

Barton created four prototypes of simple electronic drum pads. They produced static triangle or square waveforms, and the user could adjust the pitch and decay. Pollard then invited drummers he knew—including Jim Keltner, Hal Blaine, and Ringo Starr—to try them out. The product was an instant hit, and a company was formed.

Barton named the new product the "Syndrum." Then he had one final brainstorm. Playing around with a drum kit in his parents' garage, he noticed that the head on one of the toms was loose. When struck, the drum's pitch immediately jumped, then decayed. Barton decided to try a similar effect on the Syndrum. "That was the birth of the swept DEOOOM sound that became the Syndrum's signature identity," Barton recalled, "and has been copied in every drum synth ever since."

The distinctive sounds of the Syndrum, and other electronic percussion, weren't just part of those devices' sonic identities. They often became crucial elements of the songs that featured them.

3.

Sly Dunbar's manager warns that it's important to let the phone ring when calling his client.

First of all, he says, "the Jamaican phone network is for shit." The more important reason is Dunbar's long-standing love of drum programming. "He is punching in beats night and day," his manager says, "and does not always pick up his phone."

As it turns out, Dunbar answers readily this Sunday morning. But he admits he'll be programming drums before the day is through.

Lowell "Sly" Dunbar and his longtime bass-playing partner, Robbie Shakespeare, are perhaps the most famous rhythm section alive. From Bob Dylan and The Rolling Stones to dancehall performers unknown outside Jamaica, countless artists have proudly displayed the "Sly and Robbie" credit on their work.

But Dunbar has also spent a good chunk of his professional life surrounded by drum machines and electronic percussion. "He's a master in the field," says his friend, keyboardist Wally Badarou.

Dunbar's apprenticeship in this area began during the summer of 1978. He and Shakespeare were touring America with Peter Tosh, then opening for The Rolling Stones. But they had longer-term plans. The pair thriftily bagged up leftover food from their hotels and ate it on the bus. That allowed them to save their meal money for their musical endeavors.

Some of the cash helped start the duo's Jamaican label, Taxi Records. And before leaving New York, Dunbar used $500 to purchase two Pollard Syndrums at Manny's Music. At first, he wasn't sure of the best way to use the devices. But when he heard M's huge 1979 hit "Pop Muzik"—which featured his friend Wally Badarou on keyboards—something clicked.

By that point, Dunbar had also acquired a Pollard Syndrum Quad. The Model 478 had a blue control board and four drum pads. "I was on the road with Peter Tosh, and I heard 'Pop Muzik.' I heard that synthesizer sound—*boop*," Dunbar remembers. "And I said, 'I wonder if these things could play something like that sound?'

"So when I went to soundcheck, I bring the control board down, and I try to get that sound. At first it goes, *JJJUHHH*." Here Dunbar mimics a deep drum hit. "And then I tune it up, and I make that sound—*boop, boop*. And I say, 'Hey, that's the "Pop Muzik" sound!'"

Dunbar first overdubbed Syndrums on a cover of Cornell Campbell's "Queen of the Minstrels," from his 1979 album *Sly, Wicked, and Slick*. The Syndrums also appeared on "Baltimore," a version of a Randy Newman song that Dunbar recorded with vocal group The Tamlins the same year. The tune became a massive Jamaican hit, and gave Dunbar and Shakespeare's Taxi label a huge boost.

The Syndrum's *boop, boop* was fast becoming a Dunbar trademark. On Black Uhuru's "Guess Who's Coming to Dinner," "I kind of get that 'Pop Muzik' sound again," he says. But this time, Dunbar used it to play a distinctive percussive riff that bubbles underneath the entire track.

In 1980, Island Records head Chris Blackwell assembled a team of top-notch session men at his studio in Nassau. Dunbar, Shakespeare, and Badarou became part of the so-called Compass Point All-Stars. Their first assignment was to back up singer Grace Jones, an androgynous, Jamaican-born model. Jones was trying to restart her stalled musical career, and on the albums *Nightclubbing* and *Living My Life*, the All-Stars created a futuristic soundscape of reggae, dub, R&B, and new wave.

The high-pitched *boop, boop* of Dunbar's Syndrums—this time, the Model 478—provides a percussive counterpoint to his drumming on "Pull Up to the Bumper" and "My Jamaican Guy." Dunbar went in a different direction, however, on "Nipple to the Bottle." He smeared the Syndrum's white noise over his snare drum to accentuate the backbeat. The result was a major club hit, reaching Number 2 on the Billboard Dance charts in 1982.

What made Dunbar's Syndrums a truly wise investment, he thought, was not just his career as a drummer. "When you're a producer, you're trying to develop a sound. I always go back and look at Motown," Dunbar explains. "They develop a sound and continue that sound. And people grow to know that sound, and love it."

4.

To inventor Mark Barton's chagrin, the Syndrum was not adopted by progressive rock bands. It was mostly snapped up by disco artists instead.

This wasn't surprising. Disco's four-on-the-floor bass drum meant that the backbeat—the snare drum, playing on beats two and four—now needed to be reinforced, to differentiate it.

The easiest way to do this was by adding multiple handclaps. Drummer Bernadette Cooper of Klymaxx, an all-female R&B band from Los Angeles formed in 1979, remembers this process well from the band's first album, *Never Underestimate the Power of a Woman*.

"We'd all get around the mic in the studio and do the claps," Cooper says. With a laugh, she adds, "and do it again when we messed up."

Drummer Billy Amendola remembers using a slapstick—a hinged wooden device that mimics the sound of a whipcrack—in the studio during the late 1970s with his disco band Mantus. "We used that on the snare drum of just about every song," says Amendola, "to give the two and the four a little something extra."

The Syndrum and the devices that followed it could also augment the backbeat. One of the most popular of the new units was the Synare 3 Percussion Synthesizer, which appeared in 1977 from Connecticut's Star Instruments. Retailing for just under $800, the Synare 3 had two oscillators, white and pink noise generators, and a ring modulator. But it was best known for its "flying saucer" design, and for the *Star Wars*-like sound effects it created.

One of the early hits that featured the Synare 3 was the disco song "Ring My Bell" by Anita Ward. It reached Number 1 on both the pop and disco charts in 1979. Here, the Synare's trademark "pee-ooo" sound was actually heard on the first beat of certain measures, rather than the backbeat.

Stephen Morris remembers vividly seeing the machine's ancestor, the Synare 1, in a shop window in Manchester in 1978. Nose pressed to the window, he lusted after the four rubber pads, the sliders and switches, and—most of all—the handle. You could carry this drum kit anywhere.

"Luckily it was Sunday. So the shop was shut. So I couldn't go and embarrass meself," Morris recalls with a smile. Years later, he finally got this drum set of his dreams and found that "you can get some great sounds out of it. But none of them sound anything like a drum, which is a problem."

Morris had better luck with the Synare 3. It quickly became an integral part of Joy Division's repertoire, including the "chi-chi" sounds in "She's Lost Control."

Producer Martin Hannett "looked down on it," Morris recalls. "He'd say, 'You can get better sounds.' Which was true! You *could* get better sounds out of an ARP—he had the 2600. But you couldn't *hit* it! And the Synare gets louder when you play it, like a drum." He grins. "But I had to look really miserable before he'd let me play it."

Hannett wasn't the only person skeptical of the Synare. When Warren Cann of Ultravox acquired a pair of the units, he was told they were "disco in a box! The Philadelphia sound!" But when he tried them out, "it was the worst thing I'd ever heard. *Pee-ooo! Pee-ooo!*" He groans at the memory.

Determined to get something out of his investment, Cann kept fiddling with the Synare 3's controls. He finally came up with two sounds he liked: a slowly decaying fizzle of white noise, and a deeper-pitched rumble that sounded like gathering thunderheads. "That was all it was good for!" he insists. "It was a total one-trick pony."

But it was a great trick. When Cann took those two sounds to Ultravox's rehearsal studio, they helped salvage an orphaned chord progression. Just half an hour later—with the Synare reinforcing the rhythms of the Roland CR-78—it became Ultravox's biggest hit. Slow, romantic, and deliberately over-the-top, "Vienna" reached Number 2 in the UK, and was one of 1981's best-selling singles.

The Synare soon had a similar effect on an even bigger hit. In December 1980, producer Val Garay was overseeing a session at a rehearsal studio in North Hollywood. The artist was Kim Carnes, who was struggling with a cover song about a woman who had the mystery of a film icon. "Bette Davis Eyes" had a melody perfectly suited to Carnes's raspy vocals. But the singer wasn't happy with the jazzy arrangement.

Drummer Craig Krampf remembers the night well. "Kim said, 'We have a great record here, but musically, it sucks. Is there anything we can do with this song?' And we said, 'Well, let's figure out the beat first.'"

Krampf played a four-on-the-floor disco pattern, and keyboardist Bill Cuomo came up with the song's signature riff. Suddenly the song was nearly perfect. But something was still missing.

Then Krampf spoke up. "I said, 'I got this drum at home that sounds like a trash can!' And Kim said, 'Why don't you bring it?' She was up for radical things."

The drum was the Synare 3. Garay would complain later that "it was the most annoying thing I'd ever heard in my life." But he had to admit that the massive white noise handclaps Krampf created with it were exactly what the track needed.

"Bette Davis Eyes" became the biggest hit of 1981, and a worldwide Number 1. "That's a very special record," says Krampf, who points out that the week of this conversation is the fortieth anniversary of the song's release. "Forty years ago," he reflects. "Can you believe it?"

Thanks in part to the Synare, you can.

5.

The Syndrum and Synare weren't the only devices that could pump up the backbeat. Warren Cann discovered another of them one day in 1978, when he rode his motorcycle to a music shop in St. Albans, North London. When he arrived, the owner, Dave Simmons, excitedly ushered him into his workshop.

"He shows me this box. It's a little bigger than this." Cann holds up his iPhone to demonstrate. I say, 'What is it?' And he says, 'It makes handclaps. That's why I call it the Claptrap!'"

Like the Synare, the Claptrap was, as Cann observes, a one-trick pony. But like the Synare, its trick could be valuable. It simulated the sound of handclaps with white noise, allowing users a surprising amount of editing control. "You could spread the claps out, sloppy them up," Cann says. "Or you could tighten them up. Or you could try to hit that sweet spot—the sound of two or three people clapping."

The Claptrap was featured on several New Romantic hits. But the invention that followed it out of that back room in St. Albans would create worldwide reverberations.

6.

Martin "Red" Broad is seated behind his drum kit. He's looking out at the 90,000 seats of a mostly empty Wembley Stadium on this early 1980s afternoon.

Broad's band, Sector 27, will be opening for Elton John here in a few hours. But right now, he's about to enjoy one of the best parts of this gig: sound checking his electronic drums and listening to the snares and tom-toms explode like bombs across the vast arena.

"What made it exciting was hearing that sound coming through the PA," says Broad. He ruffles his spiky blonde crop and grins at the memory. "It was just like, WHOA. *Power!*"

That was the promise of Simmons electronic drums: power, both audio and aesthetic. Eventually, most drummers who heard—and saw—them were convinced by that power. Like Broad, who at one point owned the second-biggest Simmons kit in England.

He didn't even mind that the first Simmons drum pads were hard plastic, "like hitting a kitchen surface," Broad recalls, rubbing his elbow reflexively. "They were still worth it."

A Simmons kit looked great. And the sound was massive. It fulfilled the objective Richard James Burgess had when he first began thinking about electronic percussion. "I used to say that a snare drum should sound like an axe through your head," he says, "and the kick drum should be like a kick in the gut."

Simmons had developed the SDS 3 at the request of Baz Watts. Watts was a former bandmate of Simmons, who went on to play drums for Adam Ant and Paul Young. "He wanted something different," Simmons recalled. What Simmons gave him was essentially an electronic brain connected to acoustic drum heads. Each drum had its own channel, and a noise generator.

The SDS 3 was "put into short production runs in the garden shed," said Simmons. "We'd make five, sell five, make 10, sell 10." At the same time, Burgess was testing out his own ideas about electronic drums.

Born in London, raised in New Zealand, and educated at Berklee School of Music in Boston, Burgess has had a music career as colorful as the drums he helped invent. He was the drummer in the British soft-rock band Easy Street, which had a minor US hit in 1976 with "I've Been Lovin' You." Burgess also played with keyboardist Christopher Heaton in the avant-garde group Accord, an electronic act that appeared on the BBC.

Burgess and Heaton next joined forces in Landscape. This quintet made a debut album of instrumental jazz-funk for RCA, but it sold poorly. Without vocals, Burgess realized, the band was probably doomed. Meanwhile, he was also experimenting with the idea of an electronic drum kit.

Burgess heard that Simmons was working on the same problem. He paid a visit to the workshop in St. Albans, and left with several SDS 3 modules. Burgess discovered that triggering four or five modules simultaneously could "generate a single sound that was quite realistically drum-like. It didn't necessarily sound like real drums, but it had the same impact—enough to perform the function of a real drum set."

He'd recognized that every drum sound contained both pitched and unpitched elements. Triggering a single sound couldn't capture all these elements. But triggering multiple drum sounds at once could get you surprisingly close.

This was the breakthrough. Burgess travelled back to St. Albans, where he and Simmons began designing a new prototype. They used an ARP 2600 synthesizer to generate the layered drum sounds, and used crystal mics in the triggers.

The result was the Simmons SDS 5. Burgess played the prototype unit on Landscape's second album, 1981's *From the Tea Rooms of Mars … to the Hell Holes of Uranus*. This release solved both of Burgess's problems at once. His vocals and tongue-in-cheek lyrics made songs like "Norman Bates" and "Einstein a Go-Go" left-field pop hits. The Simmons drums, meanwhile, gave the album a crisp, in-your face punch.

The latter tune became a UK Top 5 hit in 1981, and Landscape were invited onto *Top of the Pops* to promote their single. This TV spot turned out to be better advertising for Simmons than money could buy.

After developing the SDS 5 prototype, Burgess and Simmons made another crucial realization. "Since the drums were not generating any acoustic sounds," Burgess says, "they didn't need to be round." Suddenly the sky was the limit, design wise.

A kit with batwing pads was developed. Then Simmons commissioned a local sculptor, Colman Saunders, to create models of human heads that could house the drum pads. The effect was both creepy and unforgettable.

Burgess played this "Mount Rushmore" kit with Landscape on *Top of the Pops*. "It caused a riot," Simmons recalled years later. "Our phones rang off the hook." However, the Mount Rushmore kit would never be mass produced. Burgess came up with a better idea while driving to St. Albans one day.

"It struck me that ergonomically, a honeycomb-shaped set would be very compact and versatile in the ways you could set it up," he says. And once customers saw prototypes of the hexagonal pads, the design "quickly went viral."

The finished kit was fully modular, with independent kick, snare and tom-toms. Drummers could store their preset sounds—a godsend for playing live.

Almost overnight, Simmons grew from a garden shed operation to a full-scale factory. "It was certainly an exciting time for all of us involved in creating the drums," Simmons remembered in 2011, "and maybe some of that excitement was reflected in the drummers who saw the kits on *Top of the Pops* and said, 'What the ***k?'"

7.

Drummers from every genre would eventually add Simmons drums to their arsenals. In those early days, however, "the majority of drummers were either anti-electronic drums," Dave Simmons claimed, "or downright hostile toward them."

So during that first year of production, Simmons created a product for a different market. The Simmons Suitcase Kit was part Syndrum, part VCS suitcase synthesizer. It was a set of seven small Simmons pads, mounted in foam rubber and housed in a hard flight case. Just like the hexagonal pads of a Simmons drum kit, the pads in the suitcase could trigger sounds from an SDS5 brain.

Not many of these kits were manufactured. But one went to an artist who managed to essentially turn the Suitcase Kit into a drum machine.

He was a London musician named Thomas Morgan Robertson. The son of a Cambridge archeology professor, he'd been fascinated by electronic music since he rescued a synth module from a garbage bin. He'd become enough of an expert that the stadium rock group Foreigner had invited him to America to play synthesizers on the platinum album 4. Now he was beginning a solo career back in England—as the synth-pop artist Thomas Dolby.

At first, Dolby simply played the Simmons pads with his fingers. "I'm not a great drummer, even with my fingernails," Dolby explains. "But when you play the pads with fingernails, you get four separate hits. Like a cluster of notes. So on a song like 'Windpower,' that's what you're hearing."

Having to physically play the Suitcase Kit, however, was limiting Dolby's live possibilities. "Then I was out one night in a nightclub. I saw these flashing red and green lights out on the dancefloor, flashing in time with the music. And I wondered how they were doing that," Dolby recalls. "It turned out that they had a little unit in the DJ booth, which converted sound to voltages. And I thought, if I could just do that, then I could maybe program my drums, instead of playing them with my fingernails."

The answer was a PPG 340/380 Wave Computer, originally designed to run the light show of the German Electronic band Tangerine Dream. The idea was similar to the box Dolby had seen in the DJ booth. "It had a VDU (visual display unit) and a keyboard, and a green screen and a cursor. You would basically program ones and zeroes," he says. "It would put out positive and negative voltages to the lighting units."

But PPG also had created a rack-mounted drum module similar to the Simmons brain. "It was very primitive," Dolby says. He discovered, however, that he could use the notes from the sequencer to trigger both the PPG and the Simmons drum sounds.

This actually made concerts *more* challenging for Dolby, however. Now he needed to lug the PPG unit, which he'd nicknamed Henry, to every gig. It was the approximate size of a refrigerator. "My lumbar region has never recovered," Dolby says with a groan.

To store the drum programs—as well as bass sequences he'd programmed—Dolby had to record them onto microcassettes. There were two cassettes for each song in his set. They had to be manually loaded into the PPG before each song.

"Then I had to type on the keyboard, 'Load,' and hit return. A series of dots would run across the green screen for exactly 52 seconds," he says.

"At the end of that time, one of two things would happen," remembers Dolby. "The cursor would either blink, which meant it was ready for me to type 'Play,' and then hit return. Or it would print out, 'Error,' and, in parenthesis, 'Reload?' And it would be about a 50/50 chance which of those outcomes I would get."

He snorts with laughter. "When you're still obscure and there's only 14 people in the audience," Dolby says, "it's slightly less humiliating when everything goes wrong.

"So I began to develop preambles for the songs," he adds. "And this informed my songwriting. When I wrote a song like 'One of Our Submarines,' it was convenient to tell the story of my Uncle Stephen, who died in a submarine in World War II. When I sat down to write a song, I had to be thinking about the backstory, for while I was minding the PPG."

These songs became Dolby's first solo album, *The Golden Age of Wireless*. They would make him a star, one of the most recognizable figures of the early days of MTV. But few people realized the singular, innovative drum sound Dolby had created—and how creating it had helped bring those songs into being in the first place.

***

Inside and Outside the Box: The Linn Revolution

1.

Drum machines have sometimes been called rhythm boxes. But this machine is, quite literally, a box, made of cardboard.

Inside the box are circuit boards. On the outside, dangling from some wires, is a control panel. You might mistake this for some overambitious kid's science project. In a way, that's exactly what it is. But the young man lugging it around is demonstrating it to some of the biggest stars in music.

Stevie Wonder's response is perhaps the most honest. He can't see the scuffed-up cardboard, or the masses of circuit boards. He just hears the sounds the box makes: the sounds of real drums, sampled but unmistakable. And he can reassemble them however he chooses.

So Stevie Wonder puts down a $2,500 deposit for those sounds. So does the great jazz pianist Herbie Hancock. So does disco pioneer Giorgio Moroder. So does guitarist Frank Zappa, and trumpeter Herb Alpert. Even Daryl Dragon—the skipper of hitmaking husband-and-wife duo Captain & Tennille—ponies up.

This cardboard box contains the technology that will change the music business for good. Not that Roger Linn, the young man who made it, is thinking those thoughts at the time.

"The phrase is, 'Necessity is the mother of invention,' and I just wanted to have a drum machine," says Linn today. "All of a sudden, I'd get these calls from famous musicians who I would have killed just to get an audition with. I'd say, 'Well, you know, I don't do this. I'm just a guitar player. I'm a songwriter.' They'd say, 'Yeah, yeah, that's fine. What about this drum machine thing?'"

"Eventually I got the message: I had a better chance of success in combining my music and technology skills, and that was better than becoming a guitar player," Linn reflects. "It took me a while to remove that ego identification, but I finally did."

Roger Linn is relaxing on the deck of his home in Los Altos, California. During this interview, he will refer several times to the mistakes he made as "a cocky 24, 25-year-old." That was how old he was when he unveiled the Linn LM-1 to a mostly unsuspecting world.

The irony is that the ego identification Linn mentions just took another form. In the music world, "Linn" remains one of the iconic real-name brands, right up there with "Moog" and "Oberheim." What Roger Linn once hoped to accomplish as a guitarist, he achieved a thousand times over as the creator of Linn drum machines.

"Have you ever read Malcolm Gladwell's book *Outliers*?" Linn asks suddenly, leaning forward in his deck chair. "You know that chapter about people born in 1955? I was born in 1955, as was Steve Jobs, Bill Gates, and a long list of other people. The idea that Gladwell presents is that if you were born in 1955 or thereabouts, then when the microcomputer revolution hit in 1975, you're old enough that you just weren't still stuck in high school, and you weren't yet old enough to have a family and kids and settle down. So it was the perfect time for people to take risks.

"If I had been born five years later, I would've missed that," Linn adds, as the California daylight begins to fade. "Now I would say I've got some talent, sure, and I happen to have two interests that happen to combine very well. But a whole lot of it was just the luck of the draw."

2.

Roger Linn's first lucky break turned out to be a cautionary tale.

Linn grew up in a musical family in Whittier, California, just east of Los Angeles. His mother was an opera singer; his father a composer and music professor at the University of Southern California. He began studying classical guitar, but switched to electric when he heard Clapton, Beck, and Hendrix. When he was fourteen, he got an after-school job at a Hollywood guitar shop.

There, Linn quickly made a name for himself—by modifying effects pedals. Even before his career had begun, the paradox of Roger Linn's professional life was apparent. The more interested he was in *playing* music, the more his fellow musicians wanted him to *invent* things for them.

One of Linn's high school friends knew the road manager of a quartet named Fanny. They were one of the first all-female rock groups, and their debut album had just been released on Reprise Records. "My friend told the road manager about this modification I had made to a stompbox—a distortion pedal," Linn recalls. "It made it sound much better, and he was very excited about it."

But disaster struck when the group tried out the new pedal in concert. "All of a sudden, apparently, a baseball game came through on a radio station." Linn shakes his head. "When it came to designing musical equipment, I didn't know anything about the reliability that's required."

The setback didn't deter him. In 1973, he began working with singer-songwriter Leon Russell. Linn played guitar, percussion, and synthesizers. He also became Russell's go-to engineer at his Oklahoma studio. It was housed in a converted church, and it was where Russell helped develop the "Tulsa Sound" as an artist and producer.

Linn spotted a place where his technological interests might be useful. "Leon used to cut tracks with the drum machine, and one of them—I don't remember what the model number was—but it was intended to sit up on top of a piano or keyboard. It was long and wide, and it had a little touch bar to start and stop it. It had a pretty good sound."

There was also a lot, Linn saw, that it *didn't* have. As a songwriter, he realized that a programmable drum machine would be an invaluable tool. "Once I got my first computer when I was probably 19 or 20, I wanted to apply it to music," Linn says. "There were all kinds of programs I was writing. And one that I *really* wanted to make was a drum machine."

3.

Steve Porcaro sheepishly apologizes.

"Am I yelling?" he asks with a grin. (He was.) "Hey, I get excited talking about this stuff!"

Steve Porcaro and his late brother Jeff were two of the founding members of the hugely popular rock group Toto. As a songwriter and session musician, Steve has been involved with dozens of other hits, including Michael Jackson's "Human Nature," which he wrote. And he's written or played on the soundtracks to a score of TV shows and films, including *ER* and *Justified*.

But you might not know that Steve Porcaro's enthusiasm for technology was one of the driving forces behind Linn drum machines. He and Roger Linn have been friends for nearly fifty years. And it's easy to imagine the white-haired, gregarious Porcaro as he must have been in the early days of the LM-1: as the more reserved Linn's hype man.

"When you're talking about drum machines as we know them now, you're talking about Roger," says Porcaro proudly. "Roland wasn't doing that. Yamaha wasn't doing that. Korg wasn't doing that. *Nobody* was doing that, except this kid in the Valley named Roger Linn. He beat 'em all to the punch by a mile."

Porcaro and his two older brothers, Jeff and Mike, grew in Connecticut. Their father, Joe, was a well-known jazz drummer. And as the three boys grew up, Joe Porcaro made sure they all took drum lessons. The tutelage helped Jeff become one of the top studio drummers in world. Meanwhile, Mike would later turn to the bass, and Steve became a keyboardist.

Steve Porcaro had seen preset drum machines used in the studio since his earliest days as a professional. He remembers that when his brother Jeff played with the soft rock duo Seals and Crofts in the mid-1970s, "they would lay down tempo maps using a Rhythm Ace.

"But ironically," he adds, "they weren't using it to keep the track steady. They wanted it to *move*. They wanted to speed up just a little going into the chorus. So they'd turn up the tempo on the Rhythm Ace, and then overdub the drums on top of it."

In 1975, Steve Porcaro visited Leon Russell's Oklahoma studio. He was amazed at the collection of gear Russell had assembled. "And here was this one guy, Roger Linn, this young kid, running all of it," Porcaro says. He became friends with the whiz kid engineer, who was just two years older. They stayed in touch when they both returned to the Golden State.

In the meantime, Porcaro took a job as the keyboardist for Gary Wright. The former Spooky Tooth keyboardist and songwriter had just made his third solo album, using a Univox drum machine in the basement of his rented New Jersey home.

The songs that resulted became 1975's *The Dream Weaver*, a Top 10 hit. The title track reached Number 2 the following year, and Wright took his show—and his drum machine—on the road. Steve Porcaro was part of this group. So was a session drummer named Art Wood, who got a crash course in electronics.

"I was grateful for the opportunity to play with the drum machine because it really it nailed down my timing," remembers Wood. "I would start off Gary's show up on a riser. I smashed a gong and then I would jump down onto the stage. And as I jumped, I'd hit the foot pedal for the drum machine, and then I'd count off the song."

Soon, Wood would get a chance to see what this mixture of playing and programming looked like to a spectator. He'd view it from a perspective almost nobody else had shared.

4.

The roots of using sampled drum sounds in programming go back to a little computer store in Studio City, California.

The shop was called COMPAL—Computer Power and Light. There, Roger Linn bought a home computer developed by the shop's owners: the COMPAL 80, powered by an Intel 88 processor. One of Linn's friends, Roger Nichols, bought the same computer. Nichols was interested in drum replacement, too.

Specifically, Nichols was trying to develop drum programming software that would satisfy his longtime clients, the duo Steely Dan. Nichols had been the engineer for the group since their 1972 debut album, *Can't Buy a Thrill*. Donald Fagen and Walter Becker had a reputation for literate, musically complex songs. They were also known as perfectionists who were especially tough on drummers—even seasoned studio pros. That persnickety streak reached its peak during the recording of their seventh album, *Gaucho*.

"We were having trouble laying down 'Hey Nineteen.' We tried it with two different bands and it still didn't work, so one of us said something like, 'It's too bad that we can't get a machine to play the beat we want, with full-frequency drum sounds, and to be able to move the snare drum and kick drum around independently,'" Fagen told *Sound on Sound* in 2006.

"Roger replied, 'I can do that.' This was back in 1978 or something, so we said, 'You can do that???' To which he said, 'Yes, all I need is $150,000.' So we gave him the money out of our recording budget, and six weeks later he came in with this machine, and that is how it all started."

The system of "digital drum replacement" that Nichols developed was nicknamed Wendel, and it debuted on *Gaucho*. The song "Hey Nineteen," a Top 10 hit in early 1981, is probably the first big hit to feature sampled, programmed drums.

"We found that there were certain feels that we couldn't get out of real drummers—they weren't steady enough," Nichols later told the Steely Dan fanzine, *Metal Leg*. "So we had to design something that would do it perfectly, but with some human feeling, the right amount of layback. Instead of just one hi-hat sound that repeats machine-like over and over, we had sixteen different ones, so it had the inflections.

"Wendel can play exactly what the drummer plays—if he plays a little early or a little hard, Wendel plays it a little early or a little hard. Play it once, Wendel memorizes the song, then you play it again and it repeats what it hears."

Fagen and Becker had gotten what they wanted. But programming a drum track, hit by hit, was too painstaking a process even for Steely Dan. Fagen remembered that Nichols "had to type all these bytes out, huge lists of numbers, which took him 20 minutes, and at the end he would hit Return, and we heard this one snare a beat. It took so long."

It was essentially the same concept Linn was starting to pursue. His own version of this system began when he called Roland to request the circuit board from one of their drum machines. He wrote a computer program in BASIC that could trigger the Roland machine's sounds, which were housed in a box with a control voltage/gate. By typing in code—"B" for bass drum, "S" for snare, and so on—onto a grid, Linn could program each individual sound.

By this point, Linn was no longer working with Leon Russell. But when he showed Russell the prototype, "Leon wanted to buy it immediately. And I said no, it's just a prototype. He says, 'I wanna buy it anyway.' And he threw a bunch of money at me, but I still said no. But he wouldn't relent."

Finally, Russell made Linn an offer he couldn't refuse: a coproducer's credit on his next album. So Linn built the machine, and used it to program the drums on Russell's 1979 album *Life and Love*. "And in typical Leon fashion, when the album came out, it says in huge letters on the back, 'PRODUCED BY LEON RUSSELL.' And way down in the corner"—Linn's voice drops to a tiny whisper—"it says, 'Engineered and co-produced by Roger Linn.'"

"Sometimes he was a real manipulator," Linn adds with a smile. "But it got him what he wanted." While the programming is deliberately simple, and the Roland sounds are obviously machine-made, *Life and Love*, like *Gaucho*, stands as a milestone of drum programming history.

By now, Linn had showed a few other people his program. Watching Stevie Wonder struggle to operate it showed its inventor some important truths.

Clearly, the visual interface meant little to a blind man. Wonder was also not going to be happy typing complex, note-by-note drum patterns onto a computer keyboard. "Real musicians," Linn realized, "should be able to play their music in real time."

This got Linn thinking about other possible flaws with his invention. "I recognized it had to sound better," he says, "and I wasn't quite sure what to do about that." Two of his friends were instrumental in helping answer that question.

5.

To this point, the sounds of drum machines hadn't changed substantially since the Chamberlin Model 100 had vanished, nearly thirty years earlier. That unit had used recordings of a live drummer. Occasionally, an oddball device surfaced that tried the same trick—like the Bandmaster Powerhouse, a Scottish-made machine from 1976 that offered taped drum loops on eight-track cassettes.

But most drum machines since the Model 100 simply contained analog sounds that were created by shaping basic waveforms and white noise. Those sounds were sometimes intriguing, and sometimes not. What they weren't—and really weren't meant to be—was realistic.

Recording engineer Gordon Rudd, who'd been working with Leon Russell since 1968, had noticed this while working on designs for a digital tape recorder. "One thing I learned from the sound synthesis business is that sounds in real life are extremely complex," he says. "Even the most complex and intricate analog synths could not really create a decent violin or trumpet. It was now my premise that it would be easier and more effective to play back a recorded sound than to try to synthesize it."

But analog tape-based drum machines, Rudd realized, "were such poor quality that they had limited usefulness." So he'd pitched the idea of a digital tape machine to his industry contacts, including Beatles producer George Martin. He also paid a visit to a home studio Russell kept in Encino, California. Rudd played both men a 16-bit digital recording of solo drums.

"This drum recording had the most presence of any drum recording I'd ever heard," Rudd says. "I like to think that my demo may have influenced Roger to try digital drum sounds."

To this point, no one except Roger Nichols had tried to digitally sample the sounds of real drums. And even his invention, Wendel, was a one-of-a-kind creation. Sampling was a game for rich professionals.

At about the same time that Linn was working on his drum machine, a pair of Australian inventors were developing an all-in-one workstation called the Fairlight CMI. This "Computer Musical Instrument" included sampling among its many features. But when it appeared, it also retailed for $35,000—more than twice the average American household income at the time.

Major expense was inevitable if you were talking about sampling violins or saxophones. But Steve Porcaro had studied waveforms that suggested that sampling drums might be different. "At one point he'd talked to some people at Roland who had the idea of having some samples at the start of a sound, then synthesis after that," Linn says. "Because often at the start of a sound, that's where you hear the realism."

Every sound has four stages: attack, decay, sustain, and release. The first stage, attack, is where the sound begins and reaches its peak volume. Sounds like a bass drum or snare drum reach their peak almost instantly. Linn realized that a short sample of a percussive sound might be enough to trick a listener's ear.

"If you don't sample the whole drumbeat, but instead sample one instance of a bass drum, one of a snare drum, one of a hi-hat, and a few other drums, you can actually get away with sampling," Linn says. "I think that was a big innovation for drum machines."

Now the question was: whose drums would Linn use to test this innovation?

6.

For the past forty years, Art Wood has struggled with a peculiar dilemma.

Music writers have often contended that the late Clyde Stubblefield is the most widely heard drummer in popular music. That's because Stubblefield played drums on James Brown's 1970 single "Funky Drummer." And Stubblefield's shuffling drum break became perhaps the most-sampled recording ever.

But Stubblefield might not be the title holder after all. Art Wood has played with plenty of heavyweights, from Tina Turner to Bette Midler to James Brown. He's also been heard on countless other recordings—though his contribution is even less recognized than Stubblefield's.

Wood's drum samples became the sounds of the Linn LM-1. They were also used on subsequent Linn products. They've been sampled innumerable times—even by other drum machines.

If you bought music or listened to the radio during the 1980s, you heard Art Wood daily, though most of those credits were never on a record sleeve. Art Wood was probably the favorite drummer of the legendarily demanding Prince, even though they never met.

But try explaining all that to the crowd at your local nightspot. Art Wood has. That's his dilemma.

"You walk into a bar and you hear Gary Wright or Peter Frampton. And you go 'Hey, that's me on the radio there, playing drums,'" Wood says. "And that opens up some conversations."

"But five or six years later, I'd go into a bar and all you hear is The Human League, 'Don't You Want Me?'" he says. "And you say, 'Hey, that's me on the radio! Well, it's not really me … but it *is* me. I played on that record, but I didn't play on it. Those are my drums,'" he says, shaking his head good-naturedly. "It opened up a sort of a confusing conundrum, you know?"

Many people do recognize that *someone* was playing those drums on the LM-1. They just don't recognize the right someone.

The list of drummers who allegedly provided samples for the LM-1 is short, but distinguished. Multiple people interviewed for this book confidently told me that session drummer Steve Gadd is the voice of the Linn. Others were just as sure it was Toto's Jeff Porcaro, or Tower of Power's David Garibaldi. One person even believed that Prince provided the samples himself.

Had he wished, Roger Linn might have been able to persuade just about any of those drummers to participate in his project. "But from an engineering standpoint, there isn't a whole lot of difference between Jeff Porcaro hitting a snare drum once and Art Wood hitting a snare drum once," Linn explains. "In fact, *I* could hit a snare drum once."

"The purpose of the drummer was mostly just to tune the drum to make it sound good," he adds. "Some of the sessions were kinda funny. Art would come in, strike it once, and I'd say, 'Thank you very much. We'll call you.'"

Actually, Linn didn't even have to call Wood. The two men had been bandmates earlier in the 1970s. They were roommates during the time the LM-1 was being developed. And the sounds of the machine were recorded in a closet of the Hollywood residence they shared.

Wood brought in a selection of drums from his kit for the recordings. Two of the most significant drums were snares. "I had a Ludwig super sensitive snare from the late Sixties. And then I had a Slingerland Radio King from the 1930s," he says. "The sound on the LM-1 always reminds me of the Radio King because it's the snare that I always used on ballads. Because it had sort of a deep, *doof* kind of sound. And the LM-1 to me, always sounded like a *doof* kind of snare, like on those Prince records."

The sound of the drums was dry, which was the preference for sessions during the 1970s.

And as Linn puts it, "You could always add ambience later, and it would cost us twice as much to put that ambience in wrong. So why add reverb?"

The dry studio sound became an advantage, since the biggest challenge facing Linn was memory. He had a fraction of a second per sound. So Wood had to keep his drum sounds tight and short. "Even the snare drum—if it rang too long, I had to mute it," Wood says.

Linn recorded the drums using a Sound Workshops console, "which had a really good EQ section. So I don't think we even compressed the drums. He would just kind of EQ them a little bit," says Wood. "And if it sounded good on the chip, then that was the sound."

The "chips" were EPROMs, which stands for "erasable programmable read-only memory." Linn had developed his own analog-to-digital converter, so that he could turn the drum sounds into data on his computer. He then burned them onto memory chips with an EPROM blower.

It became clear early on that cymbals were going to be a problem. The hi-hat cymbal might just fit into the available space. But cymbals, with their long decay times, would not. Not without doubling the cost of the machine, which was going to cost several thousand dollars already.

To save memory and money, Linn rationalized. "Nobody uses a ride cymbal in rock music," he insists. "They use a hi-hat, and people only use a crash occasionally, and you could overdub that. I thought, 'What's the point?'"

But he also innovated. Even the sound of an open hi-hat—the swishing sound that occurs when the drummer lifts his foot off the hi-hat pedal controlling the two cymbals—was taking too long. "So I just conserved memory. I had Art use mallets to do a cymbal roll on the hi-hat, so we had this continuous *shhhhh*. And I just looped that and had a little envelope generator cutting a little piece of it out."

In the end, a dozen sounds were chosen for the machine. They were split between the standard rock drum kit sounds, including high and low toms, and a selection of percussion instruments like cowbell and clave. And, in an important decision, Linn allowed users to adjust the pitch of each sound. This not only gave more freedom to fine-tune the LM-1: it also opened the door for innovative new sounds to be created.

When he and Linn were done recording, Wood says, "I was kind of excited about it because I thought, nobody's done this." However, he also admits, "I don't think I even thought about it as a commercial product, or if it would be successful, or catch on. It was just cool, you know?"

7.

The sounds of Wood's drums were the major selling point of the LM-1. But there were several other innovations that made it a revelation to musicians.

The first was the ability to program in real time—sometimes called "tap programming." To this point, the few programmable drum machines available had almost all required users to program in step time—that is, to write out patterns note by note. Even the Roland CR-78, which had a plastic pad on which users could tap out rhythms, was difficult to program in real time.

So having buttons that users could tap to program each drum sound was an incredible innovation. Linn had learned from Stevie Wonder, and gave musicians the power to play rhythms with their fingers, instead of being forced to write them in code.

This decision revealed a fundamental difference between Roland, which had been founded by a nonmusician, and Roger Linn, who played music professionally. "Roland had this idea about step programming. They thought there were a lot of musicians who don't have the programming and real-time playing skill, and it's easier for them to turn notes on and off with different switches," says Linn. He had realized, however, that musicians valued speed—especially when they were composing. It was faster to play a rhythmic idea with your fingers than program it.

That led to Linn's second and third innovations. What frustrated users of the CR-78's pad interface was that there was almost no way to correct programming mistakes.

Quantization is a fancy term that essentially means "autocorrect." It lines notes up according to a preset grid. If you play a note outside the grid, the "quantize" feature moves it to the nearest line on the grid. This has become one of the most common features of all programmable instruments. But the sequencer program Linn wrote for the LM-1 created this feature accidentally when he was trying to save memory.

"Not only was sample memory expensive, but *memory* memory was expensive. It's what they call RAM memory, into which I had to store the actual drumbeat data. I had to squeeze the information in as little space as possible," Linn recalls.

He decided that it made sense to simply store beats as sixteenth notes—the most common division of notes.

"So when the program had to store a sixteenth note, it would store it in the sixteenth note that's closest to where you actually played it. And when it would loop back around, it would correct your timing errors," he adds. "It was a fortuitous coincidence."

To further humanize the sound of the programmed beats, Linn added a feature that could delay certain notes. This mimics the tiny imperfections of a real drummer, and gives a pattern "swing." Linn realized that by delaying every other sixteenth note a fraction, it gave the pattern a more human feel.

The discovery of quantization might have been an accident. But Linn recognized immediately the significance of what he'd done. "He would always call me over when there was another big jump forward," Steve Porcaro says. "So he calls me one day. He has the click going. And he grabs his dog's paws, and starts slamming them on the buttons."

The machine's quantization kicked in, and Poracro chuckles as he recalls Linn playing back the result. "All of a sudden—*chick-aboom-a-chick-a-boom-a-chick*. It was *groovin'*!"

Both men listened to the pattern and smiled. If even a dog could create perfect rhythm, then the LM-1 was going to be very popular indeed.

8.

Most people know that the "L" in LM-1 stands for Linn. Few realize, however, that the "M" was Alex Moffet, a high school friend of Roger Linn's. Moffet was an important early investor in Linn's invention.

"He was sort of entrepreneurial and had made some money," Linn remembers, "so he said, 'Here's my deal to you: we'll start a corporation, you'll own 51 percent, and I'll set you up in a nice house in the [Hollywood] Hills and buy you a car, and you just invent, and I'll take care of all your business stuff.'"

The two men started Linn Moffet Electronics together in 1979. But as Linn recalls it, "it turns out that—and he was honest with me—his business acumen was less than we had both anticipated, so we eventually parted company. I thought he was my business partner, but it turns out he was more of a seed investor."

That left Linn needing to get a $20,000 loan from his father—and to offer up his prized 1967 Porsche in trade—to complete the LM-1. The deposits he secured from musicians—half down on the $5,000 list price—kept the project going.

The first thirty-five machines were essentially assembled by Linn and a cast of "out-of-work musician friends." But demand already exceeded supply. Then Linn was introduced to Bob Easton, an engineer who owned a company called 360 Systems. Easton was also a pioneering designer. He'd come up with a pitch-to-voltage converter that allowed guitar strings to trigger sounds from a synthesizer—making him the father of the guitar synth.

"He said, 'You know, I've got a factory down at my office down in the Valley, and we're running it about half capacity,'" recalls Linn. "'If you'd like us to manufacture your drum machines for you, that would put you at the next level.'"

Linn got more out of the deal than just increased production of the LM-1. "Bob was also was a great mentor for production engineering," Linn says. "I knew how to make a prototype, but I didn't know how to make things reliable in the field. He taught me a lot about that."

The first print ads for the LM-1 appeared in the fall of 1980. Above a photo of the LM-1 were just two words: "Real Drums." Designer Eric Wrobbel and Linn thought that this phrase, "juxtaposed with a picture of something that looked decidedly *un*like real drums, would make for a provocative headline," as Wrobbel later remembered.

They were right. More than a year before it officially arrived, buzz was building about the LM-1 among Los Angeles musicians. Steve Porcaro remembers Linn bringing his breadboarded prototype to a session for Toto's first album. Porcaro's brother Jeff was there. So was top studio pro Jim Keltner. "And they were diggin' it, in a way," Porcaro says.

But Porcaro was aware of his dilemma. "I'm in a band with a brother who's one of the greatest drummers in town," he points out. "What am *I* doing fucking with this stuff?"

Porcaro sighs. "There was always this weird thing, this drama about it," he says. "Is this going to replace drummers? And it did sometimes. And sometimes there'd be a magic there."

Within a couple of years, the LM-1's magic was no longer confined to Los Angeles. You could hear it everywhere.

***

13

Have You Seen This New Drum Machine? *Shit!*

1.

Elton John has enjoyed quite a few hits. But unless you're a diehard fan, you might not remember "Nobody Wins."

The song just missed the Top 20 when it was released in May 1981. Sir Elton hasn't played it live for nearly forty years. And while its synthesizer-dominated groove sounded contemporary on release, the melody that unfurls over its minor chords is slight.

The song is significant, however, because it's the first hit single to feature the Linn LM-1. It also exposed, early on, the tensions that arrived with the new drum machine.

The programmer on the song was Toto drummer Jeff Porcaro. That may surprise those who believe Porcaro hated drum machines. It's true that his take could be negative. Like when he told *Modern Drummer* in 1988 that "a capable drummer can record as many songs in a day and a half as it would take a week to program. And it'll feel better and won't sound like every other record on the radio."

But Porcaro's relationship with drum machines was far more ambivalent. His keyboardist brother Steve points out that Jeff, who died in 1992, was one of the first people to understand the importance of the LM-1. "He spent five grand on an LM-1," recalls Steve Porcaro. "And who better to program it than a drummer? Who better to ask, 'What would I do if I had a third arm?'"

Jeff Porcaro's mood could swing sharply in the other direction, however. That's what happened when Roger Linn decided to celebrate the success of "Nobody Wins."

"I wasn't particularly sensitive at the time," admits Linn. "I placed an ad in *Billboard* magazine, and it showed a picture of the LM-1. And it said 'The hit record,' and it showed 'Nobody Wins.' Then it said 'The drummer on the hit record,' and it showed a picture of the LM-1."

He winces. "Jeff got pissed and wanted me to retract it. I did an article and I said, 'I'm so sorry about that. It was tongue-in-cheek. Obviously, the LM-1 was not the drummer on the record. Jeff Porcaro was the drummer on the record.'"

The feelings of other drummers would be harder to soothe. Studio drummer Craig Krampf remembers vividly his first encounter with the LM-1. It was February 1981, when the machine made its debut at the National Association of Music Merchants show—NAMM for short—in Los Angeles.

"All these drummers were going, 'Damnit! Have you seen this new drum machine? *Shit!*' They were just swearing and cussing," says Krampf, who's played with Kim Carnes, Paul Stanley of KISS, and Journey singer Steve Perry. "And I couldn't believe it. So I went and saw it."

When he did, Krampf had an epiphany. "I said to myself, 'Well, you better learn this. It's not gonna go away, no matter how much you swear.'" Krampf first bought a cheaper machine, the Oberheim DMX. But he taught himself to program, and would eventually use that skill on Linn machines as well. "And I kept working through the entire technological revolution," Krampf says.

One of the other drummers at that NAMM show was Miami percussionist Joe Galdo. His disco group, Foxy, had just broken up after enjoying a couple of Top 40 hits. It was Galdo's thirtieth birthday, but he'd barely noticed: he was wandering around the show, glumly thinking about his future. Suddenly, he was jolted back to the present by a fusion-style rhythm in 6/8 time.

"So I'm quickening my pace to see who's playing this thing. And I turn the corner, and there's this empty booth with a black box there," Galdo recalls. "It kind of scared me. At first, I thought it was a recording, because it sounded like a real drummer who was playing the shit out of this thing. But unfortunately, nobody was there by this machine to tell me what it was."

Months later, back in Miami, Galdo was driving down the South Dixie Highway when an Elton John song came on the radio. The percussionist on the song, Galdo thought, sounded like fusion drummer Ed Greene or R&B session man James Gadson. "They're coming in after the fill, and they're super solid," he remembers. "Right on the money."

Impressed, Galdo stopped off at a music store to pick up the album, *The Fox*. He read the sleeve credits, and was stunned to see that the drums had been "programmed by Roger Linn and Jeff Porcaro." Suddenly, the black box he'd seen in Los Angeles made sense.

"I called my wife, and I said, 'Listen, I'm not sure how much we have in the bank. But I think this is something we have to do,'" Galdo says. With his wife's blessing, Galdo eventually tracked down a LinnDrum, the follow-up to the LM-1. And he would go on to use it on a series of hits by Miami Sound Machine and singer Gloria Estefan, making him one of the most successful drum programmers of the 1980s.

Another early adopter was New York drummer Billy Amendola. "I think the drum machine really made me a songwriter," says Amendola, who also serves as the Editor at Large of *Modern Drummer* magazine. "I might never have gotten an interest in it without the machine."

It was several months before the LM-1 truly took hold in the pop world. Herbie Hancock, the recipient of the second LM-1 manufactured, subtly debuted the machine on "Textures," the closing track from 1980's *Mr. Hands*. Meanwhile, moviemaker John Carpenter used the LM-1 on the futuristic score for 1981's dystopian fantasy *Escape From New York*.

The LM-1 did immediately find a home in the electronic music known in the UK as New Pop. John Foxx, whose former band Ultravox had been a key influence on that sound, was recording his second solo album, *The Garden*, in 1981. He'd been experimenting with the Movement Systems Drum Computer, a British-made device that looked like an orange desktop computer and featured sampled sounds. "But when the Linn arrived, that was the end of it," Foxx says.

Ultravox drummer Warren Cann was ecstatic when he first saw the LM-1. He'd been working with German film composer Hans Zimmer in an electronic side project called Helden. And Zimmer had an in with the owners of an exclusive London music store called Syco Systems.

The shop was elegant, with high ceilings and minimal decor. Cann describes it as "an art gallery for rock stars. It's all white, and there's next to nothing in it. Everything in it has pride of place.

"If you're Paul McCartney, and you want to buy a new synth, or if you're Pete Townshend, and you want to buy a new drum machine, you call up and you make an appointment," says Cann. "When you turned up, you'd be the only one there. Stay as long as you want; play whatever you want. It was heaven."

That was how Cann felt when he auditioned the LM-1 there in 1981, and bought "certainly, one of the first three or four in Britain. I thought, 'This is the future!'"

"A separate output for every channel. Wahoo! You can tune each voice! Wow!" Cann remembers. "Plus it made sense with respect to chaining patterns together into songs. You need to tailor the drum part to the song. Now you could do that with a drum machine."

Another London drummer who quickly grasped the significance of the LM-1 was Chris Merrick Hughes. One of the two percussionists in Adam and the Ants, he'd also produced the group's two biggest albums, *Kings of the Wild Frontier* and *Prince Charming*. Hughes helped provide the polyrhythmic "Burundi Beat" that took Adam to the top of the charts. But despite the Ants' reliance on live drumming, and the machine's considerable expense, "I bought an LM-1 almost as soon as I could get one," says Hughes.

Hughes was well aware of the anti-machine sentiments of some fellow drummers, and of the British Musicians Union. He was not unsympathetic—but he also wasn't threatened by rhythm units.

"Some drummers just want to drum, and then go down the bar," says Hughes. Others, like him, were curious about the new technology. "It's just rhythm. It's just music," he adds. "Let's have a look."

2.

In 1981, Adam Ant's paint-streaked face was pinned up in thousands of UK bedrooms, on the strength of two Number 1 singles. But neither of them was the biggest British smash of that year.

That honor went to Sheffield group The Human League. "Don't You Want Me" wasn't just a hit—it came to epitomize synthesizer pop. It was also the song that truly put the LM-1 on the map.

Yet when the single was released, its parent album, *Dare*, had already produced three hits and reached Number 1. "Don't You Want Me" was just an attempt by the group's label, Virgin, to get a little extra mileage out of an already successful album.

It worked beyond anyone's wildest imaginings. The song wasn't released until November. By Christmas it was on top of the charts. And by New Year's, it had become 1981's best-selling single.

David M. Allen certainly hasn't forgotten. Allen was the programmer and engineer of *Dare*. Working with producer Martin Rushent, who died in 2011, Allen played a major role in creating a sound that still defines its era.

Quick-witted and acerbic, Allen admits the contributions he made to *Dare* haven't always been acknowledged—not even by Rushent himself. "But that's fair enough," Allen says. "He was a great mentor and teacher. And he taught me about the ripoff side of the business as well, in a very gentle way. And I'm talking to you now because of that record."

Allen was in a band when he first visited Martin Rushent's Genetic studio, located in a barn next to the producer's home in Streatley. But Allen soon left the group to become Rushent's assistant.

In late 1980, Allen worked on a session at Genetic with producer Peter Collins. The band was Musical Youth, an adorable group of preteens from Birmingham. They were a couple of years away from their biggest hit, the pop-reggae smash "Pass the Dutchie." But the big news was the drum machine Collins had brought back from America—the LM-1. "I'm probably the first studio person in the UK to have touched one of them," Allen recalls.

Then Rushent asked Allen to do some night sessions, working on demos for an up-and-coming band named Down to Earth. Collins's LM-1 was still there in the studio, and Allen took full advantage of it.

"Every night, I'd be nipping into the studio and programming the drum machine. And I was telling Martin, 'We've gotta get one of these. We can fuck off the drummer, for a start.'" He guffaws. "Obviously, one has dreams of power and glory, you know."

On Allen's recommendation, Rushent purchased the LM-1. "And the very next session after that," says Allen, "was the Human League." At first, that session—to record a single titled "The Sound of the Crowd"—seemed headed for disaster.

The Human League had split with founding members Martyn Ware and Ian Craig Marsh, who'd taken their gear and songwriting ideas with them. They'd been replaced by two teenagers, Joanne Catherall and Susanne Sulley, that lead singer Phil Oakey had seen dancing at a Sheffield disco. A new keyboardist, Ian Burden, and guitarist, Jo Callis, had joined holdover Adrian Wright, who did projections for the group's live show.

The six members "had no real material, just bits of ideas," Rushent told author Simon Reynolds. "I listened to the demo and said, 'Well, that's going in the bin; we're starting again.' Their spirits picked up hugely when we'd completed 'Sound of the Crowd,' cos it did sound a hundred times better."

One reason was the MC8 MicroComposer, Rushent's secret weapon. This powerful sequencer was introduced by Roland in 1977. Its "copy/insert" function allowed users to save time by copying and pasting sequences inside a song.

Rushent and Allen were using the MicroComposer to trigger Simmons electronic drum sounds, but they could only sequence and record one drum sound at a time. "That took fucking *ages*," groans Allen.

No one had figured out how to sync up the LM-1 with all the Roland gear in the studio. That included the Roland Jupiter-4 analog synthesizer, which generated many of the sounds on *Dare*. In those days, analog electronic instruments could only be synchronized by matching the time code waveforms generated by each device. But there was no universal standard for these waveforms. So it was nearly impossible to get devices made by different manufacturers to "speak" to each other.

Then one evening, Allen examined the waveforms of the time codes generated by the LM-1 and Jupiter-4. "Obviously there wasn't a lot to do that night!" Allen laughs. "But by using EQ and compression, I made one waveform look like the other waveform.

"It wasn't clever. In fact, it was the sort of thing where, if you were clever, you wouldn't do it. You'd say, 'That is just not going to work.' But fuck me, it *did*!" he says. "So we could run the Linn with all the Roland gear. For about 18 months, we had a lead on everybody else."

Meanwhile, after leaving the Human League, Martyn Ware and Ian Craig Marsh had formed Heaven 17 with singer Glenn Gregory. They planned to go in a completely different direction than the League. But their new material would also be heavily informed by the LM-1.

"Simon Draper is the head of A&R at Virgin. And he said to us one day, there's this new machine by Roger Linn, and it uses real drum sounds. And of course, we got one," recalls Ware. "I still believe it's the greatest drum machine ever made, to be honest with you."

Ware's programming on Heaven 17's 1982 debut, *Penthouse and Pavement*, was a testament to the LM-1's possibilities. The drum sounds were recorded without reverb, so they punched right through the mix on the radio.

But Ware was also one of the first programmers to create patterns that would have been impossible for a single drummer to play. The intricate choruses of the title track from *Penthouse and Pavement*, with layers of cowbell, cascading tom-toms, and stuttering hi-hats, were a perfect example.

"I was actually listening to *Penthouse and Pavement* last night. How you going to beat that shit?" demands Ware. "I mean, I would stack up the first side against any drum programming out there.

"I remember a drummer in Sheffield who said to me once, 'It's stupid. You know, a drummer couldn't play that,'" Ware adds. "And I'm going, well, that's the point, isn't it?"

3.

Not everyone was sold on the LM-1—not even the new stars of New Pop. Thomas Dolby avoided it because he felt the machine wasn't punchy enough. "LA drummers lean back on their snare drum," he says. "The snare is inherently kind of laid back, like in the jazz sense."

Other musicians and producers eschewed the LM-1 because of its ubiquity. "All of a sudden, the Linn was all over everything," says Depeche Mode producer Daniel Miller.

Back in Los Angeles, Art Wood was experiencing some resistance himself. Located on Vine Street in Hollywood, the Professional Drum Shop is one of the oldest drum stores in the world. It's a legendary hangout for the many percussionists who pass through town. Everyone from jazz great Art Blakey to Wrecking Crew drummer Hal Blaine to The Who's Keith Moon has paid a visit.

"On Fridays, all the all the drummers would go there. There'd be a happy hour and we'd all talk about stuff," Wood recalls. But one Friday afternoon, Wood made the mistake of asking the owner, Bob "Pops" Yeager, if he could have a stand for his drum machine.

"And Pops started yelling, 'Get the F out of my store!' And then he just went into his back office and slammed the door," says Wood. "I was already intimidated enough by all these guys that had been playing in Hollywood since the Forties. So there was a real division about drum machines, I remember."

Such divisions were happening all over the world at this time. One of those arguments would help jumpstart the career of a young Australian songwriter. It also produced the song many people now consider his country's surrogate national anthem.

4.

As the frontman of the new wave band Icehouse, Iva Davies has had mainstream success in both the UK and America, including the US Top 10 single "Electric Blue" in 1987. But back home in Australia, he's an even bigger star: a Hall of Fame artist with twenty Top 40 hits.

One of the greatest honors of his career came in 1999, when the Icehouse song "Great Southern Land" was performed on New Year's Eve at the Sydney

Opera House. The performance was the culmination of a twenty-five-minute piece called "The Ghost of Time," commissioned for Sydney's millennium celebration.

"Great Southern Land" had been a Top 5 single Down Under in 1982. The song presents a postcard history of Australia, but doesn't avoid the country's complicated past. Davies references the island's founding as a prison colony and the treatment of native peoples, as well as the rugged beauty of the desert landscape.

"It was amazing to hear this song being played by the Sydney Symphony Orchestra, being seen by millions and millions of people," remembers Davies, "and then realize that it is the way it is, in part, because I didn't understand yet how to control the tempo on a drum machine." He gives a sheepish laugh.

"Great Southern Land" clocks in at exactly 120 beats per minute: the stock tempo of the LM-1. Yet the drum machine almost didn't end up on the song at all. And that might have changed everything.

Davies, a classically trained musician, had wanted a drum machine for years. He finally got one toward the tail end of Flowers, the band that preceded Icehouse. It was a BOSS Dr. Rhythm, and it helped Davies through a bout of writer's block to create Icehouse's first Top 10 Australian hit, 1981's "Love in Motion."

While he was on tour in America, Davies heard the LM-1 on The Human League's "Don't You Want Me." He bought one of the machines and took it back to Australia, where he used it to write a new batch of material. To record it, his record label Chrysalis connected him with an up-and-coming producer on the brink of the big time.

Keith Forsey had first made his name in the disco world, as Giorgio Moroder and Pete Bellotte's drummer of choice. And he was well-acquainted with programmed drums. "I found that in most bands, the drummer was the weakest link," Forsey says. "So if you could get this machine to stay in the pocket, you'd solved one of your biggest problems."

But Forsey was also one of the top drummers in the world, a timekeeper intimidating in his precision. And on the album that would become Icehouse's debut, Forsey wanted to play the drums himself. Including on the song "Great Southern Land."

"We had some ding-dong fights over the drum machine," Davies recalls. "He was determined to play live drums on the whole record."

The demo of "Great Southern Land" had instantly clicked with listeners, Davies says. "I couldn't work out what it was that people were hearing, but everyone seemed to love it."

Davies and Forsey recorded three separate versions of the song. All of them featured live drums. And all were rejected by Chrysalis. Frustrated, Davies booked time himself at Gold Star Studios in Los Angeles, with engineer Dave Jerden.

"I said, 'I'm just going to go back to the demo and record everything the same way, including the LM-1. And Chrysalis said, 'Yes, yes, yes, that's it!,'" Davies remembers. "And the only real difference—which I really hadn't been aware of—was the drum machine."

Forsey came to the rescue, however, when Chysalis demanded a more surefire single. He invited Davies to join him for a songwriting session at Giorgio Moroder's Los Angles mansion, where he was housesitting. Moroder had a twenty-four-track studio on the premises, and Davies showed up ready to write.

But when he arrived, he immediately panicked. He'd forgotten the LM-1, "which was really the starting point for me," recalls Davies. "So Keith said, `Don't worry, I'll make a call."

"So a little later the doorbell rings, and I answer it. And there's a man there, holding an LM-1 that looks very similar to my LM-1, except perhaps a little more rudimentary," says Davies. "The man was Roger Linn, and he'd brought over the prototype of the LM-1. The serial number was literally, I think, '0001.'"

Immediately, Davies wrote three songs. Two ended up being album tracks: the synth-pop shuffle "Glam," and "One to One," driven by pulsing sequencers that anticipated the sound Forsey would refine with Billy Idol.

"But it was the third one that was the important one. That was 'Hey Little Girl,' and it became a hit all over Europe," says Davies. The song was a swaying, sensuous number that could easily have fit onto Roxy Music's recent hit album *Avalon*. "And that was the song David Bowie heard, that led him to offer us the chance to open for him on the Serious Moonlight Tour.

"So it's a hell of a story: Roger Linn bringing me an LM-1 at Giorgio Moroder's house, that I use to write a song that gets me the chance to open for David Bowie," concludes Davies. "It's like Bowie told me: 'You can never tell who's listening.'"

5.

By the early 1980s, nearly everyone was listening to the LM-1's most dedicated user.

Prince Rogers Nelson's relationship with the LM-1 was a lifelong love affair. It was the drum machine he used on a series of albums that rewrote the boundaries of pop music, earned him a seemingly endless string of hits during the 1980s, and, thanks to *Purple Rain*, made him a movie star to boot. Long after dozens of other drum machines had appeared and gone, Prince remained committed to Roger Linn's original invention.

In 1999, Prince was asked why he'd pulled one of his LM-1s out of storage to use on the album *Rave Un2 the Joy Fantastic*. "Nothing has the timing of that thing. It locks up differently than any other drum machine," he responded. "And believe me, I've had every drum machine ever made. When I put my own internal rhythm on top of it, there's nothing like it."

Susan Rogers was Prince's chief recording engineer from 1983 to 1987, during the most prolific period in an incredibly prolific career. She witnessed firsthand Prince's devotion to the LM-1. "He was so incredibly brand-loyal. And I discovered that he was that way to the end of his days," Rogers says. "If he liked it, he liked it. And he stuck with it."

There was a practical side to that loyalty. During the 1980s, Prince released at least an album a year. Two of them were double LPs, and several—the soundtrack to *Purple Rain* and 1987's *Sign O' the Times*—are widely considered masterpieces. That doesn't even count the albums Prince wrote, and in some cases performed, for the stable of acts in his orbit. Nor the songs he penned for other artists, nor the unreleased albums, nor the huge collection of outtakes in his near-mythical vault.

How did he create so much music in such a short time? His familiarity with the LM-1, Rogers says, was a major reason. "That was why he could work so quickly. Because he knew his gear really, really well," she says. "He simply had zero patience for learning a new piece of gear."

"He quit while he was ahead," agrees David "Z" Rivkin, a Minneapolis native who recorded the demo that got Prince his record deal, and who continued to work with him throughout the Eighties. "He found what worked and stuck with it. Most artists don't understand when they should just lock in."

Today, Susan Rogers is the director of the Berklee Music Perception and Cognition Laboratory. She has a doctorate in psychology from McGill University, and is working on a book about how listeners visualize music.

Her work for Prince, she admits, was far less theoretical. "I didn't know how to make the aesthetic choices. He was totally fine with that. He didn't need anyone to do that for him," she says. "He was such a pure creative being—he was what the scientists would call hypercreative. What mattered exclusively was keeping current flowing in the wires."

A Southern California native, Rogers was a maintenance technician in the early 1980s at Rudy Records, the studio owned by David Crosby and Graham Nash of the group Crosby, Stills, Nash, and Young. Rogers remembers seeing a drum machine brought into the studio one afternoon. "There was a lot of grousing, a lot of complaining," she says. "It's like evil had walked into the room."

Rogers saw it differently. "I had the typical attitude of the youth of the day, which was, 'Bring it on. I don't have anything to lose!'" So when she found out Prince was looking for a studio technician, she applied immediately. Rogers was already a huge fan, and Prince—who was just finishing the *1999* tour and beginning work on *Purple Rain*—was about to become one of the biggest stars in the music business.

Lots of folks had predicted this, ever since Prince emerged from Minneapolis as a teenage prodigy at the end of the 1970s. Among the many instruments Prince could play, drums were a particular strength. Engineer Ross Pallone, who worked with Prince on his fourth album, 1981's *Controversy*, was impressed that Prince usually started songs by recording himself playing drums—and never used a click track.

However, during the recording of 1981's *Controversy*, Prince acquired an LM-1. He claimed at the time that it was "*the* first Linn," which seems unlikely. But the hopped-up new wave song "Private Joy" was definitely Prince's first recorded use of the machine. When he heard the track, Prince's drummer—David Rivkin's younger brother, Bobby Z—knew immediately that "things were going to change … He told me right away I was gonna play pads hooked up to the machine."

The next year, on the double album *1999*, Prince made far more use of the LM-1. In one interview, he said the LP was "nothing but me running all the computers myself," and that "it takes me five seconds to put together a beat" on the LM-1. That left Bobby Z "feeling like an auto assembly worker looking at a robot for the first time, wondering if I had a job." He did, but it would increasingly involve playing to a click track and using triggers to replicate the Linn sounds live.

Keyboardist Matt "Dr." Fink said Prince used the LM-1 because it was "the fattest-sounding machine" available. It was also, Fink added, "very unique sounding." But much of the uniqueness of its sound would be developed by Prince himself.

Some of the sounds he created by using the machine's tuning controls—most notably, the detuned sidestick that makes the hollow "knocking" noise on "When Doves Cry"—became as well-known as the LM-1's original voices. Prince was also fond of tuning down the LM-1's handclaps. "I remember he said if you listen to those old soul records, or if you listen to George Clinton, you'll hear the really funky records have those low-pitched claps," Rogers says.

Like drum machine users since Sly Stone, Prince was also reliant on effects to create new sounds. He used a series of BOSS guitar pedals to create many of his best-known rhythm patterns from this period. Prince and Rogers could run the signals from the LM-1's individual instrument outputs into these effects units. The treated drum sounds were then recorded straight onto tape.

These pedals came in a rainbow of colors, and perhaps it's appropriate that the one Susan Rogers calls his favorite was purple: the BOSS BF-1 Flanger. A flanger mixes two identical signals, but delays one of them slightly while varying the delay length. This produces a sweeping effect that Prince used most noticeably on the 1984 song "Erotic City." It's also employed on later tunes, like "Raspberry Beret" and "If I Was Your Girlfriend."

"He loved that flanger so much, and used flanging a lot on the hi-hat," Rogers recalls. "And if you listen to his work around the Eighties, the flanger was fairly ubiquitous in his drum machine programming. That's kind of an iconic sound for him."

Prince made heavy use of several other BOSS pedals while recording the LM-1, Rogers adds. These included the brown OC-2 Octaver, which adds a note one octave above and one octave below a sound. Prince also loved using the orange DS-1 distortion box, and the black HM2 "heavy metal" effect, on drum tracks. And "perhaps his favorite trick," Rogers adds, was recording only one channel of the BOSS CH-1 Super Chorus pedal, an effect best heard on the tom-toms of 1987's "Forever in My Life."

Another key effect used on Prince's Linn machine was a gated reverb preset called "Non Lin 2," on the AMS RMX16 digital reverb unit. This gated reverb was inspired by the accidental drum sound Hugh Padgham developed on Peter Gabriel's third album. Prince used the AMS's Non Lin 2 preset to beef up many of the drum tracks on *Purple Rain*.

Yet for all the time that they worked together, Rogers says, they rarely discussed the devices he was using. "He was so taciturn. His favorite way of working was to not talk," she says. "Which is why he liked to have so few people around him. Because if he knew you really well, you didn't *have* to talk."

Instead, Prince simply wanted Rogers to have his gear—including his LM-1—ready to capture his newest idea, as quickly as possible. "And if you could do that, he could create with the good old LM-1," she says. "It was reliable. It was trustworthy. It was one of his favorite tools for creativity."

6.

Love it or hate it, the LM-1 had changed the world. And Roger Linn believed his drum machine odyssey had come to a close.

"When Roger was finally done with the LM-1, I'll never forget him saying, 'That's the last drum machine I'm ever going to make,'" remembers Steve Porcaro. "He was just burned out."

Porcaro wasn't having it. "I got in his face, and I says, 'Dude, this thing costs *five thousand dollars*. You've already made the Rolls Royce. Now you've gotta beat the Japanese! You've gotta come out with a cheap one before they do.'"

Linn was also hearing the same thing from Bob Easton, who'd taken over the manufacture and marketing of the LM-1. "He was good at scaring me," Linn recalls. "He kept saying things like, 'You better make a cheaper one quickly!' or 'Other people will come in and wipe you out!'"

It was actually one of Linn's Japanese competitors who gave him the best advice of all. Far from treating Linn as an enemy, Roland founder Ikutaro Kakehashi tried to mentor the young creator.

So at the 1982 NAMM show, a worried Linn approached Kakehashi for advice. "I said, 'Taro, what am I doing wrong?' And he said, 'Fundamental rule of business: you must bring in more money than go out.'"

Linn smiles at the memory of Kakehashi's joke. "It was funny, but even funnier was the fact that I didn't even *consider* that!" he says. "I just thought, 'People will always buy what I want because it's so cool.' But it didn't happen that way." On a more serious note, Kakehashi convinced Linn that he needed another product. Depending on sales of a single machine, Kakehashi explained, put Linn at a disadvantage if there were production slowdowns or shortages.

Finally, Linn gave in. All the advice he'd received had "built a fire under my butt, and I worked on making a cheaper one. And Bob Easton helped me in the engineering of that as well."

The result was the LinnDrum, which debuted in late 1982 with a significantly cheaper price tag—$2,995—and some noticeable improvements. Crash and ride cymbals were now standard equipment, and there were five external trigger inputs.

Users could also create their own sounds, extending an offer that Linn had begun with the LM-1. "I created a policy that if you wanted to get your own sound in an LM-1 or in the LinnDrum, just send me in a tape, and I'll create chips of it for free. On the condition," he adds, "that I add the sounds in my library to sell to other people."

The biggest moneysaving change was to get rid of individual tuning for each drum sound. This, however, was a dealbreaker for some musicians—particularly Prince. "He did not like it as much as he liked the LM-1 because the LM-1 had tuning knobs for each individual instrument, and he made heavy use of those tuning knobs," says Susan Rogers. She remembers Prince reluctantly using a LinnDrum that belonged to Sheila E. at an Atlanta recording session for her song "A Love Bizarre," during the Purple Rain tour.

Beyond comparing the features of the two machines, however, Rogers says Prince was convinced that the *feel* of the LinnDrum was different. "It was just a little tighter and cleaner," she says. "I think the clock must have been better, but the LM-1 was funkier. It would drift a little bit, and he liked that."

But plenty of users were delighted with the LinnDrum, which quickly became the company's standard. Ads from the time marketed the LinnDrum as "The Ultimate Drum Machine," and the industry affirmed that claim. Less than 600 LM-1s had been manufactured. But between 1982 and 1985, nearly ten times as many LinnDrums rolled off the production line at Bob Easton's factory.

Three of those roughly five thousand units went to a team of musicians who created some of the biggest hits of the MTV era. Spiky-haired singer Billy Idol, his guitarist Steve Stevens, and their producer, Keith Forsey, each used the LinnDrum for making demos.

"I had a studio apartment then, and I had my little Tascam four-track recorder and my LinnDrum. And I was off and running!" remembers Stevens. "It was a great writing tool. And Keith was a really good teacher. I learned how to program the Linn from him."

Forsey might have been reluctant to use drum machines when working with Icehouse. But they became a signature element of Billy Idol's sound, a rock-disco hybrid perfectly pitched at the charts.

On the album *Rebel Yell*, songs like "Eyes Without a Face" and "Flesh for Fantasy" started out with a LinnDrum keeping time. Yet finding a drummer who could play with a machine seemed impossible until Thommy Price was recruited from another session—for the AOR band Scandal—at the same studio, Electric Lady.

"They were going through drummers left and right," Price recalls. "So I got on the elevator with my pink snare drum, went upstairs, and one of the first tracks we did was 'Do Not Stand in the Shadows.'" Keith Forsey remembers that moment well. "I can still see Thommy through the glass. He went right into the first song, and we were all like, 'Fuck, yeah!'"

Price developed a reputation for being able to coexist with drum machines. "Most of the tracks were pretty much done before I came in," he says. "But even though it sounds like there's a lot of programming, there's real drums in there somewhere. Keith Forsey taught me a lot about just grooving with the track."

The next year, Forsey transplanted Idol's LinnDrummed sound to British postpunk band The Psychedelic Furs. Price joined on drums for the hits "Heaven" and "Here Come Cowboys," although the most memorable moment might have been the programmed, deliberate tom fills on "The Ghost in You." "That song could have done with a real drummer," observes keyboardist Ed Buller, who cowrote that song, and several others on the album. "But those Linn tom fills never sounded right live!"

Though he experimented with other machines, Forsey—like Prince—found it was easy to stay faithful to Linn. "The Linn—they got it exactly right," he says. "Why the fuck do I want to re-learn everything again? There's no reason to change."

But as the 1980s sped ahead and technology made weekly leaps forward, everyone's loyalty was about to be tested.

***

14

808 State

1.

Suzanne Ciani peers closely at the track sheets on the monitor of her studio computer. "You know," she muses, "people never put dates on things."

But in this case, someone did. The scanned copy of the track sheets for her second solo album, *Seven Waves*, lists recording dates that begin on January 12, 1980.

These sheets list the instruments used on each track. Ciani reads them off, one by one. "Piano … vocoder … Oh, bass drum," she says, a little surprised. "There it is!"

The bass drum in question is actually one of the most famous sounds in popular music. It's the bass drum from the Roland TR-808 drum machine.

And the reason these track sheets are so significant is this: they suggest that Suzanne Ciani was probably the first person to use the TR-808 on a recording project.

The TR-808 is famous for more than just its booming bass drum. Today, it's undoubtedly the most famous drum machine in the world. During the 1980s, it played a major role in the formation of whole musical genres and subgenres—hip hop, most notably.

The machine has given its name to a Kanye West album (*808s and Heartbreak*), a band (Britain's 808 State), and even been the subject of a documentary. That 2015 film was titled, simply, *808*. The manufacturer and "TR" prefix are no longer necessary. Those three numbers now mean only one thing.

But it seems right that Suzanne Ciani may have been the first person to record with an 808. Ciani and the 808 were both trailblazers. Both were unfairly underrated. And both are seen now for what they always were: far ahead of their time.

Indiana-born, Massachusetts-raised, and Berkeley-educated, Ciani is one of the early innovators of electronic music. She's also one of the most decorated female composers in history, with five Grammy nominations. Her fifty-year career is all the more remarkable because of the number of musical worlds she's successfully inhabited.

Her avant-garde credentials are impeccable. When she came to New York in the early 1970s, she brought only her clothes and her Buchla modular synthesizer. For a while, she slept on the floor of composer Philip Glass's studio. The solo concerts she gave using the Buchla, however, helped her win a National Endowment for the Arts grant.

At the same time, Ciani took her love of electronic instruments into the musical mainstream. She founded a studio that created effects for companies like Coca-Cola: she's responsible for that famous pop-and-pour sound from Coke commercials.

Ciani also used the Buchla to develop the distinctive rocketship swoosh on the Starland Vocal Band's 1976 Number 1 hit "Afternoon Delight." She provided sound effects on the disco album *Star Wars and Other Galactic Funk*, which spawned another chart-topping hit, "Star Wars Theme/Cantina Band," in 1977. Her vocoderized interjections even made her the first female voice ever heard on a pinball game—the Bally classic *Xenon*.

In her solo career, Ciani created a sound for which there wasn't really a category. Today, some might describe *Seven Waves* as "ambient," or even "new age." At the time, though, no one knew what to call a female artist making instrumental electronic music.

The Buchla 200-E is still in her studio, patch cords snaking out of it like a rainbow-colored tangle of spaghetti. Its capability for creating rhythms led to Ciani's interest in drum machines. But if she's the first person to have recorded with the TR-808, it's not only appropriate, but ironic.

"It's funny to think about, because I'm not much of a drum person," reflects Ciani. "I was actually kind of *anti*-drums. They were doing a job that didn't need to be done in electronic music. The beat was already carried using other instruments."

But Ciani was naturally curious about new instruments, and the TR-808 was no exception. "And I had to build my audience, because I was lonely. I was in a world that wasn't shared, this brave new world of electronics." She smiles. "And I wanted to bring more people into that world."

2.

Tadao Kikumoto is also smiling. He's amused by a new book just published in Japan. It's called *The Gods Who Created the TR-808*.

Is the title sacrilegious? Not according to Kikumoto. "Don't worry, we have myriads of gods," he says sarcastically. "There are so many easy gods in Japan."

Humble and self-deprecating, Kikumoto calls himself one of those "easy gods." But the man most responsible for creating the Roland TR-808 certainly had a difficult path to godhood.

The machine debuted in 1980, the same year as Roger Linn's LM-1. Both devices were a huge leap forward from all that came before them. They were programmable, intuitively designed, and easy to use.

Inevitably, the 808 was compared to Linn's machine. Perhaps it was also inevitable that, in the short term, it came up second best. While they cost thousands of dollars more, the sampled drums of the LM-1 were a revelation. The synthetic sounds of the 808 took longer to be fully appreciated.

But the proximity of the 808 and the LM-1 meant that Kikumoto and Roger Linn have always had intertwined destinies. A whimsical painting that Kikumoto sends a link to is a reminder of this. It's a medieval-style triptych called "Three Kings." The painting features three of the pioneers of electronic music in robes, each holding one of their signature instruments. Bob Moog, who created the Moog synthesizer, is in the middle. Kikumoto is at his right, and Linn is at his left.

"Another laugh!" says Kikumoto. He jokes that the painting depicts him as one of the three "easy kings." That may be true, but there are unquestionably many, many subjects in Kikumoto's kingdom. It's been growing ever since someone first touched the brightly colored keys of the TR-808.

3.

In terms of exposure to music, Kikumoto had an upbringing very similar to his boss, Ikutaro Kakehashi. Both men grew up in postwar Japan, a rebuilding society where music education was almost nonexistent. "The music environment of my childhood was so poor because of World War II," Kiukmoto recalls. "My first tech and music experiences were playing with ham radios and hi-fi audio at technical high school club activities."

But this shared background gave the two men an unusual level of understanding and trust. "He was always very positive about my ideas, because he did not play any musical instruments, like me," says Kakehashi. "We both thought that too much expertise narrows one's horizon."

Besides his interest in technology, Kikumoto also enjoyed listening to Latin music—primarily for its percussion instruments. And he grew to love the baroque classical compositions of Bach. "But after joining Roland," he admits, "I was still not so familiar with pop or contemporary music."

However, music was a field in which Kikumoto had already demonstrated his inventing savvy. In 1975, he was working with early Intel microprocessors. Then he heard electronic musician Isao Tomita's version of Claude Debussy's "Clair de Lune, No. 3."

The song was from *Snowflakes are Dancing*, a collection of Debussy compositions that Tomita performed using the Moog synthesizer. In his autobiography, Ikutaro Kakehasi compared it to Walter Carlos's 1968 album *Switched-On Bach*, but "vastly more subtle ... For someone who understood the inner circuitry of synthesizers, the artistic level of this record was astounding."

One of the people who understood that inner circuitry was Tadao Kikumoto. Inspired by Tomita's work, he decided to applying microchip technology to a musical instrument. So he designed and patented a "Computer Controlled Guitar Synthesizer."

Unfortunately, "when I finished making the prototype, Roland announced their own guitar synth. My design was too advanced and expensive." But his project had nevertheless impressed Ikutaro Kakehashi. "He invited me to join Roland strongly," Kikumoto recalls.

Kikumoto understood traditional analog technology, but also the microcomputer circuitry that was rapidly becoming popular. His first assignment was for BOSS, the division of Roland that manufactured guitar effects pedals. He was asked to develop a portable, programmable rhythm unit—something guitarists could use for practice sessions.

Kakehashi wanted a smaller, cheaper version of Roland's CR-78 drum machine. He thought it could be done by using a CMOS microprocessor, which had just become widely available. The abbreviation CMOS stands for complementary metal-oxide semiconductor. It's a battery-powered semiconductor chip inside that doesn't use much power, and stores information in a computer. For years, the CMOS chip commonly held data like the time, date, and system hardware settings.

It sounds basic now. But in 1978, Kikumoto discovered that these CMOS chips were still too expensive for a cheap, portable device. "Then I invented a special unique digital circuit using a number of simple, discrete CMOS integrated circuits, combined with battery operation," says Kikumoto.

The result was the BOSS DR-55, otherwise known as the Dr. Rhythm. This drum machine was the first rhythm unit owned by a variety of musicians. Just $200 when it was released in 1979, and programmable besides, it became a favorite drum machine of gigging musicians and songwriters.

"It was so successful, and Mr. K was very surprised and happy!" Kakehashi says of the Dr. Rhythm. As a reward, he was promoted to chief engineer for a brand-new drum machine project. This device would become the first product of a new line called the "Mid-O Series." And it was driven by a specific request from America.

Early in 1979, Kakehashi returned from the Winter NAMM show in Anaheim with some news. He explained to Kikumoto that studio owners in the United States wanted a more realistic-sounding drum machine. Studio costs were high, and recording drums—a process that could now stretch into days—was a primary culprit. "If we were able to provide this for less than one thousand dollars," he told Kikumoto, "then there will be a huge market."

Kikumoto was excited. In his imagination, he and his team would actually be creating a drum *synthesizer*. It would allow users to develop their own individual drum sounds, by shaping sound waves and white noise. Just as analog synthesizers had let keyboardists create unexpected and previously unheard sounds, this new Roland machine would do the same thing for drum programmers.

But when Kakehashi returned from his next trip to America that summer, there was a major complication. He handed Kikumoto a cassette that contained recordings of a new drum machine. The machine hadn't yet been released, but it was already creating significant buzz. It was Roger Linn's LM-1.

Now a critical choice faced Kikumoto. Should his new drum machine follow the lead of the LM-1, and use digital samples of real drums? Or should he continue his dream of creating an analog drum synthesizer?

Kikumoto's engineering team duly investigated the cost of sampling. As they expected, it was immense. Just as Roger Linn had discovered, the amount of memory necessary to include sampled cymbals was a dealbreaker. It would push the cost of the machine to more than $10,000, Kikumoto says—more the double the cost of the LM-1.

But Kikumoto and his fellow Roland engineers—several of whom would later become known as the "Analog Mafia"—didn't just consider themselves problem solvers. They also thought of themselves as artists.

Kikumoto explains this by referencing the famous nineteenth-century woodblock print "The Great Wave off Kanagawa," by the Japanese painter and printmaker Katsushika Hokusai. The carving is powerful, he says, because its lines aren't exact. Instead, they're *representations* of the wave. And in those lines, you can find the artist's unique vision.

"At the time, I thought PCM sampling was like shuttering a camera. While it was photo-realistic, a single sound would use much expensive semiconductor memory," says Kikumoto. "We were synthesizer engineers. I wanted to provide a synthesizer by which the user could create various drum sounds using their sense of aesthetics, just like drawing artistic pictures."

In other words, the Roland engineers felt digital sampling was too easy, and too limiting. The truly artistic choice, Kikumoto thought, was the more "representational" analog sounds that could be created with a drum synthesizer.

"However," he admits, "this idea was too optimistic for the time." And time was working against his team. The LM-1 was on the horizon. Even using existing technology—the Roland System-700 Modular Synth—to generate the analog sounds for the drum synthesizer wasn't enough of a shortcut. And there was no room on the circuit board and front panel of the new drum machine for all the necessary controls.

Regretfully, Kikumoto abandoned his idea for a drum synthesizer. He and the Roland engineers instead made use of analog circuitry to create the new machine's sounds themselves. On a recommendation from Don Lewis, the controls for these sounds would be placed on the outside of the unit. Users wouldn't have complete freedom to shape the drum sounds—but at least the controls that were offered would be easily accessible.

Some of the 808's sounds were clear improvements on the past. Kikumoto had carefully analyzed the Roland CR-78. He'd also learned about the tricks some Roland engineers had brought with them from the Ace Tone company. One area where this study paid off was in the cymbal sounds of the 808.

Kikumoto credits the engineer Hiro Nakamura, who had worked on the CR-78, with improving the metallic percussion sounds—like hi-hats, the crash cymbal, and cowbell—on the 808. Rather than simulate these sounds with white noise, six pulse wave generators were used instead. Noise was removed from these waveforms with a low-cut filter. This cleaned up the cymbals so much that they now had a "silky, metallic" sound. Like the Hokusai woodcut of the wave, the cymbals weren't strictly realistic. But they were pleasingly distinct.

There was, however, one place where Kikumoto's original vision of a drum synthesizer survived. That was on the 808's most famous sound: the kick drum. It's the instrument Kikumoto feels is the most important on the drum machine. He especially wanted to better the kick drum sound of the CR-78, which was "toy-like," he complains. "There was no impact, partly due to the very weak attack."

So Kikumoto experimented. He hit an acoustic bass drum and measured the sound waves with an oscilloscope. He also analyzed the bass drum sounds of the LM-1 on the cassette tape he'd been given. "I discovered unique harmonic activity within the first 50 milliseconds," he says. "Based on this finding, I made some new circuits, but this was not enough."

So he argued for retaining one vestige of his drum synthesizer concept. That was a control that allowed a user to adjust the decay of the bass drum. While there was some internal grumbling, Kakehashi backed the idea.

That decay control would be used to create the booming, low-frequency bass drum sounds that helped define the 808. Somewhat ironically, this was something the Roland technicians had no idea that their invention could do.

"Truthfully, the audio system in the Roland lab was so poor that we could not listen to the very deep bass of the TR-808," Kikumoto admits. "So we actually did not even notice the signature deep bass … and we did not expect this deep bass would become the essence of the 808 and cornerstone of new music creation to come."

Meanwhile, developing the bass drum had cost the engineers so much time that other sounds, in Kikumoto's view, suffered. "Just like the bass drum, I wanted to make a realistic snare drum," he says. "My ideal snare drum for the TR-808 had controllable diameter, depth of the shell, and tension of the membrane." But there simply wasn't a chance to try out these concepts.

Handclaps had been a specific request of Don Lewis, who had simulated them with a modified clave sound on the CR-78. Kikumoto and his team developed claps by running white noise through a bandpass filter, which limits low and high frequencies. Yet Kikumoto was, once again, not satisfied. He compared the handclap sound to a "bunch of bamboo sticks."

The programming controls, however, helped the machine, called the "Rhythm Composer," live up to its name. The row of lighted, colored buttons at the bottom of the control panel made step programming the 808 an easy, and visual, experience. Each of the sixteen buttons corresponded to one beat. If you wanted to program a bass drum on every other beat, for example, you selected that sound and pressed the odd-numbered buttons, one through sixteen. There was also a tap button that could be used to play drum parts manually.

Kikumoto's team had beat the odds. They'd come up with a device that sounded like no other Roland machine—or, for that matter, any other drum machine. And the Roland TR-808 came close to its target price, listing for just under $1,200.

"Mr. K seemed very happy," Kikumoto remembers, "because the TR-808 suggested future potential with its unique programming style, using timeline switches, plus the handclap sound—also with an affordable price."

And Kikumoto was pleasantly shocked when he heard the TR-808 on the radio before it had even been released. Roland's Sales Department had provided an 808 to the group Yellow Magic Orchestra, Japan's homegrown answer to Kraftwerk. The trio used the machine on the final show of their 1980 tour, and the performance at the Nippon Budkan in Tokyo was aired around the country.

The endorsement of hometown heroes YMO was nice, but it didn't really lessen Tadao Kikumoto's disappointment. The TR-808 was leagues away from the drum synthesizer he'd envisioned. And he could clearly see that "the market was paying more attention to PCM sampling." As the first units shipped, it was difficult for him not to consider the 808 a failure.

4.

Had things worked out differently, this chapter might not have been about the drum machine Suzanne Ciani used. It might have been about the one she created, instead.

At the end of the 1970s, Ciani and inventor Richard Factor realized there was a market for a sampling drum machine, and set out to design one. Factor, one of the founders of Eventide Clockworks, had developed innovative instruments like the Eventide Harmonizer. "And just as Richard and I were finishing up the design of our machine," Ciani remembers, "Roger came along."

"Roger" was Roger Linn, whose sampling drum machine, the LM-1, preempted their plans. Ciani got an early version of the LM-1 at her studio. Not long after, she also received from Roland a TR-808. She immediately began to use this machine in her own work.

Ciani had little use in her solo compositions for a drum machine that sounded like a real drummer, like the LM-1. Even when using the TR-808, she often bypassed the stock sounds, and had the machine trigger percussion from her Buchla synthesizer instead. But on the final three tracks of *Seven Waves*—"Water Lullaby," "Deep in the Sea," and "Sail Away"—you can hear the familiar rhythms of the 808.

The album, however, took the better part of three years to release. American record companies were resistant to the idea of an instrumental album by a woman, Ciani says. "They expected me to play a guitar and sing, at least," she remembers.

Seven Waves therefore first appeared in 1982, on the JVC label in Japan. Thanks in part to this delay, Ciani's pioneering work with the 808 went largely unnoticed at the time. In fact, she only now realizes it herself. But while she's proud of the distinction, the idea of racking up another "female first" still strikes a nerve.

"It's not that women aren't capable or interested. They just had no fertile ground for doing these things," Ciani insists. "There were *always* women. We just didn't know about them."

Yet some of Ciani's aversion to drums is, she admits, a result of being female. "I always felt there was too much emphasis on the pounding"—she mimics banging on a drum—"and the tempo. That's most represented in pop music by men. I was looking for a new paradigm. The ocean, for example. It's steady. It's slow. And it's powerful."

The response to the TR-808 was a little like how Ciani describes the sea. It was slow. But it was steady. And ultimately, it would prove powerful indeed.

5.

When the TR-808 was first released, Tado Kikumoto remembers well that it was "miserably regarded as cheap sounding," when compared to the LM-1. In one famous review, the maraca sound was compared to a "horde of marching ants."

Yet when the machine made its way to music stores, the response was often ecstatic. Throbbing Gristle's Chris Carter, for example, bought his first 808 at a Denmark Street music shop owned by former Zombies keyboardist Rod Argent. He still remembers vividly that day in 1981, when the first shipment of 808s from Japan arrived. The shop "was packed with people trying to use the display model, and I gave up any attempt to try it out," he says.

When Carter got the machine back to the Crouch End flat he shared with his bandmate Cosey Fanni Tutti, they found there were no instructions. Undaunted, they took the 808 to Throbbing Gristle's studio, where there was a full PA. "We couldn't believe the range of the sound it was making," Carter remembers. "The bass was like nothing we'd ever heard. We actually blew a couple of wedge monitors and a bass bin in those early test sessions, but we didn't care."

Cosey and Carter were recording their first album as a duo, "and we ended up using the 808 on almost every track. It was so inspiring that within a couple of weeks, we'd finished the whole album, *Heartbeat*, which Rough Trade put out before the year was over," says Carter. "That first pressing sold 10,000 copies, and the album really helped us move on from Throbbing Gristle with a completely new sound."

John Foxx's 1981 album *The Garden* was a sampler for new drum machine technology. In addition to the new LM-1, Foxx was immediately taken with the Roland TR-808 he acquired. He used it on several songs—most obviously "This Jungle," where its twitching hi-hats take center stage. "I loved the 808," Foxx says. "I still think it's the best-ever drum machine—the right balance of controllability and fabulous sounds."

Even Kraftwerk, which conducted most of its drum machine experiments behind the closed doors of Kling Klang Studio, had apparently acquired an 808. Percussionist Karl Bartos remembered that founder Florian Schneider "had an engineer build a unit that synchronized our 16-step sequencers to a pre-production Roland 808 drum machine."

The most famous early use of the TR-808, however, occurred in the run-down resort town of Ostend, Belgium. In the autumn of 1981, soul legend Marvin Gaye was living there, in self-imposed exile. Gaye owed millions in back taxes and was on the run from the IRS. He was finished with his longtime label, Motown, and he was trying to conquer his addictions to booze and cocaine. "There are plenty of places I'd like to be rather than Ostend," Gaye said at the time, "but this is where I need to be."

For eighteen months, Gaye stayed in a seafront apartment, writing the songs that would become his first album for Columbia Records. When he finally began recording in Belgium, he told engineer Mike Butcher that he was going to use a drum machine and synthesizers. "He planned to do a lot himself," Butcher said, "and he wanted to have some control."

Guitarist Gordon Banks remembered that "it was basically him and I in the studio. Columbia Records gave him some new toys to play with." Two of those toys, Banks said, were a Roland TR-808 drum machine and a Jupiter 8 synthesizer. "Marvin didn't know too much about technology, so it was my job to figure out how to get the stuff working. He kind of liked the sounds that came from it and he went from there."

One of the first songs recorded was inspired by the reggae Gaye had heard during a 1981 tour of England. The spare, hypnotic drum program copies the wide-open spaces found in Jamaican music, unfolding at a leisurely 94 beats per minute.

The song evolved into a pillow-talking R&B number, and "Sexual Healing" became a monster comeback hit for Gaye. It stayed at Number 1 on the Billboard R&B charts for nearly three months at the end of 1982, and peaked at Number 3 overall.

In those days, however, the 808's reputation didn't always precede it. When keyboardist Jimmy Jam and bassist Terry Lewis flew to Atlanta in early 1983 to produce a session for The SOS Band, they arrived with songs—but few preconceived ideas about how they should sound.

"I don't even know whether we even cared at the time what kind of drum machine it was," recalled Jimmy Jam. "Because we recorded those tracks in Atlanta, they just said, 'Oh, well, we got an 808.' We're like, 'OK fine, plug it in and let's go.' And those songs hit huge."

None were bigger than "Just Be Good to Me," which reached Number 2 on the R&B charts. It also cost Jam and Lewis their day jobs. The pair were members of The Time, the flashy Minneapolis group then opening for Prince on his 1999 tour. Snow delayed their flight from Atlanta, they missed a show, and His Purple Highness delivered their pink slips.

But "Just Be Good to Me" also changed the way Jam and Lewis felt about the 808. On the next album they produced, Cheryl Lynn's *Encore*, the pair deliberately used other drum machines. "We kind of thought, that's more the SOS sound, so we don't want to really take that sound and use it everywhere," Jam explained. "I totally identify the SOS Band with the 808. And if I hear another drum machine, it kind of doesn't sound like SOS to me."

6.

Tadao Kikumoto's fears about the TR-808 wound up justified.

In 1983, Roland discontinued the machine. By that point, about twelve thousand had been manufactured. That was roughly a fifth of the amount of LinnDrums on the market. The disparity showed on the charts. In the UK, where synthpop had established a stronger foothold, the summer of 1983 was filled with LM-1 and LinnDrum-powered hits.

You could hear Roger Linn's imprint on Irene Cara's soundtrack smash "Flashdance (What A Feeling)," and on Genesis's ominous "Mama." You could hear it on near-miss Number 1s from The Human League and Heaven 17. And you certainly couldn't miss it on the litany of Michael Jackson singles from *Thriller*.

The week of July 17, however, was a definite high point for the TR-808 on the British charts. Soul crooner Paul Young reached Number 1 with a cover of Marvin Gaye's "Wherever I Lay My Hat (That's My Home)." Like Gaye's "Sexual Healing," the song was built on an 808 drum pattern with delicate clave accents.

Just below Young was the London jazz-funk band Freeez, who shed their horn section and had their biggest hit with "IOU." This sleek, synthesized tune was produced by an American named Arthur Baker, whose career was already deeply intertwined with the 808. Maybe the most surprising entry that week came courtesy of Robert Plant. The former Led Zeppelin singer's "Big Log," featuring prominent 808 handclaps, peaked at Number 11.

But back in Japan, Roland had already moved on. Kikumoto and his engineers on the Mid-O team were going to get a second crack at designing a drum machine to compete with Roger Linn.

What Kikuomoto and his team wouldn't learn for years was what was happening to their discontinued TR-808 in America. The machine Roland believed was a failure was being written into the genetic code of an entirely new genre. Together, that machine and genre would one day rule the world.

***

15

Hip Hop's Electric Guitar

1.

His name was Joe.

He lived in New York city in the early 1980s. And he owned a Roland TR-808 drum machine.

That's nearly all we know about one of the most famous drum machine owners in musical history.

There is *one* other thing we can say about Joe. If he'd owned a Linn drum machine, or an Oberheim DMX, or some other, more esoteric unit, then most of the things we take for granted about popular music today might sound very different indeed.

That's because Joe's TR-808 was the drum machine used on Afrika Bambaataa and Soul Sonic Force's "Planet Rock." Released in 1982, this single is one of the core texts of hip hop. And it's still the song most people associate with the 808 sound. So imagining the tune without those booming bass drums, those bright, brittle hi-hats, and those metallic handclaps is nearly impossible now.

Yet when Joe showed up at Intergalactic Studios in New York, producer Arthur Baker had no idea what drum machine he'd be hearing. The 808 was merely a happy accident.

"If he had come in with a Linn or a DMX, we would have used it," admits Baker. "But it would have been a completely different sound. And I don't think the record would have been as successful."

"The unlikely mix of talents was as much a phenomenon as the record itself," added John Robie, who played synthesizer on the song. "People from totally different backgrounds with completely dissimilar tastes and styles somehow came together to do this. At the time I remember it feeling pretty bizarre."

That bizarre combination of factors made a splash whose ripples are still drifting outward today. "Planet Rock" launched multiple Hall of Fame-worthy careers. It made a struggling new label legendary. It created a style of hip hop that would eventually become dominant, and birthed the electro genre to boot.

And it turned Joe's drum machine into a device that countless listeners wanted to own, or at least emulate. Joe has never come forward to claim his share of history. But the echoes of his 808, wherever it is now, keep sounding into infinity.

2.

Nearly forty years removed from his most influential hit, his trademark lion's mane of hair has gone grey. But Arthur Baker still has a younger man's enthusiasm and brashness. As he reminisces about "Planet Rock" from his Miami home office, you can still imagine the young DJ who got in on the ground floor of hip hop—and unabashedly hung his own photos on the walls.

Baker is writing his autobiography, and gives a quick, satirical sketch of his early life: "Born in Boston, Jewish, went to temple, got into music, then I moved to New York. There you go!" The next point on that truncated timeline would be "Planet Rock."

It was a life-changing record for others besides Baker, but its aftermath hasn't always been upbeat. The paths of three key architects have diverged widely. Baker, who once called John Robie his best friend, now admits they no longer speak. Those who know Robie say he feels burned and underappreciated. "He was the king of doing Arthur's music," says musician Man Parrish, a longtime friend. "If it wasn't for John, Arthur wouldn't have all those sounds. He was a genius."

Meanwhile, Afrika Bambaataa has experienced a much more radical reversal of fortunes. Bambaataa, born Lance Taylor in the Bronx, founded the Universal Zulu Nation in the late 1970s. It was a group of disc jockeys, graffiti artists, break dancers, and early hip hop enthusiasts that offered an alternative to gangs. This devoted following helped Bambaataa become one of the city's most recognizable DJs. He and his "assassins," Jazzy Jay and Red Alert, blended genres, played records at the wrong speed, and even backwards—anything to keep the dance floor packed. And with his mohawk and sunglasses, Bambaataa commanded the eye as well as the ear.

"Planet Rock" made Bambaataa one of hip hop's first stars. Later, he became one of its most respected ambassadors. For a while, he was even a visiting professor at Cornell University. But in 2016, allegations surfaced that years earlier, he'd molested several underage young men. He denied the stories and was never charged with a crime, but went from the Ivy League to untouchable. Bambaataa has done almost no interviews in recent years, but his manager agrees to this one "for the culture."

There's certainly no denying Bambaataa was an early supporter of drum machines. That was true in the music he played as a DJ, where he championed new wave acts like Yellow Magic Orchestra and Gary Numan. And like his New York rival Grandmaster Flash, who used a Vox 829 Percussion King to augment the beats in his DJ sets, Bambaataa used a similar pushbutton machine while playing live.

Of the small group of men who recorded "Planet Rock," Bambaataa insists, "I'm the one who brought the whole electro thing to them. Arthur was more into the R&B and soul."

Working in those genres, Baker had a breakthrough regional success in 1981. He'd cowritten and produced a disco single called "Happy Days." Credited to a group of Boston musicians called North End, the record became a club hit in New York, where Baker relocated.

There, Baker began writing reviews for a periodical called *Dance Music Report*, which was owned by Tom Silverman. Silverman was then starting his own dance music label, Tommy Boy. And the artist he most wanted to record was Afrika Bambaataa, who'd made the jump from block parties in the Bronx to downtown Manhattan's new wave clubs. So Silverman drafted Baker to produce.

Bambaataa had a stable of groups, and the first one Silverman chose to record was the Jazzy Five. "They wanted to do an old-school rap record," Baker recalls. This meant replaying an existing R&B riff for the rappers to use. The Sugar Hill Gang had done this on their crossover hit "Rapper's Delight," based on Chic's Number 1 single "Good Times."

Baker picked Gwen McRae's "Funky Sensation" for the Jazzy Five's source groove. The result, "Jazzy Sensation," was a Big Apple hit, selling more than fifty thousand copies. As a follow-up, Silverman suggested recording Bambaataa and his group Soul Sonic Force.

The song was going to be a number Bambaataa called "Planet Rock." It had a unity-through-partying lyric, and quoted several funk and breakbeat records, including Babe Ruth's "The Mexican" and Rick James's "Give It To Me." It might have turned out to be a live, disco-style groove like "Jazzy Sensation"—if not for the influence of another song.

That was Kraftwerk's "Numbers," which had appeared on the German quartet's 1981 album *Computer World*. It's a fairly one-dimensional track: the lyrics are simply a series of numbers recited in different languages, and there's only the slightest melody. It's the drums, scored by percussionist Karl Bartos and given a sharp, metallic edge when run through Florian Schneider's frequency shifter, that are the song's visionary centerpiece.

Bambaataa had been featuring this song regularly in his DJ sets. One of his main ideas for "Planet Rock," he says, was to combine the rhythm of "Numbers" with the melody of Kraftwerk's 1977 single "Trans-Europe Express." Bambaataa and Tom Silverman both recall that snippets of both these songs were included on the original "Planet Rock" demo.

Baker also remembers hearing "Numbers" around this time, at a Brooklyn record store called Music Factory. "The managers were these two brothers, Donnie and Dwight, who later became the group Rockers Revenge. They played me 'Numbers,' and I was like, *Fuck*! We should use that beat." But to do that, Baker realized, "We gotta have a drum machine."

Baker recalls visiting all the main music shops in Manhattan to audition drum machines. "But we couldn't afford to buy one," he says. "And a lot of the rental places didn't have 'em."

The answer came from the pages of *The Village Voice*. "We found an ad: 'Man with drum machine.' The guy's name was Joe. Twenty-five dollars a session," Baker remembers. "So we told him what to play—we played him 'Numbers'—and he programmed it.

"And he showed us what to do—I remember playing that rhythm on the cowbell. And Bam had a change of beat he wanted. He loved 'Super Sporm' by Captain Sky. So he showed the guy what to do, and the guy programmed that too."

Yet after the programming session was over, no one ever saw Joe again. Nor did they have a way to find him. That's because he—probably not unreasonably—demanded to be paid in cash. "It's one of those fucking things. He didn't trust Tom to give him a check that wouldn't bounce." Baker shakes his head and guffaws. "Tom and I don't remember him ever surfacing afterwards."

The song was recorded at Intergalactic Studios, located on the eighth floor of a building near Silverman's home. "And on the day of the session the elevator wasn't working. So John Robie and I had to walk up eight flights of stairs with his keyboards," Baker said, "and once there, we bonded really quickly."

Bambaataa had suggested Robie, recommending him as "this guy who plays keyboards like Kraftwerk." Baker quickly realized that Robie was "super-creative" and "obviously the right guy to do this." This became even more apparent when

Robie's Multimoog couldn't be synched to the Roland 808 drum track, and he was forced to play everything live.

Baker takes credit for requesting that the synth bassline double the pattern of the 808 kick drum. He would also drop the snare hits out of the mix occasionally, leaving just bass and handclaps, to create a sense of drama. "Which became a thing that everyone in hip hop did afterward," Baker points out. As a finishing touch, the studio's Fairlight CMI was used to play sampled orchestral blasts.

That night Baker brought a tape of the instrumental home to Brooklyn. He told his wife, somewhat immodestly, that he'd just made musical history. "I just knew," Baker says now. "It sounded really special. Even before the rap was put on. I was just like, fuck, we've really *done* something here."

His enthusiasm wasn't shared by all the participants. "The rappers thought they may never make another record again," Baker contends. "They thought it was gonna be nothing, for sure.

"They wanted a record like 'Jazzy Sensation.' They wanted a downtown, downtempo, funky R&B record. That's what they were expecting," adds Baker. "And when they got this instead, they had to rewrite the raps because it was so fast."

GLOBE, whose real name is John Miller, would admit this reluctance. "The first track they gave me was them redoing 'Trans-Europe Express,' but sped up, and I hated it," he said. "'Numbers' was hard, but the original track that they gave me sounded like some tin can shit."

But GLOBE worked out a strategy where the group slowed down its raps to half-time, a style he called "MC Popping." And Baker suggested some vocal hooks he'd swiped from other records. One of them was The Strikers' 1981 dance hit "Body Music," whose "Rock, rock/to the punk rock" chant was adapted for the chorus of "Planet Rock."

Still, Baker claims, "I'll be honest: I think I was the only one who actually felt we'd made history. I think Silverman had a feeling, too. But not Robie—he wasn't even into dance music."

Robie later confirmed his initial low opinion of the song. "Coming from a rock background and being a 'legit songwriter,' I thought 'Planet Rock' was silly," he said in 2016. "I was playing one-note lines and creating sound effects on a monophonic synthesizer, there was a repetitive drum machine sequence, and people were spouting stuff about saving the universe. Honestly, to me it was an embarrassment."

But when Baker took the test pressing of "Planet Rock" to the Brooklyn record store Music Factory, it created a sensation. "A guy came up to me and said, 'I wanna buy that.' I was like, 'It's an acetate!'" Baker says. "He said, 'I don't care. I'll give you a hundred bucks for it right now.'"

Once it hit the streets of New York City during the spring of 1982, the song sold out of its initial run of 50,000 copies in just a week. It also fulfilled a major goal Baker and Bambaataa shared: to make what they called an "Uptown/Downtown" record. That is, a song that would appeal to both uptown urban audiences, as well as new wave fans downtown. "I wanted a record that would break down all those boundaries," Baker says.

But it was in the clubs, with its kick drum rattling the rib cages of dancers, where the full impact of the record, and its drum machine, was truly felt. "From a technical standpoint, it was a challenge" recording the 808, says Mark S. Berry, who was the house engineer at Vanguard Records, and mixed many of Baker's early productions. "But as hard as we could get that bass drum to sound, and with that light, crisp snare—it *pounded* in the clubs.

"For me, it was all about the foot. It was just so round and fat on the 808," Berry adds. "And when Arthur did those patterns, where the bass drum wasn't just four on the floor—it just wore those speakers out."

The disc jockeys who wore out their copies of the song agreed. "'Planet Rock' was the one record that blew everything open," disc jockey François Kevorkian recalled. "It was just the most astounding, bass-drum-heavy, in-your-face, motherfucking deadly record we'd ever heard. It was a phenomenon—a tidal wave."

3.

As the tidal wave of "Planet Rock" washed over listeners, it didn't just make stars of its creators. It became a vinyl commercial for the TR-808 as well.

In late 1982, a nineteen-year-old Los Angeles DJ named Greg Broussard visited a local bar known as Club Radio. The guest behind the turntables that night was a New Yorker named Afrika Islam.

Islam took his name from Afrika Bambaataa, whom he called his "father." Sometime that evening, Islam played "Planet Rock." Knowing Islam's connection to Bambaataa, Broussard approached the DJ booth bursting with questions.

"I asked him, what kind of drum set did they use on 'Planet Rock?' And he said it wasn't a drum *set*, it was a drum *machine*," Broussard recalls. "That's when the wheels started spinning in my head. I was like, I can't play drums, but I *know* I can play a drum machine."

The very next day, Broussard visited the Hollywood Music Center. "I asked the guy if he had something called the 808. And he helped me program 'Planet Rock' right there on the spot. Then I started changing the beats around, and making it my own. And people actually started gathering around in the store."

There was a problem, however. "I only had 600 bucks. I went home, and I *begged* my mom for 600 more bucks," Broussard remembers with a laugh. "She finally gave it to me, and I went back and bought the 808. I took it home that day and started making beats."

For the next two weeks, Broussard did nothing but program his new machine. He had a powerful incentive. He and some friends— including an aspiring rapper and dancer named Tracy Marrow, who went by the name of Ice-T—were scheduled to DJ a party at the Los Angeles Sports Arena. They were part of a collective known as Uncle Jamm's Army, and they were drawing big crowds across Southern California to hear the mix of electronic dance music, early rap, and funk they played.

Finally the big night arrived. More than ten thousand people had packed the Sports Arena. Broussard cued up "Planet Rock" on the turntables, and then readied his version of the beat on his 808.

"Then I turned the volume down on the record, and the whole 10,000 people were dancing to the drum machine," says Broussard. "And then I started breakin' it down. I turned down the rimshot and made the beat just kick-snare-clap. And they were *still* partyin'!"

Now Broussard got even more adventurous. He started playing one of the original beats he'd created on the 808. "Somebody screamed out, 'What record is that?' And I was like, 'Wow, they like this drum machine!'"

Those original beats became the 1984 singles "Dial-a-Freak" and "Yes, Yes, Yes," credited to Uncle Jamm's Army. But that spring, Brousssard entered a local studio with his 808 and an idea for a solo single. "I took that little chant Prince did from 'Controversy'—'*People call me rude ...*'—and put it over the 'Planet Rock' beat," Broussard recalls. "And that was the Egyptian Lover style."

The result, "Egypt, Egypt," became a national hit for the Egyptian lover in the summer of 1984. An album called *On the Nile* followed, and soon people were calling Broussard "The King of the 808."

In a strange coincidence, another hip hop single recorded around the same time as "Egypt, Egypt" not only used the Roland TR-808, but also recycled a version of the familiar "Snake Charmer" melody. That was "Electric Kingdom," by a group called Twilight 22. Released in 1983, this song and its follow-up, "Siberian Nights," gave "Planet Rock" a widescreen revision, adding rumbling timpani and metallic percussion that made the records leap from the speakers.

The background of Gordon Bahary, the musical architect of these songs, helps explain their advanced sound. "Precocious" barely begins to describe the Long Island teenager who called Motown Records' Los Angeles office every single day in the mid-1970s, demanding to speak to his idol, Stevie Wonder.

An amused Wonder finally called Gordon Bahary back. But he was flabbergasted to learn that the kid didn't just want to speak to his hero. He wanted to *produce* him, instead.

The audacity of this confident 15-year-old touched Wonder. He flew Bahary to Los Angeles, where the youngster observed the making of the landmark double album *Songs in the Key of Life*. Bahary vowed to return as a collaborator. Four years later, he did.

In early 1979, Wonder was recording a soundtrack to the documentary *The Secret Life of Plants*. Bahary was summoned again to the West Coast. This time, he helped Wonder create a makeshift drum machine on the track "Race Babbling," by using two ARP synthesizers triggered by a sequencer.

"I even got the snares to rattle with noise," Bahary remembers. "The engineer was cracking up. He said, 'I can't believe I can hear the snare rattling.'"

Wonder wasn't Bahary's only musical mentor. His next-door neighbor on Long Island was Grammy-winning songwriter Harry Chapin, whose compositions "Taxi" and "Cat's in the Cradle" became radio classics. "He listened to my songs, he helped me edit them—he really helped me grow as a songwriter," Bahary says.

Chapin loaned the teenaged Bahary his preset drum machine. "And that became my drum set for the next six months," Bahary says.

Just shy of his fortieth birthday in 1981, Chapin was killed in a car crash, on the way to a benefit concert. But his final words to his young pupil resonated. "Harry Chapin said to me before he passed away, 'You know how you can tell a hit? It sounds like it's always been there,'" recalls Bahary. "And the last thing he told me was, 'Your music *almost* sounds like it's always been there.'"

The next year, Bahary heard "Planet Rock." He asked another trusted advisor, Ray Velasquez—an A&R representative at Vanguard Records—how the song's drum sounds were made. "He told me it was a Roland 808," Bahary says.

So Bahary went to his local Sam Ash and bought his own machine. "My heart was pounding out of my chest when I pulled it out of the box, that's how I felt," he says. "It was such a step up from Harry Chapin's little box." One of the 808 rhythms Bahary programmed led him to a familiar, Arabic-style melody sometimes known as the "Snake Charmer." He recalls, "My parents being Persian and Iraqi, we would have Arab and Iranian music in the house all the time."

By this time, Bahary had also acquired the E-MU Emulator, one of the first sampling keyboards. He used it to create dramatic timpani rolls that provided extra low end atop the 808 kick drum. "It was like the beginning of *Space Odyssey. BUM-bum-BUM-bum-BUM-bum*," Bahary says. "And my first impulse was, 'C'mon, man, don't do it. It sounds like a TV commercial.' But then I was like, 'No, it's innovative.'"

Rapper Joseph Saulter added cautionary verses about the dangers of the big city, and the song became "Electric Kingdom." Feeling confident, Bahary called Ray Velasquez at Vanguard on a Sunday. "I played it for him over the phone. He was literally screaming, saying, 'It's a hit! It's platinum!'"

Bahary had finally lived up to Harry Chapin's admonition: the familiar melody sounded like it had always been there. But the otherworldly drum sounds were purely his own.

4.

Some hip hop and electronic musicians had been working with the TR-808 even before "Planet Rock" arrived. One was Ben "Cozmo D" Cenac. A Brooklyn native and DJ, Cenac was a veteran of block party rap battles during the early hip hop scene.

He was also a gear junkie. Cenac remembers spending lots of time on the stretch of 48th Street in Manhattan where three music stores—Sam Ash, Electro Harmonix, and Manny's—were located. Cenac bought his first drum machine—a DR-55 Dr. Rhythm—at Sam Ash. Later, he traded it in for a preset unit, the Electro Harmonix DRM-16.

When Cenac took a studio engineering class at the New School, his professor was Phil Clendeninn, a well-known New York session musician. Clendeninn also had a part-time job at Sam Ash.

"So now I had an *in*," recalls Cenac, adjusting the black bowler hat that has long been his trademark. "And when the 808 came out, he told me about it. I said, 'Oh shit. I've *got* to have that.'"

As soon as he brought it home, Cenac began writing the songs that would transform his group from an R&B ensemble called Positive Messenger to a space-age hip hop group known as Newcleus. "When I got my 808," says Cenac, "I never looked back."

Cenac first heard "Planet Rock" on the radio in the spring of 1982, while he was working on a song called "Computer Age (Push the Button)." Like "Planet Rock," Newcleus's song had a futuristic theme and an uptempo, percussive 808 groove.

"I said, 'Man, if they like that, they're gonna *love* 'Computer Age,'" remembers Cenac. "I thought, 'OK, it's time to start shopping my stuff.'"

He did, and Newcleus eventually scored three hits from the 1984 debut album *Jam On Revenge*. The sped-up Munchkin vocals, sci-fi imagery, and comic book cover art made the group irresistible, but the 808 "was the heart of our production," Cenac says.

For another future titan of electronic music, however, the release of "Planet Rock"—and the sound of its 808—was a crushing blow.

In the spring of 1982, Detroit native Juan Atkins was on his way to the Big Apple. In the car was a box filled with copies of a new single from his group Cybotron. Atkins and his musical partner, Vietnam veteran Rick Davis, had recorded "Cosmic Cars" using the TR-808, which they'd purchased the year before.

"Cosmic Cars," a hard-hitting electronic dance track, had just been released on Atkins and Davis's label, Deep Space Records. "I had an auntie that lived in New York," says Atkins. "So I decided I'm gonna take this record to all the major radio stations in New York. Cause I know if we can break it in New York, we can break it nationwide.

"So we're driving down the freeway and listening to the radio. And the dude comes on and says, 'All right, here's the mystery tune!' He was *taunting* the other radio stations—like, '*Nyah, nyah, nyah, nyah, nyah,* we got this first!' And it was 'Planet Rock.'"

As the 808 beats rattled the car speakers, Atkins was both excited and angry to discover these kindred spirits. "It was a bittersweet feeling," he recalls with a sigh. "Because it sounded almost *exactly* like what we were doing. But the bitter part was, '*Damn!* They beat us to the punch!'"

All the momentum had suddenly gone out of the New York trip. "We still took the record around, but nobody paid attention to us," says Atkins. After splitting with Davis, Atkins would find better ways to get his music to the public—and a drum machine he could truly call his own.

5.

"Planet Rock" still has an air of reverent mystery about it, four decades after its release. But another huge 808 hit of 1982 is somewhat the opposite. Man Parrish not only didn't think "Hip Hop, Be Bop (Don't Stop)" had made musical history. He wasn't even sure it was music, period.

"I still don't feel comfortable with it. I still think people are crazy. Me?" Parrish asks, sitting in the outdoor garden of his Palm Beach home, where palm trees shade a glassed-in pool. "A white kid from Brooklyn? And a gay guy, which was the worst thing you could be in the hip hop world? *Nah.*"

Far more minimalistic than "Planet Rock," Parrish's single is a celebration of pure electronic rhythm. An instrumental—except for the chanted title, Munchkin giggles, and barking dogs—"Hip Hop Be Bop" puts the focus on the Roland TR-808. If Parrish was skeptical about it, clubgoers and reviewers were not. "As influential as Kraftwerk's last album was, their next will be hard pressed to match the high humor and serious groove of Man Parrish," wrote Brian Chin in *Billboard*, about Parrish's debut LP.

Six feet three inches tall and relentlessly good-humored, Manny Parrish is the perfect chatty guide to the late 1970s and early 1980s New York of his youth. A runaway at age fourteen, Parrish drifted into the outer reaches of Andy Warhol's circle at the fabled Studio 54 nightclub. It was Warhol, he proudly notes, who gave him his nickname "Man."

Parrish was also a self-described "gear whore." He built his own Radio Shack synthesizer, and began slowly acquiring equipment. Soon, he learned how to use his ARP 2600 and Moog modules to program drum sounds, preferring them to early machines like the Roland CR-78.

But when the TR-808 finally became available, Parrish immediately recognized the value of a particular feature: the fine tempo knob. It provided more precise control over the speed of a drum track than the "coarse" control, which had forty click-stop settings. This was important because when instruments couldn't be made to sync on tape, Parrish had to make minute adjustments by hand to bring everything in line. "That really made a difference," he says. "As the circuitry would heat up, as the tape would stretch, the beats per minute would go out of time. And I would ride that fine tempo knob like a DJ."

Making small corrections, Parrish would try to keep the drums locked to rest of the track for as long as possible. "Maybe you'd get 12 or 15 bars out of it, if you were lucky. Then it'd go out of sync, you'd stop the tape, roll it back a little, and start again. And I was the master of hitting the 808 on the downbeat to start it back up." He sighs. "But that was not a lot of fun."

It *was* getting him noticed, however. Raul Rodriguez was an assistant at Disconet, a subscription-only service for DJs. He'd heard Parrish's 1981 single "Heatstroke," originally written for a porn film. Rodriguez suggested that he and Parrish write a song together.

The result was "Hip Hop, Be Bop (Don't Stop)," a collage built with just three instruments. Parrish's TR-808 was augmented by metallic tom-tom fills, which John Robie sourced from his Prophet V synthesizer and played by hand. Parrish added the bassline from a monophonic Prophet I synth.

The barking dogs on the track were a tribute to clubgoers at the Funhouse, who would woof enthusiastically when DJ Jellybean Benitez played a song they liked. "We wanted to do a goof record," Parrish says, "and bark back at them and blow their minds."

Engineer Mark Berry admits his own mind was blown during the mixing of what he calls a "monstrosity." He, Parrish, and Raul Rodriguez gathered at Vanguard Studios on 23rd Street for the session. All six hands were necessary to slide faders and piece together the song, which Berry first thought was just an "amalgamation of sounds and noises."

In the clubs, all was made clear. "It was like, 'Holy fuck. We *nailed* it!" Berry recalls. "We found a six-minute dance track where no one got tired of the sounds. It was this totally chaotic record that worked when it was all edited together."

"I don't think I'm a musician. I can't read or write music. I don't know theory," explains Parrish. "But when I got the TR-808, I thought, 'OK, I'm not a drummer, but now I have drums I can program. And I can already make bass sounds, and synthesizer sounds. I've got a *band*. Let's do this!'"

6.

It didn't take Arthur Baker long to acquire his own TR-808. "I probably got mine as soon as I got the first check from 'Planet Rock' cleared, in fact," he says.

The 808 was the engine of a ridiculously busy period for Baker, John Robie, and Mark Berry. In 1982 and 1983, their names appeared on an unbroken string of dance singles. Many of them, like Freez's "IOU" and Nairobi's "Funky Soul Makkosa," were driven by that distinctive Roland rhythm.

But a proper follow-up to "Planet Rock" was proving elusive. The problem was the title. Baker wanted to call the song "Looking for the Perfect Beat." But he and John Robie simply couldn't find a beat that lived up to that name.

"We sat around for six months looking for the perfect beat to follow up 'Planet Rock,'" Baker recalls. "We were at Robie's house, working on it, and we finally realized that we're not gonna *find* the perfect beat. We should just *change* the beat we got."

That meant abandoning their experiments with another drum machine, the Oberheim DMX, and recommitting to the Roland TR-808 that had made them stars. At the rappers' request, its tempo was slowed—to about 118 beats per minute, from "Planet Rock"'s 130.

Then Baker came up with a vocal hook: a singsong repetition of "looking for the perfect beat." It was inspired, Baker says, by Thomas Dolby's "She Blinded Me With Science," a new wave hit getting club play in the fall of 1982.

But the most significant innovation came in the breakdowns of the song. The rappers shouted "Beat this!" followed by a heavily treated drum break. The treatment was partially an accident: a long reverb was used on the Roland's snare drum, but it was mistakenly applied to the bass drum as well. The reverb turned the bass drum cavernous, like a giant pounding on the door. "And I was like, that's amazing," says Baker. "We *gotta* keep that!"

That accident would help create a whole new genre. The next year, Bronx-born producer Chris Barbosa and his partner Mark Liggett borrowed "Looking for the Perfect Beat"'s reverb-heavy 808 bass drum. They used it on a single they produced for a young singer named Shannon. "Let the Music Play" not only became a Top 10 hit, it launched a movement called freestyle, which added Latin percussion to the 808 rhythms Tommy Boy had made famous.

The third Soul Sonic Force single, 1983's "Renegades of Funk," got off to an uneasy start. Baker began the song at Unique Studios, minus John Robie. "We fell out for a bit at that point," Baker recalls. Meanwhile, he claims there was initial resistance from the rappers to the idea of writing about "renegades." "They were like, 'We don't wanna be controversial. We don't wanna get in trouble,'" Baker chuckles. "I'm saying to them, 'What are you *talking* about? What's wrong with writing about Malcolm X and Martin Luther King?' And then GLOBE came up with a great rhyme."

John Robie later joined the sessions. "We used the 808, but I also had an Emulator," he said. "And even though the 808 is the foundation, there's lots of real percussion there." Besides the Emulator, there was also a lower-cost sampling technique, Baker adds, which may have been used to provide the song's bigger snare drums: an AMS Digital Delay. Canny producers had started to use this effect to digitally sample a short sound—like a drum hit—by "freezing" it, and then triggering it with another device.

Baker would continue to use the 808 on important singles, like the 1983 dance hit "Confusion" he produced for British postpunkers New Order. Many years later, he helped create the documentary *808*, which paid tribute to the machine so instrumental to his career. One of the artists he interviewed was Questlove, the drummer of hip hop band The Roots.

"What I like is what Questlove said: that the 808 is hip hop's electric guitar," Baker says. "I think that really sums up its importance.

"There's two different types of people," he continues. "People who say, 'The 808 doesn't sound like drums. I don't wanna use that.' And then there's people who say, 'That doesn't sound like drums. I *love* that!' And a lot of times, that's exactly what I wanted.'"

***

16

Worker Bees of the DMX

1.

If there's drum machine royalty, then there's only one king. His name is Jimmy Bralower.

Not everyone recognizes The King's pedigree, though he's contributed to ten Number 1 records and more than eighty gold and platinum recordings. That's because Bralower epitomizes what was, in the early 1980s, a completely new breed of session man.

Studio hired guns have always battled anonymity. But the session men who programmed the drums on some of the biggest hits of the 1980s have been condemned to a special sort of facelessness. In the minds of the public—and some musicians—it was a job not much different than data entry.

Jimmy Bralower has been challenging this misperception for decades. He was the right-hand man of superproducer Nile Rodgers, and you've heard his drum programming on hits by Madonna, Hall and Oates, Peter Gabriel, and Steve Winwood, among many others. People who know Bralower's work refer to him by his nickname, with reverence. Several musicians interviewed for this book only agreed after they found out The King was involved.

Big Apple born and raised, Bralower is certainly no shrinking violet. But he makes a deliberately modest comparison between drum programming and driving a bus. "We take people where they want to go," he says from his New York studio, "and they say, 'Thanks for the ride.'" Sometimes, he admits, there isn't even a thank you. Yet without Bralower and his fellow session men, who mastered an ever-increasing variety of drum machines, the most iconic rhythms of the Eighties would not exist.

Some of those rhythms came from the two main challengers to Linn and Roland—the Oberheim DMX, which we'll read more about here, and the E-MU SP-12, covered in Chapter 17. These new drum machines were part of a complete realignment of music technology.

It's possible that no musical era has ever seen more rapid and radical changes than the 1980s, especially during the first half of the decade. A major reason is that at this time, the entire industry was shifting from analog technology to digital.

This process occurred on several fronts at once. First, FM synthesis, and later, digital-to-analog converters, paved the way for digital synthesizers like the Yamaha DX7. This shift allowed for digital sampling devices, and full digital recording. The compact disc permitted digital data storage and playback. And a universal musical "language" known as Musical Instrument Digital Interface—or MIDI for short—was unveiled, making electronic music creation easier and more affordable than ever before.

To navigate these dizzying changes in the recording studio, you needed an expert. The role of a session man had changed: now at least half the job was knowing the new technology, with all its nuances and quirks. Many drummers had become programmers. Some even specialized in programming a particular machine, although it paid to be familiar with all of them. "In those days," says Bralower simply, "you had to learn to do a lot of stuff if you wanted to work."

It's even harder now to identify these session men, with the disappearance of the liner notes that once gave these studio "worker bees" their hour in the sun. "But worker bees," Bralower points out, "can be interesting, too."

2.

Jimmy Bralower's big break occurred, appropriately enough, on a song called "The Breaks." Yet rapper Kurtis Blow's 1980 single was nearly the beginning *and* the end of Bralower's career.

"I was basically seeing my life flash in front of me every day," Bralower says. "I finally had gotten to play on a hit record as a drummer, and it happened to be in a genre that was the first place they were going to eliminate drums."

Bralower's professional career had started at the age of fourteen. The Long Island native and some school friends formed a surf band called The Young Ones, and signed to Columbia Records. Their 1966 single "Man of Mystery" has the rumbling drums and tremolo guitar of The Ventures down pat. But the song didn't bring Bralower and his precocious bandmates stardom.

Jimmy Bralower's next chance wouldn't come for another thirteen years. It happened in the wake of "Rapper's Delight," an out-of-nowhere Top 40 hit by a trio of rappers called The Sugarhill Gang. One of the first hip hop singles, it was an instantly polarizing record. "There were two schools of thought," Bralower remembers. "One school was it's just a one-shot novelty record. The other was, it's the beginning of a whole new thing."

A former bandmate of Bralower's named J. B. Moore, who was working at *Billboard* magazine, believed the song really was the start of something big. He and a colleague, writer Robert Ford, decided to make their own rap record. They wrote a holiday-themed rhyme, then located a nineteen-year-old MC named Kurtis Blow to voice it.

Brawlower was drafted to play drums, and "Christmas Rappin'" became a 1979 hit in the UK. The follow-up single, "The Breaks," was an even bigger success, becoming the first hip hop record on a major label, and the first to go gold. But the emergence of the Roland TR-808—via singles like "Planet Rock"— was quickly changing the game in hip hop. The 808 sparked a move away from disco-based grooves like "The Breaks." And that meant musicians like Jimmy Bralower might no longer be necessary.

"When the 808 showed up, it was a curiosity for the B-boys that were hanging out in the rap world," says Bralower. "They were just into these beats. They didn't know anything about drumming, and they didn't care. They just cared about these sounds."

Now Bralower was losing sessions to drum machines. And as proficient as he was, Bralower had also recognized a difference between his playing and the more distinctive drumming of studio legends like Steve Ferrone or Jim Keltner. "I learned," he explains, "that there's a difference between saying, 'Get me a drummer' or 'Get me Steve Ferrone.'"

The answer, Bralower realized, was to commit fully to drum machines. He bought a LinnDrum, and vowed to learn how to use it better than anyone else. That, he thought, would be the thing that would make him truly distinctive.

"I didn't just wanna be, 'Get me a drummer,'" he says. "So I found a place where it could be, 'Get me Jimmy.'"

3.

The small community of musical equipment manufacturers in California was well aware of Roger Linn's drum machine success. One member who'd been observing closely from the beginning was Tom Oberheim.

Born in Manhattan, Kansas in 1936, Oberheim was older than most of the other audio manufacturers of the 1970s and 1980s. Though he was interested in singing, he wasn't a musician himself: he'd trained instead to be a physicist. However, he'd been lured to Los Angeles to study at UCLA because of an ad he'd seen in *Downbeat* magazine promising free jazz concerts.

After spending a decade designing computers, in 1969, Oberheim founded the company that bears his name. Its first product was a ring modulator, an effect that produces ringing, inharmonic overtones. In 1975, Oberheim introduced the first polyphonic synthesizer—an instrument that could play multiple notes at the same time. And in 1979, the company debuted the OB-X, which boasted a microprocessor that made it lighter and easier to program than other synthesizers.

In the summer of 1980, Oberheim hired a nineteen-year-old prodigy named Marcus Ryle, who became one of his top engineers. Ryle would go on to make his own name in the music business. Working first at Alesis, and then as the cofounder of pro audio company Line 6, Ryle developed a number of products that helped revolutionize music tech. (One of them, the Alesis HR-16 drum machine, will be covered in Chapter 20.)

Like many of his innovative peers, Ryle got early exposure to computers. His entrepreneur father brought home an Apple 2 Plus, which Ryle used to create his own primitive sequencing program. Then, as a teenager, he got a look at a much more sophisticated system, during a 1979 visit to Herbie Hancock's Beverly Hills home.

Ryle had come to Hancock's house to demonstrate a new synthesizer. He found Hancock experimenting with a computer-based drum program. "He said there was a guy named Roger Linn who was working on this," Ryle recalls. "And I thought, 'This isn't like *anything* I've ever seen before.'"

As mentioned in Chapter 12, Roger Linn soon shifted his focus to the development of the standalone LM-1 drum machine. In the fall of 1980, he demonstrated this unit to local members of the Audio Engineering Society.

"Roger's presentation just blew me away. He's such a smooth guy, first of all. He was the epitome of cool," recalls Ryle, who attended the meeting at the Sportsmen's Lodge in Studio City. "And what he showed us—these are real drum sounds, and you can program them. I was like, 'This changes everything.' And Tom was equally impressed."

Soon afterward, Oberheim invited Linn to his office and proposed they team up to build the drum machine. "We had a lovely chat," Ryle says. "And Roger said, 'I really wanna give this a go and build these machines myself.'"

In Linn's recollection, he was somewhat less gracious. "I was a cocky young 24 year old, and I thought, '*Pfft*, I can do better than this.' I think in retrospect, Tom is just such a gentleman that it was his way of being able to say he offered first," Linn says. "Then when they made their own thing, it wasn't like they were just stepping on me."

With or without Linn, Oberheim and Ryle had already made their decision. "So we got started on the DMX," Ryle says. "Obviously, it was inspired by Roger. But given our synthesizer background, there were things we wanted to do differently."

Specifically, Oberheim and Ryle were thinking about integration. In the days before MIDI, they envisioned a groundbreaking suite of electronic instruments designed to work together seamlessly.

Ryle was already working on a polyphonic sequencer called the DSX. "And we said, there should be a companion drum machine," he says. "Today, it sounds almost quaint. But back then, there was no notion of having a drum machine and a sequencer that were synchronized."

The DSX sequencer and the DMX drum machine would be joined by the OB-X synthesizer—and soon afterward, its successor, the OBXa—to complete a system known as the Oberheim Parallel Buss. ("Buss" refers to grouping multiple audio tracks together into a single signal path.) This system was a pricy $10,000. But as Ryle notes, it was targeted at professional musicians. "Honestly," he says, "there was no home recording yet."

Oberheim hired engineer Gordon Rudd, who had seen the Linn LM-1 in its early stages, to work on the DMX. Ryle's primary focus, meanwhile, was making sure the entire system functioned effectively. But Ryle proudly notes that "I'm one of the most recorded musicians in history, because I'm one of four people who was recorded to make the DMX handclap." That handclap sound was a particular favorite of early hip hop producers, in particular.

Most of the other sounds on the DMX were provided by jazz drummer Peter Erskine. Because the DMX became the second drum machine, after the LM-1, to use digital samples of real drums, comparisons between the two devices were frequent. A big part of the DMX's reputation was that compared to Roger Linn's drum machines, its sound was punchier and more in-your-face.

Many people interviewed for this book described the two in roughly the same terms as Jimmy Bralower. "DMX drums, they certainly had an attitude," he says. "The Linn really didn't. The Linn for me was more programmable and more flexible. The DMX was more aggressive. It was very clipped and very tight—a heavily compressed sound. It was kind of take it or leave it."

The comparison between the two machines is sometimes chalked up to the analog filters used to remove noise from the drum sounds. Ryle says it's less about the filters used and more about having better control over their application.

"First of all, we had the good fortune of coming second. Roger was the first to even try recording drums," Ryle says. "But we felt we could improve the noise performance, since we were a synthesizer company. Especially for things like the toms, which could get a little fuzzy sounding."

Each of the DMX drum voices was assigned its own voice card, "whereas Roger's voices were all on one board. We did that with the notion that the circuitry is now a little more customized," says Ryle. Now each drum voice could be filtered separately. "And the filtering is different for a tom than for a snare or a hi-hat," he adds.

When it debuted in 1981, the DMX listed for nearly $3,000, making it significantly cheaper than the LM-1. It also entered the market a few months before the LM-1's successor, the LinnDrum. The DMX and LinnDrum listed for about the same price, making them primary competitors for a couple of years.

But the DMX had an extra advantage: its connection to the Oberheim Parallel Buss. In the pre-MIDI era, having a set of instruments that could talk to one another was a big deal. One of the early adopters—an artist, songwriter, and producer from the suburbs of Boston—would use the Oberheim system to help transform R&B in the same way "Planet Rock" remade hip hop.

4.

David Frank remembers the date without hesitation: May 7, 1982. That was the day he and Mic Murphy went into the studio to record "It's Passion," their first song as The System.

Frank recalls the date so easily because the duo got a record deal the very next day. Within three weeks, their first single hit the record racks and the airwaves. And when it arrived, "It's Passion" was an instant dance club hit whose influence far outlasted its chart position. The minimalistic, syncopated synth-funk Frank and Murphy created became one of the dominant sounds of the 1980s. Not coincidentally, the gear that made The System possible was another system: the Oberheim Parallel Buss, including the DMX drum machine.

A conservatory-trained pianist, Frank studied at Berkelee College of Music before moving to New York. He became one of the first people in the city to own the Oberheim system. By the time he went into Sorcerer Sound studios to record "It's Passion," he'd studied each component of the Parallel Buss in minute detail.

"It was the right time for me to have it," Frank says of the Oberheim gear. "Because I learned every possible thing I could do with it that I could think of. Memorizing the manuals backwards and forwards. If you listen to 'It's Passion,' you'll hear everything I had thought of up to that day."

Had things gone a little differently, "It's Passion" might instead have been the first single for an up-and-coming female singer. She was Frank's neighbor and former bandmate, a Detroit native named Madonna Ciccone.

The first project Frank worked on, after getting the Oberheim DMX in early 1982, was with the German expatriate Otto Von Wernherr, an actor and singer. Madonna was drafted to add vocals to several songs, and Frank provided the musical backing using his Oberheim equipment.

The Von Wernherr sessions became a historical curiosity after Madonna became famous. Few realized that on these songs, Frank was using the Oberheim system to become—as he was later known—"The Godfather of Electronic R&B." As he notes, "I figured out most of the stuff that I used later while working on that project."

Frank was using the system not just to generate sounds, but also to write songs. "The first good thing I wrote on it," he remembers, was a song titled "Crimes of Passion." Frank invited Madonna to add lyrics and vocals to the tune. He'd also scored some free studio time to record it.

The day before the recording, Madonna told Frank she couldn't work on the song without Stephen Bray. Bray was Madonna's songwriting partner, her former boyfriend, and a drummer. It was the last of those details that gave Frank pause.

"I don't wanna do it with Steve. Because he's gonna want to put guitars and live drums on it, and I want it to be electronic," he told Madonna. But now Frank had a studio booked, and no singer or lyricist. So he called Michael "Mic" Murphy. The pair had recently toured with the New York R&B band Kleeer—Frank as a keyboardist, Murphy as the group's road manager.

During a studio all-nighter, Murphy rewrote the song's lyrics and delivered a vocal whose warmth provided the perfect counterpoint to the Oberheim electronics. The next morning, bleary-eyed, they took the tapes out to have a 12-inch single pressed.

Murphy and Frank thought "It's Passion" could score some airtime at new wave clubs like Danceteria. But when the clerk at the duplication service suggested they take a copy to Mirage Records, they wound up with a record deal on the spot. Founded by brothers Jerry and Bob Greenberg, Mirage was on the lookout for bands who could get club play. So The System literally got a deal before they even had a name.

Sweat, their 1983 debut album, saw Frank drawing on his knowledge of the Oberheim Parallel Buss. The DMX drum programming reflects that intense study. For example, the opening of the hit "You Are in My System" places the hi-hats in 3/4 time against a 4/4 bassline—a formula that's reversed on the song's bridge. And the crisp kick drum rolls of the title track would be copied by many other programmers. "I just said, when it comes to the drums, I'm not gonna do what's been done before," Frank says.

Frank stayed loyal to the Oberheim system through the next two System albums, 1984's *X-Periment*, and *The Pleasure Seekers* the following year. He also became a sought-after session man, and his DMX expertise found its way onto other people's records. One was Phil Collins's 1985 Number 1 hit "Sussudio."

Collins, of course, had been using drum machines for some time. And he programmed some other machines on his third solo album, *No Jacket Required*—including the Roland 808 on "One More Night," and the LinnDrum on "Don't Lose My Number." But calling in Frank to program the Oberheim DMX is a reminder of just how specialized this era had become.

"It was the last day I was in London, and his roadies had given me a gram of cocaine the day before. I was so wasted, I really didn't wanna work on the song," Frank remembers. "And he was like,"—here Frank mimics Collins's cheerful voice—"'C'mon, mate! Let's just do 'Sussudio.' I'm not even sure it's gonna be on the album.'"

So Frank retreated to a programming room and got to work. "I programmed it very simply," he says, "because Phil was gonna play on it." In the end, that simple but effective DMX pattern became the backbone of the single.

As he looks back on the 1980s, Frank admits "it was a little bit of luck" to have had the Oberheim DMX and its related gear so early. But the real good fortune, he thinks, was "to be there at that moment, without having anyone's expectations of me in the way."

"A lot of people are always at the mercy of the radio, of what other people want," Frank reflects. "I had the opportunity to do what I did best. Those moments are not that plentiful in music history."

5.

One of the people who watched the rapid rise of The System was a drummer who'd played on some of hip hop's biggest hits. Now he was, like Jimmy Brawlower, feeling his own musical mortality, as drum machines invaded his turf.

Keith LeBlanc was part of the house band at Sugar Hill Records. The New Jersey label was the home of the Sugarhill Gang, Grandmaster Flash and the Furious Five, Spoonie Gee, and The Sequence. Between 1979 and 1983, LeBlanc played drums on a series of hip hop classics.

The changing of the guard occurred while LeBlanc was on tour. All of a sudden, he was watching The System, starring his former road manager, Mic Murphy, leapfrog his group on the bill. "We were playing down south with them. And they were headlining over us, with two guys!" recalls LeBlanc, in the laid-back drawl of a true studio cool cat. "It was amazing."

Now it was 1983, and drum machines "were taking a big chunk of my income away," LeBlanc recalls. In particular, LeBlanc was losing sessions at Sugar Hill Records. The label's studio in Englewood, New Jersey, was now the home of an Oberheim DMX that session bassist Doug Wimbish had jokingly nicknamed "Willie."

Willie's primary programmer was an Indianapolis native named Reggie Griffin. He was a multi-instrumentalist in the funk band Manchild, a group best known for giving the singer-songwriter Babyface his start. Griffin had been recruited by Sugar Hill Records founder Sylvia Robinson to work on a follow-up to The Sugarhill Gang's hit "Rapper's Delight."

The result was The Sugarhill Gang's rap cover of the song "Apache." But after it became a hit in February 1982, "Planet Rock" changed the game. "Drum machines were starting to come into vogue. The 808 was already out. The LinnDrum was just coming out. The DMX had just come out," Griffin remembers. "So they asked me which one to get, knowing that I was the electronics guy. I suggested the DMX. Soon as they got it, Sylvia looked at me and said, 'Get ready. I know he's the one who knows how to program it.' And of course, I was."

Willie the DMX showed up on several songs from Grandmaster Flash and the Furious Five's 1982 debut album, *The Message*. One was the title track, which not only became a hit, but showcased hip hop's developing social conscience. The song was written by Ed "Duke Bootee" Fletcher, who performed it with rapper Melle Mel.

"Duke came to me and was like, 'I'm hearing this groove,'" says Griffin. "He knew I could program the sounds, design the sounds. And that drum machine beat became the foundation." On the single "Scorpio," meanwhile, Eddie "Mr. Ness" Morris, Melle Mel, and Griffin created a hard-hitting electro track with just three elements: a Roland vocoder, Griffin's Prophet V synthesizer, and Willie.

The DMX's kick drum, Griffin says, was the difference maker. "We'd usually tune the kick drum down. It had a dirty growl to it that the LinnDrum didn't have," he says. "The Linn was just a little too pretty."

That DMX kick drum sound was so distinctive, in fact, that its absence could be noticed—as Griffin found out to his chagrin. His 1982 single "Mirda Rock," released on the Sugar Hill imprint Sweet Mountain, featured the Roland 606, a programmable drum machine that followed the 808.

Griffin and engineer Chris Lord-Alge were happy with the song, a infectious, vocoderized dance track in the vein of "Scorpio." Then Sylvia Robinson paid a visit to the studio. "She heard the kick. And she said, 'That's not *Willie's* kick drum. You gotta put *Willie* on there.' I looked at Chris, and Chris looked at me, and we went, 'Oh boy.'"

Asked how he managed to comply with Robinson's request, in the pre-MIDI era, Griffin sighs. "If you really must know ... we tried everything we could to lock the DMX up. And nothing worked. So I ended up having to do it manually." How long did it take to punch in those DMX kick drum hits by hand? Griffin gives an even deeper sigh. "I'll make myself feel better and say it didn't take that long." Sarcastically, he adds, "Now the kick drum had a 'human feel!'"

In 1984, Keith LeBlanc joined the DMX club. But he wasn't able to afford the machine until producer Marshall Chess—the son of Chess Records founder Leonard Chess—approached him about making a solo single.

To record it, LeBlanc borrowed a DMX from a friend, songwriter Carl Sturken. "I purposely chose that machine because that was the sound right then," he says. And the DMX played a huge role in the song that resulted, a sound collage of Malcolm X speeches and programmed drums called "No Sell Out."

LeBlanc wound up putting the single out on Tommy Boy Records, after Sugar Hill was reluctant to grant Malcom X's family royalties for the vocal samples. It was a controversial release, but also a groundbreaking one. That was in part because of LeBlanc's busy drum track, which had an aggression that matched Malcom X's fiery civil rights rhetoric. The DMX tom-toms rumble between the heavy kicks and snares like thunderheads, and the song previews the crossover between hip hop and industrial music that LeBlanc would spearhead.

From this point until the end of the 1980s, he would do most of that work with the DMX. Marshall Chess bought LeBlanc one of the machines as partial payment for "No Sell Out."

"When I first got a DMX, it meant the world to me at that time. To me, it was like having a 24-track studio," LeBlanc says. "Because I was a drummer, I tried to make the machine do things that a drummer couldn't do. That's what I was into. Of course, if I was programming for a pop star, I would do whatever they wanted, as quickly as possible."

Sometimes, what the pop stars wanted was the sound of "No Sell Out." After hearing the record, Martin Fry and Mark White of the British group ABC contacted Tommy Boy to find out how to bring LeBlanc to London. They wanted his DMX sound for their third album, *How to Be a Zillionaire*. It contained several hit singles, including the Top 10 smash "Be Near Me," that drew heavily on LeBlanc's programmed hip hop rhythms.

One of the last assignments for Griffin's DMX, meanwhile, was a project that brought together several musicians on the frontline of drum programming. Joan Jett's *Good Music* featured contributions from Jimmy Bralower and "Looking for the Perfect Beat" engineer Mark S. Berry. Most notably, the song "Black Leather" was the result of a chance nightclub meeting between Jett and Furious Five member Eddie "Mr. Ness" Morris—who both had a fondness for leather gear.

The tune was a big beat DMX stomp with swaggering power chords and a half-sung, half-rapped vocal from Jett. It was reminiscent of a pair of recent songs called "Rock Box" and "King of Rock," and that was no accident. Coproducing with Reggie Griffin was Larry Smith—the man who'd overseen those songs for a Hollis, Queens group named Run-DMC Together, Smith and Run-DMC made the Oberheim the drum machine of choice in hip hop.

6.

"New wave isn't a bunch of English dudes with orange hair, fancy clothes, and lousy voices trying to catch a beat," insisted Nelson George in 1984. "The real 'new wave' happening today is about the street, about the beat of the drum machine, about hard, percussive synthesizer flourishes, and about voices that tell stories about life as seen by young men with microphones, turntables, and serious syncopation."

George, then *Billboard*'s Black Music Editor, made this declaration on the sleeve of *Rap 1*, a compilation from a brand-new label called Profile Records. And he emphasized the importance of the drum machine in these songs. The producers, George noted, "get as much *sound* and *substance* out of straight, direct rhythms" as Quincy Jones did on Michael Jackson's megahit *Thriller*.

Two of the seven songs on *Rap 1* epitomized that straight, direct rhythmic approach. They featured Joseph "Run" Simmons and Daryl "DMC" McDaniels, whose trademark stage gear—black fedoras and leather jackets—was as no-nonsense as their sound. And they were produced by Larry Smith, later known as "the Quincy Jones of rap" for his work with Run-DMC and Whodini.

"Jam-Master Jay" was a tribute to, and showcase for, the group's DJ, Jason Mizell. And "Sucker MCs" was even more minimalistic. As Smith admitted to author Brian Coleman years later, "'Sucker MCs' was honestly a really plain record. It was just them and a drum machine. Although that was really radical for that time."

This sound was a turn away from both disco-based rap *and* the 808 electro jams that had replaced it. Arthur Baker remembered impresario Russell Simmons, Run's older brother, once complaining that "Planet Rock" and its syncopated sequels were "too nervous." He told Baker, "I can't get with that nervous shit."

The sound Simmons had in mind for Run-DMC was slower, less funky, and more rock-oriented. Songs like "Rock Box" and "King of Rock" boasted metallic guitars, but the star was the drum machine.

That machine was an Oberheim DMX. No other record had given its hard, compressed sound the sonic space that "Sucker MCs" and its flip side, "It's Like That," provided. But Smith also acknowledged that the drum machine was a practical decision. He and Russell Simmons had made "Sucker MCs" with their own money, and then sold it to Profile. "To be honest, if I had had the budget," Smith said, "I would have hired live performers on the whole first Run-DMC album."

That was the old school way, which Smith knew well. He'd played bass in Orange Krush, a band formed to back rapper Kurtis Blow on the road. There was a live drummer, Trevor Gale, and a DJ and guitarist named David Reeves.

In 1982, Orange Krush recorded a song titled "Action." Smith dubbed the distinctive beat of "Action" the "Krush Groove." When programmed into the DMX—right down to the handclaps—it became the basis of "Sucker MCs" and three other Run-DMC tracks.

The member of Orange Krush who had the most experience with drum machines was David Reeves. He's even mentioned in the lyrics of "Sucker MCs"—"Dave cut the record down to the bone" refers to him stripping away all the layers of "Action" except the "Krush Groove" rhythm.

Like Grandmaster Flash and Afrika Bambaataa, Reeves had used a primitive drum machine during his DJ sets. He'd programmed the drums, and played most of the instruments, on the Jimmy Spicer hit "Money (Dollar Bill Y'All)." And Reeves had gotten his own Oberheim DMX before Smith. He used it to produce the 1983 single "The Big Beat," from "love rapper" Spoonie Gee.

"Larry Smith followed me, because he saw me with the DMX," says Reeves. "Of course I did give Larry tips. Larry was a bass player. He wasn't really a hip hop guy. So I gave him a thorough hip hop lesson." Some of those tips, Reeves says, included "syncopating the hi-hats. Pitching up the snares and lowering the kicks. Tuning the tambourine and the handclaps. And sequencing."

Owning a DMX at the time, he admits, "wasn't cheap. But I had a four track, so the DMX made it easy to make a beat, then play bass and guitar and scratch over it." In early 1984, one of these demos would become Reeves's first solo single. "One for the Treble" was an instrumental sound collage that featured his turntable skills—and, of course, his Oberheim DMX.

Reeves had gone by the nickname Davy D, but for the release of "One for the Treble," he became the first musician to take the name of a drum machine. He rechristened himself Davy DMX, which seems like an appropriate tribute to the machine's importance in hip hop.

Surprisingly, it wasn't that sort of tribute at all. Reeves admits he was paying homage instead to those English new wavers Nelson George disdained. "The drum machine—it seemed a little more arty. My whole concept was to make the song seem like it was an import. That's why I had the girl on there with the London accent," he explains. "It was kind of inspired by The Police—'Voices Inside My Head,' the echoed guitars."

The story of Davy DMX, however, is also a sobering reminder that the "worker bees" of this chapter have often gotten far less than their due. Reeves is frank when asked about the thorny issue of credits.

"I really didn't know much about the music business. Russell was my good friend," Reeves says. "Once 'Action' was done, it was on the radio. But people were like, 'Why your name isn't on this?'" The writer's credits, Reeves noted, went instead to Larry Smith and Russell Simmons.

"Then we did 'Bubble Bunch,' and my name wasn't on *that*. But when we got to 'Dollar Bill,' I played bass guitar, drums, and *everything*, so now I was wondering why [Simmons's] name was on it. But then the secret came out about writers and publishing."

Reeves discovered that Simmons had made a publishing deal with Profile, and was collecting royalties as both a writer and publisher of the songs. "But Russell doesn't write anything. And that's where the problem came," Reeves says. "That's where things started to get *funky*."

7.

Bill Laswell and Michael Beinhorn waited in the outer office. They could hear voices from the home studio inside. One was the studio's owner, jazz pianist Herbie Hancock. The other was engineer Dave Jerden.

Hancock and Jerden had just listened to two songs that Beinhorn and Laswell had created, where the dominant instrument was the Oberheim DMX. Now they were trying to make sense of what it all meant.

"Herbie said, 'Do you get this? Is this really good?'" Laswell remembers. "And Dave, who didn't really know anything about hip hop stuff, said, 'Well, people are doing things differently now. It's gonna work.'"

"Herbie didn't know what the fuck to make of it at all," insists Beinhorn. "It was just way outside of his experience."

Those two skeletal songs were called "Earth Beat" and "Rockit." And Jerden's reassurance would up being a massive understatement. "Rockit" not only revitalized Hancock's stalled career, it legitimized the still-embryonic genre of hip hop.

The accompanying album, *Future Shock*, was Hancock's highest-charting entry in years. Yet Hancock's own future shock when faced with Beinhorn and Laswell's DMX beats says something about how fast music and technology were changing during this time.

Hancock and Jerden were certainly no technological rubes. The latter had worked with Brian Eno and David Byrne on *My Life in the Bush of Ghosts*, a 1981 album of experimental sound collages that anticipated sampling technology, and made early use of a Linn LM-1 to boot. Hancock, meanwhile, owned one of the very first LM-1s. As Bill Laswell observes, "Herbie had a warehouse of stuff. He had Fairlights, and really expensive vocoders, a Clavinet. Anything that was current, he had two of 'em."

But after scoring a moderate pop hit with 1979's *Feets Don't Fail Me Now*, Hancock's next three forays into disco and R&B failed to crack the Top 100 on the Billboard album charts. "This was going to be Herbie's last record for Columbia. This was the end of the line for him," asserts Beinhorn. "So this was sort of like his 'I have nothing to lose' record."

Enter Beinhorn and Laswell, who were bandmates in Material, a New York avant-funk outfit that epitomized the collision of "Uptown" and "Downtown" that Arthur Baker and Afrika Bambaataa tried to capture with "Planet Rock." Beinhorn and Laswell had also worked on a series of 12-inch singles for the French label Celluloid. The first of these, 1982's "Change the Beat," was a cross-cultural collaboration between Fab 5 Freddy and the Gallic rapper Beside. It was also Beinhorn and Laswell's first experience programming the DMX.

Hancock had a new manager, a 25-year-old scenester named Tony Meilandt. He knew Material, and made an approach to Laswell about producing Hancock's next record. So Beinhorn and Laswell were commissioned to create two tracks for Hancock on spec.

If the resulting DMX beats were raw, Beinhorn readily admits it's because he really didn't know what he was doing. "Rockit," in particular, was the result of two happy accidents. "I decided that I wanted to have drum fills," Beinhorn says. "But it didn't occur to me that the drum fills actually need to be *inside* of a bar."

When Beinhorn heard the lengthy tom fills that resulted, "I was like, 'Oh, man, I really fucked this up.' And Bill was like, 'No, wait a minute—this is great.' And I was like, 'You know what? It *is* pretty great!'" The hiccuping drum roll that starts the song was an even more basic mishap: Beinhorn was trying to play sixteenth notes on the toms. "But I didn't play it right. I screwed up the end," he says. "And we heard it back, and we were, like, 'Hmmm … not bad.'"

Others were even more enthusiastic. Beinhorn and Laswell were signed to Elektra Records, so they played "Rockit" for A&R man Tom Zutaut, who later became famous for signings like Motley Crue and Guns N' Roses. "He did actually start to go crazy," Beinhorn admits. He said, '*I gotta have that!* What *is* it?' We were like, 'That's for Herbie Hancock.' And he was like, 'Ah, *shit!*'"

Laswell and Beinhorn were ultimately drafted to produce the remainder of *Future Shock*. But Hancock's label, Columbia, wasn't sold on the results at first. Hancock's tech guru, engineer Bryan Bell, recalls hearing "Rockit" described by label executives as "robot disco bullshit"—until it became the biggest-selling 12-inch single in the company's history. "It legitimized hip hop into a commercially accepted art form," Bell says. "It made rap interesting to the major labels."

Laswell went on to create a series of records that relied on the gritty sound of the DMX. One of them began with a phone call from Afrika Bambaataa. "He said he wanted to do a metal record. And he asked me, 'Do you know Def Leppard?'" says Laswell, clearly amused by the memory. "And I was like, 'No, I don't know them.' And he said, 'Do you know any rock singers?' And I said, 'Well, I just worked with this guy who was in the Sex Pistols. His name is John Lydon.'"

The resulting record, 1984's "World Destruction," was inspired by a documentary Bambaataa had seen about the French astrologer and doomsayer Nostradamus. Laswell's stomping DMX beat was driven by prominent cowbell and augmented by metallic guitar from Nicky Skopelitis. It showed a clear awareness of the rock-oriented direction that hip hop, and the DMX, had taken in the wake of Run-DMC.

But following the unexpected success of "Rockit," the DMX would drive a wedge between Laswell and Beinhorn. "This record was a tremendous success for us, obviously. But the problem is what happened after," says Beinhorn. "Everything that we did was using the DMX to get pretty much the same type of beat that we got on 'Rockit.' I mean, it was a great formula. But we were in a position to achieve a great deal more at that point."

The tipping point was an album Laswell began recording with the DMX and a series of top percussionists, like Aïyb Dieng and Steve Turre. It appeared in 1985 as *Down By Law*, under the name Deadline. For Laswell, it remains "a really special record." But Beinhorn had already left the partnership.

Newly solo, Beinhorn found that his major calling card—"Rockit"—meant less than he'd hoped, in a rapidly changing musical landscape. "To be perfectly honest with you, most people didn't care. I was really hard up for work," he admits. In early 1987, he found himself in the studio with Los Angeles funk-rock quartet The Red Hot Chili Peppers.

The Chili Peppers, like Beinhorn, were scuffling. Their last album, 1985's *Freaky Styley*, had sold poorly. Their third LP looked to be make-or-break, and singer Anthony Kiedis's drug addiction hung like a pall over the project. They also had no use for drum machines: the last song on the record Beinhorn ended up producing for them was called "Organic Anti-Beat Box Band."

"It wasn't my milieu at all, making records with guitars. But somehow I just managed to matriculate into it," says Beinhorn. The shift paid off handsomely for both Beinhorn and the Chili Peppers. *The Uplift Mofo Party Plan* set the group on a course to become one of America's biggest bands. Beinhorn went on to produce huge hits for Soul Asylum and the grunge act Soundgarden. All without a drum machine in sight, or earshot.

But Beinhorn throws back his head and laughs when he recalls the first thing he did upon leaving his partnership with Laswell. "I've been waiting for you to ask me that," he says, with a huge grin. "I went right out and bought a LinnDrum."

Drum machines could certainly exert a powerful pull. But as the story of Beinhorn and Laswell suggests, they could be an equally strong force that drove musicians apart.

8.

Frank Beard was furious. His fists were balled up, and he was ready to fight anybody and everybody in his living room. Especially Billy Gibbons, his bandmate in ZZ Top.

"*Who's that fuckin' drummer?*" Beard screamed at Gibbons, the veins in his neck taut.

Beard had just heard a mix of "Gimme All Your Lovin'," which would be the leadoff track and first single from ZZ Top's new album, *Eliminator*. And he knew from the first snare hit that he wasn't drummer on the track.

Gibbons mumbled an explanation. Beard's drums hadn't been replaced by a session pro. They'd been eliminated in favor of a drum machine, instead.

The man who might very well have programmed these drum parts decided to quietly exit the room. Linden Hudson was a former DJ, recording engineer, and songwriter. He'd been living at Beard's home, where he'd built a studio. And during the making of *Eliminator*, many of his ideas—and one of his songs—had been assimilated into the album. He and Gibbons, the band's primary songwriter, had spent hours together during 1982, "talking about drum tracks and alternate realities."

One of Hudson's interests was computers. Another was research. And one of Hudson's pet theories involved his careful analysis of popular dance singles. The ideal tempo for such a song, Hudson contended, was 124 beats per minute, and he had the numbers to back it up. Impressed, Gibbons began thinking about how to polish up ZZ Top's dusty desert boogie.

With Beard and bassist Dusty Hill frequently absent during demo sessions, the sound of *Eliminator* began to take shape around Hudson's LinnDrum patterns. Synthesizer basslines were locked tightly to the programmed rhythms, and Gibbons laid his blues guitar and growling vocals on top. Hudson then bowed out when recording sessions shifted to Ardent Studios in Memphis, with engineer Terry Manning and producer Bill Ham.

Years later, in a blog post credited to "Compass Point"—the name of the studio he'd taken over in 1992—a writer who appeared to be Manning claimed to have done the drum programming on *Eliminator*.

> Well, I guess it can now be told, as long as you promise not to pass it on, but yes, I played the drums on Legs, and in fact, almost the whole album. As mentioned, this song was recorded in my attic, except for Billy's lead guitar and vocal, which came from a previous studio version which was unsatisfactory. (Oh, if I could tell the whole, real story! Maybe someday)

> The drums were a combination of things. There was programming, on my Oberheim drum machine, and then a multitude of samples triggered in over the snare as well, using an AMS DMX, and very carefully manually trimming the input volume to catch every beat properly. The hat was a sound from the Oberheim mixed with some sampled things and some white noise, then gated and triggered from an arpeggiated spike. Then I one-at-a-time overdubbed certain other drums, some toms, and definitely cymbals. On some of the tracks of the album, I added to the tom sounds with a Simmons electronic kit, just barely mixed under the real ones, for tom "fatness."

There was a diplomatic caveat: "I will reiterate that this is not referring to Frank, ZZ's drummer. I stated before that I will not talk about certain aspects of the ZZ recordings, out of respect for the band and management. Frank did a marvelous job on many records, and this reflects upon him as a great drummer."

When it appeared in 1983, *Eliminator* became one of the biggest successes of the 1980s. Some of it was the videos. The band's iconic beards, sunglasses, and roles as bemused spectators amidst a landscape of scantily dressed models—it all equalled MTV crack. But the precision-tooled sound also generated hit after hit, chugging along at Hudson's recommended tempo.

One of Hudson's own songs, a funky electronic track called "Thug," turned up uncredited on the album. He sued, eventually recovering $600,000—a tiny fraction of the multiplatinum sales *Eliminator* generated.

As the decade progressed, ZZ Top would make more and more use of programmed rhythms. On the band's next album, 1985's *Afterburner*, hits like "Sleeping Bag" made no pretense of live drumming. Yet the controversy that began that afternoon in 1983 at Frank Beard's house has never been completely resolved.

Hudson has made a compelling case that his LinnDrum programming ended up on *Eliminator*. He was backed up in *Sharp Dressed Men*, a 1994 biography of the band by their former road manager David Blayney, who claimed Beard's playing on the album was primarily overdubbing tom-tom fills.

But at age seventy-three, Hudson has grown tired of the battle. Manning's blog post has disappeared. And the band's public position on the conflict has remained lawyerly, with the big questions avoided.

In a 2021 interview, Billy Gibbons called Hudson

> quite an influential, inspirational figure. He was right there with us when some of the material was developed and brought forward some production techniques that were then valuable. I still treasure the moments that he and I spent together. There was quite a bit of time that the two of us sat behind a mixing console discussing new ways to go about making popular music.

Beard, meanwhile, was dismissive. "Basically, Linden was kind of a house-sitter for me," Beard claimed. "He looked after my home when we were out on tour. What happened with him was a real drag. But you have to move on."

Moving on was easier said than done when drum machines were involved. Other MTV superstars were finding this out around the same time.

The British trio Wang Chung had signed an American record deal with the hot new label Geffen. The group had chosen producer Chris Merrick Hughes, who'd worked with Adam and the Ants and Tears for Fears. They particularly hoped Hughes could help them unlock a promising song called "Dance Hall Days." The track had a shuffling 12/8 rhythm that had resisted efforts to fit it into a drum machine.

Using his LM-1, Hughes oversaw sessions that were far more successful. "Dance Hall Days" became a Number 1 Dance hit in 1984, and its parent album, *Points on the Curve*, broke into the Top 30. "The drum machine really held that album together," observes singer Jack Hues. However, drummer Darren Costin left the group afterwards. "Being the drummer always means a lot of waiting around," Hues admits. "Now, with the drum machine, waiting to do a pass of overdubs, there was even more of it."

Yet Wang Chung discovered that if a drummer wasn't essential in the studio, he was still needed for the video. The band's A&R man at Geffen was

John Kalodner, who stressed how important a drummer was to American audiences. "He told us, 'You have to have a drum kit, or they'll think it's cheating,'" Hues says.

Meanwhile, Huey Lewis and the News had experimented with a LinnDrum while recording their 1983 sophomore album, *Sports*. But resistance from the group led to the drum machine being dropped. Then Lewis turned the tapes over to A-list mixer Bob Clearmountain. "But it just wasn't right, dammit," Lewis recalled. "I made him remix it—and he hates to remix. I'm going, 'What is wrong here? Why can't we get this thing to groove?'"

After a break of a couple of months, Lewis relistened to the *Sports* tapes and had a revelation. "I went: 'Shocking!' 'Heart Of Rock and Roll,' 'I Want a New Drug,' 'Walking on a Thin Line'... they're just too damn funky. We have to cut them again with a drum machine."

The results proved his intuition correct: *Sports* went platinum seven times over, and spawned four Top 10 singles. However, drummer Bill Gibson admitted years later that the drum machine "took a little getting used to at first."

Gibson, however, survived the transition. Acclaimed drummer Steve Smith of arena-rock superstars Journey would not be so lucky. During the making of the 1986 album *Raised on Radio*, he was asked to leave Journey—essentially, in favor of a drum machine.

Smith revealed the situation in an extraordinarily candid interview with *Modern Drummer* that summer:

> This is very hard to explain, because it's very emotional and I also have a lot of confusion about it ... Most of the material for this new record was written by Jonathan [Cain] and Steve together or Neal [Schon], Jonathan, and Steve [Perry] together. The band ceased being a band. They did very extensive demos of the songs at Jonathan's studio, complete with drum machine beats and bass parts that they specifically wanted. So I felt a lot less involved, and there was much less leeway in what I could contribute. They felt very specific about what they wanted in the drums and the bass. They also felt that the parts they had come up with were integral to the tunes. First they said, "Let's record the whole album with the drum machine and have you maybe put some parts on later." They felt that the drum machine itself was part of the compositions.

Smith admitted that "there was a lot of friction to start with, simply because of my resentment of their using a drum machine." Programming drums, Smith realized, was simply not as fulfilling as playing them.

But those were the intellectual, rational insights. The emotional side was still raw.

Modern Drummer: How did you feel about their wanting to put a drum machine on the album?

Steve Smith: I felt terrible about that.

***

17

Destination Emulation

1.

Tech guys usually don't get emotional. But Evan Brooks clearly is right now.

The cofounder of Pro Tools is remembering how he got his start in the music industry. Fresh out of college, Brooks and his partner Peter Gotcher oversaw a company that was profitable from day one. That's in part because of the revolutionary drum chips the duo created for the new drum machine called Drumulator. But it's also because E-MU Systems, the Santa Cruz-based electronics company that manufactured the Drumulator, did something few businesses today would consider.

"I have to tell you this because I don't know if a lot of people know it, and it's just extraordinary," says Brooks, from the dining room of his California home. His round glasses give him a John Lennon-esque appearance, and the eyes behind them are earnest. "E-MU not only gave us this order for chips, but they gave us their entire domestic dealer network, all of their international distributors, and then they gave us their actual warranty registration cards for every Drumulator they had sold.

"We left with a complete dealer network and distributor network and a 100 percent targeted list of potential customers," Brooks says. "And then E-MU gave us space in their trade show booths, and also space in their ads."

Brooks is still moved by the memory of that day in 1984. "They basically made it happen for us. This could not have happened without that kind of trust and generosity," he says. "I mean, granted, it was good for them, but could you imagine any company giving their warranty registration cards to anybody, much less a couple of kids?"

It's easy to forget this now, in an era of faceless multinational conglomerates, but most of the music tech industry once revolved around a small group of individuals in California. Some were ex-hippies, and others weren't. But for a short period of time, the competition that occurred between them all was—let's use the word "gentlemanly." And many of those relationships remain intact.

"We were competitors, but we were also friends," says Sequential Circuits founder Dave Smith. "We'd go to trade shows and hang out. And every time you'd go to a trade show, multiple people would have something new." Smith dates the start of this period to 1978, and the introduction of Sequential's Prophet-5, the first programmable polyphonic synthesizer. "But over the next four or five years," he says, "everything was just moving at lightspeed."

The size of the market, Smith also points out, was a factor. "Everybody forgets how tiny the industry was. There were only, like, 13,000 MiniMoogs sold. There were only 7,000 Prophet-5s sold. This is tiny compared to how big the market might be now, or compared to other sections of the music market," he says. "Behind the scenes, we might be aggressive—'Oh, the [Sequential] Drumtraks is much better than the DMX, or the LM-1.' But we didn't take it so seriously that we couldn't be cordial, or even friendly. We're all lifelong friends at this point."

The founders of E-MU Systems epitomized that friendly aesthetic. The company's business model was about finding ways to do more and charge less. The two products that put E-MU on the map in the 1980s were the perfect realization of this ethic.

2.

In 1983, the drum machine landscape was largely a battle between two titans: the LinnDrum and the Oberheim DMX. Then another game-changing device entered the market.

This machine managed to do something that had so far eluded other manufacturers. It offered sampled drum sounds while hitting the price point that Ikutaro Kakehashi had attempted for the Roland 808: less than a thousand dollars.

The E-MU Drumulator would soon be eclipsed by its successors, the SP-12 and the SP-1200. However, when it arrived, its combination of price and punch instantly positioned the Drumulator as a major player.

"Comparisons with the LinnDrum and Oberheim DMX are inevitable," a June 1983 review in *Electronics & Music Maker* acknowledged. "Although the Drumulator does not offer one hundred per cent of the features of these machines, it is much cheaper, simpler to use, and offers all the basic facilities of either."

The machine's principal designer is seated in an office littered with circuit boards. At age seventy-two, in plaid shirt and glasses, Dave Rossum still looks like the wise engineer who built E-MU into an electronic music powerhouse. But he came to his calling the long way around.

Rossum's chemist father disliked music. "He grew up raised by a single mother in Minneapolis. His mother told him she threw his father out of the house because he was a musician and a drunk," Rossum recalls. "And so Dad associated being a musician with being a drunk. And he didn't find out until he was in his sixties that she threw him out because he was two-timing my grandmother and had three children with another woman."

Both his grandsons would inherit his ability. Rossum's older brother was a guitarist who would probably have been a member of Jefferson Airplane if he hadn't been drafted during the Vietnam war. And Rossum himself was born with perfect pitch, and begged to take piano lessons as a boy. Yet he abandoned his musical dreams, attending the University of Santa Cruz to study molecular biology.

Then fate intervened. When he came to the lab one afternoon, Rossum found a note from his adviser, Harry Holier. He'd gone to the college's music department to help them unpack a new purchase: a Moog 12 synthesizer. "So I went over and helped them set it up. And by that evening, I was showing them how to use the Moog." Rossum laughs. "It's sort of like God taking you by the nose and saying, 'Here!'"

During the summer of 1971, Rossum and group of college friends constructed their own synthesizer. The students returned to school in the fall, but Rossum, his girlfriend Paula Butler, and a high school friend named Scott Wedge kept building. They constructed a synthesizer they dubbed the E-MU 25—after their drug of choice—and the next year, they formed a company called E-MU Systems.

The new company developed a polyphonic keyboard, and licensed the technology to Oberheim and Sequential Circuits. But in 1980, royalty disputes put E-MU on the ropes, and Rossum and Wedge had to innovate their way out of the predicament. The answer turned out to be the Emulator. This was a sampling keyboard that offered the functionality of the $35,000 Fairlight CMI for less than $8,000.

It was an immediate hit, Rossum says with some pride, not just for its cost, but for its simplicity. He realized that a similar set of cost-saving principles could be applied to drum machines, and he turned his sights on Roger Linn's LM-1.

Rossum knew the machine well: Linn had invited him to do a product review when the LM-1 was about to release. Rossum paid particular attention to the machine's companding digital-to-analog converters—"comdacs" for short—which compressed 12-bit dynamic range to an affordable 8 bits.

"I was astounded at how good those stupid comdacs actually sounded in the musical context," Rossum recalls. "Especially for drum sounds, where harmonic distortion isn't that much of a problem."

But Rossum had identified some possible shortcuts, based on his work with the Emulator. After the Emulator's release in 1981, he and engineer Terry Shultz holed up in a former dentist's office, located just around the corner from the Victorian house that was E-MU's headquarters.

"The brainstorm that created the Drumulator was that Roger's early instruments had separate EPROMs for each sound, separate digital to analog converters. That's what made the LM-1 cost $5,000," Rossum explains.

Saving money, he concluded, meant saving memory. "The trick was getting a single memory, a single digital to analog converter, a single CPU," he says. From a microprogramming class he'd taken in college, Rossum also realized he could "program a little tiny processor to run a program that would tell the machine how to loop these sounds. And that little 32-step program was the birth of the Drumulator."

The Drumulator's drum samples were sourced from Huey Lewis and the News drummer Bill Gibson. Gibson, however, "was surprised to discover that his 'playing' would consist of single hits of his drums. 'Those were some really strange recording sessions,'" Scott Wedge told author Greg Milner.

Rossum and Wedge successfully pared the machine's internal memory down to an economical five chips. Four of them stored the Drumulator's sounds, and the fifth chip contained a map of the system.

In early 1983, the E-MU Drumulator was introduced at the National Association of Music Merchants (NAMM) convention with a list price of $999. Rossum and Wedge had met with Roger Linn the week before to give him the news of their new drum machine. "So he wouldn't be surprised. Because he was a friend," explains Rossum. "And we weren't stealing any of his ideas."

Unlike machines such as the LM-1, the Drumulator didn't debut with any big-name endorsements. Instead, Rossum says, the focus was price: "Now there are affordable digital drums.'"

That was part of what sold Depeche Mode on the Drumulator, prior to making their third album, 1983's *Construction Time Again*. "The thing about the Drumulator was that it was substantially cheaper than the Linn," says engineer Gareth Jones, who joined the band when they began recording at John Foxx's studio, The Garden.

> That, and the separate outputs. Any individual character we were able to give the Drumulator came from the separate outputs, which was marvelous. You could send the hi-hat into the toilet, and the kick drum into an amp in the main room. And all at the same time, without the tedium of rolling the tape back and doing one track at a time.

The Drumulator had plenty of other new devotees. Two of them would help E-MU take drum machines a step further into the future.

3.

Like many musicians in the early 1980s, Evan Brooks and Peter Gotcher were tantalized by drum machines with digitally sampled sounds. When the under-a-thousand dollars Drumulator arrived. Gotcher immediately bought one. But after a couple of weeks, the novelty was gone.

"Peter came to me and said, 'Hey Ev, I'm really getting sick of these sounds. Can you put different ones in?' And I said, 'Sure!'" Brooks strokes his goatee and grins. "And I had no idea how to do it! That was the essence of our working relationship: he would challenge me, and I would have to rise to the challenge."

"So I called up E-MU, and said, 'How do you replace the sounds in your unit?'" The representative Brooks spoke with was friendly, but wary. There was a document available that explained how to change the Drumulator's EPROMs, Brooks was told. But no one who'd been given this information had ever done anything with it.

"And I said, 'You don't know me from Adam, but I promise you—cross my heart—that not only will I do something with it, but I will bring it back and show you.'"

So Gotcher and Brooks first recorded a selection of drum sounds, using the studio they'd built in a garage behind the medical office where Brooks's father worked. Then the pair pooled their money to buy an Emulator, to access the operating system it shared with the Drumulator. And then Brooks had to build his own computer *and* write software, to enable it "to take this data stream from the Emulator and format it into the way the chips needed to be for the Drumulator."

Brooks also bought an EPROM burner to make the chips, which had to be created in complete sets. "For the Drumulator you had to replace all the sounds wholesale," he says. "You couldn't just do one at a time."

It all paid off when the first set of chips were plugged into the Drumulator. "We popped 'em in there, and damn if it didn't work!" says Brooks, still marveling at the memory. "We made four different sets of chips: a couple of electronic drums and then some ethnic percussion."

In the fall of 1983, Brooks and Gotcher took their chips to E-MU. "They assembled the whole company in this room, and we demoed the chips that we had made, and jaws just dropped. The silence was deafening," Brooks recalls. "The sales guys finally said, 'You know how many more Drumulators we could sell if we could show this capability?' So they gave us an order for 20 sets of chips, right there and then. We weren't even thinking about making chips for anybody else. I was just coming good on a promise I had made to them."

The E-MU officials also turned over information about their domestic dealer network, international distributors, and warranty registration cards for all the Drumulators they'd sold. Brooks and Gotcher were amazed, but as Dave Rossum recalls it, the decision was fairly easy.

"I'm not sure it had a real big effect on sales. [The chips sets] were expensive, and esoteric. The percentage of Drumulators that got upgraded was probably less than 10 percent," says Rossum. "But from a business point of view, it was something that we weren't gonna do. So it was kind of a no-brainer."

The partnership with Digidrums also made sense on a deeper level for E-MU. Rossum and Wedge took seriously the way they'd been mentored in E-MU's early days by such industry titans as Bob Moog.

"Here were two very bright, and kind of crazy, kids coming in with an idea," Rossum says. "I have to say that Scott, maybe even more than me, appreciated the importance of those kinds of relationships, and how to foster them. If you talk to some people at E-MU, Scott drove some of them crazy. Because he would stick his nose in and offer advice. But it was all good-spirited. And the opposite side of that was that he really loved helping people get started."

The most popular set of Digidrums chips was not among those first four collections. But the next year, it took Digidrums, E-MU, and the Drumulator to the top of the charts.

The "Rock Drums 1" chips simulated live drums with ambience. It was a sound descended from the legendarily huge kit of Led Zeppelin's John Bonham. Many listeners and users are convinced that the drums are samples of Bonham's kit from the opening of the song "When the Levee Breaks," in fact. Evan Brooks says he simply can't remember where those sounds came from. "I think we got things from various and different sources," he says.

What Brooks will say is that on the Rock Drums chips, he and Gotcher focused on creating fewer sounds of longer duration. "So even though they were gated, they were still allowed to develop and to get big," Brooks says, "and we had room to let them decay properly."

The massive, metallic snare drum became a staple of pop, rock, and hip hop. Scotland's Cocteau Twins were one of the groups who fell for it the hardest. The Rock Drums chips supplied crushing beats beneath the ethereal textures of 1984's *Treasure*. And guitarist Robin Guthrie prizes those chips to this day.

"I'm going into the drawer by my mixing desk," says Guthrie from his Paris headquarters, rustling audibly for a moment, "and I have in my hand now all the Rock chips from the Drumulator." He laughs, then turns wistful. "I don't actually own a Drumulator any more. But I'd like to borrow one for an afternoon." Meanwhile, in London, singer-songwriter Howard Jones made the Drumulator the core of his live sets during this time.

Across the Atlantic, a group of abrasive Jewish rappers from New York and their long-haired, metal-loving producer used the Drumulator and Rock Drums to begin nailing down their signature sound. On the 1984 Beastie Boys song "Beastie Groove," Rick Rubin played up the chips' Zeppelinesque big beats. The song, the B-side of the similarly stomping "Rock Hard," created a template the trio and Rubin would take to the top of the charts three years later with *Licensed to Ill*.

But the most famous appearance of the Rock Drums chips also occurred in 1984, on the song "Shout." Written by Tears for Fears singer Roland Orzabal, "Shout" was clearly special from the outset. Yet it took a marriage of two drum machines to bring it to fruition.

Producer Chris Merrick Hughes remembers hearing about the song from keyboardist Ian Stanley. "He said, 'I was at Roland's at the weekend. He's working on this new piece. Tell him to play it for you.'" When Hughes asked to hear the song, Orzabal played a rattling percussion pattern on his LinnDrum. "It was absolutely transfixing," Hughes remembers.

Yet Hughes could hear that there was a rock anthem in "Shout" waiting to emerge. "Within a day or two, I got my Drumulator—yes, it had the 'When the

Levee Breaks' drum samples in it," says Hughes. "Then we put the two rhythm boxes together and said, 'Yep. That'll do!'" (Actually, it didn't: Hughes later added live drums to the track. He explains, "It just had to escalate.")

"Shout" escalated into a Number 1 hit in several countries, including the United States. Its ubiquity is probably what led Peter Gotcher to say, years later, that "every Tears for Fears and Howard Jones song" used the Rock Drums sound. He joked, "Sometimes you feel like you've unleashed something into the world that you shouldn't have."

Gotcher may have been overstating the case, but the sounds he and Brooks created did spread quickly. "Pretty soon the other drum machine companies started coming to us and saying, 'Hey! We want replaceable sounds for our machines, too,'" Brooks remembers.

As Digidrums sounds became more popular, Brooks says, the irony was that he and Gotcher "ended up really not using drum machines in our own personal work after that." He admits that he, too, got burned out by programmed rhythms. "Roger Linn has a great saying: 'We make the music that our instruments want us to make,'" Brooks says. "And that's really, really true with drum machines."

4.

At the same time Dave Rossum and Scott Wedge were working on the Drumulator, they were also developing an upgraded version of the Emulator. The Emulator II, which debuted in 1984, was a sampling keyboard that offered polyphonic sampling and eight simultaneous voices. It was a further upgrade on the Fairlight CMI.

However, it's worth considering the Fairlight as perhaps the ultimate "drum machine that wasn't." While, as author Greg Milner points out, the Fairlight "never really caught on in the United States," and "was mostly a synthesizer with a bit of sampler thrown in," the number of records which sourced their drum sounds from a Fairlight is probably much higher than we realize.

To cite just one famous example, in 1983, producer Mutt Lange and engineer Mike Shipley used the Fairlight to create the drum sounds on Def Leppard's multiplatinum *Pyromania*. A year before a car accident that cost drummer Rick Allen his arm, and forced him to begin using a custom electronic kit, Lange and Shipley were already creating one of the first metal albums where the percussion was, in essence, provided by a drum machine.

"There are no real drums. The cymbals are played, but the bass drum, snare, and toms are all machine," recalled Shipley, who passed away in 2013. "We had all kinds of drums in there, and I sampled them into the Fairlight and detuned them … It was pretty unnatural, but that was kind of the point."

The Fairlight had been developed in Australia in the mid-1970s by a pair of friends, Kim Ryrie and Peter Vogel. The duo were trying to create a hybrid synthesizer, using analog oscillators controlled by digital circuitry.

The experiment did not succeed. While Rylie and Vogel were working Down Under, an American company, New England Digital, released a machine called the Synclavier. It arrived in 1978 as the first all-digital synthesizer, and was widely praised for the quality of its synthesized sounds. Rylie and Vogel, who had been struggling to create realistic synthesized sounds, needed another angle. They found one through digital sampling.

Just as Roland Electronics and Roger Linn had created two paths for drum machines—one based on sound synthesis, the other based on sound samples—so the Fairlight and the Synclavier diverged. The Synclavier was a high-end synthesizer that didn't add a sampler until 1982, when the company felt it could offer high enough sound quality. The Fairlight, although it had a keyboard, was significant from the beginning because of its sampling capability.

The Fairlight's sampling rate "was very low, and if you wanted a sound more than one second long, the rate was even lower. Since the samples were only 8 bits long, the sounds were very crude," Greg Milner notes. But Linn, Oberheim, and E-MU had shown that crunchy 8-bit samples could create satisfying drum sounds. So the Fairlight made sense as a surrogate drum machine.

Sometimes, the Fairlight was overkill. In 1984, a Norwegian pop trio called a-ha was struggling to record a promising song called "Take on Me." They were working with British producer Tony Mansfield, who had overseen a Top 10 cover of "Always Something There to Remind Me" for synth-pop duo Naked Eyes.

"Tony used a Fairlight for most of the drum sounds," recalls guitarist and programmer Paul Waaktaar-Savoy. "It was a bit frustrating because we didn't know how to use one, so everything would go through him. It sounded more lumpy and less joyful … just repetitive."

The band's label, Warner Brothers, believed in the song, and gave a-ha a chance to re-record it with producer Alan Tarney. This time, Waaktaar-Savoy did the LinnDrum programming. "I've never seen anyone as good as him at programming a Linn," Tarney said later.

Waaktaar-Savoy's secret was "imagining I'd be sitting behind a drum kit going for a great take, rarely repeating a pattern, and not putting in things that couldn't be achieved with two hands and two feet. It was all about finding the right feel, making sure any fills or flourish wouldn't stop the groove, but only add to the excitement."

For others, however, the Fairlight was heaven-sent. Boris Blank, Dieter Meier, and Carlos Perón were a Swiss electronic group whose first two albums as Yello had been modestly successful. Then Blank heard about the Fairlight, and felt he had to act. The problem was the price tag.

Luckily, he knew someone who could help: the wealthy banker father of Meier, the group's vocalist. But Blank had to make the pitch himself. It was a little intimidating at first, Blank admits, as he jokingly imitates Mr. Meier's deep, growling voice. "I managed to convince Mr. Meier," Blank says, "that the music we're making will be successful someday."

Meier's father loaned the group 250,000 Swiss francs, the price of a Fairlight and a mixing desk. His bet ultimately paid off. After a transitional album, 1983's *You Gotta Say Yes to Another Excess*, where the LinnDrum provided most of the percussion, Blank dove full-on into sampling with his new Fairlight.

"That was like Christmas, birthday, marriage, all together," Blank jokes. "Because I could just sample *anything*!" He launches into some enthusiastic demonstrations. "I could smash a snowball into a wall. Transpose it three octaves down, and cut it left and right, and then have a proper attack at the beginning. And you have the best bass drum in the world, made out of a snowball!"

The resultant album, 1985's *Stella*, was the group's first release after the departure of Perón. It became an international hit, thanks to the single "Oh Yeah," which appeared in the film *Ferris Bueller's Day Off*.

The proceeds helped Yello pay back Dieter Meier's father. But for Blank, the truly priceless investment was in sound creation. "I'm a hunter and collector. I collect a lot," explains Blank, who still owns his Fairlight and the massive libraries of sounds he's created. "You can get deep into the molecular structure of a sound and play God with it! With the Fairlight, I had the world to make my own."

That same thought, expressed as a song called "The World Is My Oyster," leads off Frankie Goes to Hollywood's *Welcome to the Pleasuredome*, a 1984 album that's certainly one of the most famous examples of Fairlight technology. The team who created it—and a number of other landmark albums—built a musical pleasuredome that endured long after the groups who inhabited it went extinct.

5.

If you made a list of milestone recordings in 1980s music technology, a common denominator would be the names of programmer J. J. Jeczalik and engineer Gary Langan. ABC's *The Lexicon of Love*. Malcolm McClaren's *Duck Rock*. The Art of Noise's *Into Battle with the Art of Noise* and *(Who's Afraid of) The Art of Noise*. And, of course, Frankie Goes to Hollywood's 1984 debut LP, *Welcome to the Pleasuredome*.

Jeczalik and Langan are also exceptionally funny, especially when they're together. Langan is the chain-smoking straight man, while Jeczalik's perpetually puckish grin makes him boyish, despite his grey hair. Their repartee, as they describe the pains of being on the front lines of electronic music in the 1980s, has an Abbot and Costello-style charm.

J. J.:	It was all a mess. An absolute mess.
Gary:	It was hell, looking back on it. Absolute hell.
J. J.:	There were no manuals back then, you know.
Gary:	Well, there *were* manuals. But they were like the manuals for a 747. [He leans back on the couch and covers his eyes.] You couldn't actually *read* them. All those wasted hours, waiting and waiting for things to sync up. There has to be a payback somewhere, J. J., for all those hours you and I spent.
J. J.:	It would be all right until you got to the third chorus, and then everyone would look at each other and say, "It's not in sync, is it?"
Gary:	We were like alchemists. [He groans.] It's awful just sitting here talking about it.
The Author:	I don't want to pick at a scab—
Gary:	Well, you are!
J. J.:	It's not a scab. [He smiles.] It's a wound.

* * *

The other common link between Langan, Jeczalik, and all those albums above is producer Trevor Horn. Horn's drum programming philosophy was central to the way they all sounded—and to the way records sounded throughout the 1980s.

"Trevor was always looking for the perfect drum track. For him, the bass drum and snare was the essence of everything. That was the strong foundation on which you could build," recalls Jeczailk. "Early on, I remember him going on about that, the importance of locking everything down."

Horn had developed this idea while living with the singer Tina Charles. One night, she brought home the backing track to "I Love to Love," which became a hit for her in 1976. "I'd never heard a backing track before done by a hit producer," Horn said. "It was dead simple, there wasn't a spare thing on it. I must have listened to that about 30 times."

The next year, Horn made himself a makeshift drum machine on a twenty-four-track tape. "I recorded everything separately, just a very basic beat—eighths on the hi-hat, off beat on the snare, four on the floor, done to a metronome with a very grumbly drummer who I had to pay over the odds to do it," he said. "And then you could make a drum track by speeding it up or slowing it down to your tempo, and then editing it."

As Langan recalls it, Horn wanted to apply his ideas to a drummer in the studio. "Trevor had this notion that to make big-sounding records, every beat had to be completely locked in. And so before we got LinnDrums, the thing with Trevor was to make drummers play like what was going to become a drum machine."

But there was a reason for this precision, Jeczailk notes. "When you've got that uniformity, you create vast amounts of space. Whereas if you've got something flim-flamming around, you have no space to fill. You have no choice."

"Drum machines have a defined start and end time," Langan adds. "Every sound has a mathematical start and end. In the 1980s, we discovered mathematics."

***

The Author: Did you ever own a drum machine?
Gary: Why, Dan, why? After they gave me so much shit in the studio, why would I want one in the bloody house?
It would be like having your worst aunt come stay. You've gone over and had tea with her, and she's come back home with you!

***

Although limited by its sampling time and rate, the Fairlight CMI could create precise beats and fill the spaces they created. Jeczalik's former boss, Richard

James Burgess, had been one of the first people in England to use the machine, on Kate Bush's 1980 album *Never For Ever*. Burgess had also convinced Jeczalik that the future lay in technology. He recommended that his roadie lean to type, and convinced him to read the 1979 book *The Mighty Micro: The Impact of the Micro-Chip Revolution*, by Christopher Evans.

"It blew my mind. I still have it somewhere," Jeczalik says. "He was making all these predictions, all of which turned out to be wildly inaccurate by a power of about a hundred. Because things happened so much faster than he predicted."

So Jeczalik took over Fairlight programming duties on *The Lexicon of Love*, as well as Malcolm McClaren's mashup of hip hop and Appalachian music, *Duck Rock*. "When I was jobbing on the Fairlight, people just thought you plugged it in, and off you went. But what Gary and I did, I suppose, was developed a sort of rulebook," says Jeczalik. "And that gave you a fighting chance to get everything to work. But if you took that model somewhere else, you ran up against a situation where people had no clue whatsoever."

***

J. J.: A pivotal moment for me was a session with Paul McCartney. We sampled a trombone with the Fairlight, which I think I did pretty successfully. And he played this massive chord with it, and he said, "Well, it doesn't sound much like a horn section." And I said, "You're right. It sounds a bit like a Hoover. But that's because it's not a horn section." And I suddenly realized, well, there's no point putting musical instruments into this thing. Because it's crap.

Gary: Input didn't meet output with the Fairlight, did it?

J. J.: But once you realized that the magic was the stuff that you didn't know and couldn't predict, that became the whole thing.

Gary: We like it when things go wrong, don't we, J. J.? When you've got a drum machine that goes rogue, we're in our element. [He laughs.] That's why we stuck with the Fairlight for so long. It had a great error factor to it.

***

There may be no better example of a Fairlight-created happy accident than the one that happened one afternoon in 1983, at London's AIR Studios. It created multiple hit records, and a brand-new group. It also ties together many of the drum programming and recording philosophies of the 1980s.

"What you used to use to gauge the brilliance of your engineering at this time was how good your drums sounded," Gary Langan explains. "And my nemesis was a guy named Hugh Padgham." Padgham, as we saw in Chapter 9, had developed a gated drum sound for Phil Collins that revolutionized the industry. Padgham had also worked with Trevor Horn in the early days of his career, and a sort of rivalry had developed between him and Langan.

"Hugh had done 'In the Air Tonight' with Phil Collins. And I went and got a copy and played it in the control room. And it just sounded awesome." Langan laughs as he admits his jealousy. "I was *sick* when I heard it. Sick as a dog."

Not long afterward, Langan was engineering a session at AIR Studios for Yes, whom Horn was producing. "They spent a whole day cutting this track, and then realizing that they didn't actually have a song to go with it—it was just basically drums and some guitar noodles," Langan recalls. "However, the drums sounded like bloody cannons.

"And Trevor said, 'Well, we're going to scrap this. It's not going anywhere.' So I was supposed to erase the multitrack. But I didn't." Langan grins slyly. "I *stole* the multitrack, and hid it amongst the others. And then one afternoon, Trevor and the band buggered off. And I got the multitrack out, and I said to J. J., 'We're going to put these drums into the Fairlight.' And that's how it started. And the rest, as they say, is history."

The mistake occurred when Jeczalik sampled the wrong segment of Alan White's massive-sounding drums. Instead of starting the loop on the first beat, he began it on the third beat, instead. "I had no idea it was starting in the wrong place," he says.

"Which was genius," Langan counters.

Jeczalik rolls his eyes. "Absolute genius. Which is why we spent the next two hours trying to get it to loop. So it was a fight, straightaway. It was a bit slow, a bit fast. Trim a bit off the front, trim a bit off the back. There was no notion that it was *anything*."

But eventually, those sampled, looped drums turned into a song—"Beat Box"—and a new musical project called The Art of Noise. Langan and Jeczalik were joined by composer and keyboardist Anne Dudley, who had done string arrangements on ABC's *The Lexicon of Love*. For a while, they were also joined by Trevor Horn himself.

Horn and Langan were in the car together one afternoon when Horn confessed that he missed being in a band. Langan decided the moment was right to make a confession of his own. He played Horn a cassette that included Alan White's sampled drums.

"When I played him that cassette, he had not a clue what he was listening to. And that's when I had to fess up about what J. J. and I had done." Langan pauses and grins. "He went a bit silent on me."

However, Horn was intrigued enough to eventually join forces with The Art of Noise, bringing in journalist Paul Morley as a nonmusical member. This would lead to tensions that caused Horn and Morley to depart after just one album. But the relationship among the core trio would continue for three more LPs and several significant hits, including covers of "Peter Gunn" and Prince's "Kiss."

Jeczalik explains, "The way we post-rationalized it was that you had Gary doing the sonics. You had me sampling things the wrong way round. And you had Anne's musical ability to pull it all together. It never would have worked any other way."

Before the split, Horn and Morley, along with Horn's wife, Jill Sinclair, formed a label called Zang Tumb Tuum—or ZTT for short. It boasted several notable acts, including Grace Jones, The Art of Noise, and the German synthpop group Propaganda. But the Liverpool quintet Frankie Goes to Hollywood would take the label's philosophies and technologies to their absolute limits.

***

Some songs that define their eras arrive fully formed and perfectly realized. "Relax," by Frankie Goes to Hollywood, was not one of those songs.

A worldwide Number 1 single in 1984, "Relax" generated equal amounts of record sales, related merchandise (including the well-known "Frankie Say" T-shirts), and infamy over its homoerotic lyrics and video. But the song had a tortured birth. Two versions were recorded and scrapped, the second using musicians from Ian Dury's Blockheads. Horn kept trying to simplify the sound, at one point instructing Blockheads bassist Norman Watt-Roy to pare his riff down to a single E note. Nothing had worked.

The answer turned out to be a combination of the Fairlight and Horn's LinnDrum. "Trevor was ace on the drum machine because he was a bass player. And he knew what to play on the drum machine to make him sound even better," notes Gary Langan. "His drum programming was always exemplary."

But even Horn wondered if the pattern he had in mind was too simple. "It was like my pet drum pattern which I fiddled about with," he said. "I thought it was more like an English square dance than anything else, but when I saw the effect that this had on the guys in the band, I realized that it was probably going to be a very good dance record."

Other than vocal contributions from lead singer Holly Johnson and backing vocalist Paul Rutherford, the other three members of the group didn't appear on the track. It was put together instead by Horn, keyboardist Andy Richards, J. J. Jeczalik on Fairlight, and an engineer and guitarist named Stephen Lipson.

Version three of "Relax" was being recorded when Lipson joined up, but even that was going badly. "It was rubbish, really," he recalls. "We spent ages on it, and then Trevor came in one night and said, 'Let's try this.' And he played the rhythm he had on the LinnDrum.

"By that time, he knew I could play guitar, and I played a bit for the middle eight. Andy was in the room. And J. J. It was the four of us. And we just did it. It happened really quickly."

The tool that allowed Horn's LinnDrum to link up with the Fairlight CMI II that Jeczalik was using was called Page R, the "Real Time Composer." While sampling capability was the Fairlight's calling card, Page R might have been its true innovation.

Page R was a sequencer that stored data from songs and digital instruments. It had a primitive visual interface—via the Fairlight's computer screen—where users could see information like drum patterns and song data. It was a descendant of the computer-based drum machines that Roger Nichols and Roger Linn had created, and the forerunner of just about every digital workstation and computer-based recording program used today.

The interface was made possible through a circuit board known as the Conductor. Manufactured by a company called Syco Research, the Conductor was first discovered by Horn at the end of the sessions for Yes's *90125*. The ability to lock the LinnDrum to the Fairlight via Page R, Horn later recalled, was "breathtaking."

It would be Lipson, not Horn, who went on to produce the next, and final, Frankie Goes to Hollywood album, 1986's *Liverpool*. Lipson also oversaw Propaganda's acclaimed debut, *A Secret Wish*. While working with Horn, Lipson had learned how to program the Synclavier, and it was that device that featured heavily on *A Secret Wish*.

"The Synclavier just sounded better than the Fairlight," says Lipson. That's not to say he enjoyed the experience of working with it. "It was like programming a computer. It's terrifying, really," he says. "Whatever anyone might tell you about the Synclavier, it was not fun. You didn't get inspired with the Synclavier. It was a lot of input."

Gary Langan agrees. "The Synclavier was something very precious. It wasn't very robust. If you tried to push it, it wasn't your friend. There wasn't any grit or energy in it. For me, the Fairlight was rock 'n' roll."

***

Gary: I think we knew this technology was going to go somewhere. But to actually relive those days—no thank you.
 Youngsters don't have to explore. J. J. and I were always pushing things to their breaking point. Nobody does that anymore. They have it put before them on a platter.
J. J.: And that's the trouble with the youth of today. [He grins.]
Gary: We're just two grumpy old men, J. J.

***

18

Mr. K's Last Laugh

1.

He looked just like any other student.

Skinny, angular, and bespectacled, the new journalism major was dwarfed by the buildings of Northwestern University and the Chicago skyline. As he walked from class to class, this slight figure bobbed and weaved to the sounds pumping into his headphones. In the Walkman Age of the early 1980s, it was a perfectly unremarkable sight.

But the *sounds* passing through those earpieces were remarkable indeed. There was nothing but drums—programmed drums, harsh, mechanical, and loud. They were coming from a battery-operated Roland TR-606 drum machine the thin young man carried in a vinyl case slung over one shoulder.

"I was captivated by it," recalls Steve Albini. "I would listen to the rhythms as though they were a complete piece of music. I wore that drum machine like an accessory, with headphones, and I would just walk around campus. I would spend all day, editing and manipulating a drum pattern until it was satisfying to listen to on its own."

Almost exactly forty years later, Albini is seated in the control room of Electrical Audio, the Chicago studio complex he owns. He's filled out a little since those college days, and the hair beneath his woolen skullcap is now graying. The past four decades have been crammed with noteworthy musical accomplishments. But it all really started with those campus drum machine adventures.

Albini will always be, for casual listeners, "the guy who produced Nirvana"—specifically, the band's 1993 album *In Utero*, released the year before frontman Kurt Cobain's suicide. But that was only one of thousands of records Albini has overseen, engineered, or recorded during his career. And of all those projects,

Big Black—the band Albini started with his drum machine—may well have had the most lasting influence.

The rhythms Albini scrupulously reworked on his walks around Northwestern became the basis for the first Big Black songs. Those songs, in turn, became a seedbed for American industrial music. In a broader sense, they also engineered what you might call a Midwestern resurrection.

In the early 1980s, it seemed the Roland Corporation had been decisively defeated by its drum machine peers. Then a new generation of musicians took its abandoned devices and used them to create entirely new styles of music. "Irony" barely captures this fact: as the US factories of the heartland were being hollowed out by foreign competitors, an untutored group of young American creators used a failed line of Japanese machines to create industrial music, house, and techno—and to pursue great innovations in hip hop as well.

An iconoclast famous—and sometimes infamous—for his uncompromising stances about music and how it's made, Steve Albini had strong ideas about drum machines from the start. "Even at the time, there had started to develop a string of cliches about the drum machine. And even at that stage, I could recognize them as cliches, and I was desperate to avoid those cliches," he says.

"The end result would be that you'd get to the bit where the drummer was supposed to play a fill, and there would be some crudely programmed drum fill. The kind of fill that a proper drummer would hang his head in shame over," adds Albini. He grimaces. "Those things, I thought, were just sinful misapplications of the technology—having the drum machine mimic a human drummer as a kind of labor-saving device.

"So I always tried to make some distinction between what I was hearing from moment to moment versus what I had heard the rest of the previous twenty years of my life. I always wanted what I was working on to be different from what I had heard previously."

Though perseverance, anger, and sometimes just plain luck, Big Black—and the other artists in this chapter—managed to assemble rhythms exactly as Albini describes.

2.

Albini's bandmate in Big Black, guitarist Santiago Durango, once described the group's 1982 debut, *Lungs*, as "completely unlistenable. That's one of its saving graces—that it's probably the worst piece ever put together by a human mind. It's horrible. But it's so horrible that there's something there. It transcends horrible."

Based on that review, you might expect a din of distortion and broke-backed rhythm. Instead, *Lungs*—essentially recorded solo by Albini on a four-track—is atonal but well-organized, given a surprisingly professional sheen by the Roland TR-606.

Durango and bassist Jeff Pezzati, both members of the Chicago band Naked Raygun, soon joined Albini to make Big Black a trio. But in truth, the group was always a quartet. The TR-606—christened "Roland"—was the fourth member.

Albini had bought the TR-606 Drumatix, which Roland debuted in 1981, brand new at a Chicago guitar shop. "The 606 didn't have a particularly large song memory," says Albini. "I think it only held four or five songs." So the group had to find ways to make the most of that limited memory over the course of a concert.

"For some of the songs, we were just using a single pattern for the duration of the song," Albini remembers. Another trick was to lower the tempo. "If you had a pattern that was four bars long and you lowered the tempo by a quarter, suddenly you'd have a 16-bar pattern to work with," he says. "Which would often be enough for you to build a complete verse-chorus structure."

By the time of 1984's *Racer-X* EP, the Roland 606 had been replaced by the E-MU Drumulator. The machine inherited the name Roland. More importantly, it remained an equal member of Big Black.

"I remember when we were working on *Songs About Fucking* with John Loder in London. He was mocking the sound quality of the samples in the machine, and I sort of jokingly defended Roland as though he was my friend. Like, *C'mon, man. That's just what he sounds like. Get off him!*" Albini laughs at the memory, but his loyalty was serious. When Loder suggested using the AMS Digital Delay to sample other drum sounds, "we weren't interested, really."

"I was really into the idea that this drum machine was a band member, and we respected him. And we were just going to let him do what he wanted to do." Albini pauses and smiles. "To the extent that he did exactly what we told him to do, of course."

3.

The Roland 606 was a favorite machine of several bands besides Big Black, including British synthpop acts A Flock of Seagulls and Orchestral Manoeuvrers in the Dark. But the other group who imbued it with an actual personality was the Leeds goth outfit Sisters of Mercy.

Like Big Black, the Sisters had a single name for a succession of drum machines. They were all called Doktor Avalanche, and the machines eventually even got their own minder: technician Dave "Ravey Davey" Creffield.

The Doktor who joined the fledgling group in 1980 was a humble Boss DR-55 Dr. Rhythm. In its second incarnation, it was a Roland TR-606 for a couple of years, before transitioning to a Roland TR-808, an Oberheim DMX, and then an Akai S900 sampler, by the time of 1988's *Floodland* album.

Whatever his brand and specs, Doktor Avalanche became an even more famous descendant of Kingdom Come's "Ace Bentley," and gave the Sisters some of their undeniable mystique. But frontman Andrew Eldritch, who began his career as the group's drummer and later became its deep-voiced singer, once revealed how accidental the whole thing had been.

"Because I can't drum and sing at the same time, we bought a machine," Eldritch reflected. "Had we been able to buy a machine to do the singing, it might have turned out different."

4.

The budget-priced TR-606 had its fans—especially when paired with its companion piece, the Roland "Transistor Bass" TB-303 bass synthesizer. But following the failure of the 808, Roland engineers were determined to take another swing at the top end of the drum machine market. The next installment of the Mid-O Series, the TR-909, became one of Roland's most high-pressure projects.

Engineer Tadao Kikumoto had discovered a technique called "down chirp oscillation" that he thought would be perfect for the project. In simple terms, down chirp oscillation means a signal that quickly, but smoothly, transitions from high to low frequencies.

"I thought the technique could synthesize not only realistic drums, but also idealistic sounds which would allow the user to transcend realism," Kikumoto explains. The drum sound he felt might benefit the most from this technique was the one he thought was most important: the bass drum. As Kikumoto had already observed, the bass drum has complex harmonic activity in the beginning, or attack, part of its signal. But it rapidly tails off into lower frequencies.

Still dreaming of creating a genuine drum synthesizer, Kikumoto persuaded his boss, Ikutaro Kakehashi, to adopt down chirp oscillation as the basis for the new drum machine. But it took some convincing. Kakehasi had seen the success of drum machines with sampled drum sounds, like the LinnDrum and Oberheim DMX, and he hoped Roland would adopt PCM sampling for this new project.

Sampled sounds ultimately did end up as part of the 909, because time was once again working against Kikumoto and his Mid-O team. The challenge of creating the metallic cymbals, in particular, was so great that Kakehashi advised the engineers to sample those sounds, to avoid further delays.

Engineer Atushi Hoshiai—who Kikutaro notes is the "last legendary engineer of the Mid-O Series" still employed by Roland—came up with the solution. He used low-cost 6-bit memory chips for the cymbal sounds.

"The technique was smart to reduce the cost of expensive digital memory," admits Kikumoto. This decision looked even smarter when Roland adopted the technique for its next drum machines in 1984: the TR-707, and the TR-727, a companion device which featured Latin percussion.

By that point, however, the TR-909 was effectively dead. Rushed to market in 1983, it was officially discontinued just two years later. The fact that it was the first MIDI drum machine, as well as the field's first true analog and digital hybrid, had not given it an edge on its competitors. Neither had its drum sounds, more powerful and punchier than the 808's. Not even its "shuffle" and "flam" features, which gave the programmed rhythms a note of realism, were enough to sway buyers. Once again, comparisons with the digital drum samples of other drum machines were unavoidable—and largely unfavorable. As with the TR-808, it was easier to focus on what the TR-909 was not.

What it *was*, in the eyes of Tadao Kikumoto, "was another failure, expensive and less realistic compared to many PCM drum machines." It was also a personal loss for Kikumoto, who had nurtured for half a decade the dream of a true drum synthesizer. Now the Mid-O staff was reassigned. The wave of the future clearly was digital sampling. Analog technology appeared officially dead.

"Mr. K never complained about my decision and failure," reflects Kikumoto. "Mr. K believed in my technical vision and philosophy of scientific approach, I supposed." The proof of this was that "the various studies of drum sounds I had worked on with Mid-O had become [the] basis of the fundamental R&D for the next digital generation."

That must have been cold comfort in 1985. But though just 22,000 TR-808s and 909s had reached the world, they were beginning to mutate the musical landscape.

5.

The Roland 808 had already carved out a significant role in pop music. As "The King," drum programmer Jimmy Bralower, observed, it functioned best in genres where realistic sounds weren't the objective. That explains the perfect marriage of hip hop and the 808 bass drum.

As Tadao Kikumoto recognized, the bass drum was the cornerstone of the TR-808. And the decay function he'd insisted upon, when applied to the 808 kick drum, became the instrument's signature: a woofer-rattling thud that is now one of music's most recognizable sounds.

The artist who usually gets credit for this innovation is Rick Rubin. On the 1984 T La Rock single "It's Yours," Rubin opened the decay on the 808 he kept in his dorm room at New York University, accentuating the bass drum's low frequencies. The single was the first release on Def Jam Records, the label that would come to define hip hop.

"If you don't have it, it's not authentic," producer Hank Shocklee said of this sound, in the documentary *808*. The kick drum from "It's Yours," sampled and processed, became a key ingredient of Public Enemy's in-your-face bouillabaisse. Shocklee spoke for many when he insisted, "It's not hip-hop without that sound."

Yet ownership of that sound kick drum is contested. In that same year of 1984, Brooklyn-born artist and producer Steve Standard released an electro single called "Set It Off" under the name Strafe. It was overseen by famed disco producer Walter Gibbons, who'd become a devout Christian. Two years later, however, Standard said he'd intended the 808 bass drum to feature that deep decay. But Gibbons, he claimed, dialed back those frequencies, fearing them an instrument of Satan. "I was ashamed of the mix," Standard said.

For further insight into that iconic 808 bass drum sound, it's also worth listening to a hip hop record recorded in 1985. The artist was a rapper named Tricky Tee. And the label was Sleeping Bag Records, a New York imprint founded by another disco innovator, Arthur Russell.

On "Leave it to the Drums," the 808 kick drum had the longest decay heard to date, fading out over almost a full bar. The cowriter and producer was a Big Apple teenager named Sam Citrin, whose stage name was Sam Sever.

"The 808 on that song is ringing like a motherfucker," Sever says. "For a long time, people would tell me 'That's the 808 sound I used on all my records.'"

At the time, Sever shared an apartment above Sleeping Bag Records with his "big brother and mentor," Kurtis Mantronik. The Jamaican-born Mantronik was an A&R man for Sleeping Bag. He was also an artist: recording as Mantronix, he cracked the dance charts in 1985 with his debut "Fresh Is the Word."

In their apartment studio, Mantronik and Sever experimented with the 808 and Roland 909. One of their favorite pastimes was seeing how far they could push the 808 kick drum's decay. "Back then when you opened up the decay," Sever says, "most engineers would go, 'No, man, that's too much! You're gonna blow the speakers!' And Kurtis and me would go, 'Nah, that's the shit, bro!'"

"Point being, we were doing that shit on tapes and things that were going around. The Beastie Boys were friends of mine, but I think those dudes caught wind of what we were doing. Then they started opening up the decay," adds Sever. "I'm not arrogant. I'm not gonna say me and Kurtis were the first to open up that decay. But we were definitely doing it very, very early."

6.

If there's a drum machine that defines the genre of techno, which set the industrial rhythms of Detroit to music during the 1980s, it's the Roland TR-909. And if there's an artist who can claim to be techno's true godfather, it's Juan Atkins.

Atkins is the oldest of the Belleville Three, the trio of producers who created techno and put Detroit at the center of an international phenomenon. He was also the first one to record: in the duo Cybotron, with his partner Rick Davis, Atkins released futuristic electro tracks that used the Roland TR-808. National success eluded the group, but Atkins became, as he matter-of-factly states, "a local superstar," one whose steadying influence was suggested by his *Star Wars*-inspired nickname: "Obi Juan."

When the Roland TR-909 hit the market in 1983, Atkins and Davis were among the first buyers. "We came across the 909 the same way we came across the 808: we knew it was coming," Atkins recalls. "The 909 was the next step."

There was just one catch: Atkins *hated* the machine on first listen. "I didn't like the bass drum sound, compared to the 808," he says. "It sounded clunky, you know?" Atkins disliked it so much, in fact, that he ended up returning the

909 to the music shop where he bought it, trading it in for a Sequential Circuits Drumtraks.

That might sound like heresy to those who find the 909, techno, and Atkins almost interchangeable terms. But it took a credit card scam to reintroduce Atkins to techno's signature machine.

Derrick May was the second member of the Belleville Three. The group got its name because May, Atkins, and the third member, Kevin Saunderson, were all living in Belleville, a suburb 25 miles southwest of the city.

A few months younger than Atkins, May bounced back and forth between Chicago and Belleville, and sometimes stayed with Atkins and his grandmother. The two friends encouraged one another's musical experiments, and shared dreams of owning their own labels someday. Then May came to Atkins with a dilemma.

"Derrick didn't have money to pay his rent. He needed to find something to sell to get rent money," says Atkins. "At the time, these guys were using a credit card scam to order equipment. So Derrick must have ordered about eight or nine TR-909 drum machines, on other people's credit cards.

"That's basically what made me get back to the 909. These guys needed somebody to help them learn how to use this gear. They'd bring the stuff over to me and let me work with it for a while."

Atkins, May, and Saunderson already understood the power of drum machines. Deep Space was the name of the label Atkins had set up to distribute his own electronic work with Cybotron. It was also the name of a DJ collective that included the Belleville Three. The trio were trying to break into the heavily competitive "social club" scene in Detroit, where trend-conscious, middle class black teens demanded a soundtrack of disco and new wave instead of funk.

But Deep Space were outsiders from the suburbs, and their DJ company was only getting jobs no one else wanted. "We were in competition with this other company, Direct Drive. They were like the Empire," Atkins says, referring to the villains of *Star Wars*. "They had the whole thing wrapped up, and we were the new kids on the block."

So one night in 1982, during a battle with Direct Drive in the basement of Detroit's Saint Andrews Hall, Deep Space unveiled their secret weapon. "Which was the TR-808," Atkins says. "We used it to play rhythm tracks in between songs. And of course, people went crazy. And of course, all the other DJs in the city wanted to get drum machines."

Kevin Sanderson points out that those DJ gigs with the 808 contained the raw ideas of the music that would become techno. "It got a little boring after a while with no music, so you'd mix a track back in," Saunderson says. "But that really helped us. Because you'd be saying, 'I've got these hot rhythms. Now what else can I add to this?' That really led us to taking the next step and making our own music."

But Atkins knew Deep Space's drum machine edge was worth protecting. So later, when May was looking to unload his surplus 909s, Atkins issued a stern warning. One of Deep Space's competitors was an architecture student named Jeff Mills, who wowed everyone who heard his acrobatic DJ sets. Mills even had his own radio show on WDRQ, where he was known as "The Wizard."

Atkins did not want to see Mills end up with a drum machine. "I said, 'Derrick, I know you gotta pay your rent, and I know you want to sell one of these 909s, but I wouldn't sell it to *nobody* in Detroit.'" Honoring that request would have some unexpected repercussions.

In the meantime, Atkins overcame his reservations about the 909. It helped that he now owned the first two MIDI-equipped drum machines: the 909 and the Sequential Circuits Drumtraks. Chaining them together, he created a kit with the Drumtraks kick and snare, and all other sounds from the 909. This hybrid provided the rhythm of "No UFOs," the 1985 single Atkins released as Model 500. "MIDI came along and changed the game," Atkins observes.

Kevin Saunderson used MIDI to create a different sort of hybrid on "Good Life," the 1988 hit from his group Inner City. The duo featured Saunderson and vocalist Paris Grey, and was techno's earliest crossover success story. "Good Life" topped the Billboard Dance chart by combining a 909 with Latin percussion from the Roland 727.

Saunderson's older brother was a musician who recommended that he buy a LinnDrum. "But when I heard a 909, I just had to have it," Saunderson recalls. "The LinnDrum, it was an interesting machine, but the kick just wasn't right for dance. You could use toms or other parts of it. But when the 909 came along, it just took over."

Saunderson stayed loyal to the 909 throughout the Eighties. "Eventually I got an SP12," says Saunderson. "Sometimes you want a different dynamic, a different inspiration. Then I got the [Akai] MPC and started sampling my 909."

"But in the end, I always went back to the 909. Those key sounds—the clap, the kick, the hi-hats. Even the toms." Saunderson smiles at the memory. "Even if I tried, nothing could give me that same warmth. Nothing could match it."

7.

Derrick May has always been the larger-than-life member of the Belleville Three. That's been clear since the 1987 single "Strings of Life," built on a riff by pianist Michael James, and punched into the stratosphere with string samples and a driving 909 beat. That extravagant quality is evident on a February evening in 2021. As night descends, May putters around his warehouse studio, high above the Motor City streets. He's wearing a fur cap and scarf, and punctuates his recollections by waving a smoldering cigar.

If anyone from the techno world would be likely to say that "I was able to make the 909 sing," it would be Derrick May. And he does say exactly that.

The list of Roland drum machines that May has used is long. It includes the 808, of course, as well as later 1980s machines like the TR-707, the TR-626, and the TR-505. "But for me, the 909 was a blank canvas," he explains. "Unlike the 808, which is really colored—it has this mechanical sound, and it's soft and sexy, but powerful and fierce—the 909 was *dry*. It was more of a challenge. It had a raw blankness to it. You could create your own painting on this canvas."

May painstakingly filled in that blankness by using effects. One was a little-remembered processor made by Ibanez, best-known for guitar effects: the DM1100 Digital Delay. May swept the ticking delays across the 909 drum tracks of techno classics like Rhythim is Rhythim's "Kaos" and "Beyond the Dance," released on his Transmat label. Though he didn't know it then, May was actually helping the 909 realize Tadao Kimumoto's dream: a drum machine with sounds entirely customized to the user.

May is what author Malcolm Gladwell would undoubtedly call a "connector." The proof of this innate connector-ness comes in what May did with one of his surplus 909s: he took it to Chicago. There, May had become a weekend regular at dance clubs like the Power Plant, the Playground, and the Warehouse—later renamed the Music Box. In these venues in the early 1980s, DJs such as Ron Hardy, Jesse Saunders, and the late Frankie Knuckles were editing records on the fly. Out of those sets came the electronic style that would become known as house music.

At the Power Plant one evening in 1983, May approached Craig Loftis, a DJ who also served as the engineer for Frankie Knuckles. "I said, 'Does Frankie want a 909? I got one. For $400.' And Frankie did something he never did: he invited me into his DJ booth."

May returned to Chicago the next week, "and Frankie was using the drum machine. He had realized that the 909 would be difficult to use live, because the pitch control was very sensitive. So he had recorded the drum machine tracks onto reel to reel, and he played them in the party." Then in 1985, Knuckles let Chip E.—sometimes known as "the Godfather of House Music"—use his 909 on the single "Like This." And shortly after that," May adds, "it was everywhere."

One of the creators of this new dance music was a Chicago post office employee and aspiring musician named Marshall Jefferson. On the strength of his day job, Jefferson was offered a $10,000 line of credit at a local Guitar Center.

Jefferson walked out of the shop with armfuls of tech—including several pieces of Roland's discontinued Mid-O Series. Two of the instruments were drum machines: the TR-808, and the TR-707. And one device was a piece of gear absolutely nobody else wanted: the TB-303 Bass Line. Its oscillator generated two simple waveforms, and neither sounded anything like a bass guitar.

"You couldn't *throw* 'em away," says Jefferson, still looking disgusted. "I paid $150 for it, and that salesman thought he did a great deal." In the end, it *was* a great deal—for Jefferson.

Unknowingly, Jefferson had also done the right thing by purchasing two drum machines.

The TR-707, which was MIDI capable, could be linked to most of the other gear Jefferson purchased, including the Yamaha QX1 sequencer. So the 707 became the anchor of "Move Your Body," Jefferson's 1986 debut single. Dubbed the "House Music Anthem," its piano melody and uninhibited vocal (from Jefferson's friend Curtis McClain) quickly defined the genre.

The 808, however, wouldn't sync with any of the other devices Jefferson had bought—except the 303. So he used just those two instruments to create a minimalistic, haunting track that was voiced by his friend, scenester Derrick Harris, a.k.a. Sleezy D. Recorded in 1984 after an all-nighter at the Power Plant, Sleezy D's single "I've Lost Control" lives up to Jefferson's goal: capturing "a nervous breakdown on vinyl." And the wild, squelchy bass sound of the TB-303 became the foundation stone of acid house, a harder, sparser dance music that soon exploded in the UK.

So Jefferson's mismatched drum machine haul produced at least two transformative singles. Yet one thing seems to make him nearly as proud.

"I never owned a 909," Jefferson says, breaking into a throaty chuckle. "I guess I'm just a born contrarian."

8.

Kevin Crompton *did* own a 909, but like Juan Atkins, it took him some time to warm up to it. As the drummer for the Vancouver new wave band Images in Vogue, Crompton had gotten used to seeing all the latest electronic percussion gear during the early 1980s. He was an early adopter of Simmons electronic drums, and knew all about the Roland 808.

But after leaving Images in Vogue, Crompton asked vocalist Kevin Ogilvie to sing on some of his demos. The new songs were harsh and clangorous, and the project evolved into an industrial group called Skinny Puppy. The pair of Kevins took new identities—Crompton became cEvin Key, while Ogilvie adopted the name Nivek Ogre. Their interest in the latest technology, however, remained unchanged.

"Ogre had some money, so we bought the 909 the day it came out," recalls Key. The machine showed up on their debut EP, 1984's *Remission*, meaning that Skinny Puppy is credited as the first group to record with the 909. But Key admits, "Everyone wasn't as excited about the sound of it right off the bat. It was a flatter sound. And I remember our first challenge was thinking, we'll work around that. Because it still had the triggers, and we were always triggering new kicks and snares and stuff like that anyway."

Those sampled sounds, Key adds, were often triggered via a Korg SDD1000 Digital Delay. "So that's how we got those massive Skinny Puppy drum sounds," he says. "We would have the drum machine, it would be triggering a sample for the kick and the snare, and it would get built up to be this huge monstrosity of a sound, with the magic of Mushroom Studio," where the group recorded.

Other musicians, meanwhile, were happily snapping up 909s—especially if they could be found secondhand. The stories of discontinued Roland instruments from the Mid-O Series instruments being sold for peanuts at pawn shops "were not just legends," insists techno artist Richie Hawtin. "They were *reality*. A 303 was 50 bucks. This happened not just once, but time and time again." As a teenager, the British-born, Ontario-raised Hawtin made a regular weekend circuit of all the pawn shops in his hometown of Windsor. Then he'd cross the Detroit River to do the same in the Motor City.

Hawtin assembled a collection of secondhand Roland drum machines. In 1993, he chained together three of them—the 808, the 909, and the 606 Drumatix—to create his first single as Plastikman. "Spastik" became a defining moment in the second-wave techno of the Nineties. Released on the Plus 8 label Hawtin had founded with fellow musician John Acquaviva, "Spastik" was a nine-minute asteroid storm of electronic percussion generated by this trio of rhythm boxes.

"It was very rarely just one machine," Hawtin says of his early singles. The 909, however, was the drum machine that fascinated him the most. His father, a robotics technician at General Motors, not only introduced his son to electronic music, via Kraftwerk and Tangerine Dream—he also helped modify one of his son's 909s.

The 909's appeal quickly spread beyond Detroit. Around the time he played his first gig in 1990 at New York's Palladium, techno artist Moby purchased his first 909 at a Manhattan shop called Rogue Music. "I don't know if I had a 909 for that show," he says, "but if I didn't, then I certainly got one soon after."

It was the beginning of a long, productive relationship. "Every record I made from 1990 until about 2000 featured the 909 in some capacity," recalls Moby. "Obviously, I used the kick drum. I had a song called 'Thousand' that goes up to a thousand over a thousand beats per minute, and that's just all 909. Well, 909 *energy*."

That 909 energy became unique to techno and house, Moby thinks, "because hip hop producers didn't want it. Every hip hop producer in the late Eighties, early Nineties wanted an 808. So the 808s were always sort of prohibitively expensive." But another reason, he contends, was "because the sounds were just more usable and less distinctive. You know, an 808 only sounds like an 808 and it's amazing, but if you want an 808 kick drum to be super solid, like a 909 kick, it just can't do that.

"I mean, we're talking hundreds of thousands of tracks, from so many different producers, all centered around the 909," adds Moby. "But you could listen to it and not know that's what you were hearing."

The appeal of the 909 and the rest of the Mid-O Series has taken on a chicken-or-the-egg quality for many of these artists. Richie Hawtin, now fifty-one, admits, "I find myself asking the question a lot: did these Roland instruments just have the right frequencies for me? Or were they cheap and just what I could afford?"

"Did they *define* my frequency range," he muses, holding up both palms and shrugging, "or it was just a happy accident that I found Roland?" The Mid-O Series, it seemed, was a natural generator of happy accidents. One of the happiest, and strangest, involved a 909, an unlikely artist, and an even more unlikely locale.

9.

The shuddering beats punched through a pungent curtain of marijuana smoke. The haze was so thick you could barely see the man behind it.

Violins were the instruments most commonly heard in this Philadelphia recording studio. But it was now long past midnight. And the center of attention was a Roland TR-909, a drum machine that had yet to make an impact in hip hop.

The person operating the machine was 23-year-old Jesse Bonds Weaver, Jr., an aspiring rapper who went by the name Schoolly D. And on this magical night in 1985, Schoolly tapped himself and the 909 into the history books. He recorded three songs about navigating the seamy side of West Philly—including the classic "PSK What Does It Mean?"—that featured him playing the 909 live while he rhymed.

"You can *hear* it's live. The tempo goes from 96 to 98 to 93. If you listen, you can even hear my fingers hittin' the start and stop," recalls Schoolly. "I wanted the drum machine to sound just like a drummer was playin'. Only better."

The plan had always been for Schoolly and his DJ, Code Money, to record everything live that night. "All those blues recordings, all those jazz recordings, all those old rock 'n' roll records—a lot of them were recorded live, with two or three microphones," Schoolly explains. "It had to be that simplistic and that raw for it to last forever."

But the raw sound was sweetened by a surprising ingredient. Through the smoke that night, a huge flat panel would have just been visible. It was a plate reverb, commonly used to add ambience to classical recordings. Sound bounced off the thin metal sheet inside the unit's casing, producing a dense, bright reflection. Engineer Jeff "Cheesesteak" Chestek was running the 909 through an amp that night, and the plate reverb turned every beat cavernous.

"It was special," reflects Schoolly, now fifty-nine years old and taking a break from painting in his Philadelphia studio. "But we didn't know *how* special it was gonna be."

Schoolly had used a LinnDrum on some early singles. Then he and the members of his Parkside crew pooled their money to buy their own drum machine. The first was a Roland Dr. Rhythm, but it was the second, the TR-909, that captured Schoolly's attention. He borrowed it from his friend Royal Ron, "and I just took it home and nobody ever asked for it back." He laughs. "Once they started hearing my beats, it was decided. Everybody else just gave up."

In fact, Schoolly even remembers bringing the machine to meals, where he'd program beats with headphones on until his irate mother told him "to get that shit away from the table!"

Schoolly realized the 909 would allow him to create an authentic brand of Philadelphia hip hop. In particular, he says, it was the machine's kick drum that made it unique. "That mid-low sound was killin' it," he explains. "If you really wanted to be distinctive, *that* was the Philly sound." Once he'd created some songs with the 909, however, the question of where to record them became problematic.

"People were still musically segregated," Schoolly recalls. "A lot of the R&B studios, like Sigma—unless you was with someone, you wasn't gettin' in." That left an unlikely option: a local classical studio, where engineer Jeff Chestek would have to smuggle Schoolly and Code Money in after dark.

"Us being little black boys from West Philly—they *did* have a reason not to trust us. We just looked like a bunch of thievin'-ass kids, *which we were*"—here Schoolly roars with laughter—"but we didn't *go* there to steal. We *went* there to record. Somebody *did* steal an $80,000 microphone, but I made 'em take it back."

On the appointed night, joints were quickly skinned up, and the weed-inspired work commenced. "The fog was so thick, you could barely see. If the board didn't have lights on it, we wouldn't have been *able* to see," Schoolly recalls.

He wasn't too high, though, to abandon his plan. When a curious Chestek saw that Schoolly intended to play the drum patterns live, "I remember him saying, 'Is that how you wanna do it?' And I was like, 'How *else* would you do it?'" Schoolly remembers. "Thank God for that ignorance."

As the hours slipped past, Schoolly, Code Money, and Chestek tracked "PSK", named after the Parkside Killers gang. Next was the braggadocious, X-rated "Gucci Time," then the self-explanatory "Freestyle Rappin'." After that, "I fell asleep around 6 or 7," Schoolly says. "I woke up to Jeff cleaning up, and I was like, shit. The people with the bow ties and the blue suits are gonna be here soon."

After the bow ties and blue suits showed up, Chestek would lose his job. "People found out that a gangsta rap group had recorded there. And the people was like, 'Those niggas were down here touching our white pianos? For white people?'" Schoolly cackles. "*Hell* no."

When Schoolly awoke that evening after a long nap, he found a crowd outside his house anxious to hear the results of the session. Cueing up the cassette, he cringed: the massive plate reverb on the 909 now sounded like overkill. "I was like, 'Fuck! I must've been *dusted*!' I called Cheesesteak, told him I'm gonna come back down and remix it."

Then one member of the Parkside crew played a fateful role in drum machine history. He was Schoolly D's friend Lynn, a 6-foot, 6-inch, 280-pound man-mountain. "Lynn said, 'Motherfucker, if you take that reverb out, I'm gonna *stab* your ass. Didn't you see the look on everyone's face? Don't change *shit*!" So the reverb stayed. And "PSK" would inspire a million gangsta rappers, including Ice T, who used it as the basis for his own breakthrough hit, "6 'N the Morning."

Schoolly went on to use other machines—notably, the Latin percussion of the Roland 727 on his second LP, 1986's *Saturday Night—The Album*. But his loyalties are still with the 909, a machine as important to Philadelphia hip hop as it was to Detroit techno.

"Because it sounds so fuckin' good at a block party," Schoolly explains. "Parliament can be playin', Grandmaster Flash can be playin', but when you put that fuckin' 909 on—BOOM-pow, BOOM-BOOM-pow. Man!

"You gotta do a lot of shit to make an 808 sound good outside," he says. "But that 909, that kick. That Philly *mid-low*." He exhales dramatically, then laughs once more. "*Boy!*"

***

19

The Mammals Arrive: The Linn 9000 and the End of the Drum Machine

1.

By 1984, drum machines had infiltrated just about every musical genre.

Even musicians' unions had acknowledged—with grumbling—that drum machines were not just the future, but the present. And in genres like soundtracks and advertising, which were dependent on trends, drum machines were quickly accepted. Jingle writers, the session bassist Will Lee remembers, "had to present something to clients beforehand. The more it sounded like the real thing, the better chance you had of getting the gig. So guys who could program were getting lots and lots of work."

Sometime during the height of this drum machine dominance, Roger Linn made a fateful decision. Linn had never given up his musical dreams, and having a drum machine in his home studio had been as helpful as he'd predicted. "But I thought, 'Wouldn't it be great if I could do the bass parts? Some keyboard parts, too. What if I were to take some of the advantages of the drum machine, like the ability to automatically repeat notes, and apply that to playing pitch notes as well?'" he recalls. "It made sense to extend the metaphor of looping and swing from drum beats only, to doing sequenced musical parts.

"So the Linn 9000, that was the idea," says Linn.

This invention, however, was like the arrival of mammals in a dinosaur-dominated landscape. The Linn 9000 contained the seeds of destruction for Roger Linn's company—and, though almost no one realized it at the time, for that dinosaur, the standalone drum machine, as well.

2.

The Linn LM-1 had revolutionized drum machine technology, and the LinnDrum consolidated those advancements to become one of the dominant sounds in popular music. But that hadn't always led to success for Roger Linn's company.

Linn is candid about a major mistake he repeated twice: stopping manufacture of his old machines to make way for the new. "Stupid me: I discontinued the LM-1 and almost went out of business because of that," he recalls. "People said, 'I still want the LM-1,' and I said, 'Why would you want it? It's more expensive. So what if you're missing a few tuning knobs?' But I had no awareness of what people wanted. I just wanted to focus on what was interesting to *me*.

"And then after the LinnDrum, I discontinued it, thinking everyone would want to buy the Linn 9000," he adds, "which was another stupid move."

It might have worked, if the Linn 9000 had been more reliable. Yet as forward-looking as its design was, the thing most people seem to remember about the machine today is the system crashes and memory dumps that made it such a risky proposition.

Art Wood used just about every major drum machine during the 1980s. He calls the Linn 9000 his favorite machine of all time—and not just because, as with the LM-1 and LinnDrum, he supplied some of its drum sounds. But he acknowledges, "The bastard never really worked while Roger was there." Yet Wood, like many frustrated users, could see its immense potential. "I knew what it was *supposed* to do," he says, "and I knew that was going to be *the* machine."

One of the major problems with the 9000, Linn acknowledges, "was that I still wasn't a great production engineer. At this point, I wasn't working with my mentor, Bob Easton, and that was a problem. I thought I knew it all. I was, you know, a cocky kid." The business lesson that Ikutaro Kakehashi of Roland had tried to jokingly impart to Linn back in 1982—"you must bring in more money than go out"—still had not taken hold.

"I was spending far too much money while I was ignoring the existing sales, and eventually it was too complex," says Linn. "That caused unreliability. That caused my reputation to suffer. And finally, it brought down the company."

It didn't seem that way when the Linn 9000 was introduced in 1984. In a glossy brochure, Linn wrote, "The Linn 9000 is a dream I've had for a long time. It answers nearly all of the requests I've received from top recording artists over the years. To a far greater degree than has existed before, it allows the non-technical artist to quickly and accurately realize the music which exists in his mind."

The eighteen velocity- and pressure-sensitive pads were key. For the first time, programmers could punch in rhythms on something other than tiny buttons. "Because the pads are big enough for the user to have a fair go at, you can use the 9000's velocity-sensitivity to capture the instantaneous dynamics of live programming," wrote Paul Wiffen in the April 1985 edition of *Electronics & Music Maker*. "So if your table-tapping is fairly accurate, then the programming style offered by the Linn is ideal."

There was more: if a user varied the pressure on a pad while the Linn 9000's "note repeat" function was turned on, the machine would duplicate notes at different velocities, creating realistic hi-hat patterns and tom fills "that you couldn't play as easily with your fingers or repeated strikes," as Linn notes. For Paul Wiffen, "more than any other feature, this is the one that substantiates Roger Linn's claims. It's quick, accurate and very impressive."

The 9000's sampling option was also a game-changer. "The great thing about the 9000 was it was a sampling machine. So you just hit record on the machine and put whatever you want in it," says Art Wood, who made the machine his go-to device for sessions. "By the time it was done, you could load whatever you wanted into any pad, or combine the pads to load longer sounds."

The machine's software shortcomings, however, were the main complaint of Linn 9000 users. Engineer Gordon Rudd, who'd worked on the DMX at Oberheim, had left to join Linn Electronics. Rudd, who wrote the original Linn 9000 software, believes the problems began with the decision to abandon the LinnDrum, which was "selling well, and trouble-free. There was no compelling reason to discontinue it, and would not be a problem selling both at once, due to the price difference," Rudd says. "The Linn 9000 was a complex machine, and a little more time would have made a big difference."

The original Linn 9000 software was written in a language called FORTH, which was often used for systems that had to interact with hardware. "I was introduced to FORTH by Tom Oberheim," Rudd says. "I was interested in creating a programming language for musical instruments, and FORTH had a lot of great features. Until then, musical instruments were programmed in assembly language, mostly because of speed and memory limitations of the microprocessors." Rudd adds that the main issue when he left Linn, in his view, was hardware-related: a flaw that caused the 9000 to crash while recording.

However, Linn engineer Bruce Forat claims that FORTH was a big part of the problem: it was simply too slow to respond. "Nobody had ever created a sequencer using that language," he says. Forat had been skeptical of the decision to hire Rudd in the first place, because of Rudd's background working on the Oberhaim DMX. "The LinnDrum was the king," Forat says. "My personal thing was, why would you hire somebody who worked on something inferior to make something superior? Why hire somebody from Ford to work on a Ferrari?"

The same time pressures that had worked against the Roland 808 and 909 were now rushing against Linn, who desperately needed a new product on the market to generate cashflow. Rudd left the company before the Linn 9000 was released, but remembers "there was more and more pressure to hurry up and finish. At one point we hired two more programmers to speed up the software development. It is well known," he notes drolly, "that adding more programmers does not speed up development."

Other complaints about the machine were bigger-picture. In his perceptive review, Paul Wiffen noted several flaws, like the limited tuning and the lack of step programming. He felt the Linn 9000's advancements didn't justify its $5,000 price tag.

The 9000 "has too many operational omissions to make it every man's answer to electronic music recording," Wiffen added. He acknowledged that some of those omissions could be cured by software updates. But "as it stands at the moment, the Linn 9000 is a dinosaur that'll need every update it can gets its hands on if it's not to become extinct."

Prescient as that comment was, the Linn 9000 had a short but incredibly productive run in the late 1980s. The pinnacle may have occurred in a South London studio complex, where the 9000 became the brain of a thoroughly modern Motown.

3.

If you were aware of pop music between 1984 and 1993, then you probably spent a fair amount of time listening to the work of Stock, Aitken, and Waterman. They're one of the most successful production teams in history, overseeing more than 100 Top 40 hits and more than $40 million in sales.

The trio's successes included Dead or Alive, Bananarama, Rick Astley, and Kylie Minogue. Stock, Aitken, and Waterman gave those acts, and many others, a slick, uptempo sound that drew on the Linn 9000's programming and sequencing capabilities.

Phil Harding was the studio engineer who helped shape the sound of those hits—a vital cog in the Motown-style assembly line at the "Hit Factory." In 1986, he was joined by programmer Ian Curnow, and the two became top remixers in the subbasement of Pete Waterman Limited—or PWL for short—Studios. For anyone interested in the history of this era, Harding's own books—*PWL from the Factory Floor* and *Pop Music Production*—are essential reading.

It's easy to imagine someone of Harding's easygoing demeanor thriving in the hothouse environment of the Hit Factory. Especially when you remember the amount of technological challenges he had to surmount.

Many of those challenges came directly from the Linn 9000. "The worst thing was it would just crash and freeze up," Harding recalls. "More serious was if we had the whole bass part sequenced and you hadn't laid it to tape. You've just wasted two or three hours' studio time."

Harding gives an example: one of the most famous Stock Aitken Waterman tracks, Rick Astley's 1987 worldwide Number 1 hit "Never Gonna Give You Up." The song, like many SAW productions of this period, has a bass sound generated on the Yamaha DX7 synthesizer, and sequenced through the Linn 9000. "And you're all sitting there praying," Harding says with a knowing smile. "If you got something down, you'd *never* just walk away and think about recording it tomorrow. You had to stripe it to tape ASAP."

The hassles of the Linn 9000, Harding is quick to point out, were worth it. "It was such a solid workhorse. For us, it was only unreliable maybe 5 or 10 percent of the time. And because it was unreliable, we had five or six of them lying around. And quite often, our own maintenance people would fix them."

While the drum programming at PWL was primarily done by Matt Aitken, Harding and Curnow customized the sounds of the Linn 9000 they used for remixes. For kick and snare sounds, they often used processed samples from the LinnDrum. "The internal drum chips in the 9000 weren't as good, in my view, as the LinnDrum," Harding says. "It went a bit backward; it was softer." He also notes, "As we got more into sampling, the snares might have come from anywhere."

Pete Waterman, who oversaw the entire operation, had a particular interest in bass drum sounds. The bass drum was always recorded on Channel One of the mixing desk. "And it was always, *Channel One, 2 or 3 decibels up*," Harding says. "All of us would learn to mix the kick a bit lower because we knew Pete would come in to nudge it up. And if he thought things didn't sound right—if you had used a different kick or whatever—it just wasn't worth the fight."

When PWL's Fairlight programmer, Mike Gill, left in 1986, Harding proposed his friend Ian Curnow for the job. Curnow had just finished working with the synthpop band Talk Talk, running a revolutionary live programming system made by Kurzweil.

After mastering the Fairlight, Curnow sometimes used it for drums. "It made a really effective drum machine," he says, "because it made everything grainy. For drums, that's nice." But a more significant change was taking place in the "Bunker" studio that Curnow and Harding used for remix work. Curnow was a beta tester for Cubase, a software sequencing program run through an Atari computer. He and Harding began transitioning away from the Linn 9000 and into the early stages of computer-based recording.

As Harding describes it, an "upstairs–downstairs" divide began to open up at PWL. "Stock and Aitken had a resistance to going to Atari and Cubase," he says. "They couldn't really get their heads round it." Harding acknowledges that there was more than just comfort behind the decision to stay with the familiar Linn 9000. "We worked fast. And anything that's going to slow you down—well, the Atari and Cubase would break down as often as the Linn 9000. And they'd got used to the bloody 9000 crashing."

However, younger assistants were surprised by the reliance on the Linn 9000. "What began to happen, let's say around '88, is you'd have studio assistants who'd be working with me and Ian," says Harding. "Then they'd go upstairs and do a session with Mike [Stock] and Matt. And they'd go, 'Where's the Atari? Where's Cubase? Why are they struggling along with this Linn?'"

"The boys upstairs thought they were cutting edge with the Linn 9000. And the sounds just weren't that special," Curnow contends. "They were the presets. They'd just adjust the pitch of the snare drum, as far as I know. But I had a better version of it downstairs with the Fairlight and Cubase."

By the early 1990s, the pipeline of PWL hits had dried up. Perhaps not coincidentally, this happened just as music technology shifted decisively from hardware to software. "I think they regret staying with the Linn so long," Harding reflects. "But it was a bit of a jump into the darkness, moving from a drum machine and built-in sequencer on to a computer."

Curnow adds, "I was trying very hard to convince them to broaden the palette. And Waterman kept wanting to narrow it down again. After a couple of years, there was a public realization: 'Oh God, all these records sound the same.' And that contributed to the end of their reign."

4.

Although he's one of the major figures in drum machine history, Bruce Forat has rarely sat for an interview of any duration. The reason is simple. "The people who need to know me already know me," he says. "And the people who don't know me will find out about me from their friends."

That word-of-mouth claim is true. Several people interviewed for this book credit Forat with saving their Linn 9000s. But ever since he and his brother Benny joined Linn Electronics in 1982, Forat has been making repairs and custom modifications to Linn machines—including the LM-1 and the LinnDrum.

He's still doing it, though he admits it's not his favorite activity. "Lately I'm hating it. To really fix these older machines up, it just takes so long," Forat says, the sounds of soldering in his Studio City workshop occasionally drowning out his voice.

Forat started fixing drum machines immediately after being hired at Linn as a twenty-year-old college student. In his first months of work, he says, he solved a problem that was threatening sales of the LinnDrum: a glitch that was causing "high frequency background noise," and led to returns of the machine. The solution, Forat recalls, "cost less than 50 cents for each machine." It also led to a face-off with his boss in a crowded tech room.

"Roger said, 'How many hours did you work on this?' So I said, 'I didn't time myself, but maybe 18 hours,'" Forat remembers. "And he said, 'If you knew what you were doing, it should only have taken you two hours. And then he went into his office and closed the door."

Linn's brother Steve, who was managing the company, counseled Forat not to take the snub personally. And the next day, Roger Linn called Forat into his office to give him a pat on the back, and a raise to boot. But the incident exposed tensions between the two men that seem to have resurfaced at various points over the years. Forat prefaces these anecdotes with, "I'm not sure if you want to put this in there. . ."

Some of those stories come from the final days of Linn Electronics. Through the end of 1985 and early in the new year, Roger Linn and his team were frantically making software updates to the Linn 9000. After Gordon Rudd's departure, new programmers had switched from FORTH to assembly language. That was improving the 9000's performance, says Forat. The problem was that as soon as one bug was fixed, a new one would appear. The process Forat describes sounds tragicomic.

"One guy would fix one part of the code. But doing this fix wouldn't take into account what the next guy might be doing with the same code," says Forat. "And that would cause *more* bugs. It was nuts." The final problem ended up being insoluble: there was no room left on the 9000's memory chips for more fixes.

The situation became so hopeless, Forat recalls, that some employees were simply shipping defective Linn 9000s back to customers in unopened boxes. Forat sighs deeply. "It was pretty crappy days, you know? We knew we couldn't fix it. People had gave up."

The updates that did get made were too slow to save Linn Electronics, which shut down in early 1986. Bobby Nathan, a musician who ran Unique Studios, reprinted in *Keyboard Magazine* a letter that Linn had sent to dealers and service centers. Nathan called the company's closure "a great tragedy that has befell [*sic.*] us all … If it had not been for Roger Linn's invention the drum machine, I would not be here to tell this tale."

Under the heading "What Happened," Linn explained, "We simply ran out of money and were unable to get more." Under "Why?", Linn blamed the 9000. "The 9000 had technical problems early on and was expensive to re-engineer, manufacturer and service; we had strong competition; we had no investment financing; and we were experiencing all the classic 'growing pains' of a new business." Bugs or no bugs, when some users heard that Linn was closing, they acted fast. Stevie Wonder immediately bought twenty of the machines, cleaning out the stock of several Los Angeles Guitar Centers.

It was not, in a sense, the end of the company. Bruce and Benny Forat outbid a number of other electronics companies and bought Linn's remaining stock. A little more than a thousand Linn 9000s had been sold to that point. But everyone realized if they could debug the machine, they would own a tremendous asset. Bruce Forat remembers auction day as "very tense. There was people from all over the world trying to get this stuff." He and his brother, however, walked away with the remaining Linn 9000s, plus some LM-1s and LinnDrums.

Ultimately, it was Bruce Forat who fixed the bugs in the 9000. He taught himself code and learned about microprocessing, to rethink the machine from the ground up. "I printed this stuff out, and I would read it every day," Forat says. "And the more I read it, the more it made sense."

Meanwhile, the Forats continued to service existing Linn 9000s. Producer and songwriter Glen Ballard, who used the machine to write Michael Jackson's 1988 Number 1 single "Man in the Mirror," regularly brought his 9000 to Bruce Forat during this period. "Literally, it was like doing drug deals," Ballard said. "I would meet him and get these chips to keep my Linn 9000 going."

When the Forats unveiled their own take on the machine, the Forat 9000 realized Roger Linn's ambitions. "They fixed it," says Art Wood, "and it became a great machine." In 1987, the Forats quickly released a follow-up device: the F16, a rack-mounted sampler and "brain" for electronic drums. It offered 16-bit sampling targeted at the new digital generation. Users included Jimmy Jam and Terry Lewis, Def Leppard drummer Rick Allen, and Babyface, who used it on the 1992 smash "End of the Road," by Boyz II Men, which spent a record-breaking thirteen weeks at Number 1.

The F16, though, was yet another move away from the standalone rhythm box. One person who wasn't sorry to see them go was engineer Gordon Rudd. "I think Roger deserves credit for perceiving that with a microprocessor-based product, software features are free. We packed an amazing amount of features into the Linn 9000," Rudd says. "I feel bad that it was such a fiasco, as it was basically a great product. I guess it kinda changed my life too, but it all worked out in the end."

And after working on the DMX and Linn 9000, Rudd adds, "I was pretty sick of drum machines."

5.

The single biggest problem that bedeviled electronic musicians had finally been solved by 1984. After decades of frustration in getting electronic instruments from different manufacturers to talk to one another, MIDI— short for Musical Instrument Digital Interface—became the universal language of the industry.

The invention of MIDI revealed the competitive stubbornness beneath the companies' gentlemanly veneer. Engineer Bryan Bell recalled proposing a universal system like MIDI to manufacturers during the 1970s. Bob Moog's answer was to simply buy more Moog instruments. Tom Oberheim, meanwhile, threatened to void Bell's warranty if he tried tinkering with his Oberheim devices.

Ultimately, it was Sequential Circuits' Dave Smith who became the "Father of MIDI," with help from Japanese companies like Roland. Though he was friendly with other American manufacturers, Smith saw firsthand that getting them to agree to such a system would be no easy task. Each company seemed to have a different idea about the kind of system that would be best.

In 1980, Ikutaro Kakehashi of Roland proposed a worldwide standard digital music communication system. The next year, at the annual conference of the Audio Engineering Society, Smith presented a paper touting a "Universal Synthesizer Interface." Two years later at NAMM, Smith gave an updated pitch for what he now called MIDI. But there was significant resistance.

"It became clear that United States manufacturers were not going to get involved. They wanted something that was absurdly overkill," recalls Smith. "But after the meeting, the Roland guys came to me and said, 'We still want to do this.' And so we had a separate meeting at NAMM with just us and the four Japanese companies. So we just started from there and ignored everybody else."

Fresh off developing the Roland TR-808 drum machine, Roland engineer Tadao Kikumoto was asked to write the MIDI protocol. As Kikumoto recalls, it was "not only for synthesizers and computers, but also for drum machines." Both Roland and Sequential Circuits would also lead the way in manufacturing MIDI-equipped drum machines: Roland with the TR-909, and Sequential Circuits with the Drumtraks.

"I knew with those five companies involved—it was us, Yamaha, Korg, Kawai, and Roland—nobody else would have a choice. I knew they'd all get dragged screaming into it," Smith recalls. "The first couple of years, it was everybody bitching about what's wrong with MIDI. But it was the right thing to do."

The proof can be boiled down to a simple detail. Unlike just about every other computer program and interface in existence, MIDI is still used in its original version, nearly forty years after its introduction. "It's completely unthinkable," says Smith. "It's still version 1.0, and it's used every single day, everywhere. Every studio, every university, every musician's house."

The key letter in MIDI, however, was "D." This new musical language both reflected the industry's move from analog to digital technology, and helped drive that shift. It happened at the same time that another digital technology—sampling—was about to transform drum machines, and music itself.

6.

While Roger Linn was rushing the Linn 9000 into production, the company that had become his primary competitor was also working on its own sampling drum machine. Up the Pacific coast, E-MU Systems had weathered a tense 1984. The company had laid off employees due to delays in getting its upgraded sampling synthesizer, the Emulator II, to market.

The E-MU braintrust was also feeling pressure from Sequential Circuits, which had released its Drumtraks drum machine. Some of the Drumtraks' sounds had actually been lifted from the LinnDrum and DMX, but it was far cheaper than those units—just $1,295 retail—and had MIDI. That was no coincidence, thanks to the involvement of Sequential's Dave Smith in MIDI's development.

However, the arrival of Drumtraks motivated Dave Rossum at E-MU to update the successful Drumulator. Sampling was clearly going to have to be part of E-MU's new machine, which became known as the SP-12.

Rossum and the crew at E-MU were able to offer 12-bit sampling capability (the "12" in the machine's name; "SP" stands for "sampling percussion") with 1.2 seconds of sampling time. A decision Rossum made to keep the price below $3,000 was a sample rate conversion technique known as "drop sampling." The "drop" refers to the fact that parts of a sample are dropped or repeated to save memory. It's a crude but effective technique to extend sampling time.

Engineers at E-MU had investigated drop sampling for the Emulator line, but had ultimately rejected it. "It really badly distorts the sound," Rossum says. "We just felt the fidelity change was unacceptable." But now they were making a drum machine—where a certain amount of distortion was not only acceptable, but could even add a gritty character to the sounds.

With a list price under $3,000, the SP-12 was successfully launched at the 1985 Summer NAMM show in New Orleans. Some early buyers discovered the circuit boards of their SP-12s were inscribed with the legend, *Paul is dead. The Walrus is Paul*, a reference to a famous Beatles conspiracy theory. Rossum smiles as he pulls one of the circuit boards out from under a desk in his office. "We wanted to have fun," he recalls, "and there was so much of a spirit of humor in the company."

There were more than laughs inside the SP-12. In its Turbo version, memory could be increased to about five seconds. The E-MU engineers believed this would offer plenty of time for long samples—like cymbals—to decay. But no one expected what happened next.

Musicians—hip hop musicians in particular—didn't seem to care about the SP-12's two dozen stock drum sounds. They also weren't trying to sample individual drum hits. Instead, they were using the sampler to lift entire loops, riffs, and grooves from records, and using these bits to create new songs.

If they'd had an ear to the streets, manufacturers might have heard what was coming. A Queensbridge DJ named Marlon Williams had helped lead the charge toward sampling in hip hop. Williams had happened onto sampling accidentally while interning at Unique Studios in the early Eighties. He found that he could replace the snare sound from a drum machine with a more satisfying drum hit from a record.

As the producer Marley Marl, Williams would build an empire on this discovery, using the Korg SDD-2000 Digital Sampling Delay to lift drum loops from old soul vinyl. His favorite source was the 1973 Honey Drippers single "Impeach the President." Marley used those drum samples dozens of times, most notably on the 1986 hip hop hits MC Shan's "The Bridge" and Eric B. & Rakim's "Eric B. is President."

Dave Rossum was initially surprised that producers began using the SP-12 in this way. But he also realized this development was good for business. "Ultimately, it was just people being creative," Rossum reflects.

One of the first groups to use the SP-12 was the Beastie Boys. The trio and Rick Rubin unveiled it in 1986 on "Rhymin and Stealin," from their multiplatinum debut, *Licensed to Ill*. Meanwhile, an aspiring producer named Matt Dike would acquire his own SP-12 a couple of years later. That machine became the cornerstone of Delicious Vinyl, a Los Angeles label that achieved worldwide success through huge hits like Tone-Loc's "Wild Thing." On that song, Dike used his SP-12 to sample drumbeats from Bizzy B and a guitar riff from Van Halen's "Jamie's Cryin'."

Thanks to those successes, the SP-12 also led indirectly to a partnership between Dike, engineer Mario Caldato Jr., and the Dust Brothers—a pair of aspiring producers named Mike Simpson and John King. And that collaboration, in turn, would lead to the four men joining forces with the Beasties for their collective masterpiece, 1989's *Paul's Boutique*.

Just two years later, the SP-12 was replaced by the E-MU SP-1200. Responding to the marketplace, E-MU dumped the drum presets and upped the sampling memory to allow for thirty-two custom sounds. Hip hop producers fell in love with the combination of grungy 12-bit samples and the freedom to construct entire songs on a single piece of gear. It was this machine, more than any other, that provided the heartbeat of hip hop's late Eighties, early Nineties Golden Age.

The 1200's increased sampling memory—a maximum of 2.5 seconds per sound, and 10 seconds in total—still fell short of what increasingly ambitious musicians needed. So in a further repurposing of the product, savvy producers began sampling records at faster speeds—most often at 45 RPM, instead of 33 1/3—and then playing them back at slower speeds on the SP-1200. This ingenious time-compressing and stretching technique had a similar effect to drop sampling: it created distortion. But the ability to sample bigger chunks of old records was worth the tradeoff in sound quality. Especially to hip hop artists, who wore the digital grit as a badge of honor.

Their enthusiasm was, however, one of the reasons that E-MU decided to phase out the SP-1200. Author Greg Milner explained this seeming paradox:

> As technologists, the E-MU crew was baffled by their customers' attraction to the SP-1200 and its inferior technology. As mild-mannered Santa Cruz neohippies, they were even more flummoxed by what their customers were doing with the SP-1200. "We tried to stuff it back in the closet," [Scott] Wedge admits. "Rap had a bad ..." His voice trails off. "Politically, it was really ugly stuff. We kind of pulled [the 1200] out of retirement, but when we learned that what it was being used for was this rap music, we went, 'Well, let's discontinue it, maybe that'll stop it.'"

There were other reasons E-MU wanted to kill the SP-1200. Replacement parts were becoming hard to find, and sales had eventually slowed. Yet despite E-MU's reservations, the list of producers and artists who created classic hits with the 1200 reads something like a who's who of hip hop.

The most ambitious users of the machine were an incendiary quartet from Long Island. These future Rock and Roll Hall of Famers pushed the SP-1200 to its limits on their masterwork, a record that showed how far hip hop could go, musically and politically.

7.

Not many people realize comedian Eddie Murphy's role in drum machine history. But the roots of iconic hip hop act Public Enemy stretch back to the former *Saturday Night Live* funnyman.

The connection is Eric "Vietnam" Sadler, a Long Island friend of Murphy's. Sadler was also a member of the Bomb Squad, the group of producers that created Public Enemy's dense, pugnacious sound.

Specifically, Sadler was the Squad's "Chef"—the musician who stirred the deliberately unpalatable ingredients assembled by Public Enemy frontman Chuck D, and producers Hank and Keith Shocklee into digestible songs. "Chuck and Hank had these radical ideas. They didn't want *any* type of music. No strings. No niceness. *Fuck* all that," recalls Sadler. "So my gig from the beginning was making the blend work sonically." Chuck D explained the relationship more succinctly to author Brian Coleman: "Eric was the musician. Hank was the antimusician."

Sadler has rarely been interviewed, and zealously guards his privacy in retirement. Yet while he's quick to credit Chuck D and the Shocklees for their vision—"Without Hank and Chuck, none of this would exist," he says. "*I* wouldn't exist musically in this way."—Sadler's own story shines a fascinating spotlight on the schisms that prematurely ended the Bomb Squad.

In the early 1980s, Sadler and his friend, fellow Long Island musician Charles Cassius, opened a rehearsal studio in a local dentist's office building. Eddie Murphy was then starring each week on *Saturday Night Live*. But he was also writing songs with Cassius in preparation for a solo album. Murphy left some of his musical equipment at the rehearsal studio, and an eager Sadler pounced on the Oberheim DMX.

"I stayed up 24 hours a day, messing with this drum machine that was worth thousands of dollars," he remembers. Sadler's programming experience came in handy when a pair of local brothers—Hank and Keith Boxley, later known as Shocklee—came looking for a place to conduct their own musical experiments. The Shocklees moved their studio gear into an upstairs office in the same building. A frequent guest was their friend Carlton Ridenhour, better known as Chuck D, who had a successful show with Hank Shocklee on Adelphi University's radio station, WBAU.

Out of these gatherings emerged a group called Spectrum City. In 1984, the collective recruited Sadler—they called him "Vietnam" because he liked to wear old army jackets—to help them record a single called "Lies" for Vanguard Records. The session set a pattern for the partnership that emerged between Chuck D, the Shocklees, and Sadler.

When they got to Vanguard Studios, Sadler was told the group had decided to use Vanguard A&R man Ray "Pinky" Velasquez as their producer. "They said, 'He makes hits.' So they sent me home. I caught the subway and the bus and walked back to Long Island," Sadler remembers. "That night, Chuck came back and was like, 'Yo, man, the stuff came out horrible. Can we just do one song?' So we used the Emulator." In half an hour, they had a rock-rapping B-side called "Check Out the Radio."

Renamed Public Enemy, the group got a deal with up-and-coming Def Jam Records. Sadler was again recruited to help record the debut album, *Yo! Bum Rush the Show*. For the princely fee of $100 per song, Sadler "programmed basically everything on there, except for Terminator X's song ['Terminator X Speaks with His Hands'] and the original 'Public Enemy No 1,' which Keith had basically done."

The main drum machine Sadler used was the E-MU SP-12, but he employed a variety of other devices. The Korg DDD-1 drum machine, introduced in 1986, was a favorite of Public Enemy: it had eighteen drum sounds and the option to add more via ROM cards. Other drum sounds came from the Ensoniq Mirage sampling keyboard, and an Oberheim DX that Sadler liked for its tunable shaker. Sadler even played a set of Simmons drum pads "for accents" on some songs. "We used a little bit of everything we could."

But when the album was finished, Sadler still hadn't been paid. "I made $100 a song. It ended up being $1,200. I was good with that. I was making no money. But we were done, and I was supposed to get paid before Christmas," he says. "October comes around, November comes around, I have no money. So I raised all living hell two weeks before Christmas. I went down to Def Jam and raised enough hell that I got my $1,200.

"And I was happy as a pig in shit," he insists. "I was in the studio, having fun. We were all just buddies and pals." But Sadler's musician friends, who all liked to play Spades with him in the office's downstairs rehearsal area, weren't as sanguine.

"All my friends were mad at Chuck and Hank after that first album. I got credit for 'minimal synth programming.' And it said 'Drum programming: Hank Shocklee and Eric Sadler.' And my friends said, 'You gotta be kidding me. You did the whole thing.' I said, 'I got paid. I am fine.' Although in the back of my head," Sadler admits, "I was like, *Minimal synth programming*. What the hell is that?"

The modest success of the first Public Enemy album meant that for the follow-up, *It Takes a Nation of Millions to Hold Us Back*, the group got new equipment. Part of this arsenal was the E-MU SP-1200, which quickly became the group's go-to piece of gear. Hank Shocklee would say years later that he admired the machine's clunky feel. "It quantized sound very abruptly," Shocklee explained. "It was the thing that gave the SP-1200 its soul."

But the man who programmed the 1200 nearly didn't get the gig—again. "Chuck and Hank came to me. And when I say, 'Came to me,' I mean, they're just coming down to the rehearsal studio in the dentist's office building from upstairs," says Sadler. "I'm playing cards. We're getting ready to start the next album. And I said, 'I want $5,000. I want producer [credit]. And I want one point.'"—that is, a percentage of the total royalty.

"And they said, 'Nah, man, screw that. You ain't gettin' that. No way.' And I said, 'OK, then, I'll catch y'all later.' And my boys playin' cards were like, 'That's hilarious. They can't even turn on the equipment.'" That might not have been literally true, but it didn't take long for Chuck D and Hank Shocklee to realize they needed Sadler. "Couple days later, they came back down, and it was fine," says Sadler. "And that was it."

Now the Bomb Squad was in place. *It Takes a Nation of Millions* would be the only album that Sadler, Chuck D, and the Shocklees would work on in equal partnership. And its sound is a testament to the oddly perfect dynamic they shared. A major component was Sadler's intricate rhythms, which blended sampled beats and drum machine sounds.

"Whatever sample we had always had to have drum [programming] lined up with it. And then the decision was, do I want to line it up exactly? Do I want to keep it the same pitch? Slow it down? Do I want to break the sample that's 10 seconds long into four 2.5 second pieces?" says Sadler. "Sometimes you had to find the frequencies to take out the kick drum on a sample and replace it with your kick drum. It's a process, but it was always fun to do it."

Hank Shocklee, meanwhile, often astounded Sadler with his sample choices, like the screeching saxophone glissando from "The Grunt" by the J.B.s. "He throws on that horn," Sadler recalls. "I thought, '*What in the fuck in life is going through his head?*' So I sample it. Then I said, 'What now?' And he said, 'Put "Funky Drummer" behind it.' And the rest, I'm just programming." The result was the insistent, militant "Rebel Without a Pause" one of the highlights of Public Enemy's catalog.

The songs demanded a vocalist who could meet their aggression, and Chuck D delivered. But Sadler points out that Keith Shocklee, the fourth Bomb Squad member, shouldn't get short shrift. "Keith is more of a DJ. But his ideas were always great. They were just fewer. But he's the main guy behind 'Fight the Power,'" Sadler says. "When he did come up with an idea, it was phenomenal."

If critics thought the first record was militant and abrasive, they certainly weren't ready for this new release, where every song sounded like patched-together shrapnel that might detonate again. The SP-1200 was the container that stored all these incendiary fragments.

The SP-1200's appeal "was user friendliness. How fast you can grab samples. How fast you could put 'em on the pads," Sadler explains. "It was very easy to get your ideas across very quickly." Pumping up the tempos well above 100 BPMs, and sampling source material like Slayer's "Angel of Death" (with Slayer producer Rick Rubin's blessing), *It Takes a Nation of Millions* showcased a group unafraid to challenge listeners, tout black power—and confront its critics.

The album topped the Black Albums chart in 1988 and just missed the Pop Top 40, an astounding feat for a record so confrontational. It made the Bomb Squad one of the hottest commodities in urban music. The next year, the Squad scored two major outside projects— Ice Cube's *AmeriKKKa's Most Wanted*, and *Poison*, by ex-New Edition members Bell Biv DeVoe—and also had to follow up *Nation*. And those pressures, according to Sadler, are what ultimately drove the four men apart.

Sadler still sounds disappointed, more than thirty years later, as he recalls Public Enemy's follow-up LP, 1991's *Fear of a Black Planet*. "It was a disaster to me," he admits. "We never got the sequencing right. I wasn't happy with all the songs we had done. And Chuck wasn't happy either. I felt like it was a weird sort of Beatles album—everything coming from different directions."

By the end of the millennium, Sadler had largely bowed out of the music business. "One of the reasons is that it became about lawyers and money and making hit singles, and not about the art," he says. "And I was spoiled. When you work with people like Chuck D and Ice Cube and LL [Cool J] to start your career, where else can you go after that?"

But if there's anything that makes him nostalgic, it's thoughts of his old SP-1200. "My 1200, I sold a long time ago. I wish I hadn't, though," Sadler admits. "I think about buying one because of the memories—programming it. I used to go and go and go. It was so much fun.

"It's like a guitar, you know?" he says with a sigh. "When you get used to something, it becomes like your baby."

8.

"The MPC," Steve Porcaro says simply, "was just a Linn 9000 that worked."

If the Linn 9000 was like the arrival of prehistoric mammals, and the E-MU SP-1200 was an asteroid that wiped out many of the old drum machine dinosaurs in a sampling explosion, then the MPC series could be considered the mammals' final triumph.

As much as anyone, Roger Linn realized the unfulfilled possibilities of the Linn 9000. After Linn Electronics dissolved, Linn decided he needed a partner to fully unleash that potential. Enter Akai, the Tokyo-based electronics manufacturer, which was looking to make a splash in the music world.

"It was an obvious choice, surely," Linn says. "Akai had seen my success in drum machines. They had seen there was demand for something like the Linn 9000. In other words, a production-engineered machine that could do drumbeats and maybe sequencing."

Linn's goals were similar to his objectives in creating the Linn 9000. He wanted to combine a drum machine and a MIDI sequencer. He wanted it to be intuitive to operate, so the touch- and velocity-sensitive pads of the Linn 9000 were retained. But a significant difference was that Linn could now focus, for the first time, on the product, rather than on sales and marketing as well. The MPC—which stands for MIDI (later, just "Music") Production Center—product line was the result.

The Akai MPC60, the first fruit of this new partnership, emerged in 1988. Musicians began using the machine as they had E-MU's SP-1200. The thirteen seconds of sample time, which could be divided among the MPC's different pads, allowed even more freedom to create sampled rhythms.

One loop-based artist whose career changed because of the MPC60 was San Jose native Josh Davis, who went by the handle DJ Shadow. Davis felt he'd exhausted the limits of creating music with his four-track cassette recorder. Now he had the studio-in-a-box of his dreams. "I'd fantasized about the MPC for so long that when I got it, I took it home and I was shaking and sweating," he recalled. "I stayed up all night reading the manual front to back. I had to use it immediately because I was bursting with all these ideas."

Many of those ideas became *Endtroducing*, Shadow's cut-and-pasted 1996 debut. The record, the world's first entirely sampled album, was an astonishing collage of source material assembled with the MPC60. Other producers also saw the MPC as an answered prayer. Bomb Squad member Eric Sadler used the machine heavily on new jack swing trio Bell Biv DeVoe's 1990 debut, *Poison*. "I used it to sequence my basslines and things like that," Sadler says. He also used the MPC60 to create the final song on the album: the Number 1 single "I Thought It Was Me."

Even today, the MPC60 still boasts legions of fans. Bernadette Cooper of R&B group Klymaxx proudly declares, "I'm an MPC girl all the way." Reggae drummer Sly Dunbar admits he regularly spends hours hunched over his MPC in his studio. And David Frank of the System stuck with his MPC60 for years "because I just wasn't confident about the feel of computer drums."

A major competitor of the MPC60 turned out to be Roger Linn himself. Or at least, his Linn 9000, as reworked by the Forat brothers. Unsurprisingly, Bruce Forat believes the Forat 9000 was the superior machine—partly because of sound; partly because of feel. "The 9000 sounds like an SP-1200. It was in your face," Forat contends. "And the feel of the 60 was a lot more mechanical. Things *sounded* sequenced. That was what everybody's gripe was at that time."

The partnership between Linn and Akai would become more successful than anyone imagined. But faultlines emerged in 1991, when Akai debuted the MPC60 Mark II. The changes were mostly cosmetic: a plastic chassis, a new paint job, and a headphone jack, as well as a lower price. Linn sarcastically suggested calling it the MCPNPHP—the "NP" standing for "new paint," and "HP" for "headphones."

A bigger problem came, Linn claims, when Akai officials began to investigate ways to avoid paying him his agreed-upon royalty for the MPC design. "They were trying to mince words and trying to reinterpret words in the contract," he says. "They were just trying to get rid of me because I had shared the source code with them—because it was a collaborative adventure.

"So they figured they could do it themselves, and eventually they thought that they would just rewrite the entire source code, just to make their own machines. I reminded them when they were about to sell it that my designs were protected in the contract, and so they finally acquiesced," Linn adds. "They paid my royalties, but it was a bit of a difficult time there."

The MPC line eventually expanded to several different machines. Foremost among them is the MPC3000, released in 1994 as the latest and greatest successor to the MPC60. With 16-bit stereo sampling, a powerful sequencer, and the timing that Linn's drum machines have been famous for since the LM-1, the 3000 became a favorite of top session musicians like keyboardist Jason Miles, who kept using it on sessions well into the new millennium.

Bruce Forat soon began to service Akai machines, as well as Linn products. If you visit the Forat brothers' website, forat.com, you can see dozens of their colorful, custom MPC casings—many created for hip hop royalty.

Those artists were among the most enthusiastic adopters of Akai's MPCs. The units became indispensable to hip hop producers like Dr. Dre, J. Dilla, and

Kanye West. As many people have pointed out, this positions Linn as one of the most important figures in hip hop history.

He seems nonplussed by the idea. "I didn't know anybody in hip hop," says Linn, "and a lot of the ways they used these machines were different than I had anticipated." Considering the idea further, he turns to one of his favorite metaphors. "You make the brush," he says, "and the painter decides what to paint with it."

***

20

Computer Love

1.

The standalone drum machine was on the verge of extinction almost as soon as it conquered pop music.
There were many reasons. Sampling, which allowed musicians to use loops of live rhythm, was certainly high on that list. So were hybrid machines like the Linn 9000 and its successor, the MPC60, which made the all-in-one digital workstation a compelling alternative. And while computer recording was still in its infancy, the options and control it could provide would clearly soon outpace any piece of hardware.

But could a single person really be responsible for the demise of the drum machine? Producer Bill Laswell argues that it's possible. "To me, Jason Corsaro replaced the drum machine," Laswell says. "He wasn't totally technical. He wasn't really musical. But somehow, he had this quality."

Corsaro, who died of cancer in 2017, was best known for the work he did at New York's Power Station studio. There, he engineered and mixed a series of records that defined the musical 1980s. Working with such artists as David Bowie, The Rolling Stones, Madonna, Duran Duran, and Hall and Oates, Corsaro developed a drum sound bigger and badder than anyone had imagined possible. The only real precursor was the work of Led Zeppelin's John Bonham. And, as Laswell points out, when Led Zeppelin reformed in 1985 to play at Live Aid, they hired drummer Tony Thompson of Chic "because they heard the drum sound Jason got."

A source of that huge sound was the Power Station itself. Located in Hell's Kitchen, the studio started life as a Con Edison power plant. It was repurposed as a recording studio in 1977 by Bob Walters and Tony Bongiovi, whose cousin Jon would later achieve fame as the leader of the hair metal band Bon Jovi.

Programmer Jimmy Bralower remembers,

The Power Station rooms were so definitive. Studio C was where the Duran stuff happened, and Madonna. There's a certain sound in that room. Then Studio A was the big rock room. That's where Billy Squier was done, and also Bruce Springsteen's "Hungry Heart." A lot of big rock records from that era were done in Studio A. You couldn't help but get a great sound in that room. It was just built for speed.

Engineer and mixer Bob Clearmountain, whom Bralower calls "the king of the big Eighties drums," did much of his best work at the Power Station. Sometimes Clearmountain combined drum machines and live drumming, as he did on the 1984 Hall and Oates single "Adult Education." Bralower, who did the drum programming, notes, "It's all drum machine until the end, then live drums take over. Those guys didn't give a shit if it was a drum machine or a live drummer. All they knew was that this worked."

The drum sound Clearmountain helped get for Tony Thompson on David Bowie's *Let's Dance* album—big, natural, powerful—would be refined by Jason Corsaro on subsequent releases. One was Madonna's 1984 album *Like a Virgin*, produced—like *Let's Dance*—by Chic's Nile Rodgers.

Corsaro took that sound even further on *The Power Station*, the 1985 collaboration between Thompson, Duran Duran's John and Andy Taylor, and vocalist Robert Palmer. Each gigantic drum hit captures the controlled fury of Thompson's playing, which was so overwhelming that it often destroyed microphones. "He didn't do it on purpose, he was just very powerful," Corsaro later said. "He had long arms and long legs, and he used every bit of them." To maximize this natural ability, Corsaro performed an intricate series of punch-ins to Thompson's drum tracks. He added precise dollops of reverb that threaded a tiny needle: the drums were enormous, yet each strike remained distinct.

Laswell recalls vividly his first meeting with Corsaro.

> I was waiting in reception at the Power Station. And two guys came in carrying him, one on each side. He looked like he was asleep. And I went to the receptionist and said, "Is that Jason Corsaro?" She said yes, and I said, "Well, I guess I'll come back tomorrow, because it looks like he's going home." And she said, "Oh, no—he's just arrived to work." Jason was insanely into drugs and alcohol. But that began this long relationship.

Laswell loved Corsaro's drum sound so much that he sampled it directly on "Make 'Em Move," the leadoff track of *Language Barrier*, a 1985 album he produced for reggae duo Sly and Robbie. "That snare sample on Sly and Robbie, that's a sample of Tony Thompson from the Power Station," he says. Corsaro mixed the album, but it got middling reviews. *Rolling Stone* even gave the record demerits for borrowing Thompson's drum lick from The Power Station's "Some Like It Hot."

The musicians, who knew the album was on the cutting edge, were unfazed by the critics. "I just thought, these are people who are stuck in the past," Laswell reflects. "And it turns out I was right."

2.

What no one could deny, as the 1980s progressed, was that drums were getting bigger and bigger—seemingly every week. Pop music had become a sort of arms race, where the goal was to develop the most massive drum sound possible.

"It was a healthy thing, that competition," contends producer David Rivkin, better known by his handle David Z. A Minneapolis native, Rivkin engineered the demos that got Prince his record deal with Warner Brothers, and his younger brother Bobby became the drummer in Prince's band, the Revolution.

David Rivkin continued to work with Prince throughout the 1980s. He recorded and engineered the *Purple Rain* soundtrack. And his contributions to Prince's 1986 song "Kiss"—originally slated for Mazarati, a Minneapolis funk group Rivkin was producing—helped make it a Number 1 single.

But Rivkin also produced two hits that are certainly contenders for the unofficial title of Biggest Snare Drum Sound of the Decade. The first reached Number 2 on the Pop charts in 1987: R&B singer Jody Watley's "Looking for a New Love." And the second was "She Drives Me Crazy," a 1989 chart-topping single from British trio Fine Young Cannibals.

"This was my philosophy: you know in the first two bars because of that snare sound, it's that artist," says Rivkin. "Every kick and snare sound defines that artist."

To create those snare sounds, Rivkin explains, "I was building sandwiches." In other words, a great snare sound came in layers. The first layer, for Rivkin, often began with one of his two drum machines of choice: the Linn 9000, and the E-MU SP-1200. He would then build up those percussion sounds with a variety of other sources. On "Looking for a New Love," the secret snare ingredient was surprisingly low-tech. "I probably used a non-broadcasting channel on the radio, because I used to do that a lot," Rivkin says. "And I gated that white noise to make it extend."

"She Drives Me Crazy" was a more intricate process. "I took a drumhead off the snare drum and hit it with a wooden ruler, and then I gated that," Rivkin explains. "Then I EQed that sound with two different graphic equalizers, which boosted the midrange and made it sound almost like a crash. Then I combined that with an electronic sound from the Linn 9000. And a lot of times, I'd take a small speaker out in the studio and put it on the snare drum, so when the snare drum hits, it'll trigger the real snare sound." That blended sound rattled the real snare drum's wires, adding an extra layer of ambience.

Another influential snare sound is the one that turned up on Cameo's 1986 *Word Up* album. This collection made the veteran New York funk group the hottest band in urban music for a season. And the walloping snare of title track was a big reason.

The drum sound came from Sammy Merendino, one of the world's top session percussionists. But Merendino gives much of the credit to Cameo's leader, Larry Blackmon—a drummer himself.

The band had just finished touring its eleventh album, 1985's *Single Life*. On the plane back from England, "Larry told me, 'This next record is going to be *big*,'" Merendino recalls. "I already hear it." What Blackmon heard was an album with absolutely no reverb. "He actually fired an engineer who put reverb on something. Larry said, 'The sound of this record's going to be in your face, tight. And the drums are gonna be *so* upfront.'"

By the time of *Word Up*, Merendino had built up a massive percussion rig that included the Linn 9000, a couple of Akai S900 digital samplers, and some Simmons drums. Merendino also had an early Macintosh computer with the recording program Sound Designer, which allowed him to edit his own samples.

The whole caboodle had been customized by a Chicago "tech savant" named Vince Gutman. "My stuff would go into a session," Merendino says proudly, "and it was just spotless, quiet, perfect." The bass drum used on "Word Up," however, was an exception. It was one of the first samples Merendino ever made, and was heavily distorted. He decided to keep it anyway, and for the "Word Up" session, he paired it with a snare drum sample from *Single Life*.

Blackmon, though, wasn't happy with the result. "We were at Quad Studios in New York," Merendino remembers. "And so Eric Calvi, the engineer—who was instrumental in that snare sound—recorded Larry clapping his hands out in the hallway. There's this huge stairwell that just went all the way downstairs."

"So we recorded Larry clapping his hands into an AMS digital reverb. And then we laid that on top of all the other songs—on 'Candy,' and on 'Word Up.' And immediately, you get this low-high contrast between the *jjjuuuh* of the bass drum and the snare. It became a signature thing for Larry."

Merendino is acknowledged by many of the people interviewed for this book as not only one of the world's great session pros, but one of the great drum programmers as well. But while he's appeared on hundreds of commercials, and has drummed for the likes of Billy Joel, Michael Jackson, and Cyndi Lauper, he says *Word Up*, "I'm afraid, is the only perfect record I've ever done. I wouldn't change one single thing. Sometimes I'm like, how can I get back to that? I get close to it sometimes. But that was just an amazing moment where everything aligned."

3.

As the 1980s waned, there was an inevitable backlash against the sound and aesthetic of drum machines. It took many forms, including a resurgence in hard rock and "authentic" musical forms. That helped drive the success of mainstream acts like Bon Jovi, Guns N' Roses, and a second wave of hair metal bands who dominated MTV.

The irony was that many of these artists were using drum machines and electronic sounds. A common practice was attaching triggers to a drum kit to generate electronic sounds that would become a major part of the final mix.

"At a certain point in my career, I *wanted* a real drummer. Because I had a batch of samples and sounds that were just *monstrous*," says producer and engineer Mark S. Berry. "So you drum it, we'll get the triggers right, and I'll put the sound on afterwards. We put a little bit of the real drum in there, so we have the sonic quality of a sample, but so you can still hear the foot pounding the bass drum."

Beginning in the late 1980s, drummer David Frangioni became one of the industry's go-to technologists. An early adopter of drum triggering, especially in the live setting, Frangioni worked with artists like Aerosmith and Ozzy Osbourne to develop the right blend of acoustic and electronic sounds.

Frangioni, an author and entrepreneur who's also the CEO of *Modern Drummer* magazine, admits that "early on, triggering was a huge challenge." He became a fan of the Dynacord ADD-One drum synthesizer and sampler, although he notes, "I would just look at the project, the drummer, and figure out what the right triggers were. I did all my homework ahead of time."

One common technique—especially on metal albums, where huge drum sounds were a requirement—involved a sort of after-the-fact triggering. "The drums would get recorded, and then the producer—and a guy like me—would trigger the sounds off the tape. And that would be added to the blend that would become the final sound," Frangioni recalls. "That was actually more commonplace at that time than triggering while the drummer was playing.

"And of course, that got your drums done a lot faster. The drummer could play exactly as he wanted, and then it was all in the hands of the producer and the mix engineer and the technologist, which was my main role."

One of the masters of this technique, Frangioni adds, was Beau Hill, the producer of such successful metal bands as Ratt, Winger, and Warrant. "Beau was known for his great ability to take drum sounds after they were recorded, and hear how they were sitting in the track, and then figure out how to trigger the sounds," Frangioni recalls.

Drum machines were also doing more than just providing drum sounds. The Akai MPC60 became the brain of the live setup that engineer Bryan Bell designed for the band INXS, during the group's 1900–91 world tour. "Their system had real drums with triggers on every drum. They had a guitar rig where all of the switching between the pedals and the pedal boards and the directs were all automated. The keyboards were all automated. And the master drum machine gave the cues to the whole stage. So they'd play to an arrangement that was in the drum machine," Bell explains.

Yet modest little drum machines were still finding their way into the studios of pop's elite. Stephen Lipson recalls programming a shuffling reggae rhythm into the Yamaha RX-5 on the Paul McCartney song "Rough Ride," from 1989's *Flowers in the Dirt*. Meanwhile, a Yamaha drum machine provided the basic track for U2's 1987 Number One hit "With or Without You."

The machine in question—it might have been the RX-11, which was Yamaha's first machine of the 1980s—"was not a particularly great sounding thing. A pretty dead sound. But it was perfect. Just kick, snare and hi-hat," says producer Daniel Lanois, mimicking the rhythm and singing the first lines of the song. "It's just that simple."

A couple of years later, Lanois would use a Roland 808 on the basic tracks for Bob Dylan's *Oh Mercy*. Recorded at a New Orleans mobile studio, the album was widely viewed as a comeback for Dylan, a return to roots. But the machine, Lanois says, was integral to the project.

"We cut most of that record with an 808," he says. "I just had it coming through a wedge, an Electro Voice stage monitor, at Bob's feet." Lanois later overdubbed live drums from Mean Willie Green, but the 808, he says, set the tone. "A good point of reference is a song called 'Most of the Time.' Because it has just a simple little beat, and we just fell right into it," he says. "That's quite a soulful song, and it's a nice reminder that you can get soulful results with a beatbox keeping the time."

The "back to basics" movement remained alluring. Ultravox drummer Warren Cann remembers vividly one early 1980s afternoon at London's AIR Studios. During a break, he was commiserating with session pro Mark Brzezicki. The two drummers shared their frustrations with the time it took to get drum sounds, and the sometimes-disappointing results. Cann thought back on this conversation often, and it helped convince him that a drummer with his programming expertise could, and should, tap into the wide variety of sounds that sampling had made available.

Following Ultravox's appearance at Live Aid in 1985, the group was at a crossroads. The backlash to synthpop had already begun in Britain. So Cann's suggestion that the group use more drum machines was not well received by his bandmates. The next year, he was ousted from the band, with the usual explanation of musical differences.

The truth of his dismissal, Cann says, is more complicated than the pat public statement. "I just think all our wires were crossed," he says. "The technology was just starting to get to the point where there were some killer drum sounds. I didn't want to *trigger* them, because the technology just wasn't there yet," he says. "But I could program them. I wanted to program the drums for more of our music. Because even if it's not an electronic drum machine kind of song, a drum machine could have done it. That's what I was trying to explain to them."

On the group's subsequent album, the folk-rocking *U-Vox*, Cann was replaced by none other than Mark Brzezicki. And it was with a sense of dread that Cann attended the tour's opening in London. "I thought, 'What if they sound amazing?'" he confesses. As it turned out, he needn't have worried.

"They *didn't* sound amazing. And I realized that even somebody as great a drummer as Mark Brzezicki is can't be me." Cann smiles. "It made me finally appreciate this weird niche I'd found for myself."

Without Cann, the band seemed to lose its own place. *U-Vox* generated a couple of minor hits before sinking out of sight. The band would essentially split for two decades, and even Ure later disowned *U-Vox* as "an album that never should have been." Withdrawl from the "hypnotic drug" of programmed rhythm turned out to be fatal for Ultravox.

4.

As one of the founders of Digidesign, Evan Brooks had played an important role in popularizing drum machines. Now he and his partner Peter Gotcher were inadvertently about to deal them a death blow.

In 1985, the pair developed a software program called Sound Designer. Brooks had hit on the idea of using his Mac to edit drum sounds, since the computer could provide a visual interface similar to the one found on the Fairlight CMI. But he and Gotcher quickly realized that this interface could edit more than just drum samples.

"So we adapted the program to work with the Emulator 2," Brooks says. And after giving E-MU exclusive rights for a while, "we started making versions of Sound Designer that worked with six or seven other different samplers that were out there."

The breakthrough occurred when a former E-MU employee named Terry Shultz sent Brooks a new chip he was working on. Brooks realized he could use the chip to speed up the processing inside Sound Designer.

He designed a buss card that fit into one of the open slots in his Mac II. "I hacked up Sound Designer to talk to the card. And lo and behold, it was doing all of its processing in real time," Brooks says. "You could hear differences in the sound as you're turning the knob. It was like the heavens opening up! And I realized that this is where we had to go."

It wasn't just Brooks and Gotcher who went there: it was an entire industry. Sound Designer became Sound Accelerator, which became Sound Tools. This program debuted in 1989 as the world's "first tapeless studio." Two years later, Sound Tools became Pro Tools—a software-based digital workstation that became one of the most popular computer recording programs in the world.

Even Brooks seems surprised by the musical environment he helped create. "Now we're at the point you almost don't need hardware for most of the stuff that you do," he says, shaking his head. "You can do all the processing, all the mixing, everything, just with your native computer with this native hard drive. You don't need anything special." Including a drum machine.

5.

Lots of people had been waiting for Evan Brooks's world. One of the most eager was David Gamson. His work with the band Scritti Politti, in particular, has made Gamson's name familiar within the music industry. Some of that is because of the memorable songs he helped create, with candyfloss melodies that twine together elements of pop, R&B, hip hop, and reggae. And some of it is his reputation for studio exactitude.

Not since Steely Dan has there been a group so associated with its perfectionist streak. Scritti's lead singer, Green Gartside, is well known for taking his time to deliver material; at the time of this writing, it's been fifteen years since his last full-length release. But Gamson is regarded as the group's true sonic scrupulist. Some producers, like Chris Merrick Hughes, even describe using Gamson's name as code for a particularly precise arrangement—as in, "We need to Gamson-ize this song."

Gamson laughs when this detail is shared. But ever since he and drummer Fred Maher joined forces with Gartside—a Welshman who was assembling a brand-new lineup for the postpunk band he'd started at Leeds Polytechnic—their pursuit of sonic excellence was an earnest endeavor.

"At the time, we were quite snobby about those drum machines," says Gamson, whose father Arnold was a composer and the founder of the American Opera Society. "The only drum machines around were 8-bit drum machines—the Linn, the DMX. And we hated the way 8-bit drum machines sounded. So as fast as we could move away from drum machines, we did."

That move took several forms. On the trio's first recordings together, the singles "Wood Beez (Pray Like Aretha Franklin)" and "Absolute," the drums were provided by session drummer Steve Ferrone. The Power Station's Studio C added the huge reverb the group wanted.

"At the time, the Holy Grail was that Power Station, ambient, Bob Clearmountain sound," says Gamson. "It's pretty hard to get that sound on a drum machine."

The group found other ways around the 8-bit limitations of drum machines. On the American Top 10 hit "Perfect Way," they sampled Maher's drum hits individually into multiple AMS Digital Reverbs, which had 16-bit sound. Those drum samples were then triggered by a drum machine, to create a higher-bandwidth percussion track.

Maher didn't mind this reliance on technology. "I was very much into drum machines," says Maher, who also drummed with Lou Reed and the band Material. "I never really considered myself a great drummer. I was competent, and I could get the job done. But with Scritti, my role was less as a drummer and more as a conspirator. For me, the real fun was in the control room."

But precious little fun occurred during the protracted sessions for Scritti Politti's 1988 album, *Provision*. Maher's drum tracks were sampled into the Synclavier II, which provided the required 16-bit sound. However, "the sequencer on the Synclav was not intuitive whatsoever," Gamson recalls. "We even had a programmer. But it just took forever. You'd have slight errors in timing when you'd transfer the stuff in, and you'd have to make corrections." To make matters worse, those corrections had to be done using timecode, which meant "a lot of calculating where that beat would fall numerically."

And then there was MIDI. While for many people in the music industry, it was an answered prayer, Gamson grew frustrated with what he calls "MIDI slop"—miniscule delays he says would throw off a track. "For those of us who came up with CVs and gates, you're used to very precise timing," says Gamson. "Nobody really talked about it. We tried to figure it out on our own. *Why doesn't this feel good?*"

What Gamson really wanted was more precise control over the elements of each track—including the drums. Software seemed to have promise. "I had a Mac Plus, running Performer Version 1. There was Southworth's Total Music. There was Opcode. I had 'em all." Gamson gives a pained grin. "And they all sucked."

The studio hours piled up. Maher went home. Gamson became ill. And it would be more than a decade before the next Scritti album appeared. *Provision* was a hit—but there was nobody left to appreciate it. "We had completely gone off the deep end in terms of machines," Gamson admits.

Technology eventually caught up to Gamson's imagination. In the early 1990s, he began using Digidesign recording software when producing the debut album of bassist Meshell Ndgeocello.

Plantation Lullabies is something like the payoff of the philosophy Gamson developed in Scritti Politti—especially when it comes to the drums. The new technology allowed him to make microscopic adjustments to each drum part, just as he'd always dreamed.

That might seem to confirm Gamson's reputation for chasing audio perfection. But he insists the legend is a little overblown. "I never wanted to push the technological envelope," Gamson says, chuckling ruefully. "I just want my shit to be in time!"

6.

As drum machines began to near extinction, the ace programmer became an endangered species as well.

"The King," Jimmy Bralower, largely withdrew from the session scene in the early 1990s. Thanks to workstations and computers, "it was clear that people would rather do programming themselves," Bralower says. "Even if it was not better—it didn't matter."

Until the end of the 1980s, he reflects, "you had to be good enough to play your music. So there were experts manning all the seats in the room. You had a great bass player, guitar playing, programmer, arranger, engineer, producer—these were all professional jobs.

"But when the workstation came in, it was like everything was on training wheels," Brawlower adds. "It looked like you were riding a bike, but something's holding you up. You couldn't do it on your own."

7.

The 1980s would produce one last great standalone drum machine. If we continue the dinosaur analogy from the last chapter, this one is something like a crocodile: a surviving descendant of a now-vanished lifeform.

The Alesis HR-16 began as a conversation between former Oberheim employee Marcus Ryle and the late Keith Barr. Barr, like Ryle, had been an electronics whiz from an early age. He'd co-founded MXR, known for its guitar effects, but Barr had also developed a drum machine called the MXR 185. About 1,200 of the units were sold before the company went bankrupt in 1984.

But Barr, who had started a new company called Alesis, was hoping to take another shot at the drum machine market. Ryle, who'd founded a new business called Fast Forward Designs with his wife and another former Oberheim engineer, was the perfect person to help build this new device.

"Keith said, 'I really liked doing that MXR drum machine. I'd really like to do one that sounds really good, but is really affordable,'" Ryle recalls. Barr was also interested in replicating elements of the Oberheim Parallel Buss system that Ryle had helped design.

The Alesis HR-16, which debuted in late 1987, was a breakthrough device. Offering forty-nine digitally sampled sounds at a list price of less than $500, the HR-16 opened up the drum machine market to any last holdouts. "If you haven't got a drum machine at all yet, then you have to examine this one because it is a serious contender," David Mellor wrote in *Sound on Sound*. He added a caveat: "Don't be swayed by the spec, because '16-bit' is not necessarily a synonym for 'seriously wonderful.'"

The 16-bit samples were one of the major selling points of the HR-16. That bitrate was technically accurate, but it was achieved by a clever allocation of resources. "What people are surprised to find out is that they're really 8-bit samples," Ryle acknowledges. He and Barr had figured out that it was possible to use only the top 8 bits of a sample during the attack phase, because the human ear couldn't register a difference.

The distortion of the first part of those samples was high, but the ear couldn't detect it. As the sample decayed, however, the software was programmed to increase dynamic range. "Because memory was expensive," Ryle says, "that meant that the HR-16 had twice as much sounds for the same amount of memory."

There were other innovations. Barr suggested installing a pair of tiny piezo microphones in the machines, to make the HR-16's pads velocity sensitive. "I learned a lot from Keith Barr. He was brilliant. He got the notion, 'Why don't we just stick a couple of piezos in the panel, and sense the vibration of how hard you're hitting it?'" Ryle recalls.

> And the light bulb went off for me. Even a drummer, if you play two drums at the same time, it's very unnatural to play one hard and one soft. So the HR-16 has what you could call "mono velocity." You could play all 16 buttons at the same time. The velocity will be the same. But if you do a flam, the piezos will sense two different volume levels.

> Even the look of the machine was unique. It had a gray plastic, diamond-shaped cabinet, with a flip-up lid that contained instructions underneath. But the sound, Ryle says, was deliberately nondescript. "It was intentionally trying to be stealth," he says. "You'd say, ideally, 'OK, that could be real drums.' It's just not as recognizable as a Linn or a DMX."

The HR-16 nonetheless turned up on numerous recordings. Two of the most significant were hits in 1993: the Bruce Springsteen song "Streets of Philadelphia," and the Arrested Development hip hop smash "Mr. Wendal."

Some groups, like the British industrial metal band Godflesh, made the HR-16 a virtual band member. Frontman Justin Broadrick is open about his debut to Marcus Ryle: "We would never have had our 'sound,' possibly, if it wasn't for that guy!"

But by the early 1990s, drum machines were increasingly viewed as an artifact of the past. Chuck Surack, who founded Sweetwater Sound, one of the nation's top audio retailers, first sold the Alesis HR-16 and its companion sequencer, the MMT-8. "I was selling thousands of those a year," recalls Surack, who became a licensed Alesis dealer.

However, by the mid-1990s, Surack admits the bottom had fallen out of the drum machine market. "At that point, people are doing sequencing with software like Performer, and OpCode," says Surack. "And you're doing all your drums there too, instead of on a drum machine, because you have a lot more control."

Even at Alesis, by 1990, "some people were like, 'Is there really a need for another drum machine? Aren't drum machines kind of done? We've said our piece,'" remembers Marcus Ryle. "But I felt strongly that a drum machine could be even more performance-oriented than the HR-16 was. And that we could go further with the sounds without having to use a new custom chip."

The resulting machine, the Alesis SR-16, was a modest upgrade on its predecessor. "The innovation there was that I did dynamic voice allocation," says Ryle. "The library appeared to be much bigger. And it was, to some extent. But I was combining voices. You could have a snare drum with reverb, and that's because there was a snare drum sample and a reverb sample. There wasn't an effects chip in it. So I would trigger two voices at once.

> And then I had the software written so that it would know where sounds were in their decay, in order to be clever about which voices I could steal back. If I'm using two or three or even four voices for a single drum, with only 16 voices, you could run out of voices quickly. I think I did a pretty good job of masking that.

As Ryle notes, the Alesis SR-16 has had a shelf life longer than just about any other drum machine. It's still for sale today, more than thirty years after it was introduced. It still comes in a black plastic case, and while some internal parts have been replaced, the architecture of the machine remains almost unchanged. You can still buy one at your local Guitar Center or Sam Ash store. For about

$150, you can own an authentic piece of drum machine history—an artifact with ancestry that stretches back across not just decades, but centuries.

"I still see people in a bar, playing guitar, and they've got their SR-16," says Ryle. "That's a thing I'm pretty proud of."

Perhaps the greatest endorsement comes from a drummer who has worked with—and can point out the flaws of—nearly every major drum machine. It might seem surprising, but Warren Cann of Ultravox readily names the SR-16 as his favorite rhythm box.

"It's cheap," he explains. "It's cheerful." Cann pauses, perhaps reflecting on his years of struggle with music technology "that was only matched by the military and NASA."

"And," he adds pointedly, "the SR-16 *works*."

***

21

Time Out of Time

1.

One evening in late 1990, a young man enters a foggy, deserted alley in London.

He heads for a Dumpster in the back of a large office complex owned by the BBC, and lifts the lid. His eyes light up, and he carefully lifts out a bulky piece of gear.

Maybe tonight it's an old drum machine. Maybe it's an analog synth module, or an effects processor. Whatever it is, the young man will take it to his flat, and add it to his growing collection.

Nobody wants this stuff anymore, at the dawn of the digital era. But the young man, Ben Edwards, will give it a good home. He's a little like the monks who preserved books and Western history during the so-called Dark Ages, sheltering these artifacts in their monasteries.

Edwards will eventually begin releasing music under the name Benge. It will be built on analog sounds, many from these devices he saved from destruction.

"Benge rescued an entire generation from the skip," musician John Foxx had told me earlier. At the time, this sounded like hyperbole. It turns out Foxx was being quite literal.

"I found stuff in the skip, yes," agrees Benge. He's speaking from his studio in Cornwall, on the south coast of England. There are racks and racks of gear, including many of the drum machines discussed in this book. But not all the items had to be liberated from the garbage.

"People would give stuff to me. Or I'd find things in corridors. People would leave stuff outside their office doors that they didn't want anymore," Benge says. "In the early Nineties, people certainly didn't want drum machines anymore. They wanted real drums, or they wanted the new stuff. But I was never into that. I was always interested in how it *used* to be done."

Benge is so interested in those old ways that he does some drum programming on a modular synthesizer. He loves creating drum sounds with the Serge Modular synth, which he steps back to reveal, colored patch cords threading like whiskers across its face.

He also proudly shows off some other items from his collection, including a Linn LM-1 that he purchased for $200 through a free newspaper called *Loot*. The machine had been used, Benge was told, to program drums on Michael Jackson's 1987 album *Bad*. "But I didn't buy anything thinking it would be valuable," he clarifies.

It seems only right that Benge often works with such first-generation drum machine users as John Foxx (in the band The Maths) and Stephen Mallinder (as part of the Wrangler project). They, in turn, are grateful not just for Benge's musical acumen, but for his love of history. John Foxx explains this in terms of what you might call a lost analog generation.

"There was such a rush of digital innovation after 1982 that analog equipment was abandoned before it had been properly explored," Foxx says. "That's what Benge is all about. He wants to complete the exploration."

2.

There are others like Benge, of course. Conversations for this book reveal a yawning divide between older musicians—many of whom are glad to see the back of drum machines, and hardware generally—and younger artists, who perhaps weren't even born during the short reign of standalone rhythm boxes, yet remain fascinated by them.

Some who used this technology the first time around feel they've suffered enough. "I don't need to do that shit *no more*," says Ben Cenac of Newcleus, roaring with laughter. "I paid my *dues* with that shit!" More seriously, Cenac says, computer plug-ins that simulate the sound of drum machines and other instruments "are getting better and better all the time." The average listener, he points out, can't tell the difference, especially in a world where users are used to the compressed sound of MP3s and streaming audio.

But the Lost Analog Generation is out there. It includes Roy Mayorga, the mohawked drummer of Ministry and Stone Sour. Mayorga has been intrigued by the sound of drum machines since he heard Kraftwerk's "Trans-Europe Express" on the radio at age seven. "I was like, 'What is that rhythm? It's so *perfect*," he recalls.

For his twelfth birthday, Mayorga's best present was a set of Mattel Synsonics drums, a cheap but programmable machine with four plastic pads that could be played like drums. "I flipped out. There's my answer to Kraftwerk!" Mayorga grins. "Of course I destroyed it within two weeks because I was hitting the pads so hard. But eventually, I got another one." As an adult, Mayorga purchased many of the great drum machines of his youth, along with several analog synths. (And a new set of Synsonics Drums, of course.)

Singer-songwriter Chrissi Poland is also part of that Lost Analog Generation. "The first time I was really drawn in by drum machines, that made me whip my head around, was Whitney Houston's 'I Wanna Dance with Somebody (Who Loves Me)', when I was just a little kid," remembers Poland. She mimics the "di-dink-dink" of the 808 cowbell that opens the song. "That still gets me so stoked," says Poland with a smile.

Poland's friend, drummer Joe Goretti, is a member of this generation too. He's a fellow Berklee graduate who ended up in Moby's touring band because of his ability to play with drum machines. Goretti learned how during weekend gigs with a Russian wedding band that used a preset rhythm box.

"There were no click tracks, no headphones. There was just a monitor, and I had to play over top of it," Goretti recalls. "I was miserable. But I didn't realize how valuable a skill I was developing. How I would entertain myself on these gigs was to see how precisely I could sync things up. I would try to be so precise that you couldn't even hear the machine in the monitor."

When Goretti auditioned for Moby's North American tour in 2011, the band's gear was still in Europe. "He was very apologetic because all they had was the monitors," Goretti remembers. "But I was like, 'Hey, just like the Russian wedding band!'"

Moby noticed immediately. "We were playing 'Go,'" says Goretti. "He stopped me and said, 'I've never heard a drummer do that before. You don't have a click, you don't have monitors, and you're playing perfectly.'"

Another member of this generation is Manchester native Julie Campbell. The Christmas she was ten, her family bought a Yamaha keyboard with an onboard drum machine. "And I just commandeered it," Campbell says in a gentle brogue. "I distinctly remember playing around with this bank of drum patterns. That Yamaha keyboard was everything to me. I used to play guitar to those drum patterns for hours and hours."

Those preprogrammed rhythms saw Campbell through a series of solo gigs that she laughingly describes as "stark," and her first album, 2010's *Nerve Up*.

Recording as Lonelady, she used the Yamaha to generate a variety of beats that she embellished with bristling guitar riffs.

In mid-2021, Campbell released an EP recorded with Benge and Cabaret Voltaire's Stephen Mallinder. Besides a love of programmed rhythm, Campbell shares another quality with older artists like Mallinder: gratitude for how drum machines allowed her to become a musician in the first place.

Calling herself Lonelady was more than just a clever handle. "I was pretty shy. I couldn't imagine myself putting up signs saying 'Drummer Wanted,' or hanging out and jamming with people. That's not really me," admits Campbell. "So a drum machine was just perfect. That was always my surrogate bandmate."

3.

"There's nothing less cool than a drum machine," declares Moby.

If you know Moby's background, that statement might sound odd. Not only did drum machines like the Roland TR-909 help launch his career, but until recently, Moby had one of the largest collections of drum machines in the world.

Then he reached the sad realization that "99 percent of the time, I wasn't using them." So in 2018, Moby sold more than two hundred machines on the website reverb.com. The proceeds went to benefit the Physicians Committee for Responsible Medicine.

Moby kept just five drum machines, including four Electro-Harmonix units that he loves for their "disco swing," and which he once said would be the first things he'd save if his apartment were on fire. But he explains that it wasn't just the sound of drum machines that made him a collector.

"It's very easy to focus on the cool side of drum machines, whether it's Kraftwerk or New Order or early hip hop or house music or techno," Moby says. "But I also really loved the aspect of drum machines that was the guy playing organ in a church basement with them.

"One of the best things was that they came with literal and inscribed history," he adds. "They'd be covered in pen and pencil marks from whoever had been using them in a church basement or a hotel lounge somewhere. In a weird way, that was one of the most precious aspects, thinking of the history."

It's this gap between the two worlds of drum machines—the cool and the uncool, the pioneering and the practical—that Moby finds most remarkable. "While the old lady at church was playing hymns with her drum machine," he imagines, "Sly and the Family Stone were using the exact same drum machine on the other side of town. And to me, both are just as special and important in the history of drum machines."

4.

Now that Moby's collection has been sold, the person who owns the most rhythm boxes might be Wouter "Wally" De Backer—a Belgian native known to the world as Gotye.

"I recognized early on this propensity that I had to collect gear, but I quickly realized the danger of disappearing down that rabbit hole. Spending a lot on gear, but not making music with it, in other words," says De Backer. It's early 2020, just before the global pandemic will shut the world down, and De Backer is in his New York studio, which houses many of the machines in his collection.

De Backer grew up in Australia as a drummer and member of a pop-rock trio called The Basics. As Gotye, he became a household name in 2011, when his hypnotic single "Somebody That I Used to Know" became a Number 1 hit in eighteen countries. The song's parent album, *Making Mirrors*, is the last Gotye solo release to date, however. The success of "Somebody That I Used To Know," he admits, has simultaneously sped up his drum machine collecting and slowed down his recording.

De Backer's drum machine collection began with a Roland TR-77 that he bought in Australia. "It needed some servicing. And finding machines and getting them serviced expanded quite a lot when I moved to the States because … well, better technicians, I guess."

These days, De Backer has a regular—and busy—drum machine technician. "He really looks forward to my visits," De Backer jokes. "He'll say, 'I *guarantee* you nobody's ever thought of bringing me a Nintendo Ele-Conga. People think I'm *lying* when I tell them what I'm working on for you!" (The Ele-Conga is a Japanese preset machine from 1972 that plays conga-like patterns.)

De Backer owns one of the handful of Italian-made EKO Computerhythm machines in existence, as well as a functional Wurlitzer Side Man. But the most singular item ion his collection is undoubtedly the recreation of Henry Cowell and Leon Theramin's Rhythmicon—the world's first real drum machine.

De Backer and instrument designer Mike Buffington constructed the new Rhythmicon from scratch, then debuted it publicly at Tufts University in

2019. It was accompanied by the Tufts Electronic Music Ensemble, led by Paul Lehrman. The resurrected instrument played Cowell's "The Rhythmicana"—the composition he wrote for the Rhythmicon and orchestra back in 1931—fart noises and all.

The challenge now is finding the right vehicle to share his collection with the world. "It does mean something to me to find these beautiful things, to restore them and maintain them and ensure that they're preserved," De Backer says. "But the idea of public museum is a whole other energy." YouTube, he muses, might turn out to be the answer.

If De Backer turns his collection into a series of videos, expect to see a burgeoning collection of metronomes. "Partly I appreciate the perverse nature of collecting something that almost no other musician considers a musical instrument!" De Backer laughs. "But the more I've collected them, and the more I've found these sorts of oddball, outlier metronomes—like the electromechanical ones from the early 20th century—the more I think you could make the case for saying, 'These are drum machines.'"

De Backer launches into an enthusiastic description of one of his favorites. Otto Meissner's Rhythophone was a 1932 windup device that ran on a clock-like spring and struck a doorbell-like chime on each downbeat. But it also accommodated hand-punched paper discs that could trigger the chime according to the punches.

"You could punch *patterns*, in other words, and the Rhythophone could play them." De Backer sounds triumphant. "That's a programmable drum machine, in my book!"

5.

"Technology," offers Robert Margouleff, "creates a certain set of limitations through which we can create our tribal noises."

Margouleff is eighty-one years old, but his mind remains lively. As the cocreator of TONTO, the world's largest synthesizer, Margouleff and his partner Malcolm Cecil revolutionized music in the early Seventies. Margouleff and Cecil's creation became the basis for TONTO's Expanding Head Band, which released the influential electronic album *Zero Time* in 1971. And the next year, the duo joined Stevie Wonder, programming TONTO on a series of seminal records that include *Music of My Mind*, *Talking Book*, and *Innervisions*.

When Margouleff describes today's artists "writing music that unfolds in your head," he could be also be talking about the work he did with TONTO, which helped sketch out that sort of audio inner space. But when he considers the role of drum machines, he takes an even longer view.

"Think about a trap set in the time of Glenn Miller," he says. "The drums have evolved because of electricity. The kit has evolved. Drums and percussion have evolved into sounds that don't exist in the real world. And that's really what we did with TONTO, with Stevie. We created sounds of the moment. Did we think we were changing the world? Not a chance. We didn't know what we the hell we were doing. It's like sex—you're living purely in the moment."

Ultimately, many discussions of drum machines circle back to that same concept of the moment: the concept of time.

Mike Garson, David Bowie's longtime "piano man," is thinking about it one afternoon in the summer of 2021. "I could talk to you for 400 years about rhythm and time," insists Garson. "Because that's the most important element if you're gonna make something feel good."

Peering through the pink-tinted, futuristic glasses that have become a trademark, Garson uses his keyboard to make his points. "If I'm playing the piano and I'm laying behind the beat"—here Garson plays a relaxed stride riff—"there's a whole *world* of time in there. It's the science of rhythm, and rhythm is one-third of music."

Garson has used drum machines on his own recordings. "They keep me on target," he says. But he gives a more recent example of the concept of timekeeping, programmed rhythm, and how it can affect an entire band. The occasion was David Bowie's 1995 *Outside* tour. The album, Bowie's creative reunion with Brian Eno, was an ambitious sprawl of live and programmed elements. Garson says it was the first time Bowie used a click track onstage.

"The drummer, Zack Alford, wanted the click in his ear. Some of the guys didn't want it. David didn't want it. *I* wanted it. I wanted to be lined up with the drummer," says Garson. "Because there's a million places you could put the beat."

The first month or two of the tour, Garson says,

> we were shaky. We were not locked to the beat. Didn't sound good. Then the next couple of months, we were stiff to the beat. Didn't like that, either. But the last three months of the tour, we were like rubber bands. We could be behind the beat, on top of the beat, anywhere in-between. And you would never know there was a metronome going.

Garson's former bandmate Carlos Alomar, the guitarist who was Bowie's right-hand man during the 1970s and 1980s, was never fond of click tracks. But while drum machines regimented time, Alomar points out that they sometimes unlocked another abstract concept: space, which he says got squeezed out of music during the heavily reverbed 1980s. "That Power Station sound, man. You have a three-piece band that sounds so fuckin' huge that there's no space to put anything else!" exclaims Alomar.

"But music needs *holes*," he explains. "Silence in music is just as powerful as the beat. And hip hop, in particular, afforded us a way of looking at where those holes are, and going minimalistic. So for that, the drum machine was the perfect thing to use."

These days, Alomar creates electronic music, and finds that the softer pulse that drum machines can create suits his purposes. "The implied note," he says, "is what I'm really looking for. Sometimes a drum machine will do just that." He displays a "Vintage Funk Box" plug-in he's using currently using, which simulates classic sounds like Sly Stone's Maestro drum machine.

Garson, too, has gone mostly virtual musically, especially as recording has become increasingly remote. "These days, during COVID, *everyone* has to play to a click," says Garson.

So perhaps even a global pandemic can reveal the triumph of electronic percussion? Pushing back from the keyboard, Garson pauses to consider the thought. "All the drum machine is, is a glorified metronome," he offers at last. "It just sounds better."

6.

That glorified metronome, whether it comes from hardware or software, has become the norm in popular music.

Just look at the wide selection of classic drum machines in a software program like Ableton Live, which offers virtual versions of most of the units mentioned in this book. Witness the return of many classic machines, such as Roland's TR-8 update of the 808, and the new millennium birth of authentically new drum machines. There's Arturia's Drum Brute, a purely analog unit, or Roger Linn and Dave Smith's return to the field, the Tempest. This dream team invention offers both analog synthesis and sampling, for a best-of-both-worlds machine.

Or listen to Steven Wolf. Name a female pop star of the last twenty years, and chances are, Wolf has provided her percussion. Beyoncé, Katy Perry, Miley Cyrus, Pink, Avril Lavigne, Britney Spears, Celine Dion, Alicia Keys—they've all summoned Wolf. But in most cases, though his drumming chops are world-class, they've asked for his drum programming expertise as well.

Wolf, like Joe Goretti and Chrissi Poland, had a childhood interest in drum machines. Like them, he's a Berklee College of Music graduate. But when he was twenty, Wolf had a setback that opened his eyes further to the field of programmed rhythm.

"When I was at Berkelee, I was a fusionhead," he admits. "Drummers played a lot of notes. It was like a jock thing. But I woke up one day and I could barely move my hands. I went to a sports doctor, and they were like, 'Your drumming career is done.'" Wolf delved into alternative medicine to treat his tendonitis, and defied the prognosis. "But from then on, there was always pain when I played. And so I had to learn how to do more with less notes."

That pain also led him to investigate drum machines further, and he became a fan of the Akai MPC3000. And when Wolf decided, years later, to stop touring, it was clear that programming was going to become a substantial part of his livelihood. "This wasn't the heyday of session musicians, where you could be booked morning, noon, and night playing acoustic drums," he says. "That was no longer a thing."

The transition was rocky at first. "People didn't want to hire me to just program drums because they were used to paying a programmer to program drums and all the synths on records," he recalls. "So I had to invest in a full synth setup. I'm not a virtuoso keyboard player, but when I used the sequencer on the MPC, I could make it sound like I can really play."

Then Wolf discovered a Canadian producer named Henry Russell Walter, who records as Circuit and has worked with Katy Perry and Kanye West. "He's a virtuoso Mac player," says Wolf, who watched Walter create a track in real time using only his computer's mouse.

"He's doing this in real time, on his laptop, as quickly as most people would just be playing things on an MPC," marvels Wolf. "Circuit made me say I need to retire my MPC because I want to be able to just do that."

The musical landscape has titled so much towards programming, in fact, that Wolf thinks he needs a new job title. "Session drummer," he believes, no longer describes what he does. "I've been trying to rebrand myself," he explains. "At this point, I just call myself a 'rhythm maker.'"

The rhythm makers of urban music offer a particular window into the takeover of electronic beats. Producer Sam Sever might be deliberately exaggerating when he says that "nine out of every 10 songs these days is using a fuckin' 808 plug-in," but the rise of trap music and its 808-inspired patterns has made the statement at least plausible. Writing in *The Face* in 2019, Simon Reynolds chronicled the origins of trap, which he noted "has dominated popular music all through the 2010s."

> The abiding cornerstone of trap is the beat. Its roots go far back, all the way to '80s electro and the Roland 808 drum machine. Where New York rap followed the path of sampled and looped breakbeats, the South stuck with programmed rhythms. When the party-oriented, shake-that-ass sounds of Miami bass and New Orleans bounce fused with gangsta rap lyrics, trap was born. You recognise trap as a sound, or an influence, from the hi-hats, which run at double-time (or even faster) to the 75-beats-per-minute of the hard-hitting kick drums. There's a coiled tension and snake-like hiss to those rapid, intricate hi-hat patterns, while rat-a-tat snares conjure a military, parade-ground feel. Today's trap producers don't use hardware drum machines anymore, but they create that same dead-and-dry grid-like sound within their computers. On the most fundamental level of function, the bass-boom, the ear-tickling hi-hats, and the louche swagger of the music make trap the go-to party sound of the 2010s.

Now that the 808 has become the world's dominant drum machine, what does the man who played such a huge role in creating it think about its success?

Not a lot. Tadao Kikumoto is busy building a robot, for starters. He's also working on a new project, Silent Street Music, which envisions an outdoor concert experience where the audience wears earbuds. And he's preparing for the release of the RC-808, a virtual rhythm programmer that finally achieves his longtime goal of combining classic Roland analog sounds with a true drum synthesizer.

You might imagine, when he looks back, that Kikumoto would feel some pride in his accomplishments. But you'd be wrong. "It was a miracle," he says simply. "We are very happy that 808 is loved in the world of music, but not very proud of our contribution to the miracle because that was not our initial intention. In fact, some people say that was just happy accident. We agree."

It wasn't until the early 1990s that the creators of the Mid-O Series first learned of the widespread love for their machines. On a visit to Roland's Tokyo sales office, Kikumoto was told that many Western musicians had begun using the 808 and 909. Specifically, he was informed about Madonna's

"Vogue," a house music track with a 909 beat that had become a worldwide Number 1 hit. That was a stunning revelation to Kikumoto and the other members of Roland's Analog Mafia. And in the thirty years since, the legend of the Mid-O Series instruments—especially the 808—has only continued to grow.

Did those machines make the music, or did the music make the machines? The question is impossible to answer, even for Tadao Kikumoto. He contents himself with a typically modest observation.

"It is interesting to see the music is changing to minimal, cyclic, rhythmic, dance-oriented. The simpler the music," Kikumoto says, "the more the TR-808 is becoming essential."

7.

It's the spring of 2021, and producer Daniel Lanois is on the phone from his Toronto studio. He's talking about his new solo album, *Heavy Sun*. Specifically, he's talking about the way he used drum machines—a subject near and dear to his heart.

Lanois has been an enthusiastic user of beatboxes since he was a kid, who got his start recording local artists in Hamilton, Ontario. "The first drum machine I was exposed to was one that was part of an organ," he recalls. "I was recording a guy who was an organist—he was actually a one-man band. I never knew what the drum machine was—I think he had a Lowrey organ. But I've been using drum machines ever since."

Some of the most storied artists in popular music—Bob Dylan and U2 come to mind—have used drum machines on Lanois's watch to build iconic songs. Lanois has kept two of those machines, a Roland TR-808 and a Maestro Rhythm King. Both of them show up on *Heavy Sun*. On one song, "Every Nation," he laid down a preprogrammed beat on the Maestro, and then hand-played the 808 on top of it.

Lanois rustles around his studio for a moment, then unearths the Rhythm King. "Let's see what it's got to say," he suggests.

Down the phone line, a familiar cha-cha beat rises, burbling cheerfully. Over it, Lanois begins to play a slow, stately set of organ chords. The effect is both futuristic and timeless: this melody and rhythm could have originated at any point over the past hundred years. After a couple of minutes, the organ ceases, and the Rhythm King continues to speak its transistorized language—a language older than many of us realize.

"That's a little gospel number I'm working on," Lanois says, switching off the drum machine. For those who think "that something that's static in timekeeping would make things static and stiff," he begs to differ.

"That's a little bit of a folly," says Lanois earnestly. "The discipline that the machine operates by allows other emotions to come through on the overdubs. It can allow for other flavors to flourish."

Yet the drum machine's flavor is no longer the property of a specific era, if it ever really was. The sound of programmed percussion is a sound that man has been seeking for centuries. It was instantiated in a set of boxes for a short while, and it still lives there on occasion. But its promise of perfection is seductive and eternal, which is how it conquered the world. Whatever form it takes, automatic rhythm is always surprisingly—sometimes maddeningly—human.

Call it a drum machine or by a hundred other names; it will always find another host. It is, truly, the sound of time out of time.

***

Appendix

I Am Echo

I Am Echo is a forty second play by Tenzing Scott Brown.

I Am Echo has been written in response to Dan LeRoy asking Bill Drummond if he would be interviewed for a book he was writing with the title *Dancing to the Drum Machine: How Electronic Percussion Conquered the World*.

I Am Echo has two principal characters, one is Echo and the other is Dan LeRoy. And this is the play:

Echo:
I am Echo and I am the drum machine.

Dan LeRoy:
I know that is why I asked to interview you.

Echo:
No you didn't, you asked to interview Bill Drummond.

Dan LeRoy:
Yes but …

Echo:
"Yes but" nothing.
I am the Echo of Echo & The Bunnymen.
If I did not exist that band would not have existed.
They were my band.
In fact if they did not exist you would never have wanted to interview Bill Drummond in the first place.
I am classic, with only four settings, but I think you will find that four is the perfect number.
Nilsson got it wrong.
One is not the loneliest number, every number that is not four is the loneliest number.
Without me the cultural landscape of the world would be a different place.

I mean how many other drum machines have you met, that have not only fronted their own band, but been the leader of a movement?

In fact I don't think you should bother interviewing any other drum machines, especially those dreary ones from Sheffield.

And definitely not those Kraut Rock Posers.

I mean none of them ever actually led their own band.

Your book should be about me.

Me and my influence.

In fact without me you would not have even thought about writing this book.

At this point Dan LeRoy gets up from his chair in front of his laptop in his room in his home from home, somewhere in The Atlantic Archipelago and goes and puts the kettle on.

And …

Echo lies in the bottom of a drawer near Town Green Aughton, waiting to make his long awaited return to the world stage. Echo's ego knows no bounds.

And …

Somewhere in suburban North London someone clicks on *Different Drum* as performed by the Stone Poneys on their Spotify app and listens. And cries.

The End

Post Script:

It will be noted by those that feel the need to know these things, Echo made no passing comment about the music of the Wirral, that is because Echo is in denial of Orchestral Manoeuvres in the Dark and Dalek I Love You ever having existed. As for A Certain Rational from the other end of the East Lancs—they never did exist.

This case is closed.

Index

ABC (band) 195, 217, 219–20
  "Be Near Me" 195
  How to Be a Zillionaire 195
  Lexicon of Love, The 217, 219–20
Ableton Live 282
"Ace Bentley" (drum machine) 40–5, 228
Ace Electrical Company
  Ace Tone FR-1 Rhythm Ace 17–21, 23–4, 33–4, 36–8, 40, 57–8, 132
  Ace Tone FR-2L 21
  founding of 15
  influence on later drum machines 164
  takeover of 22
Adam Ant (Adam and the Ants) 124, 146, 203
a-Ha
  "Take on Me" 215
AIR Studios 219–20, 267
Aitken, Matt 245
Akai 228, 233, 258–9, 264, 266, 283
  MPC series 233, 258–9, 266, 283
  S9000 sampler 228, 264
Albini, Steve 76, 225–7
Alesis 115, 188, 271–3
  HR-16 (drum machine) 188, 27–2
  MMT-8 (sequencer) 273
  SR-16 (drum machine) 115, 273
al-Jazari, Ismail 2, 3
Allen, David M. 146–8
Allen, Rick 214, 249
Alomar, Carlos 282
Amendola, Billy 121, 145
American Federation of Musicians (AFM) 19
AMS effects units 154, 184, 202, 227, 265, 270
ARP 2600 (synthesizer) 81–2, 89, 121, 125, 178, 181
Art of Noise, The 217, 220–1
  "Beat Box" 220–1
  Into Battle with the Art of Noise 217
  "Kiss" 221
  "Peter Gunn" 221
  (Who's Afraid of) The Art of Noise 217
Arturia Drum Brute (drum machine) 282
Astley, Rick 244–5
  "Never Gonna Give You Up" 245
Atkins, Juan 180, 231–3, 236
automata 2–3

Babyface 193, 249
backbeat, enhancement of 105, 120–1, 123
Badarou, Wally 106, 119–20
Bahary, Gordon 178–9
Baker, Arthur 170–6, 182–4, 196, 199
Ballard, Glen 249
Bambaataa, Afrika 171–4, 176, 197, 199–200
  "Jazzy Sensation" (with the Jazzy Five) 173
  "Looking for the Perfect Beat" (with Soul Sonic Force) 183, 195
  "Planet Rock" (with Soul Sonic Force) 171–83, 187, 190, 193, 196, 199, 257
  "Renegades of Funk" (with Soul Sonic Force) 183
Bandito the Bongo Artist (drum machine) 10–11
Bandmaster Powerhouse (drum machine) 135
Banks, Gordon 169
Barbosa, Chris 183
Barr, Keith 271–2
Barrett, Aston "Family Man" 55–6
Barton, Mark 118, 120
Bartos, Karl 49, 52, 168, 174
Beard, Frank 201, 203
Beastie Boys 213, 231, 252
  "Beastie Groove" 213
  Licensed to Ill 213, 252
  Paul's Boutique 252
  "Rhymin and Stealin" 252
  "Rock Hard" 213
Beatles, The 6, 89, 105, 112, 135, 251, 257
  "Strawberry Fields Forever" 6
Becker, Walter 133–4

Bee Gees, The 24–5, 87
   "More Than a Woman" 87
   "Stayin' Alive" 87
Beinhorn, Michael 198–201
Bell, Bryan 199–200, 249, 266
Bell Biv DeVoe 257–8
   "I Thought It Was Me" 258
   Poison 258
"Belleville Three," The 231–2, 234
Bellotte, Pete 59–63
Benge (Ben Edwards) 275–6, 278
Bentley Rhythm Ace 40–5, 56, 74, 228
Berklee College of Music 124, 152, 277, 283
Berry, Mark S. 176, 182, 195, 265
Big Black (musical group) 226–8
   Lungs 226–7
   Racer-X 227
   Songs About Fucking 227
Billboard 31–3, 57, 61, 90, 120, 143, 169, 187, 196, 199, 233
Blackmon, Larry 264
Black Uhuru
   "Guess Who's Coming To Dinner?" 120
Blank, Boris 216
Blondie
   "Heart of Glass" 103
Blow, Kurtis 187, 196
   "Breaks, The" 186–7
   "Christmas Rappin'" 187
Bogart, Neil 60
Bomb Squad, The 254–7
Bonham, John 213
Book of Knowledge of Ingenious Mechanical Devices, The 2
BOSS 84, 113, 154, 162–3, 228
   DR-55 Dr. Rhythm 84, 113, 162–3, 228
   effects pedals (used by Prince) 154
Bowie, David 36, 44, 52, 78, 92, 100, 151, 261–2, 281–2
   Let's Dance 262
   Outside tour 281
Bralower, Jimmy 185–7, 189, 195, 230, 262, 271
Broad, Martin "Red" 123–4
Broadrick, Justin 273
Brooks, Evan 207, 211–14, 268–9
Broussard, Greg (Egyptian Lover) 176–8
   "Egypt, Egypt" 177–8

Brown, Arthur 1, 40–5, 74–5
Brown, James
   "Funky Drummer" 136, 256
Brzezicki, Mark 267
Buchanan, Paul (The Blue Nile/The White Hats/McIntyre) 112–13
Buchla (modular synthesizer) 160, 167
Buffington, Mike 279
Buller, Ed 157
Burgess, Richard James 117, 124–5, 219

Cabaret Voltaire 70–3, 75, 80, 83
   "Control Addict" 72
   Extended Play 72
   "Nag, Nag, Nag" 72
   "Seconds Too Late" 72
Caldato Jr., Mario 252
Cale, John Weldon ("J.J.") 27, 33–4
   "Crazy Mama" 33
   Naturally 33
Callomon, Cally (Nigel Simpkins)
   "Time's Encounter" 87–8
Cameo 264–5
   "Candy" (Cameo song) 265
   "Word Up" 264–5
   Word Up (Cameo album) 264–5
Campbell, Julie (Lonelady)
   Nerve Up 277–8
Can 48–9, 80
   "Peking O" 48
   "Spoon" 48–9
   Tago Mago 48
Cann, Warren 94–9, 102, 122–3, 145, 267–8, 274
Cara, Irene 170
   "Flashdance (What a Feeling)" 170
Carlos, Wendy (Walter)
   Switched-On Bach 90, 162
Carnes, Kim 122, 144
   "Bette Davis Eyes" 122
Carpenter, John 145
   Escape from New York 145
Carter, Chris 44–5, 74–5, 106, 167–8
Casey, Harry Wayne ("K.C.") 58
Cassius, Charles 254
Cecil, Malcolm 280
Cenac, Ben (Cozmo-D) 179–80, 276

Chamberlin, Harry C. 6–8
   Model 100 (drum machine) 7–8
   Rhythmate (drum machine) 8
Chapin, Harry 178
Charles, Tina
   "I Love to Love " 218
Chess, Marshall 194–5
Chestek, Jeff "Cheesesteak" 238–40
Chip E.
   "Like This" 235
Chris & Cosey
   Heartbeat 166
Christopherson, Peter ("Sleazy") 73–4
Chuck D (Carlton Ridenhour) 254–7
Ciani, Suzanne 159–60, 166–7
   Seven Waves 159–60, 167
   "Deep in the Sea" 167
   "Sail Away" 167
   "Water Lullaby" 167
Circuit (Henry Russell Walter) 283
Claptrap 123
Clash, The 69, 76, 83
Clayton, Kenny 25
Cleaners from Venus 113–15
   "I Can't Stop (Holding On)" 115
   Midnight Cleaners 115
   On Any Normal Monday 115
   Songs for a Fallow Land 115
   "This Rainy Decade" 115
Clearmountain, Bob 204, 262, 269
Clendeninn, Phil 179
Cluster (Kluster) 52–3, 56, 98, 106
   Cluster II 53
   "Im Süden" 53
CMOS chips 162–3
Cocteau Twins 113–15, 213
   Garlands 114
   Treasure 213
Collins, Peter 147
Collins, Phil 92–4, 104–5, 192, 220
   "Don't Lose My Number" 192
   Face Value 105
   "Hand to Hand" 105
   "In the Air Tonight" 104–5, 220
   "One More Night" 192
   No Jacket Required 192
   "Sussudio" 192
   "This Must Be Love" 105

"Tomorrow Never Knows" 105
COMPAL (Computer Power and Light) 133
Compass Point All-Stars 120
Cooper, Bernadette 121, 258
Cope, Julian 87–8
Corsaro, Jason 261–2
COUM Transmissions 73–4
Cowell, Henry 4, 5, 279
   New Musical Resources 4
Creffield, "Ravey" Davey 228
Cubase recording software 246
Curnow, Ian 245–6
Cybotron 180, 231–2
   "Cosmic Cars" 180
Czukay, Holger 49

Dalby, Andy 41–4
Davies, Iva 149–51
Davis, Hal 9
Davis, Miles 37–40
   "Hip Skip" 40
   "Turn of the Century" 40
Davis, Rick 180, 231
De Backer, Wally (Gotye; The Basics) 279–80
   Making Mirrors 279
   "Somebody That I Used to Know" 279
Debris, Eric 76–8
Deep Space (record label and DJ collective) 180, 232–3
Def Jam Records 230, 255
Def Leppard 200, 214, 249
   Pyromania 214
Delicious Vinyl 252
Depeche Mode 79, 82, 97, 149, 211
   Broken Frame, A 82
   Construction Time Again 211
   "Photographic" 82
   Speak and Spell 82
Destri, Jimmy 103
Devo 85–7
   In the Beginning Was the End: The Truth About De-Evolution 86
   "Secret Agent Man" 86
   "Whip It" 85
Digidesign 268, 270
Digidrums 212, 214
Dike, Matt 252

Dinger, Klaus 47, 50, 53
DJ Code Money 238–9
DJ Shadow (Josh Davis)
   Endtroducing 258
Doctor Mix and the Remix 78
Doktor Avalanche (Sisters of Mercy drum machine) 228
Dolby, Thomas 126–7, 149
   Golden Age of Wireless, The 127
   "One of Our Submarines" 127
   "She Blinded Me with Science" 183
   "Windpower" 126
Dragon, Daryl (The Captain & Tennille) 129
drop sampling 251
Drummond, Bill 88, 111–12, 287–8
drum replacement 133, 265–6
drum triggering 5, 11, 17, 71, 118, 126–7, 134, 141, 147, 156, 167, 264, 266, 273, 280
Dudley, Anne 220
Dunbar, Lowell "Sly" 55, 119–20, 259
   "Queen of the Minstrels" 120
Duran Duran 109–110, 261–2
Durango, Santiago 227
Dust Brothers, The 252
Dylan, Bob 119, 267, 285
   "Most of the Time" 267
   Oh Mercy 267

Easton, Bob (360 Systems) 141, 155, 242
Echo and the Bunnymen 70, 110–12, 287–8
   "Echo" (drum machine) 110–-12, 287–8
   Edmunds, Dave 44
808 (documentary) 159, 184, 230
Egan, Rusty 99–100
EKO ComputeRhythm (drum machine) 55, 91, 279
Eldritch, Andrew 228
Electro-Harmonix DRM-16 (drum machine) 72, 179
Elka Drummer One (drum machine) 53, 106
Emerson, Lake, and Palmer
   "Tocata" 118
E-MU Systems 179, 185, 207–12, 215, 227, 251–3, 255, 257, 263, 268
   Drumulator 210–12, 214
Emulator 179, 183, 209, 210–11, 255
   Emulator II 214, 251, 268

SP-12 (drum machine) 185, 251–2, 255
SP-1200 (drum machine) 252–3, 255, 257
Eno, Brian 56–7, 83, 87, 95, 98, 110, 198, 281
   Another Green World 56
   "Burning Airlines Give You So Much More" 56
   "Great Pretender, The" 56
   My Life in the Bush of Ghosts (with David Byrne) 198
   Taking Tiger Mountain (By Strategy) 56
EPROM chips 138, 212
Errico, Greg 30, 32, 36
Estefan, Gloria (and Miami Sound Machine) 145

Fab 5 Freddy
   "Change the Beat" (with Beside) 199
Factor, Richard 166
Fagen, Donald 133–4
Fairlight CMI 135, 175, 209, 214–16, 218–23, 246, 268
Fanny (musical group) 130–1
Farfisa company 47–50, 52–3, 67, 69, 71–2
   Rhythm 10 (drum machine) 47–50, 52–3, 71–2
Fast, Larry 89–93
Ferrone, Steve 187, 269
Finch, Rick 58
Fine Young Cannibals
   "She Drives Me Crazy" 263–4
Fink, Matt ("Dr.") 153
Fletcher, Edmond "Duke Bootee" 193
Flock of Seagulls, A 227
Flür, Wolfgang 49–52
Forat, Benny 247–8
Forat, Bruce 244, 247–9, 259
Forat 9000 (drum machine) 248–9, 259
Forat F16 (sampler) 249
Forsey, Keith 59, 61–2, 150–1, 156–7
FORTH (programming language) 243–4, 248
Foxx, John 94–8, 102, 145, 168, 275–6
   Garden, The 145, 168
   "Jungle, The" 168
   Metamatic 97
Foxy (musical group) 144
Frangioni, David 265–6

Frank, David 190–2, 259
Frankie Goes to Hollywood 216–17, 221–2
  Liverpool 222
  "Relax" 221–2
  Welcome to the Pleasuredome 216–17
Freez
  "IOU" 170, 182

Gabriel, Peter 90, 92–4
  "Biko" 92–3
  "Games Without Frontiers" 92–3
  "Intruder" 92–3
  "No Self Control" 92–3
  Peter Gabriel (third album) 92–3
  Security 93
Galdo, Joe 144–5
Galuten, Albhy 87
Gamson, David 269–71
Garay, Val 122
Garibaldi, David 137
Garson, Mike 281–2
Gartside, Green 269
Gaye, Marvin 168–9
  "Sexual Healing" 169
Genesis 92, 104–5
  "Duchess" 104
  "Mama" 170
Genetic Studios 100, 146–7
George, Nelson 195–7
Gibb, Barry 24–5, 87
Gibb, Maurice 24–5
Gibb, Robin 24–5, 87
  "One Million Years" 24–5
  Robin's Reign 24–5
  "Saved by the Bell" 24–5
Gibbons, Billy 201–3
Gibson, Bill 204, 210
GLOBE (John Miller) 175, 183
Goretti, Joe 277–83
Gotcher, Peter 207, 211–14, 288
Grandmaster Flash (and the Furious Five) 173, 193, 197, 240
  The Message 193
  "The Message" 193
  "Scorpio" 194
Griffin, Reggie 193–5
  "Mirda Rock" 194
Guitar Center 235, 248, 273

Guthrie, Robin 113–15, 213
Gutman, Vince 264

Hall & Oates 55, 102–3, 185, 261–2
  "Adult Education" 262
  "I Can't Go for That (No Can Do)" 103
  "Kiss on My List" 103
  "Soldering" 55
Hammond organs 7–8, 17–18, 20–2
  X77 organ 20–2
Hancock, Herbie 129, 145, 188, 198–200
  "Earth Beat" 198
  Future Shock 198–9
  "Rockit" 198–200
  "Textures" 145
Hannet, Martin 121–2
Harding, Phil 245–6
Harmonia 52–3
  De Luxe 52
  Musik von Harmonia 52
Hawtin, Richie (Plastikman) 236–7
  "Spastik" 236
Heaven 17, 148
  Penthouse and Pavement 148
Hendrix, Jimi 23, 130
  "Angel" ("Sweet Angel") 23
Horn, Trevor 217–22
Hudson, Linden 201–3
Hues, Jack 203–4
Huey Lewis and the News
  Sports 204
Hughes, Chris Merrick 146, 203, 213–14, 269
Human League, The 83–5, 100, 137, 146–8, 170
  "Being Boiled" 84
  Dare 146–8
  "Don't You Want Me" 137, 146
  "Empire State Human" 84
  Reproduction 84
  "Sound of the Crowd, The" 147
  Travelogue 84
Hütter, Ralf 47, 49–50, 52
Hyman, Dick
  "The Minotaur" 23–4

Ice Cube 257
Icehouse 149–51, 156
  "Glam" 151

"Great Southern Land" 149–50
"Hey Little Girl" 151
"One to One" 151
Ice-T (Tracy Morrow) 177
Idol, Billy 69, 151, 156
    "(Do Not) Stand in the Shadows" 155
    "Eyes Without a Face" 156
    "Flesh for Fantasy" 156
    Rebel Yell 156
Images in Vogue 236
Inner City
    "Good Life" 233
Intergalactic Studios 171, 174
INXS 266
Ives, Charles 4–5
I Was a Robot 49–51

Jackson, Michael 9, 131, 170, 265
    "Human Nature" (Michael Jackson song) 131
Jam, Jimmy and Lewis, Terry 169, 249
James, Michael 234
Jeczalik, J.J. 217–23
Jefferson, Marshall
    "Move Your Body" 235
Jerden, Dave 151, 198
Jett, Joan
    "Black Leather" 195
John, Elton 55, 59, 123, 143–4
    Goodbye Yellow Brick Road 55
    "Nobody Wins" 143–4
Jones, Gareth 97–8, 211
Jones, Grace
    "Nipple to the Bottle" 120
    "Pull Up to the Bumper" 120
Jones, Howard 213–14
Jones, Quincy 196
Journey (musical group) 204–5
    Raised on Radio 204
Joy Division 117, 121
    "She's Lost Control" 121

Kakehashi, Ikutaro ("Mr. K") 13–19, 21–3, 25, 84, 96, 155, 161–3, 165, 208, 229, 242
    creation of Ace Tone FR-1 Rhythm Ace 18
    creation of BOSS Dr. Rhythm 163
    creation of MIDI 250
    creation of Roland TR-808 165, 208
    creation of Roland TR-909 229
    early life 14–15
    electronic experiments 15–16
    first drum machine 17
    health of 13, 15
    invention of diode matrix circuit 18
    mentoring of Roger Linn 155
Karoli, Michael 49
Katoh, Tsutsomu 17
Kay R-8 Rhythmer (drum machine) 109–10
Keio-Giken company 16–17
    Donca-Matic (drum machine) 17
Key, cEvin (Kevin Crompton) 236
Kikumoto, Tadao 161–7, 170, 228–30, 250, 284–5
    drum synthesizer plans of 163–6
    early life of 162
    guitar synthesizer built by 162
    and MIDI 250
    response to reception of Mid-O Series 166–7, 170, 229–30, 284
    Silent Street Music project 284–5
    synthesis versus sampling, beliefs about 164
    work on the BOSS Dr. Rhythm 162–3
    work on the Roland TR-808 163–7, 170
    work on the Roland TR-909 170, 228–30
Kingdom Come 40–5, 74, 228
Journey 40, 44–5
    "Time Captives" 44
Kirk, Richard H. 70, 72, 83
KLF, The
    "Doctorin' the Tardis" 88
Klymaxx
    Never Underestimate the Power of a Woman 121
Knuckles, Frankie 234–5
Korg 60–1, 75–8, 81, 101, 110, 132, 236, 250, 252, 255
    700s (synthesizer) 81
    DDD-1 (drum machine) 255
    KR-55 (Rhythm 55 drum machine) 80
    MiniPops (drum machine) 60–1, 75–8, 110

SDD1000 Digital Delay 236
SDD2000 Digital Sampling Delay 252
Kraftwerk 47–50, 52–3, 62, 71, 80, 82–3, 85, 98, 100, 166, 168, 173–4, 181, 237, 276–8
"Autobahn" 52
"Klingklang" (Kraftwerk song) 50
Kraftwerk 2 50
"Numbers" 173–5
"Tanzmuzik" 50
Trans-Europe Express 52, 83
"Trans-Europe Express" 62, 174–5, 276
Kramer, Eddie 23
Krampf, Craig 122, 144

Landscape 124–5
  "Einstein a Go Go" 124
  From the Tea Rooms of Mars…to the Hell Holes of Uranus 125
  "Norman Bates" 125
Langan, Gary 217–23
Lange, Robert "Mutt" 214–15
Lanois, Daniel 266–7, 285–6
  "Every Nation" 285
  Heavy Sun 285
Laswell, Bill 198–201, 261–3
  Down By Law (as Deadline) 200
LeBlanc, Keith 193–5
  "No Sell Out" 194–5
Led Zeppelin 170, 213–14, 261
  "When the Levee Breaks" 213–14
Lee, Will 241
Lennon, John 62–3
Leon, Craig 69
Lewis, Don 19–23, 96, 164–5, 169
  advisor to Roland Corp. 22–3, 96, 164–5
  early life 20
  experiments with drum machines 21–2
  LEO (Live Electronic Orchestra) and battles with musicians' union 19
Liebezeit, Jaki 48–9
Linn, Roger 34, 129–41, 143–5, 151, 155, 163, 166, 170, 188–9, 210, 214–15, 222, 241–4, 247–9, 251, 258–60, 282
  closure of Linn Electronics 247–8, 258
  development of LinnDrum 155–7
  development of Linn 9000 241–4, 247–9

development of LM-1 drum machine 129–30, 131, 133–41, 166, 188–9
  early drum machine experiments 34, 131, 133–5, 188
  early life of 130–3
  innovations of 136–40, 241–3
  partnership with Akai 258–60
  problems with Linn 9000 243–9
Linn Electronics (Linn Moffatt Electronics) 82, 140–1, 143–5, 148, 149, 153–61, 163, 170–1, 185, 194, 198, 210–11, 215, 241–51, 257–8
LinnDrum drum machine 145, 155–6, 187, 190, 192–4, 201, 203–4, 208, 213, 215–16, 221–2, 229, 233, 238, 243–5, 247, 251
Linn 900 drum machine 241–51, 257–9, 261, 264
LM-1 drum machine 82
Linn, Steve 247
Lipson, Stephen 222, 266
Little Sister 29, 31–2
  "Somebody's Watching You" 31–2
Loftis, Craig 234
looping 7, 87, 140, 210, 220
Lowrey organs 7, 8, 17, 57–8, 285
Lydon, John 200

M (Robin Scott)
  "Pop Muzik" 119–20
Madonna 185, 191, 261–2
  Like a Virgin 262
  "Vogue" 284–5
Maestro Rhythm King 29–30, 32, 37, 56, 282, 285
Maher, Fred 269–70
Malcolm X 194
Mallinder, Stephen 70–3, 276, 278
Manning, Terry 202
Manny's Music 103, 119, 179
Mantronik, Kurtis (Mantronix)
  "Fresh Is the Word" 231
Mantus (musical act) 121
Margouleff, Robert 280–1
Marley, Bob and the Wailers
  "No Woman No Cry" 56
  "So Nah S'eh" 56
Marley Marl (Marlon Williams) 255

Mattel Synsonics Drums 277
May, Derrick 232–5
Mayorga, Roy 276–7
McCartney, Paul 6, 92, 145, 219, 251, 266
    "Rough Ride" 266
McClaren, Malcolm
    Duck Rock 217, 219
McRae, George 57–8
    "Rock Your Baby" 57–8
Meier, Dieter 216
Melle Mel (Grandmaster) 193–4
Mellotron 6–8, 44
Merendino, Sammy 264–5
Métal Urbain 76–8
    "Ghetto" 76
    "Lady Coca-Cola" 76
    "Panik" 76–7
    "Paris Maquis" 78
MIDI (Musical Instrument Digital Interface) 186, 189, 229, 233, 235, 249–51, 258, 270
Miles, Jason 259
Miller, Daniel 79–82, 149
Mills, Jeff 233
Moby 58, 79, 237, 277–8
    "Go" 277
    "Thousand" 237
Model 500
    "No U.F.O.s" 233
Modern Drummer magazine 145, 204–5, 266
Moebius, Dieter 52–3
Moffet, Alex 140
Moody Blues, The
    "Procession" 118
Moog, Robert "Bob" 10–11, 61, 90, 161, 212, 249
Moog synthesizers 24, 41, 61–2, 86, 89–90, 101, 130, 162, 181, 209
Moog 1130 Percussion Controller 118
Moroder, Giorgio 59–63, 129, 150–51
Morris, Eddie "Mr. Ness" 194–5
Morris, Stephen 117, 121–2
Morrison, Jim 41–2
Mothersbaugh, Jim 86–7
Mothersbaugh, Mark 85–7
Mtume, James 38–40
Murphy, Eddie 253–4

Murphy, Michael "Mic" 191–3
Music Box (nightclub; formerly The Warehouse) 234
Music Factory, The (record store) 174, 176
Mute Records 79, 81–2
MXR 185 (drum machine) 271

Nairobi
    "Funky Soul Makkosa" 182
Nakamura, Hiro 164
Nathan, Bobby 248
National Association of Music Merchants (NAMM) 14, 17–18, 144, 145, 163, 210, 250–1
Ndgeocello, Meshell
    Plantation Lullabies 270
Newell, Martin 114–16
Neu! 47–8, 53, 80
Newcleus 180, 276
    "Computer Age (Push the Button)" 180
    Jam on Revenge 180
Newmark, Andy 35–8, 55
New Order 117, 184, 278
    "Confusion" 184
Nichols, Roger 133–5, 222
Normal, The 79–81
    "TVOD" 80–1
    "Warm Leatherette" 81
Numan, Gary 100, 102, 173

Oakey, Phil 83–4, 147
Oberheim Electronics 130, 144, 171, 183, 185, 187–98, 202, 209, 215, 228–9, 243, 249, 254–5, 271–2
    DMX (drum machine) 144, 171, 183, 185, 189–98, 208, 228–9, 243, 254
    DSX (sequencer) 189
    DX (drum machine) 255
    Parallel Buss system 189–92, 272
Oberheim, Tom 187–8, 249
Ogre, Nivek (Kevin Ogilvie) 236
OpCode (recording software) 270, 273
Orange Krush
    "Action" 196–7
Orchestral Manoeuvres in the Dark 101, 227, 288
    "Enola Gay" 102
Osanai, Tadashi 16

Padgham, Hugh 92–4, 105, 154, 220
Page R ("Real Time Composer," sequencer) 222
PAiA Electronics 90–4, 96, 101
   Drummer Boy (drum machine) 91
   Programmable Drum Set 91–4, 96, 101
Palao, Alec 29–30
Parrish, Man 172, 181–2
   "Hip Hop, Be Bop (Don't Stop)" 181–2
Payne, Chris 100
Perry, Lee "Scratch" 55
Perry, Steve 144, 204
Pezzati, Jeff 227
Plank, Conny 47–8, 53, 56, 98
Plant, Robert
   "Big Log" 170
PPG 340/380 Wave Computer ("Henry") 126–7
Poland, Chrissi 277, 283
Police, The 92, 197
Pollard, Joe 118–19
Porcaro, Jeff 132, 137, 141, 143–4
Porcaro, Steve 131–2, 136–7, 140–1, 143, 155, 257
P'Orridge, Genesis (Neil Megson) 73–5
Power Station (studio) 261–2, 269, 282
Power Station, The (musical act) 262–3
Price, Thommy 156–7
Prince 136–7, 152–7, 169, 177, 263
   1999 153
   Controversy 153
   "Controversy" 177
   "Erotic City" 154
   "Forever in My Life" 154
   "If I Was Your Girlfriend" 154
   "Kiss" 221, 263
   "Private Joy" 153
   Purple Rain 152, 263
   Rave Un2 the Joy Fantastic 152
   Sign O' the Times 152
   "When Doves Cry" 154
Professional Drum Shop 149
Profile Records 195–6, 198
   Rap 1 (compilation album) 195–6
Propaganda (musical group) 221–2
   A Secret Wish 222
Psychedelic Furs
   "The Ghost in You" 157

Public Enemy 253–7
   Fear of a Black Planet 257
   "Fight the Power" 256
   It Takes a Nation of Millions to Hold Us Back 255–7
   "Rebel Without a Pause" 256
   Yo! Bum Rush the Show 255
PWL Studios 245–6

quantization 139–40
Questlove (of The Roots) 184

Red Hot Chili Peppers 200–1
   "Organic Anti-Beat Box Band" 200
   Uplift Mofo Party Plan, The 200–1
Reeves, David "Davy DMX" 196–8
   "One for the Treble" 197
Reininger, Blaine L. 101–2
Rev, Martin 65–70
Reynolds, Simon 59, 67, 74, 85, 147, 284
Rhodes, Nick 109–10
Rhythim is Rhythim 234–5
   "Beyond the Dance" 234
   "Kaos" 234
   "Strings of Life" 234
Rhythmicon 4–5, 279–80
Rhythophone (metronome) 1932
Robie, John 171–2, 174–5, 182–3
Robinson, Sylvia 193–4
Rockfield Studios 44
Rodgers, Nile 185, 262
Roedlius, Hans-Joachim 52–3
Roger Linn Design
   Tempest (drum machine) 282
Rogers, Susan 152–6
Roland Corporation 22, 55, 75, 82–4, 95–6, 103–5, 111–14, 122, 132, 134, 136, 139, 147–8, 155, 159, 161–71, 175, 178, 181–3, 185, 187, 192, 194, 208, 213, 215, 225–31, 233–8, 240, 242, 244, 250, 267, 278–9, 284–5
   "Analog Mafia" 164, 285
   CR-78 (CompuRhythm drum machine) 96–107, 122, 139
   CR-5000 (drum machine) 112
   Jupiter-4 (analog synthesizer) 148
   MC8 MicroComposer 147–8

Mid-O series 163, 170, 228–9, 235–7, 284–5
naming of company 22
RC-808 (drum machine) 284
System 100 83–4
System 700 Modular Synth 164
TB-303 (bass synthesizer) 235–6
TR-8 (drum machine) 282
TR-66 Rhythm Arranger (drum machine) 23, 75, 111
TR-505 (drum machine) 234
TR-606 (Drumatix) 194, 225–8, 236
TR-626 (drum machine) 234
TR-707 (drum machine) 229, 234–5
TR-77 (drum machine) 22, 95, 279
TR-727 (drum machine) 229, 233, 240
TR-808 (drum machine) 114, 159, 161, 164–72, 175–84, 187, 192–4, 196, 208, 228, 230–1, 233–37, 240, 244, 267, 277, 282, 284–5
TR-909 (drum machine) 229, 231–40, 244, 284–5
Rolling Stones 37, 119, 261
Rossum, Dave 209–10, 212, 214, 251–2
Rother, Michael 47–8, 50–51, 53–4, 56
Rough Trade (shop and label) 72, 77–8, 81, 88, 168
Roxy Music 56, 83, 100, 102, 151
Rubin, Rick 213, 230, 252
Rudd, Gordon 135, 189, 243–4, 249
Rundgren, Todd
  Todd 55
Run-DMC 195–7
  "Jam Master Jay" 196
  "King of Rock" 195
  "Rock Box" 195
  "Sucker MCs" 196
Rushent, Martin 100, 146–7
Russell, Leon 33–4, 131–2, 133, 135
  Life and Love 134
Ryle, Marcus 188–90, 271–4
Ryrie, Kim 215

Sadler, Eric "Vietnam" 254–8
sampling 6, 79, 87–8, 135–6, 163–4, 166, 179, 183, 186, 198, 209, 214–16, 218, 211, 222, 229, 233, 243, 245, 249–253, 255, 257–9, 261, 267, 282

Sauer, Michael 47–8
Saunderson, Kevin 232–3
Schillinger, Joseph 5
Schmidt, Irmin 49
Schneider, Florian 47, 49–50, 52, 168, 174
Schoolly D (Jesse Bonds Weaver, Jr.) 238–40
  "Freestyle Rappin'" 239
  "Good Time" 239
  "P.S.K What Does It Mean?" 238–9
  Saturday Night—The Album 240
Scott, Raymond (Harry Warnow) 10–11
  Bandito the Bongo Artist (drum machine) 10–11
  "Bandito the Bongo Artist" 11
  Rhythm Synthesizer 11
  Soothing Sounds for Baby (Raymond Scott albums) 9, 11
Scritti Politti 269–70
  "Perfect Way" 269–70
  Provision 270
Seals and Crofts 132
Seeburg company 20, 65, 67
  Kinsman Rhythm King 20
  Rhythm Prince 65, 67–9, 78
Selmer MR-101 Auto Rhythm (drum machine) 72
Serge Modular (synthesizer) 276
sequencers 11, 75, 80–1, 84, 103, 127, 139, 147, 178, 189, 222, 235, 244, 246, 258–9, 270, 273, 283
Sequential Circuits 208–9, 232–3, 250–1
  Drumtraks (drum machine) 208, 250–1
Sergeant, Will 70, 110–12
Sever, Sam (Citrin) 230–1, 284
Sex Pistols 76, 78, 83, 200
Shakespeare, Robbie 119–20
Shannon
  "Let the Music Play" 183
Sharkey, Noel 3
Sheila E.
  "Love Bizarre, A" 155
Shipley, Mike 214–15
Shocklee, Hank (Boxley) 230, 254–6
Shocklee, Keith (Boxley) 254–6
Shutt, Phill (nee Curtis) 41–2
Silverman, Tom 173–7

Simmons, Dave 123–6
Simmons electronic drums 82, 117, 123–7, 147, 202, 236, 255, 264
    Simmons Suitcase Kit 126–7
Simmons, Russell 196–8
Simonton, John Jr. 91–2
Sisters of Mercy 228
Skinny Puppy 236–7
    Remission (Skinny Puppy album) 237
Sleeping Bag Records 230–1
Sleezy D
    "I've Lost Control" 235
Sly and the Family Stone 28–32, 35, 36, 55, 279
    "Family Affair" 32
    Fresh 36–8
    "If You Want Me to Stay" 37
    "In Time" 37
    "Let Me Have It All" 37
    There's a Riot Goin' On 27, 29–32, 34, 36, 56
Sly and Robbie
    "Make 'Em Move" 262–3
Smith, Dave 208, 250–1
Smith, Larry 195–7
Smith, Steve 204–5
"Snake Charmer" melody 178–9
S.O.S. Band
    "Just Be Good to Me" 169
Sound Designer (recording software; also Sound Accelator, Sound Tolos, and Pro Tools) 264, 268–9
Sound Master SR-88 (drum machine) 114–15
Spectrum City
    "Check Out the Radio" 254–5
Spicer, Jimmy 197
    "Money (Dollar Bill Y'All)" 197–8
Spoonie Gee
    "The Big Beat" 197
Steely Dan 112, 133–4, 269
    Gaucho 133–4
    "Hey Nineteen" 133
Steer, Martin "Slim" 40
Stevens, Steve (Schneider) 69, 156
Stock, Aitken, and Waterman 244–7
Stone, Sly (Sylvester Stewart) 27–32, 34–6, 38–9, 49, 55–6, 59, 154, 279
    personal problems of 27–9
    recording experiments of 30–2
    Stone Flower label 29, 31
Strafe (musical artist; Steve Standard)
    "Set It Off" 230
Strange, Steve 100
Stubblefield, Clyde 136
Sugar Hill Records 193–4
Sugarhill Gang 186, 193
    "Rapper's Delight" 186, 193
Suicide 65–71, 77–8, 113
    "Frankie Teardrop" 68–9
    "Rocket USA" 68
    Suicide 68–9
Summer, Donna 59–62
    "Hot Stuff" 62
    "I Feel Love" 61–3
    "Love to Love You Baby" 60–1
Surack, Chuck 273
swing (drum machine feature) 140, 229, 278
Syco Systems (music store) 145
Syco Research (The Conductor) 222
Synare 121–3
Synclavier 215, 222–3, 270
Syndrum 118–21, 123, 126
Synergy (musical group)
    Electronic Realizations for Rock Orchestra 90
    Sequencer 90
System, The (musical group) 190–3, 259
    "It's Passion" 191–2
    "Sweat" 192
    Sweat 192
    "You Are in My System" 192

Tago Mago (Can album) 48
Taylor, John 109–10
Tears for Fears 203, 213–14
    "Shout" 213–14
Thau, Marty 69–70
Theremin, Leon 4–6
Thomas, Timmy 57–8
    "Why Can't We Live Together" 57
Thompson, Tony 262–3
Throbbing Gristle 45, 73–5, 80, 106, 168
    "AB/7A" 75
    "Dead on Arrival" 75

Third and Final Report of Throbbing Gristle, The 75
20 Jazz Funk Greats 106
Tietchens, Asmus 106–7
Tilles, Richard 27–32, 36–7
Time Zone
  "World Destruction" 200
TK Records 57–8
T La Rock
  "It's Yours" 230
Tomita, Isao
  "Clair de Lune, No. 3" 162
  Snowflakes Are Dancing 162
Tommy Boy Records 173, 183, 194–5
Tone-Loc
  "Wild Thing" 252
TONTO (syntheiszer) 280–1
TONTO's Expanding Head Band (musical act) 280
  Zero Time 280
Toto 131, 137, 141, 143
Tovey, Frank (Fad Gadget) 81–2
  "Back to Nature" 81
transistors 9, 16–17, 22, 91, 96
trap music 284
Travis, Geoff 77–8, 81, 88
Tricky Tee
  "Leave It to the Drums" 230–1
Tutti, Cosey Fanny (Christine Carol Newby) 73, 168
Tuxedomoon 101–2
  Half Mute 101–2
  "Loneliness" 102
Twilight 22
  "Electric Kingdom" 178
  "Siberian Nights" 178

U2 266, 285
  "With or Without You" 266
Ultravox 94–102, 122, 145, 267–8, 274
  "Astradyne" 98
  "Hiroshima Mon Amour" 95–6
  "Metal Beat" 98
  "Mr. X" 98
  Systems of Romance 97
  U-Vox 267–8
  Vienna 98

"Vienna" 98–9, 122
Uncle Jamm's Army 177
  "Dial-a-Freak" 177
  "Yes, Yes, Yes" 177
Unique Studios 183, 248, 252
Univox SR-95 (drum machine) 70
Ure, Midge 98, 100, 268
Upsetters, The
  "Chim Cherie" 55

Vanguard Records 176, 178–9, 254
Vanguard Studios 182, 252
Vega, Alan 66–9
Velasquez, Ray "Pinky" 178–9, 254
Village Recorder 29
Visage
  "Fade to Grey" 100–1
Vogel, Peter 215
Von Wernherr, Otto 191

Waaktaar-Savoy, Paul (Pal) 215
Wang Chung (Huang Chung)
  "Dance Hall Days" 203
  Points on the Curve 203
Ward, Anita
  "Ring My Bell" 121
Ware, Martyn 83–5, 147–8
Waterman, Pete 245–7
Watley, Jody
  "Looking for a New Love" 263–4
Watson, Chris 70–1
Wedel, Robbie 61–2
Wedge, Scott 209–10, 212, 214, 253
Wendel (drum machine) 133–5
West, Kanye 159, 260, 283
  808s and Heartbreak 159
Wiffen, Paul 243–4
Willie (Sugar Hill Records drum machine) 193–4
Wimbish, Doug 193
Wolf, Steven 282–3
Wonder, Stevie 9, 112, 129, 134, 139, 178, 248, 280
  Journey Though the Secret Life of Plants 178
Wood, Art 132–3, 136–8, 149, 242–3, 249
Wood, Ronnie 37–8
  "Crotch Music" (Ronnie Wood song) 38

I've Got My Own Album to Do (Ronnie Wood album) 38
"Shirley" (Ronnie Wood song) 38
Wright, Gary 132, 137
  Dream Weaver, The 132
Wrobbel, Eric 141
Wurlitzer company 8–9
  Side Man (drum machine) 8–9, 16–7, 279

Yamaha 39–40, 182, 186, 235, 245, 250, 266, 277–8
  EM-90 Ensemble Mixer 39–40
  RX-5 (drum machine) 266
  RX-11 (drum machine) 266
Yeager, Bob "Pops" 149
Yello
  "Oh Yeah" 216
  Stella 216
Yellow Magic Orchestra (YMO) 166
Young, Paul 124, 170
  "Wherever I Lay My Hat, That's My Home" 170

Z, Bobby (Rivkin) 153, 263
Z, David (Rivkin) 152, 263–4
Zappa, Frank 129
Zimmer, Hans 145
Zuckerzeit (Cluster album) 53, 56
ZZ Top 201–3
  Eliminator (ZZ Top album) 201–3
  "Gimme All Your Lovin'" 201
  "Legs" 202